“This timely and thorough study revisits the elusive *Apostolic Tradition* once associated with Hippolytus, discussing the implications of the Ethiopic Aksumite evidence as well as Arabic witnesses. An Asiatic rather than Roman origin is agreed upon now by most scholars, and Johnson and Chase mount a compelling argument for an Egyptian provenance. Discussing this composite work in themes rather than chapters makes this study easier to follow than previous studies, and it will be a crucial book for early Christian liturgy.”

—Bryan D. Spinks, Bishop F. Percy Goddard Professor Emeritus of Liturgical Studies and Pastoral Theology, Yale Divinity School and Yale Institute of Sacred Music

“In this substantial and complex study, Nathan Chase and Maxwell Johnson present a major advance in the understanding of the *Apostolic Tradition*. In particular, they argue that Egypt was its place of origin. The ambitious character of their work cannot but have an impact on the whole field of study of early Christian worship.”

—Paul F. Bradshaw, Emeritus Professor of Liturgy, University of Notre Dame

“The *Apostolic Tradition* is a key source for our understanding of the early development of the liturgy, but with its many witnesses and their complex redactional processes interpretation of the text can be bewildering. Chase and Johnson do liturgical historians a great service in this excellent piece of scholarship, not only by introducing readers to two new sources but also by their careful reassessment of the scholarly consensus in light of them. The clearly presented English translations of the newly discovered Ethiopic and Arabic versions—together with a detailed commentary on ordination, initiation, Eucharist, and daily prayer—in *The Apostolic Tradition* will provide an essential starting point for all future research on early Christian liturgy.”

—Juliette J. Day, University Lecturer and Docent in Church History, Helsinki University

"The *Apostolic Tradition* remains a key document for the early history of liturgy and ecclesiastical institutions. Formerly unknown testimonies have changed the state of research. With English translations and profound investigations, this volume provides comprehensive information on all liturgical topics and a solid basis for any future study."

—Professor Dr. Harald Buchinger, Chair of Liturgical Studies, Faculty of Catholic Theology, University of Regensburg, Germany

"A document of enormous complexity, the *Apostolic Tradition* has long been considered one of the most important sources for the study of early Christian liturgy. With a new commentary that takes into account hitherto untranslated manuscripts from Ethiopic and Arabic, Nathan Chase and Maxwell Johnson have made a valuable contribution to the study of this ancient source. They demonstrate a likely Egyptian provenance of its earliest layers and the slow and complex development of this work of this church order as 'living literature.' It is a work of extraordinary scholarship and should be included on the shelf of every serious scholar of Christian antiquity."

—John F. Baldovin, SJ, Boston College, Clough School of Theology and Ministry

# The Apostolic Tradition

## *Its Origins, Development, and Liturgical Practices*

With English Translations of
the Version Contained in the Aksumite Collection (Ethiopic I)
by Alessandro Bausi
and
the Arabic Version of the *Clementine Octateuch* (Arabic I)
by Martin Lüstraeten

Nathan P. Chase
and
Maxwell E. Johnson

LITURGICAL PRESS
ACADEMIC

Collegeville, Minnesota
litpress.org

Cover art: Detail of Christ teaching the Apostles. Fresco in the Catacombs of Domitilla, Rome. Wikimedia Commons (CC0, PD-Art).


Published by Liturgical Press, Collegeville, Minnesota.  Printed in the United States of America.

**Library of Congress Cataloging-in-Publication Data**

Names: Chase, Nathan, author. | Johnson, Maxwell E., 1952- author. | Bausi, Alessandro. Ethiopic I. English. | Lüstraeten, Martin. Arabic I. English.

Title: The apostolic tradition : its origins, development, and liturgical practices : with English translations of the version contained in the Aksumite Collection (Ethiopic I) by Alessandro Bausi and the Arabic version of the Clementine Octateuch (Arabic I) by Martin Lüstraeten / Nathan P. Chase and Maxwell E. Johnson.

Description: Collegeville, Minnesota : Liturgical Press Academic, 2025. | Summary: "In recent years, a number of new witnesses to the so-called Apostolic Tradition have been discovered or freshly edited for the first time. Based on these new witnesses, as well as new secondary literature, the translations and commentary provided in this book updates and challenges earlier and more recent studies with special regard to liturgical practices"—Provided by publisher.

Identifiers: LCCN 2024049252 (print) | LCCN 2024049253 (ebook) | ISBN 9798400801839 (trade paperback) | ISBN 9798400801846 (epub) | ISBN 9798400801853 (pdf)

Subjects: LCSH: Canon law—Early church, ca. 30-600. | Hippolytus, Antipope, approximately 170-235 or 236. Traditio apostolica. | Church orders, Ancient. | Catholic Church—Liturgy.

Classification: LCC KBR196.2 .C43 2025 (print) | LCC KBR196.2 (ebook) | DDC 262.9/22—dc23/eng/20241113

LC record available at https://lccn.loc.gov/2024049252

LC ebook record available at https://lccn.loc.gov/2024049253

# Contents

# Abbreviations

ACO = *Apostolic Church Order*

ACW = Ancient Christian Writers

AIRI = Edward Yarnold, *The Awe-Inspiring Rites of Initiation: The Origins of the R.C.I.A.* Collegeville, MN: Liturgical Press, 1994.

ANF = The Ante-Nicene Fathers

ApCons = *Apostolic Constitutions*

ApTrad = *Apostolic Tradition*

Arabic I = The Arabic version of the *Clementine Octateuch*

Arabic II = The Arabic version of the *Alexandrian Sinodos*

Arb-TD = The Arabic version of TD

Arb-TD.B = The Arabic version of TD, recension B

Arb-TD.M = The Arabic version of TD, recension M

BARC = The Anaphora in the "Barcelona Papyrus"

BR-AC = The "Baptismal Ritual" alongside Ethiopic I in the Aksumite Collection

Bradshaw, *Apostolic Tradition* = Paul F. Bradshaw, *Apostolic Tradition: A New Commentary*. Collegeville, MN: Liturgical Press Academic, 2023.

CA = *Canons of Athanasius*

CB = *Canons of Basil*

CH = *Canons of Hippolytus*

CR = Coptic Rite (initiation), includes CR 1 and 2

CYRIL = The Coptic version of the Anaphora of St. Mark (see the Greek version, MARK)

D = Hugo Duensing, *Der aethiopische Text der Kirchenordnung des Hippolyt*, Gesellschaft der Wissenschaften zu Göttingen, phil.-hist. Kl. 3/32. Göttingen: Vandenhoeck & Ruprecht, 1946.

DBL = E. C. Whitaker and Maxwell E. Johnson, *Documents of the Baptismal Liturgy*, 3rd ed. Collegeville, MN: Liturgical Press, 2003.

Ethio-AA I = The Ethiopian Anaphora of the Apostles in Euch-AC

Ethio-AA II = The Ethiopian Anaphora of the Apostles in the *textus receptus*

Ethio-MARK I = The Ethiopian version of MARK in the Aksumite Collection

Ethio-MC = The Ethiopian Mystagogical Catechesis

Ethio-TD = The Ethiopian version of TD

Ethiopic I = The Ethiopic version of ApTrad contained in the Aksumite Collection

Ethiopic II = The Ethiopic version of ApTrad contained in the *Sinodos*

Euch-AC = The "Euchologion" alongside Ethiopic I in the Aksumite Collection

GCN = The *Gnomai* of the Council of Nicaea

H = George Horner, *The Statutes of the Apostles or Canones Ecclesiastici*. London: Williams and Norgate, 1904.

*Herm.Com.* 2002 = Paul Bradshaw, Maxwell E. Johnson, and L. Edward Phillips. *The Apostolic Tradition: A Commentary*. Hermeneia—a Critical and Historical Commentary on the Bible. Minneapolis: Fortress Press, 2002.

JAS = The Anaphora of St. James

LWSS = Maxwell E. Johnson, ed., *Living Water, Sealing Spirit: Readings on Christian Initiation*. Collegeville, MN: Liturgical Press, 1995.

M1-5 = Manuscripts 1-5 of Arabic I

MARK = The Greek version of the Anaphora of St. Mark (see the Coptic version, CYRIL)

MC 5 = Cyril of Jerusalem's *Mystagogical Catechesis*, Ch. 5

NPNF = Nicene and Post-Nicene Fathers

PEER$^{3e}$ = Ronald Claud Dudley Jasper and G. J. Cuming, *Prayers of the Eucharist: Early and Reformed*, 3rd ed. Collegeville, MN: Liturgical Press, 1990.

PEER$^{4e}$ = Paul Bradshaw and Maxwell Johnson, eds., *Prayers of the Eucharist: Early and Reformed*, 4th ed. Collegeville, MN: Liturgical Press, 2019.

$^{R}$CN = the author of *Contra Noetum* in the Hippolytean school, and also a redactor of ApTrad according to Stewart[1]

$^{R}$El = the author of *Elenchus* in the Hippolytean school, and also a redactor of ApTrad according to Stewart[2]

SAR = The Anaphora of Sarapion of Thmuis

SC = *Sources Chrétiennes*

SD = *Syntagma Doctrinae*

Stewart, *On the Apostolic Tradition* = Alistair Stewart, *On the Apostolic Tradition*, 2nd ed. Crestwood, NY: St. Vladimir's Seminary Press, 2015.

Syr-TD = The Syrian version of TD

TD = *Testamentum Domini* (both the church order and anaphora)

1. Alistair Stewart, *On the Apostolic Tradition*, 2nd ed. (Crestwood, NY: St. Vladimir's Seminary Press, 2015), 13.

2. Stewart, 13.

# Introduction

## 1. Introduction

The recent discovery of a new version of the *Apostolic Tradition* (ApTrad) in the Aksumite Collection (see Ethiopic I below) as well as recent work on the Arabic version of the *Clementine Octateuch* (see Arabic I below), which has been known for some time but only recently received a preliminary edition and English translation, necessitates a new commentary on ApTrad, particularly its dating and provenance. While a handful of new studies and commentaries have sought to incorporate Ethiopic I into the discussion, including those by Alistair Stewart,[1] Reinhard Meßner (Messner),[2] and Paul Bradshaw,[3] these studies have departed from the arrangement of the document in the now standard commentary published in 2002, *The Apostolic Tradition: A Commentary* (henceforth *Herm.Com.* 2002),[4] often in order to reconstruct the original sequence of chapters in

1. Alistair Stewart, *On the Apostolic Tradition*, 2nd ed. (Crestwood, NY: St. Vladimir's Seminary Press, 2015); henceforth Stewart, *On the Apostolic Tradition*. For the earlier edition, see Alistair Stewart-Sykes, *On the Apostolic Tradition*, 1st ed., St. Vladimir's Seminary Press "Popular Patristics" Series (Crestwood, NY: St. Vladimir's Seminary Press, 2001). Unless otherwise noted, all citations are to the 2nd edition.

2. Reinhard Messner, "Die Angebliche *Traditio Apostolica*," *Archiv Für Liturgiewissenschaft* 58–59 (2016): 1–58.

3. Paul F. Bradshaw, *The Apostolic Tradition Reconstructed: A Text for Students*, JLS/Joint Liturgical Studies 91 (Norwich: Alcuin Club and the Group for Renewal of Worship, 2021); Paul F. Bradshaw, *Apostolic Tradition: A New Commentary* (Collegeville, MN: Liturgical Press Academic, 2023); henceforth Bradshaw, *Apostolic Tradition*.

4. Paul Bradshaw, Maxwell E. Johnson, and L. Edward Phillips, *The Apostolic Tradition: A Commentary*, Hermeneia—a Critical and Historical Commentary on the Bible (Minneapolis: Fortress Press, 2002).

ApTrad. However, this makes it difficult at times to corollate their studies to the useful and thorough *Herm.Com.* 2002. Some of these studies, like that of Meßner, have only looked at parts of ApTrad, and others, like Stewart's updated edition, put forward a different date and provenance for the document than that advanced in *Herm.Com.* 2002. As a result, we believe a new commentary that updates *Herm.Com.* 2002 in light of Ethiopic I is warranted.

At the same time, this study will take a different approach from previous studies, and even that of *Herm.Com.* 2002, which have focused on studying ApTrad chapter by chapter. This type of approach is very fruitful in trying to find the redactional layers in the text through a close textual study of each of the witnesses to the text. The church orders are often considered pieces of "living literature" that respond to liturgical changes in the community/communities using the text. This results in various redactional layers from different times and places.[5] This has often also meant that it is difficult to determine if the church order actually ever represented the lived experiences of a particular community. This is made even more difficult to conceive of, especially in ApTrad, since the text was widely disseminated in the early church. At the same time, the document does attempt to provide a mostly coherent vision of the central rituals and rules of the Christian ritual system, even if it ultimately does not succeed in creating a coherent vision.[6] These early church orders and euchologia give somewhat systematic presentations of the Christian ritual system that allowed for wholesale borrowings of texts, phrases, and practices between Christian collections and even rituals (see Table 1). As a result, this study will look at ApTrad thematically in order to try to highlight the connections between the various parts of the document and the vision put forward by the compiler(s).

5. For an overview, see Paul Bradshaw, *Ancient Church Orders*, Joint Liturgical Studies 80 (Norwich: Hymns Ancient and Modern, 2015).

6. Kimberly Hope Belcher, "Ritual Systems, Ritualized Bodies, and the Laws of Liturgical Development," *Studia Liturgica* 49 (2019): 89–110; Kimberly Hope Belcher, "Ritual Systems: Prostration, Self, and Community in the Rule of Benedict," *Ecclesia Orans* 37 (2020): 321–56.

**Table 1: Material in the Church Orders and Early Euchologia**[7]

| | Initiation | Eucharist | Ordination/ Ministry | Daily Prayer | Rites of Healing/ Restoration | Funerals/Rites of the Dead |
|---|---|---|---|---|---|---|
| ***Didache*** | X | X | X | X | X | |
| ***Didascalia*** | R[8] | R | R | | R | R |
| ***Apostolic Church Order*** | | X | X | | | |
| **ApTrad** | X | X | X | X | X | X |
| ***Canons of Hippolytus*** | X | X | X | X | X | X |
| ***Testamentum Domini*** | X | X | X | X | X | X |
| ***Apostolic Constitutions*** | X | X | X | X | | X |
| **Barcelona Papyrus** | X | X | | | X | |
| **Euchologion of Sarapion** | X | X | X | Possibly | | X |
| **Euchologion in the Aksumite Collection (Euch-AC)** | X | X | (X) | X | | |

7. For more on each of these texts, see the Sources section below.

8. The *Didascalia* presents us with liturgical evidence only in passing. As a result, the material in this row is designated with an "R" indicating a reference to the material in the document.

Ultimately, this study has three interrelated goals: (1) to analyze ApTrad in light of this new witness and in light of the new scholarly commentaries that have already begun to address this witness, (2) to do so with an eye toward the place of the final redaction of this document, and (3) to provide an English translation of Ethiopic I and Arabic I that corresponds to the chapters and verses outlined in *Herm.Com.* 2002 for ease of comparison.[9]

## 2. Provenance and the Attribution to Hippolytus

Questions about the provenance of ApTrad have swirled around the text since its discovery. There is no need to rehearse again the whole history of how this document came to be viewed as the work of Hippolytus of Rome in the third century, but a brief sketch will be of use to the reader.[10] The document was originally known as the "Egyptian Church Order," given that the first complete form of the text was Coptic in language. Eduard von der Goltz was the first to suggest "that the 'Egyptian Church Order' might in reality be a work by Hippolytus of Rome, the *Apostolic Tradition*, previously believed to have been lost."[11] This theory gained traction and was supported by the mention of Hippolytus in derivative documents like the *Canons of Hippolytus* (CH) and the *Epitome* of the *Apostolic Constitutions* 8 (ApCons), as well as the reference to "the apostolic tradition" at the end of the document in Ch. 43. This reference to "the apostolic tradition" in Ch. 43 was correlated to a statue discovered in Rome, which contained a list of Hippolytus's works, including one titled "[ΑΠ]ΟΣΤΟΛΙΚΗ ΠΑΡΑΔΟΣΙΣ" or "*Apostolic Tradition.*" Some support was also sought in the reference to "gifts" and "tradition" in Ch. 1, since another of Hippolytus's works listed on the statue was thought to be titled: "Of the gifts." There are a number of issues with both the list and the statue, as well as the attribution to Hippolytus in derivative documents, making it dubious that this document can be placed in third-century Rome based on these tenuous connections.

To add to the difficulties in studying the document, every scholar now accepts some form of developmental layering in the text. This includes

9. *Herm.Com.* 2002.

10. For a more detailed discussion, see *Herm.Com.* 2002, 1–6. More recently this has been taken up again in András Handl, "A Heavily Bearded Philosopher in Women's Underwear: Deconstructing and Reconstructing the Identity of the So-Called Hippolytus Statue," *Louvain Studies* 44 (2021): 340–64.

11. *Herm.Com.* 2002, 2.

those scholars who attribute the work to the third-century Roman school of Hippolytus, a position best represented by Allen Brent[12] and Alistair Stewart,[13] as well as those who argue that the document is a composite document from various times and places, a position typified by *Herm. Com.* 2002.[14] Bradshaw has most recently even gone so far as to say that "there is so little of [ApTrad] that implies a particular geographical region that most of it could have originated anywhere."[15] He then goes on to note the few instances in the text that he feels might be attributable to particular regions:

- The anaphora in Ch. 4 may possibly come from West Syria
- The original core of the rites of initiation in Ch. 21, which could point to North Africa or Rome
- A later redactional layer in the rites of initiation in Ch. 21 that point to somewhere in the East

Bradshaw concludes his analysis by suggesting that this "is probably about as much as can be said."[16] More, however, can be said. It is worth noting an earlier observation in *Herm.Com.* 2002, namely that "the document apparently circulated more widely in the East than in the West, which has led some to suggest an Eastern provenance."[17] To this we might add that it appears to have circulated and been particularly influential in Egypt, where we have a number of linguistic witnesses and a derivative document, namely CH, and in the region of Syria, as exhibited by its influence on ApCons and another closely derived document, *Testamentum Domini* (TD). Interestingly, however, no Syriac witnesses to ApTrad have been discovered. At the same time, it is also worth noting that "the absence of parallels with later Roman liturgy may not be quite as damaging to the traditional attribution as might appear. Since so little is known about Roman liturgical practice prior to the fifth century, it is impossible to say how great the changes might

12. Allen Brent, *Hippolytus and the Roman Church in the Third Century: Communities in Tension before the Emergence of a Monarch-Bishop*, Supplements to Vigiliae Christianae 31 (Leiden: E.J. Brill, 1995).

13. Stewart, *On the Apostolic Tradition*.

14. *Herm.Com.* 2002. See more recently Bradshaw, *Apostolic Tradition*.

15. Bradshaw, *Apostolic Tradition*, 10.

16. Bradshaw, 10.

17. *Herm.Com.* 2002, 5.

have been in the intervening period."[18] However, the absence of Roman sources that can provide parallels to this document make it difficult to positively affirm a Roman provenance. Interestingly, Stewart, who argues that this document is a product of the Hippolytean school in Rome, also notes that ApTrad is "the product not of a united Roman church but of a culturally Asian community within the city of Rome. There is nothing in *Apostolic Tradition* which absolutely *cannot* be Roman and third-century, and much that points to this date and setting."[19] But this cuts precisely to the heart of the matter. If ApTrad is from a culturally Asian community in a non-unified Rome, then even if finally redacted in Rome it does not represent Roman practice, and mostly represents practices from elsewhere.

While also attributing the document to Hippolytus, Jean Michel Hanssens had earlier suggested that Hippolytus was not a Roman, but possibly an Alexandrian/Egyptian.[20] He suggested that Hippolytus brought the liturgy/his tradition with him from Egypt to Rome. He also put forward a number of reasons why he thought the document appeared not as a Roman document, but more as an Alexandrian/Egyptian document. This mostly focused around:

- Chs. 2–4 and 7–8 – the form and prayers of the ordination rites for bishops, presbyters, and deacons[21]
- Ch. 4 – the anaphora, which particularly in its Preface, epiclesis, and doxology, as well as some of its phraseology and reception history, appears closer to the Alexandrian than Roman tradition[22]
- Chs. 5–6 – the blessing of oil and other foodstuffs[23]
- Ch. 11 – the treatment of readers and the ordering of the ministries[24]

18. *Herm.Com.* 2002, 6.

19. Stewart, *On the Apostolic Tradition*, 26.

20. Jean Michel Hanssens, *La liturgie d'Hippolyte: Ses documents, son titulaire, ses origines et son charactère*, Orientalia Christiana Analecta 155 (Rome: Pontificium Institutum Orientalium Studiorum, 1959), 283–340.

21. Hanssens, *La liturgie d'Hippolyte*, 379–94.

22. Hanssens, 352–70 and 426–41. Some of this is supported by the evidence; see Ch. 6 of our commentary.

23. Hanssens, 411–24.

24. Hanssens, 371–76. This seems supported by the evidence; see Ch. 3 of our commentary. See also *Herm.Com.* 2002, 74–75.

- Ch. 20 – the preparatory rites for initiation[25]
- Ch. 20.9 – the possible celebration of the baptismal vigil from Friday to Saturday[26]
- Ch. 20.10 – location of the prebaptismal anointing after the renunciation[27]
- Ch. 21.9 – the renunciations in their declaratory form[28]
- Ch. 21.12-14 – the syntaxis[29]
- Ch. 21.15-18 – the creedal formulae[30]
- Ch. 21.22 – the second postbaptismal chrismation[31]
- Ch. 21.27-29 and 33-37 – the triple cups[32]
- Ch. 40 – similar Roman and Egyptian burial customs[33]

Hanssens's interpretation has not received widespread scholarly approval, but the recent Ethiopic I witness to the document, alongside Arabic I, reopens this possibility. Thus, while Bradshaw is not entirely wrong that there is very little in ApTrad that can help with determining provenance, there is a bit more that can be said. This study will explore all the possible indications of provenance in the text before ultimately suggesting that Egypt may be the place of ApTrad's final redaction.

25. Hanssens, *La liturgie d'Hippolyte*, 442–47 and 451–52.

26. Hanssens, 447–51. This is still possible; see *Herm.Com.* 2002, 110.

27. Hanssens, *La liturgie d'Hippolyte*, 452. This is more or less affirmed in the early Egyptian evidence as well; see Ch. 5 of our commentary.

28. Hanssens, 452–56. It is far from certain that this is an exclusively Egyptian feature; see *Herm.Com.* 2002, 130–32.

29. Hanssens, *La liturgie d'Hippolyte*, 457–61. See Ch. 5 of our commentary.

30. Hanssens, 461–70. This is not an exclusively Egyptian feature; see *Herm.Com.* 2002, 125–26. See Ch. 5 of our commentary.

31. Hanssens, *La liturgie d'Hippolyte*, 471–80.

32. Hanssens, 481–88. This is more or less affirmed in the early Egyptian evidence as well; see Ch. 6 of our commentary.

33. Hanssens, 492–93. This does seem supported by the evidence; see Ch. 7 of our commentary.

## 3. Sources[34]

ApTrad was originally written in Greek, but with the exception of a few fragments, only a few examples of the Greek original are still extant. As a result, extant translations of the text have to be used in order to attempt to uncover the original form(s) of the Greek. There are two main sets of witnesses to the text of ApTrad. The first witnesses, which are listed below as "Primary Witnesses," "testify to a relatively clearly identifiable textual phase and go back to a common archetype, dating to the fourth century at the latest," while the other witnesses, which are listed below as "Secondary Witnesses," are derived from the *Alexandrian Sinodos* and "testify to a different textual phase and depend upon the common archetype of the *Synodus Alexandrina*" that "is the result of a systematic updating and revision."[35] Other Secondary Witnesses include Ethiopic II from the *Ethiopic Sinodos* and the Arabic version of the *Clementine Octateuch* (Arabic I). Finally, there are the derivates of ApTrad, namely CH, TD, and ApCons. There are reasons, however, to be cautious that a single Greek archetype even existed, because no two versions of the document are exactly the same.

### *3.1. Primary Witnesses*

#### *3.1.1. The Latin Version (Latin)*

One of the primary witnesses to ApTrad is the Latin version preserved as a palimpsest in the Verona Cathedral library, *Veronese* LV (53). The palimpsest material dates to the late fifth century based on the semi-uncial hand in a list of *fasti consulares* that goes to 494 CE. The palimpsest material contains a number of texts, of which ApTrad was a part. The Latin text of ApTrad is, however, incomplete. The manuscript was erased in the eighth century when Isidore of Seville's *Sentences* was copied. The Latin translation preserved in *Veronese* LV (53) appears to date from the "last quarter of the fourth century" based on "the Latin style and vocabulary and also because the form of the scriptural citations reflects a Latin text of the Bible older than that known to Jerome."[36] The translation from the Greek was, however,

34. For a more detailed summary of each source, see *Herm.Com.* 2002, 6–13. See also Messner, "Die Angebliche *Traditio Apostolica*," 1–21.

35. Alessandro Bausi, "The >so-called *Traditio apostolica*<: Preliminary observations on the new Ethiopic evidence," in *Volksglaube im antiken Christentum*, ed. Theofried Baumeister and Andreas Merkt (Darmstadt: WBG, Wissenschaftliche Buchgesellschaft, 2009), 304–5.

36. *Herm.Com.* 2002, 7–8.

fairly literal. Before the discovery of the Ethiopic version of ApTrad contained in the Aksumite Collection (Ethiopic I), this witness represented the primary witness to ApTrad. The edition used here is that of Erik Tidner.[37] All English translations of this source in this commentary are taken from corresponding passages in *Herm.Com.* 2002 to maintain consistency.

*3.1.2. The Ethiopic Version in the Aksumite Collection (Ethiopic I)*
The most complete witness to ApTrad is the newly discovered Ethiopic translation contained in the Aksumite Collection.[38] The manuscript, which dates to the thirteenth century or earlier, preserves a translation of ApTrad that "seems to have been translated into Ethiopic directly from an Egyptian *corpus canonum* in Greek."[39] Alessandro Bausi, who has been entrusted with the manuscript's publication, has argued that the translation dates to the end of the fifth or beginning of the sixth century.[40] This new witness is of immense value not only because of its early date, but also because it is the earliest *nearly complete* witness to ApTrad. It is, however, part of thirty-six texts preserved in the collection, of which only the first ten will be consulted here.[41] It is worth noting, however, that the treatise "On the One Judge" (Text 17) also bears a number of connections to liturgical texts, particularly from the Egyptian milieu.[42]

37. Erik Tidner, *Didascaliae Apostolorum Canonum Ecclesiasticorum Traditionis Apostolicae Versions Latinae* (Berlin: Akademie, 1963), 117–50.

38. Bausi, "The >so-called *Traditio apostolica*<"; Alessandro Bausi, "La 'nuova' versione ethiopica della *Traditio apostolica*: Edizione e traduzione preliminare," in *Christianity in Egypt: Literary Production and Intellectual Trends. Studies in Honor of Tito Orlandi*, ed. Paola Buzi and Alberto Camplani (Rome: Institutum Patristicum Augustinianum, 2011), 21–69.

39. Bausi, "The >so-called *Traditio apostolica*<," 291.

40. "In terms of dating, this collection was probably arranged after the middle of the fifth century and probably no later than the end of that century or the first half of the sixth century." Alessandro Bausi and Alberto Camplani, "New Ethiopic Documents for the History of Christian Egypt," *Zeitschrift Für Antikes Christentum* 17 (2013): 217.

41. Alessandro Bausi, "La *Collezione Aksumita* Canonico-Liturgica," *Adamantius* 12 (2006): 43–70; Alessandro Bausi and Alberto Camplani, "The *History of the Episcopate of Alexandria (HEpA): Editio minor* of the fragments preserved in the *Aksumite Collection* and in the *Codex Veronensis* LX (58)," *Adamantius* 22 (2016): 249–302.

42. Alessandro Bausi, "The Treatise *On the One Judge* (CAe 6260) in the *Aksumite Collection* (CAe1047)," *Adamantius* 27 (2021): 215–56; Nathan Chase, *The Anaphoral Tradition in the "Barcelona Papyrus,"* Studia Traditionis Theologiae 53 (Turnhout: Brepols, 2023), 151, 159, 194n168, and 207.

The relationship between Ethiopic I and Ethiopic II (version preserved in the *Ethiopic Sinodos*) is complex (see Stemma 1 below), but as Bausi notes Ethiopic II is in some places "directly depended upon 'Ethiopic I'" while also "add[ing] a number of 'innovations' of its own."[43] Bausi has yet to publish a full edition of all the texts of the Aksumite Collection, but he has given a number of detailed overviews of the collection.[44] He has, however, produced a full Ethiopic and Italian edition of the text of ApTrad, as well as providing the English translation of Ethiopic I used here.[45] He has also published other liturgical portions of the Aksumite Collection, like the "Baptismal Ritual" (BR-AC, see below); however, he has not yet published an edition of the "Euchologion" of the collection (Euch-AC, see below). The latter sheds a great deal of light on some of the missing prayers in Ethiopic I, in particular the eucharistic prayer in ApTrad Ch. 4. All English translations of this source come from Ch. 1 of our commentary.

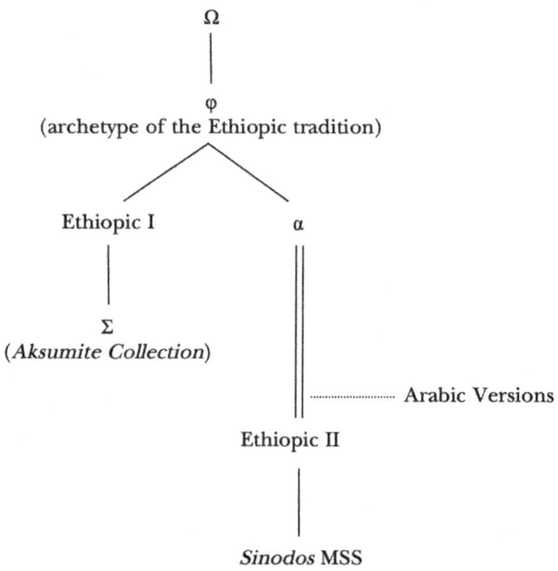


Stemma 1. A hypothetical *stemma codium* of the relationship between the *Aksumite Collection* (Ethiopic I) and the *Sinodos* (Ethiopic II). Reprinted with permission from Alessandro Bausi, "The *Baptismal Ritual* in the Earliest Ethiopic Canonical Liturgical Collection," in *»Neugeboren aus Wasser und Heiligem Geist« Kölner Kolloquium zur Initiatio Christiana*, ed. Heinzgerd Brakmann, Tinatin Chronz, and Claudia Sode (Münster: Aschendorff Verlag, 2020), 50.

43. Bausi, "The >so-called *Traditio apostolica*<," 297.
44. Bausi, "La *Collezione Aksumita*."
45. Bausi, "La 'nuova' versione."

### *3.1.3. Greek Fragments*

There are a number of Greek fragments that preserve a Greek original of ApTrad. The first set of Greek fragments is that of the *Epitome* of ApCons 8. The edition of this text often used by scholars is that of Franz Xavier Funk.[46] Part two of the *Epitome* likely had access to the Greek text of ApTrad, though this is disputed.[47] There are also two Greek fragments of ApTrad Ch. 23 and 41.9 alongside the *Epitome* in Vienna *gr.* 7.[48]

A Greek adaptation of the prayer in ApTrad Ch. 5 is preserved in Sinai gr. 973, a twelfth-century Palestinian manuscript from the Monastery of St. Catherine on Mount Sinai, where ApTrad Ch. 5 serves as part of the anointing of the sick.[49] A corrupted form of ApTrad Chs. 31-32 is also found in the eighth-century Barberini *gr.* 336, a Byzantine euchologion.[50] Finally, ApTrad Ch. 36 is preserved in two manuscripts—Ochrid, *Mus. nat.* 86 (84); Paris, BN *gr.* 900—containing an "eighth-century collection of patristic quotation."[51]

## ***3.2. Secondary Witnesses***

### *3.2.1. Alexandrian Sinodos*

#### 3.2.1.1. SAHIDIC

The primary manuscript to the Sahidic translation of ApTrad is BM *or.* 1320, which dates from 1006. A number of other Sahidic manuscripts are extant, but they are all copies of this older manuscript. The Sahidic version is missing part of ApTrad Ch. 21. The current edition of this source

46. Franz Xaver Funk, *Didascalia et Constitutiones Apostolorum*, 2 vols. (Turin: Bottega d'Erasmo, 1979), 2:72–96.

47. *Herm.Com.* 2002, 6.

48. Funk, *Didascalia et Constitutiones Apostolorum*, 2:112; Richard Connolly, "An Ancient Prayer in the Mediaeval Euchologia," *Journal of Theological Studies* 19 (1918): 132–44.

49. Eric Segelberg, "The Benedictio Olei in the Apostolic Tradition of Hippolytus," *Oriens Christianus* 48 (1964): 268–79. For the text, see A. Dmitrievsky, *Описанiе литургическихъ рукописей, хра нящихся въ библiотекахъ Православнаго Востока. Томъ II* (Kiev, 1901), 104.

50. Stefano Parenti and Elena Velkovska, eds., *L'Eucologio Barberini Gr. 336* (Rome: C.L.V. - Edizione Liturgiche, 1995), 258–59.

51. *Herm.Com.* 2002, 7. For those texts, see Marcel Richard, "Quelques fragments des Pères anténicéens et nicéens," *Symbolae Osloenses* 38 (1963): 76–83; Marcel Richard, "Le florilège eucharistique du Codex Ochrid. Musée national 86," in *Charistêrion eis Anastasion K. Orlandon*, vol. 4 (Athens: Publications de la Société archéologique d'Athènes, 1966), 3:47–55.

was produced by Walter Till and Johannes Leipoldt in 1954.[52] Gregory Dix and Botte included Greek retrotranslations of the Sahidic in their translations.[53] All English translations of this source in this commentary are taken from corresponding passages in *Herm.Com.* 2002 to maintain consistency.

#### 3.2.1.2. Arabic of the Alexandrian Sinodos (Arabic II)

The Arabic II translation of the *Alexandrian Sinodos* of ApTrad is contained in a number of manuscripts, and at least three different recensions can be seen.[54] This is the Arabic text that appears in *Herm.Com.* 2002. Arabic II is based on the Sahidic and must have been made by at least the mid-thirteenth century. In general, the Arabic II translation "follows the Sahidic closely but has the advantage of having been made from a text that did not exhibit the lacuna in the baptismal material, nor does it have all the copyists' errors exhibited by the extant Sahidic manuscripts."[55] The most recent edition of Arabic II was published by Jean Périer and Augustin Périer,[56] though further work is needed on the Arabic witnesses to ApTrad, including the Arabic version of the *Clementine Octateuch* (Arabic I). All English translations of this source in this commentary are taken from corresponding passages in *Herm.Com.* 2002 to maintain consistency.

#### 3.2.1.3. Bohairic

There is also a Bohairic version of ApTrad preserved in one manuscript: Berlin *or.* Quarto 519 (9488). That manuscript is thought by some to be a translation from the Sahidic dated to 1804 and does not contain any

52. Walter Till and Johannes Leipoldt, *Der koptische Text der Kirchenordnujng Hippolyts* (Berlin: Akademie, 1954). The text only includes ApTrad proper, Chs. 31–62. For more on the whole collection, and an English translation, see George Horner, *The Statutes of the Apostles or Canones Ecclesiastici* (London: Williams and Norgate, 1904), 295–363.

53. See Gregory Dix, *Apostolike Paradosis: The Treatise on the Apostolic Tradition of St. Hippolytus of Rome* (New York: Macmillan, 1937; 2nd ed. with preface and corrections by Henry Chadwick, London: SPCK, 1968; reprinted Ridgefield, CT: Morehouse, 1992); Bernard Botte, *La Tradition apostolique de saint Hippolyte: Essai de reconstitution* (1963; 5th ed. with addenda by Albert Gerhards; Liturgiewissenschaftliche Quellen und Forschungen 39; Munster: Aschendorff, 1989).

54. *Herm.Com.* 2002, 8.

55. *Herm.Com.* 2002, 9.

56. Jean Périer and Augustin Périer, *Les "127 Canons des Apôtres,"* PO, 8:4, 1912, 590–622.

significant variants from the Sahidic. It is possible, however, that the Bohairic is also a version of the *Clementine Octateuch*, and is dependent on the Arabic version of the *Clementine Octateuch* (Arabic I).[57] The Sahidic translation has priority over the Bohairic, except in Ch. 21.18-30 where the Sahidic is lacking. The only edition of this translation is that of Henry Tattam published in 1848.[58] All English translations of this source in this commentary are taken from corresponding passages in *Herm.Com.* 2002 to maintain consistency.

### *3.2.2. Ethiopic II (Ethiopic Sinodos)*

One of the most complete sources of ApTrad is found in the Ethiopic translation in the *Sinodos* (Ethiopic II); however, this source is a translation from an Arabic version of the *Alexandrian Sinodos* that likely dates to the thirteenth/fourteenth century. It represents "a contaminated witness: largely a recent translation from an Arabic *Vorlage*, it retains elements of an ancient layer, that in turn go back to the earlier 'Ethiopic I' version."[59] Parts of Ethiopic II preserve ancient forms not found in Ethiopic I:

> There are also a few passages in 'Ethiopic II' that may be ancient remnants, although they [are] miss[ing] in 'Ethiopic I': they are verified by the strict correspondence with the Latin version and the divergence from the Coptic and Arabic ones. They could derive from a third different Ethiopic recension (independent from both 'Ethiopic I' and from the Arabic-based 'Ethiopic II'), or, even more likely, from a more complete witness of the *Aksumite collection* than the only one known to us at present.[60]

The text also contains a number of later developments and additions. In particular, there are a number of issues with the texts after ApTrad in Ethiopic II that have parallels to the texts after ApTrad in Ethiopic I. All of the

57. Martin Lüstraeten, "The Arabic Versions of the So-Called *Traditio Apostolica*: Preliminary Observations," prepared by Martin Lüstraeten for the *Society of Oriental Liturgy* at The Catholic University of America in Washington, DC, in May 2024.

58. Henry Tattam, *The Apostolical Constitutions or the Canons of the Apostles in Coptic with an English Translation* (London: Oriental Translation Fund of Great Britain and Ireland, 1848), 31–92.

59. Bausi, "The >so-called *Traditio apostolica*<," 309.

60. Bausi, 296.

evidence suggests that parts of Ethiopic II are based on Ethiopic I, while Ethiopic II is also a witness to further developments and innovations.[61]

Ethiopic II has been published in two editions, one by George Horner (henceforth H)[62] and the other by Hugo Duensing (henceforth D).[63] Horner's edition was based on BM *or.* 793, which dates from 1730–1735, while Duensing's edition was based on a collection of eight manuscripts, the oldest dating from the fifteenth century. The translation by James VanderKam used in *Herm.Com.* 2002 is based, primarily it seems, on Duensing's edition. All English translations of this source in this commentary are taken from corresponding passages in *Herm.Com.* 2002 to maintain consistency.

### *3.3. Arabic Version of the Clementine Octateuch (Arabic I)*

Bausi and Meßner have both observed the need to pay more attention to a particular strand of the Arabic versions of ApTrad, namely that contained in the *Clementine Octateuch* (Arabic I),[64] a textual tradition that has recently begun to be studied by Martin Lüstraeten.[65] Book 3 of the *Clementine Octateuch* represents what appears to be a unique Arabic version of ApTrad, different from the *Alexandrian Sinodos* and now referred to as Arabic I. This requires some rethinking of the relationship between a few parts of the *Alexandrian Sinodos*, the Syriac *Clementine Octateuch*, the Arabic *Clementine Octateuch*, and also the Bohairic witness to ApTrad above.[66]

As Bradshaw notes, the Syriac version of the *Clementine Octateuch* does not contain ApTrad.[67] Rather, it contains TD (in two books), the

61. Bausi, 297–99.

62. Horner, *The Statutes*.

63. Hugo Duensing, *Der aethiopische Text der Kirchenordnung des Hippolyt*, Gesellschaft der Wissenschaften zu Göttingen, phil.-hist. Kl. 3/32 (Göttingen: Vandenhoeck & Ruprecht, 1946).

64. Bausi, "The >so-called *Traditio apostolica*<," 299 and 302–5; Messner, "Die Angebliche *Traditio Apostolica*," 16–18.

65. Lüstraeten, "The Arabic Versions of the So-Called *Traditio Apostolica*."

66. For the current overview, see Paul Bradshaw, *The Search for the Origins of Christian Worship: Sources and Methods for the Study of Early Liturgy*, 2nd ed. (New York: Oxford University Press, 2002), 87–91. See also Lüstraeten, "The Arabic Versions of the So-Called Traditio Apostolica."

67. For a general overview of the versions of the *Clementine Octateuch*, see Bradshaw, *The Search for the Origins of Christian Worship*, 88–89.

*Apostolic Church Order* (ACO), and ApCons 8. ACO has traditionally been ascribed to third-century Egypt, though Syria has been proposed as has an "Asian/Cappadocian" origin by Stewart, who has also recently argued that the text is dated to the fourth century.[68] The Arabic version of the *Clementine Octateuch*, which comes from Egypt, does include ApTrad between ACO and ApCons 8. This would seem to suggest that TD, ApTrad's derivative, was more popular in Syria than ApTrad, something that may explain why no Syriac translations of ApTrad have been found. In fact, ApTrad's omission may point to ApTrad not being part of the "living literature" in Syria, or at least Syriac-speaking circles. The same is not the case in the Arabic, where ApTrad is included. This, along with connections between the Arabic version of the *Clementine Octateuch* and the Sahidic and Bohairic versions of ApTrad, undoubtedly points to Egypt as the place of the Arabic version of the *Clementine Octateuch*'s final composition, especially since it would be commented upon by Abu-l-Barakat, the Coptic author of *The Lamp of Darkness* in the fourteenth century.[69] Further study is, of course, needed.

The five witnesses of Arabic I are: Paris, BN, ar. 251 (1352 CE) [Arabic I M1]; Rome, BAV, Vat. Ar. 150 (1371/1372 CE) [Arabic I M2]; Mardin, Church of the Forty Martyrs, Ms. 311 (not dated) [Arabic I M3]; Paris, BN, ar. 252 (1664 CE) [Arabic I M4]; and Oxford, Bodleian Library, Cod. Arab. Hunt. 32 (1680/1681) [Arabic I M5]. The latter two texts were determined to be part of recension 2 in Périer and Périer's edition of the Arabic version of ApTrad.[70] This version has not been separately edited, which Meßner notes is regrettable and desperately needed as this version might agree more closely with the primary witnesses of ApTrad. Lüstraeten has undertaken such a study, and his preliminary results will

68. For a general overview, see Bradshaw, *The Search for the Origins of Christian Worship*, 80. For a new edition, translation, and commentary, see Alistair Stewart-Sykes, *The Apostolic Church Order: The Greek Text with Introduction, Translation and Annotation* (Strathfield: St. Pauls Publications, Centre for Early Christian Studies, Australian Catholic University, 2006). See his most recent edition, Alistair Stewart, *The Apostolic Church Order: The Greek Text with Introduction, Translation and Annotation*, rev. ed. (Macquarie Centre: SCD Press, 2021).

69. Cf. Arsenius Mikhail, *Guides to the Eucharist in Medieval Egypt: Three Arabic Commentaries on the Coptic Liturgy*, 1st ed., Christian Arabic Texts in Translation (New York: Fordham University Press, 2022).

70. Périer and Périer, *Les "127 Canons des Apôtres."*

be included here along with his preliminary English translation.[71] A look at the text reveals an early version of ApTrad with similarities to the CH, as well as the Latin and Ethiopic I witnesses, while also bearing some connections to the Sahidic and Ethiopic II. All English translations of this source come from Ch. 1 of our commentary.

Taken together, the various witness to ApTrad appear to be related as follows (see Stemma 2 below):

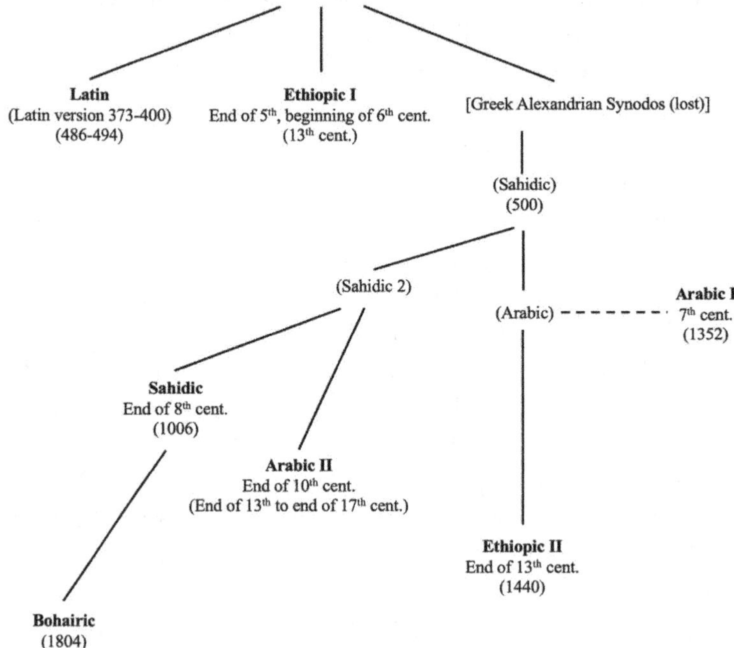


Stemma 2. Translated and adapted from Alexandre Faivre, "La Documentation Canonico-Liturgique," in *La Documentation Patristique: Bilan et Prospective*, ed. Jean-Claude Fredouille and René-Michel Roberge (Paris: Les Presses de l'Université Laval, 1995), 33.

## 4. Derivatives of ApTrad

There are a number of derivates of ApTrad that can shed light on ApTrad's development. CH, for instance, might even at times preserve older readings of the text. The two derivatives most dependent on ApTrad are CH

71. Lüstraeten, "The Arabic Versions of the So-Called Traditio Apostolica."

and TD. ApCons also shows dependency on ApTrad, but is not as close a derivative as CH and TD. On the whole, TD and ApCons have expanded their received texts of ApTrad much more than CH.

### *4.1. Canons of Hippolytus (CH)*

This text is traditionally thought to have been composed between 336 to 340 CE in Northern Egypt. As such, it is the first of ApTrad's derivatives. However, this has recently been challenged by Stewart, who has argued that CH is the result of two redactional layers in the text. The first is an older "Asian or Antiochene" reworking of the material contained in ApTrad, and the second is a lighter Egyptian editing.[72] This leads him to a dating between 340 and 380 CE, rather than the 336–340 CE traditionally ascribed to the work.[73] More recently, we have argued for the scholarly consensus that CH was composed in Egypt.[74] Furthermore, CH cannot be much later than the mid-fourth century, as indicated by the treatment of ordination in the text. Additionally, in line with the work of Heinzgerd Brakmann[75] and Stewart on CH, it is unlikely that CH emerged from Alexandria, though it clearly emerged somewhere within the Egyptian orbit. Instead, CH reflects Egyptian practice in either the *chora*, Pentapolis/Cyrenaica, or possibly even further afield—Nubia cannot be discounted.

The only preserved text of CH is in Arabic, and it is thought to be a translation from a Coptic version which itself was a translation from a Greek original. In many places the author of CH has rearranged and supplemented his source, but at other times appears to preserve an early form of ApTrad.[76] The only critical editions of the text are by René-Georges Coquin[77] and Stewart.[78] The English translation here is taken from Bradshaw and Carol Bebawi's edition of the text as adapted in places by us in

72. Alistair Stewart, *The Canons of Hippolytus: An English Version, with Introduction and Annotation and an Accompanying Arabic Text* (Macquarie Centre: SCD Press, 2021), 61–62.

73. Bradshaw, *Ancient Church Orders*, 18.

74. Nathan P. Chase and Maxwell E. Johnson, *The Origins of the Canons of Hippolytus* (Collegeville, MN: Liturgical Press Academic, 2024).

75. Heinzgerd Brakmann, "Alexandreia und die Kanones des Hippolyt," *Jahrbuch für Antike und Christentum* 22 (1979): 139–49.

76. Chase and Johnson, *The Origins of the Canons of Hippolytus*.

77. René-Georges Coquin, *Les Canons d'Hippolyte*, PO 31/32 (Paris: Firmin-Didot, 1966).

78. Stewart, *The Canons of Hippolytus*.

our commentary on CH.[79] All English translations of this source come from our commentary *The Origins of the Canons of Hippolytus*, unless the text does not appear in that commentary or unless explicitly noted that it comes from Stewart's edition. In a number of instances in our commentary on CH, we have also subdivided the canons of CH for ease of reference. Those subdivisions will be employed here.

### *4.2. Testamentum Domini (TD)*

TD is based on ApTrad but is dramatically expanded. Originally written in Greek, TD is preserved in a number of different versions:[80] two Syriac ones;[81] several Arabic;[82] an Ethiopic;[83] and a Georgian;[84] as well as a Latin fragment[85] and a Greek fragment.[86] The Syriac witnesses show a great deal of variety and do not always appear faithful to the original Greek text.[87] The Arabic and Ethiopic translations appear to be based on a lost Coptic

79. Paul F. Bradshaw, ed., *The Canons of Hippolytus*, Alcuin/Grow Liturgical Study 2 (Bramcote: Grove Books, 1987); Chase and Johnson, *The Origins of the Canons of Hippolytus*.

80. There are three main witnesses to this church order: the Syriac, the Ethiopic, and the Arabic, as well as a number of fragmentary witnesses in Greek (the original language), Georgian, Coptic, and Latin. The Arabic is itself divided into four separate recensions: B, L, M, and D. For an overview of the sources, see Martin Lüstraeten, "Edition und Übersetzung der Euchologie der Eucharistiefeier der Redaktion 'M' des arabischen *Testamentum Domini* (I.23-I.28)," *Ex Fonte - Journal of Ecumenical Studies in Liturgy* 2 (2023): 65–179; Martin Lüstraeten, "The Eucharistic Prayer in the Arabic Tradition of the Testamentum Domini," forthcoming in the proceedings from *The Eighth International Congress of the Society of Oriental Liturgy; 13–18 June 2022, Thessaloniki, Greece*.

81. The first version is published in I. E. Rahmani, *Testamentum Domini nostri Iesu Christi* (Moguntiae: F. Kirchheim, 1899). The second is published in Arthur Vööbus, *The Synodicon in the West Syrian Tradition*, CSCO 367, 368 (Louvain: Secrétariat du CorpusSCO, 1975).

82. The Arabic form is unpublished, but has been discussed by René-Georges Coquin, "Le Testamentum Domini: Problèmes de Tradition Textuelle," *Parole de l'Orient* 5 (1974): 165–88. As noted above, the Arabic is itself divided into four separate recensions: B, L, M, and D. For more on these recensions, see Lüstraeten, "Edition und Übersetzung"; Lüstraeten, "The Eucharistic Prayer in the Arabic Tradition of the *Testamentum Domini*."

83. Robert Beylot, *Testamentum Domini éthiopien* (Louvain: Peeters, 1984). Some have questioned the reliability of this edition.

84. Tinatin Chronz and Heinzgerd Brakmann, "Fragmente Des *Testamentum Domini* in Georgischer Übersetzung," *Zeitschrift Für Antikes Christentum* 13 (2009): 395–402.

85. Montague Rhodes James, *Apocrypha anecdota*, Texts and Studies II:3 (Cambridge: Cambridge University Press, 1893), 151–54.

86. Simon Corcoran and Benet Salway, "A Newly Identified Greek Fragment of the *Testamentum Domini*," *Journal of Theological Studies* 62, no. 1 (2011): 118–34.

87. *Herm.Com.* 2002, 11.

translation. This text is thought to be one of the last church orders to have been written, and is thought to be from Syria, though Egypt, Asia Minor, and Palestine have also been suggested.[88] In general its provenance remains in dispute. Nevertheless, it likely dates to end of the fourth or beginning of the fifth century. The English translation used in *Herm.Com.* 2002, as well as here, is taken from the translation of the Syriac witnesses by James Cooper and Arthur Maclean;[89] however, more recent translations from the Syriac have been made by Arthur Vööbus[90] and Alistair Stewart.[91]

### *4.3. Apostolic Constitutions (ApCons)*

One of the sources paralleling ApTrad is ApCons. This source, likely written in Antioch between 375 and 380 CE, was compiled from three older sources:

- Books 1–6 are based on the *Didascalia Apostolorum* (see below)
- Book 7 is based on the *Didache* (see below)
- Book 8 is based on ApTrad

The material in Book 8 based on ApTrad has, however, often been substantially expanded. The English translation used here is taken from *Herm.Com.* 2002 and is based on Marcel Metzger's edition of ApCons.[92]

## 5. Additional Texts Frequently Consulted

### *5.1. Other Church Orders*

A few other church orders will be consulted throughout this study, some of which have already been mentioned above.[93] These include: the

88. For an overview of provenance, see Lüstraeten, "Edition und Übersetzung," 65–179, especially 67–93; Lüstraeten, "The Eucharistic Prayer in the Arabic Tradition of the *Testamentum Domini*." See also Michael Kohlbacher, "Wessen Kirche ordnete das Testamentum Domini Nostri Jesu Christi? Anmerkungen zum historischen Kontext von CPG 1743," in *Zu Geschichte, Theologie, Liturgie und Gegenwartslage der syrischen Kirchen. Ausgewählte Vorträge des deutschen Syrologen-Symposiums vom 2.-4. Oktober 1998 in Hermannsburg*, ed. Martin Tamcke and Andreas Heinz, SOKG 9 (Münster: LIT, 2000), 55–137.

89. James Cooper and Arthur John Maclean, *The Testament of Our Lord* (Edinburgh: T&T Clark, 1902).

90. Vööbus, *The Synodicon in the West Syrian Tradition*, II:27–57.

91. Alistair C. Stewart, *The Testament of the Lord: An English Version* (Yonkers: St. Vladimir's Seminary Press, 2018).

92. M. Metzger, *Les Constitutions Apostoliques*, SC 320, 329, 336 (Paris: Editions du Cerf, 1985).

93. For an overview, see Bradshaw, *Ancient Church Orders*.

*Didache*, first/second-century Syria;[94] the *Didascalia Apostolorum* (also known as the *Didascalia*), third-century Syria;[95] and the *Apostolic Church Order*, often given a late third-century date from Egypt (though Stewart argues it is fourth-century "Asian/Cappadocian" in his revised edition).[96]

### 5.2. Other texts in the Aksumite Collection: "Baptismal Ritual" (BR-AC) and "Euchologion" (Euch-AC) in the Aksumite Collection

The material in the "Baptismal Ritual" (or Text 9) in the Aksumite Collection (henceforth BR-AC) contains the catechumenal rites, as well as the pre- and postbaptismal rites and the reception of the initiatory Eucharist. The structure of the ritual shows signs of development from the outline of the rites of initiation in ApTrad. BR-AC has recently been published by Bausi[97] and commented on by Brakmann.[98] It draws from ApTrad and provides a helpful point of comparison for ApTrad's reception in Egypt and Ethiopia. It also represents an earlier version of the baptismal ritual that accompanies ApTrad in Ethiopic II.[99] It will be dealt with in much more detail in Ch. 5 in our commentary.

94. Critical edition: Willy Rordorf and André Tuilier, *La doctrine des douze apôtres (Didachè)* (Paris: 1988). For a detailed commentary and English translation, see Kurt Niederwimmer and Harold W. Attridge, *The Didache: A Commentary* (Minneapolis: Fortress Press, 1998).

95. Critical editions—Syriac: Arthur Vööbus, *The Didascalia apostolorum in Syriac*, CSCO 401/407 (Leuven: 1979); Latin fragment: E. Tidner, *Didascaliae apostolorum, canonum ecclesiasticorum, traditionis apostolicae versiones Latinae*, TU 75 (Berlin: 1963); Coptic fragment: A. Camplani, "A Coptic fragment from the Didascalia Apostolorum (M579 f. 1)," *Augustinianum* 36 (1996): 47–51. For a detailed commentary and English translation, see Alistair Stewart-Sykes, ed., *The Didascalia Apostolorum: An English Version*, Studia Traditionis Theologiae 1 (Turnhout: Brepols, 2009).

96. Stewart, *The Apostolic Church Order*, rev. ed.

97. Alessandro Bausi, "The *Baptismal Ritual* in the Earliest Ethiopic Canonical Liturgical Collection," in *»Neugeboren aus Wasser und Heiligem Geist« Kölner Kolloquium zur Initiatio Christiana*, ed. Heinzgerd Brakmann, Tinatin Chronz, and Claudia Sode (Münster: Aschendorff Verlag, 2020).

98. Heinzgerd Brakmann, "ⲃⲁⲡⲧⲓⲥⲙⲁ ⲁⲓⲛⲉⲥⲉⲱⲥ: Ordines und Orationen kirchlicher Eingliederung in Alexandrien und Ägypten," in *»Neugeboren aus Wasser und Heiligem Geist«*, ed. Brakmann, Chronz, and Sode, 104–14.

99. For the relationship between BR-AC and the corresponding baptismal ritual contained alongside ApTrad in Ethiopic II, see Bausi, "The *Baptismal Ritual*," 47. Bausi provides a chart outlining the corresponding passages in Horner and Duensing, while

The text of the "Euchologion" (or Text 10) from the Aksumite Collection (henceforth Euch-AC) has, however, not yet been published by Bausi, but Bausi was generous enough to share it with us in advance.[100] A number of descriptions of the Euchologion have already been published, but since the text remains unpublished in full, we have provided a comprehensive overview of the text, an overview of where portions of the text have been published, and also parallels to other published texts in Table 2 below. A number of translations of the anaphoras of St. Mark (MARK/CYRIL, this version is known as Ethio-MARK I) and the Ethiopian Anaphora of the Apostles (this version is known as Ethio-AA I), as well as their accompanying prayers, have also been published by Emmanuel Fritsch.[101] The Ge'ez of MARK/CYRIL (Ethio-MARK I), along with a Greek retrotranslation, has recently been published by Valerio Polidori.[102] There is a forthcoming English translation of the baptismal portion of Euch-AC.[103]

---

also noting the earlier work of Antoine Salles, *Trois antiques rituels du baptême*, SC 59 (Paris: Les Éditions du Cerf, 1958). See also the Excursus in Ch. 5 of our commentary.

100. For a description of the collection, see Bausi, "The *Baptismal Ritual*"; Ágnes T. Mihálykó, *The Christian Liturgical Papyri: An Introduction*, Studien und Texte zu Antike und Christentum 114 (Tübingen: Mohr Siebeck, 2019), 43–44. There are also prayers for the sick and the dead, but no rituals for them. The ministerial prayers apparently relate only to the consecration of virgins and monks. For a discussion of the dating of the whole collection, see Bausi and Camplani, "New Ethiopic Documents for the History of Christian Egypt."

101. Emmanuel Fritsch, "New Reflections on the Image of Late Antique and Medieval Ethiopian Liturgy," in *Liturgy's Imagined Past/s: Methodologies and Materials in the Writing of Liturgical History Today*, ed. Teresa Berger (Collegeville, MN: Liturgical Press, 2016), 39–92; Emmanuel Fritsch, "How the Antiochene Anaphora of the Apostolic Tradition Became the Ge'ez Anaphora of the Apostles," in *Holy Spirit University of Kaslik, Faculty of Religious and Oriental Sciences, Institute of Liturgy and Department of Syriac and Antiochian Sciences, International Conference "Anaphora in Syriac Rites" 26–28 April 2017* (Beirut: USEK, 2017), 115–58; Emmanuel Fritsch, "Two Ancient Ge'ez Witnesses of the Anaphora of Saint Mark," in *Explorations in Eastern Christian Liturgy: Selected Papers of the Sixth International Congress of the Society of Oriental Liturgy, Etchmiadzin, Armenia, 11–16 September 2016*, ed. Nina Glibetic and Gabriel Radle, Studies in Eastern Christian Liturgies 4 (Münster: Aschendorff Verlag, 2022), 297–323.

102. Valerio Polidori, *Alexandria Unveiled: An Exploration of the Most Ancient Recension of St. Mark's Liturgy*, Studi sul Cristianesimo Primitivo 4 (Coppell: Kindle Direct, 2023).

103. Alessandro Bausi and Nathan P. Chase, "Rite for Christian Initiation from Alexandria," in *Prayer in the Ancient World*, ed. Daniel Falk and Rodney Werline (Leiden: Brill, forthcoming).

**Table 2: Euch-AC**

| **Prayer** | | **H** | **D** | **Folio in Euch-AC** |
|---|---|---|---|---|
| First prayer of the morning | | 79.1–82.29 | | $\Sigma 46^{rb}$-$46^{vb}$ |
| Prayer for the sick | | " | | $\Sigma 46^{vb}$-$47^{rb}$ |
| Prayer for those who make a journey | | " | | $\Sigma 47^{rb}$-$47^{va}$ |
| Prayer for rains | | " | | $\Sigma 47^{va}$-$47^{vb}$ |
| Prayer for the fruit of the earth | | " | | $\Sigma 47^{vb}$-$48^{ra}$ |
| Prayer for the waters of the rivers | | " | | $\Sigma 48^{ra}$-$48^{rb}$ |
| Prayer for the kings | | " | | $\Sigma 48^{rb}$-$48^{va}$ |
| Prayer for the catechumens | | 83.25–84.11 | | $\Sigma 48^{vb}$-$49^{ra}$ |
| Prayer for the laying on of hands upon the catechumens | | 36.13-23 | 102.14–104.6 | $\Sigma 49^{ra}$ |
| Prayer for those who offer an offering | | 83.1-24 | | $\Sigma 49^{rb}$-$49^{va}$ |
| Prayer for those who have fallen asleep | | Parallelism in 84.12–85.9[104] | | $\Sigma 49^{va}$-$49^{vb}$ |

104. Cf. Ignazio Guidi, "Due antiche preghiere nel Rituale abissino dei Defonti," *Oriens Christianus* NS 11 (1911): 20.

| | | | | |
|---|---|---|---|---|
| Prayer for peace | | 85.10-29 | | $\Sigma 49^{vb}$-$50^{rb}$ |
| Prayer for the congregation | | 86.1-16 | | $\Sigma 50^{rb}$-$50^{va}$ |
| Prayer for those who gave their names | | 30.5-21 | 82.6–84.2 | $\Sigma 50^{va}$-$51^{ra}$ |
| Prayer for the Papas | | 86.17–87.8 | | $\Sigma 51^{ra}$-$51^{va}$ |
| Prayer for the laying on of hands on the faithful | | | | $\Sigma 51^{va}$-$51^{vb}$ |
| Prayer for the water of baptism | | 31.19–32.3 | 88.5-16 | $\Sigma 51^{vb}$-$52^{ra}$ |
| Prayer for the holy oil for anointing him who is to be baptized | | 34.10-19 | 96.8-15 | $\Sigma 52^{ra}$ |
| Apotaxis and Syntaxis | | 37.27–38.11 | 108.15–110.9 | $\Sigma 52^{ra}$-$52^{rb}$ |
| Prayer for laying on of hands | | ( )[105] | ( )[106] | $\Sigma 52^{rb}$-$52^{va}$ |
| Anointing | | 39.7-12 | 114.2-8 | $\Sigma 52^{va}$-$52^{vb}$ |
| Prayer after anointing | | 39.12-20 | 114.9-16 | $\Sigma 52^{vb}$ |

105. Not the same prayer as the prayer in this location in H 36.13-23 (p. 171). H 36.13-23 appears earlier in the intercessions; see the "Prayer for the laying on of hands upon the catechumens" (Σ49ra). However, this prayer is very similar to the handlaying prayer in H 38.25–39.6 = 173.27–174.9. H seems to have been duplicated here.

106. Not entirely the same as 112.10–114.2, but very similar. This is the prayer in the BR-AC (69.6-16).

**Table 2: Euch-AC** (cont.)

| **Prayer** | **H** | **D** | **Folio in Euch-AC** |
|---|---|---|---|
| Baptism | 39.20–40.2 | 114.17–116.9 | $\Sigma 52^{vb}$-$53^{ra}$ |
| Prayer of the holy chrism | 34.19–35.18 | 96.16–100.6 | $\Sigma 53^{ra}$-$53^{va}$ |
| Laying on of hands[107] | 40.2-13 | 116.10–118.3 | $\Sigma 53^{vb}$ |
| Prayer of the oil for the new ones. Entrance of the catechumens to the sick | 33.25–34.10 | 94.15–96.7 | $\Sigma 53^{vb}$-$54^{ra}$ |
| Exorcism of the water | 32.3-11 | 90.1-8 | $\Sigma 54^{rb}$ |
| Ethio-MARK I | Ethiopic in Polidori;[108] English translation in Fritsch[109] | | $\Sigma 54^{rb}$-$56^{va}$ |
| Fraction Prayer and Communion rites | | | $\Sigma 56^{va}$-$57^{va}$ |
| Laying on of hands on virgins and nuns | | | $\Sigma 57^{va}$-$57^{vb}$ |
| Imposition of hands in marriage | | | $\Sigma 57^{vb}$ |

107. But it omits: "wie durch dich, dein einzelner Sohn Jesus Christus versprach, indem sie neu geboren aus Wasser und aus Geist waren" which appears in BR-Euch (75.13–77.10).

108. Polidori, *Alexandria Unveiled*, 112–21.

109. Fritsch, "New Reflections," 47–54; Fritsch, "How the Antiochene Anaphora"; Fritsch, "Two Ancient."

| | | | | |
|---|---|---|---|---|
| Evening Prayer | | | | $\Sigma 57^{vb}$-$58^{rb}$ |
| Prayer at Night | | | | $\Sigma 58^{rb}$-$58^{va}$ |
| Prayer of supplication | | | | $\Sigma 58^{va}$-$59^{rb}$ |
| Prayer of the house | | | | $\Sigma 59^{rb}$-$59^{va}$ |
| Prayer of the infants | | | | $\Sigma 59^{va}$-$59^{vb}$ |
| Prayer when they gird a monk | | Grébaut 1940[110] | | $\Sigma 59^{vb}$-$60^{rb}$ |
| Prayer of marriage | | | | $\Sigma 60^{rb}$-$60^{va}$ |
| Morning Prayer | | | | $\Sigma 60^{va}$-$61^{ra}$ |
| Evening Prayer | | | | $\Sigma 61^{ra}$ |
| Prayer for travels | | | | $\Sigma 61^{ra}$-$61^{va}$ |
| Ethio-AA I | | English translation in Fritsch[111] | | $\Sigma 61^{va}$-$62^{va}$ |
| Fraction Prayer | | | | $\Sigma 62^{va}$-$62^{vb}$ |

110. Sylvain Grébaut, *Rituel éthiopien de prise d'habit* (Paris: Firmin-Dibot, 1940), 234.5–235.2.
111. Fritsch, "New Reflections," 47–54; Fritsch, "How the Antiochene Anaphora."

Euch-AC, like BR-AC, will help provide further information about the reception of ApTrad in Egypt and Ethiopia. A more thorough study will have to await the publication of the text. However, there is one key part of Euch-AC that can already be investigated, and that is the two anaphoras within the Euchologion, as well as the accompanying prayers for the Eucharist—fraction prayer, prayer of inclination, call to communion, prayer after communion, and dismissal prayer. Also, some of Euch-AC is paralleled in the prayers accompanying Ethiopic II. Indications of the initiatory materials in Euch-AC have also been noted by Bausi alongside his publication of BR-AC and will be mentioned further in the chapter on initiation.

### *5.2.1. Other Sources*

A few other sources are worth comparing to ApTrad. The first is the Syriac *Epitome*. This text is contained in Book 5 of the *Clementine Octateuch* and Vatican MS. *Borgia syr.* 148 f. 91v-92r, dated to 1575/1576.[112] This text combines the prologues of ApTrad and ApCons.

Second, there are a number of sources that parallel the baptismal rites. This includes the prayers in the sacramentary of Sarapion of Thmuis (mid-fourth century, Egyptian—Thmuis),[113] the *Canons of Basil* (CB)—Canons 101–106 (a sixth-century text, possibly from Syria but which circulated in Egypt),[114] Arabic *Testamentum Domini* II.B also known as "Baumstark's

112. Richard Connolly, "The Prologue to the *Apostolic Tradition* of Hippolytus," *Journal of Theological Studies* 22 (1921): 356–61.

113. Maxwell Johnson, *The Prayers of Sarapion of Thmuis: A Literary, Liturgical, and Theological Analysis*, Orientalia Christiana Analecta 249 (Roma: Pontifico Istituto Orientale, 1995). For a new edition, translation, and updated commentary, see Maxwell E. Johnson, *The Prayers of Saint Sarapion of Thmuis: A Revised Greek Text and Translation of the Euchologion Sarapionis*, Popular Patristics Series 65 (Yonkers: St. Vladimir's Seminary Press, 2023).

114. This text is thought to have emerged in Syria but was likely in circulation in Egypt in the sixth century where it was also given an Egyptian reformulation; see Alberto Camplani and Federico Contardi, "Remarks on the Textual Contribution of the Coptic Codices Preserving the Canons of Saint Basil, with Edition of the Ordination Rite for the Bishop (Canon 46)," in *Philologie, herméneutique et histoire des textes entre Orient et Occident: Mélanges en hommage à Sever J. Voicu*, ed. Francesca Prometea Barone, Caroline Macé, and Pablo Alejandro Ubierna (Turnhout: Brepols, 2017), 139–59; Mihálykó, *The*

liturgy" (dated at the latest to the eighth/ninth century—possibly as early as the sixth century, Egypt),[115] and the initiatory rituals of the more recent liturgical books of the *Coptic Rite* (henceforth CR),[116] which has been recently studied in detail by Brakmann.[117] More work is needed on the medieval Coptic manuscripts, but the CR appears to follow the earliest Bohairic sources. Another Egyptian initiatory text with the description of an anaphora worth including is the Ethiopian Mystagogical Catechesis (henceforth Ethio-MC), which is thought to have been copied from a Greek exemplar in Alexandria in the fifth century (possibly late fourth).[118]

---

*Christian Liturgical Papyri*, 45. The Sahidic version differs from the Arabic, which has been published by Wilhelm Riedel, *Die Kirchenrechtsquellen des Patriarchats Alexandrien* (Leipzig: A. Deichert, nachf. G. Böhme, 1900), 278–83. A summary of the differences in the Sahidic and Arabic has been made by Camplani and Contardi; see Camplani and Contardi, "Remarks on the Textual Contribution," 145–47. In general, the Coptic provides the structure of the rite, while omitting the prayers. Camplani and Contardi believe that the Arabic is the better witness with regard to the prayers.

115. Anton Baumstark, "Eine ägyptische Mess- und Taufliturgie vermutlich des 6. Jahrhunderts," *Oriens Christianus* 1 (1901): 1–45; Brakmann, "ⲃⲁⲡⲧⲓⲥⲙⲁ ⲁⲓⲛⲉⲥⲉⲱⲥ," 129–37; Mihálykó, *The Christian Liturgical Papyri*, 45–46.

116. For an overview, see Maxwell Johnson, *The Rites of Christian Initiation: Their Evolution and Interpretation* (Collegeville, MN: Liturgical Press, 2007), Ch. 7. All English translations taken from DBL, 132–39. DBL's translation more or less corresponds to the two long versions of the Coptic Rite (CR 1 and 2) in Heinrich Denzinger, *Ritus Orientalium, Coptorum, Syrorum et Armenorum, in administrandis sacramentis*, 2 vols. (Graz: Akademische Druck - U. Verlagsanstalt, 1961). For CR1, see pp. 192–214. For CR2, see pp. 214–21. CR1 is based on the eighteenth-century *editio princeps* by Joseph Aloysius Assemanus; see Brakmann, "ⲃⲁⲡⲧⲓⲥⲙⲁ ⲁⲓⲛⲉⲥⲉⲱⲥ," 150. CR2 is copied from Codex Paris copt. 72 (14th to 17th centuries) via the edition by Eusèbe Renaudot; see Brakmann, 148. CR1 and 2 are very similar, especially in the parts of the initiatory ritual analyzed in this study. CR1 and CR2 appear to be very similar to the earliest Bohairic manuscript of the Coptic Rite: Codex Borg. copt. 112 (dated 1307/08); see Brakmann, 148 and 157–94 (passim). Coupled with extra-liturgical sources, this suggests that the CR had entered a more or less stable tradition before the 13th/14th century; see Brakmann, 154.

117. Brakmann, "ⲃⲁⲡⲧⲓⲥⲙⲁ ⲁⲓⲛⲉⲥⲉⲱⲥ," 145–94.

118. Emmanuel Fritsch, "The *Order of the Mystery*: An Ancient Catechesis Preserved in BnF Ethiopic Ms d'Abbadie 66-66bis (Fifteenth Century) with a Liturgical Commentary," in *Studies in Oriental Liturgy: Proceedings of the Fifth International Congress of the Society of Oriental Liturgy New York, 10–14 June 2014*, ed. Bert Groen et al. (Leuven: Peeters, 2019), 241; Mihálykó, *The Christian Liturgical Papyri*, 44–45.

All English translations of these sources in this commentary are taken from the translations given in the footnotes for each source.

Third, there are some parallels to other prayers like the Eucharist and anointing of the sick. This includes the sacramentary of Sarapion of Thmuis (see above); the materials in the so-called "Barcelona Papyrus" (P.Monts.Roca), dated to fourth-century Upper Egypt;[119] as well as some anaphoral texts like *Mystagogical Catechesis* Ch. 5 (MC 5), MARK, and the anaphora of St. James (JAS).[120] There are also some parallel texts in Euch-AC, which will not be used in this study. This includes the prayers in the *Maṣḥafa genzat* "The Funeral Book"[121] and the *Maṣḥafa qeddāsē* "Book of the Liturgy."[122]

Finally, there are parallels to the *Gnomai of the Council of Nicea* (GCN), which is from mid-fourth-century Egypt;[123] the *Canons of Athanasius* (CA), which is pseudo-Athanasian and dated from the fourth/fifth century and is from somewhere in Egypt;[124] and the *Syntagma Doctrinae*

119. For a summary of the papyrus, as well as the Greek and English translations of the liturgical portions of the text, see Chase, *The Anaphoral Tradition*, Ch. 3.

120. For a helpful summary of those sources and their editions, see Chase, *The Anaphoral Tradition*, Appendix C.

121. Cf. Bausi, "La *Collezione Aksumita*," n. 32. For the edition of the *Maṣḥafa genzat*, see V. Six, *Aethiopische Handschriften vom Ṭānāsee. Teil* 3. *Nebst einem Nachtrag zum Katalog der äthiopischen. Handschriften deutscher Bibliotheken und Museen* (Stuttgart: Steiner Verlag, 1999).

122. Cf. Bausi, "La *Collezione Aksumita*," n. 33. For the edition of the *Mäṣḥafä Qəddase*, see V. Six, *Aethiopische Handschriften vom Ṭānāsee*. See also *Mäṣḥafä Qəddase*, *መጽሐፈ፡ ቅዳሴ። በግዕዝና፡ በአማርኛ። አዲስ፡ አበባ፡ ፲፱፻፶፩፡ ዓመተ፡ ምሕረት።* *Mäṣḥafä Qəddase. bä-Gəʿəz-ənna bä-Amarəñña [Book of the Liturgy. In Gəʿəz and Amharic]* (Addis Ababa: Täsfa Press, 1958). English translation Marcos Daoud and H. E. Blatta Marsie Hazen, *The Liturgy of the Ethiopian Church* (Cairo: Egyptian Book Press, 1959).

123. Alistair Stewart, ed., *The Gnomai of the Council of Nicea (CC 0021): Critical Text with Translation, Introduction and Commentary*, Texts from Christian Late Antiquity 35 (Piscataway, NJ: Gorgias Press, 2015).

124. For the text, see Wilhelm Riedel and W. E. Crum, *The Canons of Athanasius of Alexandria: The Arabic and Coptic Versions* (London: Williams and Norgate, 1904). For discussions of dating and provenance, see Ewa Wipszycka, "A Certain Bishop and a Certain Diocese in Egypt at the Turn of the Fourth and Fifth Centuries: The Testimony of the Canons of Athanasius," *U Schyłku Starożytności: Studia Źródłoznawcze = Late Antiquity: Studies in Source Criticism* 17/18 (2018/2019): 91–115.

(SD), which is dated to fourth-century Egypt.[125] All English translations of these sources in this commentary are taken from the translations given in the footnotes for each source.

## 6. Sources and Materials Behind the Formation of ApTrad

*Herm.Com.* 2002 has persuasively argued that this church order is not the work of Hippolytus, or any one individual; rather, it is a composite document made up of a number of layers and strands of diverse provenance that were compiled over time. Thus, it does not represent the practice of any one Christian community, but rather it is a piece of "living literature."[126] The text contains a number of layers discernable through internal and external comparison.[127] *Herm.Com.* 2002 argued that the document consisted of three core sections, likely three sources of original material, that were combined together:[128]

- Directives about appointment to ministry:
  - 2.1-4; 7.1; 8.1; 9.1-2(?); 10.1-3; 11; 12*; 13; 14
- Directives about the initiation of new converts:
  - 15; 16; 17; 18; 19; 20; 21.1-5, 12-18, 20, 25-26
- Directives about community meals and prayer:
  - 23*; 24 (=29B); 25 (=29C*); 26(?); 27; 28.4-6; 29A; 30A; 31; 32; 33; 35

125. H. Hyvernat, "Le Syntagma Doctrinae," in *Studia Patristica: Études d'ancienne Littérature Chrétienne*, ed. Pierre Batiffol (Paris: Leroux, 1890), 118–60.

126. *Herm.Com.* 2002, 13–14. For debates on authorship, see also Christoph Markschies, "Neue Forschungen zur sogenannten 'Traditio Apostolica,'" in *Comparative Liturgy Fifty Years after Anton Baumstark (1872–1948), Acts of the International Congress, Rome, 25–29 September 1998*, ed. Robert Taft and Gabriele Winkler, OCA 265 (Rome: Pontificio Istituto Orientale, 2001), 583–98; Christoph Markschies, "Wer schrieb die sogenannte *Traditio Apostolica*? Neue Beobachtungen und Hypothesen zu einer kaum lösbaren Frage aus der altkirchen Literaturgeschichte," in *Tauffragen und Bekenntnis*, ed. Wolfram Kinzig, Christoph Markschies, and Markus Vinzent (Berlin: De Gruyter, 1999), 1–74; Stewart, *On the Apostolic Tradition*, 15–63; Messner, "Die Angebliche *Traditio Apostolica*," 1–3.

127. *Herm.Com.* 2002, 6–13.

128. *Herm.Com.* 2002, 14–15.

The rest of the material found in ApTrad represents expansions[129] or additions[130] to this earlier core.

The chapters above with an asterisk (*) may not, however, have been part of the original source material used to initially compile ApTrad. With the witness of Ethiopic I, there is a need to reassess the earlier core of ApTrad. It is very possible that Chs. 12, 23.4, and 29C.10-15 are later additions to the text, since they are not in Ethiopic I and were possibly not in the Latin version either (here there is a lacuna in the Latin). Ch. 12 does not make its way into CH either, except possibly in CH 7. Ch. 29Ab is very likely a later addition since it is not contained in either the Latin or Ethiopic I sources or in any of ApTrad's derivatives. A few other chapters/verses need to also be accounted for. Ch. 7.2-5 is in the Latin and Ethiopic II and is also paralleled in ApCons and TD, but it is not in Ethiopic I or CH. Ch. 8.9-12 is in the Latin and Ethiopic II, but is not in Ethiopic I and is substantially different in CH 5. Ch. 35 is in all sources but Ethiopic I and CH, but this is already largely a duplication of Ch. 41.[131] This preliminary comparison of Ethiopic I, with both the Latin version and *Herm.Com.* 2002's hypothetical core, suggests that Ethiopic I may at times be preserving an older set of readings than the Latin version of ApTrad;[132] however, its use of the long ending may indicate some development as well (see Ch. 2 of our commentary).

## 7. Comparison of the Sources and the Original Order of ApTrad

The following table (Table 3) provides an overview of the various versions of ApTrad and related sources. The chart begins with a few documents that precede ApTrad in Ethiopic I. Then it switches to ApTrad and the chapter order as given in *Herm.Com.* 2002, with chapters 29B and 29C restored to their proper order as chapters 24 and 25. Ethiopic I and the

129. 2.5; 7.2-5; 8.2-12; 9.2-5; 10.4-5; 21.6-11, 19, 21-24, 27-40; 28.1-3.

130. 1; 3; 4; 5; 6; 22; 29D; 30B; 34; 36; 37; 38A; 38B; 39; 40; 41; 42; 43.

131. Nathan Chase, "Another Look at the 'Daily Office' in the *Apostolic Tradition*," *Studia Liturgica* 49 (2019): 5–25.

132. Messner, "Die Angebliche *Traditio Apostolica*," 21–25.

Arabic I confirm that this is the original placement of these chapters.[133] The chart then concludes with a few of the additional documents that follow ApTrad in Ethiopic I. Two places where Ethiopic II significantly differs from the order in *Herm.Com.* 2002 and Ethiopic I have been noted below. Here we follow the order outlined by Meßner, which largely follows the *Alexandrian Sinodos*. Meßner debated between whether to follow the *Alexandrian Sinodos* or Ethiopic I. However, he noted a few things that we also should note in adopting the following order. Ethiopic I in the first part of ApTrad (Chs. 4–14) has omitted some materials (Ch. 4),[134] displaced others (Chs. 5 and 6),[135] and rearranged still others (the chapters on orders, Chs. 9–14).[136] Arabic I largely supports the order below.

Meßner has, however, cautioned against attempting—at least with the current witnesses—to create a single archetype. Rather, he thinks that several different recensions can be seen.[137] This likely confirms the layered and patchwork quality of ApTrad, and also provides an opening for some of its derivatives, like CH, to preserve older readings than the received witnesses of ApTrad.

133. This has been further affirmed by Lüstraeten, "The Arabic Versions of the So-Called *Traditio Apostolica*."

134. For the reasons why, see Ch. 6 of our commentary.

135. For the reasons why, see Ch. 6 of our commentary.

136. For more on this rearrangement, see Ch. 3 of our commentary.

137. Messner, "Die Angebliche *Traditio Apostolica*," 26.

**Table 3: Comparison of the Different**

{ } General Remarks in absence of title
" Same title/category
[ ] Transposed passages
- Absent

| **Title** | ***Herm. Com.* 2002 Numbering** | **Latin** | ***Alexandrian Sinodos*** | | **Arabic version of *Clementine Octateuch* (Arabic I)**[139] |
|---|---|---|---|---|---|
| | | | **Sahidic/ Bohairic(?)**[140] | **Arabic II** | |
| | | | | | **Ethiopic I** |
| {*Canones ecclesiastici*} | | 65.1–67.30 | § 1-30 | § 1-20 | Included |
| {*Alexandrian History*} | | - | - | - | |
| {*Epistle 70* by Cyprian} | | - | - | - | |
| **ApTrad (Text 4 in Ethiopic I) Ordering** | | | | | |
| {Prologue} | § 1 (= §30B) | 67.31–68.13 | - | - | § 30 |
| Concerning Bishops | § 2 | 68.14-25 | § 31 | § 21 | § 31 |
| {Prayer for the Ordination of a Bishop} | § 3.1-4 | 68.26–69.13 | - | - | § 32 |
| " | § 3.5-6 | 69.13-24 | - | - | - |

138. Adapted and expanded from Bausi, "The >so-called *Traditio apostolica*<," 293–95. The chart has also been expanded with reference to Messner, "Die Angebliche *Traditio Apostolica*", particularly pp. 23–24.

139. Messner, "Die Angebliche *Traditio Apostolica*," 17–18 and 23–24. Additional edits and additions by Martin Lüstraeten; see Lüstraeten, "The Arabic Versions of the So-Called *Traditio Apostolica*." The numbering is based on the numbering given in Riedel (*Die Kirchenrechtsquellen des Patriarchats* Alexandrien, 70–72) according to Abu-I-Barakat (Diez A quart. 111, fol. 159a–159v), and corresponds for the most part to the oldest witness Arabic I M1. The Abu-I-Barakat numbering will be used here. For more on the numbering of Arabic I, see Ch. 1 of our commentary.

140. For the edition of the whole collection, see nn. 52 and 58.

**Versions of ApTrad**[138]

= Textual identity between Ethiopic I and II

\+ Partial textual identity between Ethiopic I and II

// Parallelism of contents between Ethiopic I and II

? Information not known

lac. lacuna

| **Ethiopic I (*Aksumite Collection)*** | | **Ethiopic II (*Sinodos*)** | | **ApCons** | **CH**[141] | **TD** | **Other Sources** |
|---|---|---|---|---|---|---|---|
| | | Horner[142] | Duensing | | | | |
| **Ordering** | | | | | | | |
| Text 1 | // | 1.1–10.4 (§ 1-21) | | | | | |
| Text 2 | - | - | | | | | |
| Text 3 | = | (in some manuscripts) | | | | | |
| **According to *Herm.Com.* 2002** | | | | | | | |
| Introduction | = | [29.5-17 (§ 40)] | [78.12–80.6 (§ 39)] | 8.3.1-2 | § 1 | I.14 | Syriac Epitome |
| § 1 | // | 10.5-15 (§ 22) | 16.1-11 (§ 21) | 8.4.2-6 | § 2 | I.20 | |
| § 1 | // | 10.15–11.3 (§ 22) | 16.11–18.12 (§ 21) | Epitome 4.1-4 | § 3 | I.21 | |
| § 1 | = | 11.3-9 (§ 22) | 18.12–20.1 (§ 21) | " | " | " | |

141. The material noted as parallels between ApTrad and CH throughout *Herm.Com.* 2002 is placed outside ( ) in the text. Additional parallels noted in Chase and Johnson, *The Origins of the Canons of Hippolyt*us have been placed in ( ).

142. Horner, *The* Statutes, 1–88 (Ethiopic text), 127–232 (English translation of Ethiopic text), and 365–420 (notes to the Ethiopic text).

| Title | *Herm. Com.* 2002 | Latin | Sah/Boh | Arb II | Arb I |
|---|---|---|---|---|---|
| {Eucharistic Prayer} | § 4 | 69.25–70.35 | § 31 | § 21 | - |
| {Concerning the Offering of Oil} | § 5 | 71.1-9 | - | - | - |
| {Concerning the Offering of Cheese and Olives} | § 6 | 71.10-19 | - | - | - |
| Concerning Presbyters | § 7.1 | 71.20-25 | § 32 | § 22 | § 33 |
| {Prayer for the Ordination of a Presbyter} | § 7.2-5 | 71.25–72.5 | - | - | " |
| Concerning Deacons | § 8.1-8 | 72.6-28 | § 33 | § 23 | § 34 |
| {Prayer for the Ordination of a Deacon} | § 8.9-12 | 72.29-35 (lac.) | - | - | § 35 |
| Concerning Confessors | § 9 | (lac.) | § 34 | § 24 | § 36 (with added material) |
| Concerning Widows | § 10 | (lac.) | § 37 | § 25 | § 37 |
| Concerning a Reader | § 11 | (lac.) | § 35 | § 26 | § 38 |
| Concerning Virgins | § 12 | (lac.) | § 38 | § 26 | § 39 |
| Concerning a Subdeacon | § 13 | (lac.) | § 36 | § 26 | § 40 |
| Concerning the Gift of Healing | § 14 | (lac.) | § 39 | § 26 | § 41 |

| Ethio I | | Ethio II | | ApCons | CH | TD | Other |
|---|---|---|---|---|---|---|---|
| - | - | 11.9–12.16 (§ 22) | 20.1–24.2 (§ 21) | 8.5.9-10; 8.12.7-50 | " | I.21, I.23 | |
| [§ 8] | // | 12.16-23 (§ 22) | 24.3-9 (§ 21) | - | " | I.24 | Manuscript from St. Catherine's |
| [§ 9] | - | - | - | - | " | " | |
| § 2 | // | 14.12-15 (§ 23) | 30.8-9 (§ 22) | 8.16.2-5 | § 4 | I.30 | |
| - | - | 14.15-28 (§ 23) | 30.10–32.6 (§ 22) | " | - | " | |
| § 3 | // | 14.29–15.18 (§ 24) | 32.7–34.7 (§ 23) | 8.17 | § 5 | I.33-34, I.38 | |
| - | - | 15.19–16.3 (§ 24) | 34.8-18 (§ 23) | - | " | I.38 | |
| [§ 7] | // | 16.4-18 (§ 25) | 36.1-17 (§ 24) | 8.23.1-4 | § 6 | I.39 | |
| [§ 6] | // | 16.22–17.3 (§ 26) | 38.1-10 (§ 25) | 8.25.1-3 | § 9 | I.40 | |
| [§ 5] | // | 17.4-7 (§ 27) | 38.11-13 (§ 26) | Epitome 13 | § 7 | I.45 | |
| - | - | 17.7-8 (§ 27) | 38.13-15 (§ 26) | 8.24 | Parallels to § 7 | I.46 | |
| § 4 | - | 17.8-10 § 27) | 38.15-17 (§ 26) | 8.21 | " | I.44 | |
| [§ 11] | // | 17.10-13 (§ 27) | 38.17–40.2 (§ 26) | 8.26.2 | § 8 | I.47 | |

| Title | *Herm. Com.* 2002 | Latin | Sah/Boh | Arb II | Arb I |
|---|---|---|---|---|---|
| Concerning a presbyter or a deacon who travels | - | (lac.) | - | - | § 42 |
| Concerning Newcomers to the Faith | § 15 | (lac.) | § 40 | § 27 | § 43 |
| Concerning Crafts and Professions | § 16 | (lac.) | § 41 | § 27-29 | § 44 |
| Concerning the Time of Hearing the Word after the Examination of Crafts and Professions | § 17 | (lac.) | § 42 | § 30 | § 45 |
| Concerning the Prayer of Those Who Hear the Word | § 18 | (lac.) | § 43 | § 31 | § 46 |
| Concerning the Imposition of Hands on Catechumens | § 19 | (lac.) | § 44 | § 32 | § 47 |
| Concerning Those Who Are to Receive Baptism | § 20 | (lac.) | § 45 | § 33 | § 48 |
| Concerning the Tradition of Holy Baptism | § 21.1-18 | (lac.) 73.1-13 | § 46 | § 34 | § 48 |
| " | § 21.19-40 | 73.13–74.35 (lac.) | § 46 | § 34 | § 48 |
| {Concerning Communion} | § 22 | (lac.) | - | - | § 48 |
| Concerning Fasting | § 23.1-3 | (lac.) | § 47 | § 35 | § 49 |

| Ethio I | | Ethio II | | ApCons | CH | TD | Other |
|---|---|---|---|---|---|---|---|
| - | - | - | - | - | (§ 9) | | |
| § 10 | // | 17.14–18.1 (§ 28) | 40.3–42.10 (§ 27) | 8.32.2-6 | § 10 | II.1 | |
| § 12 | // | 18.1–19.8 (§ 28-30) | 42.11–46.11 (§ 27-29) | 8.32.7-13 | § 11-16 | II.2 | |
| § 13 | // | 19.9-13 (§ 31) | 46.12-16 (§ 30) | 8.32.16 | § 17 | II.3 | |
| § 14 | // | 19.14-25 (§ 32) | 46.17–48.9 (§ 31) | - | § 18 | II.4 | |
| § 15 | // | 19.26–20.6 (§ 33) | 48.10-17 (§ 32) | 8.32.17 | § 18-19 | II.5 | |
| § 16 | // | 20.6–21.4 (§ 34) | 48.18–52.5 (§ 33) | - | § 19 | II.6-8 | |
| § 17 | // | 21.5–22.25 (§ 35) | 52.6–58.7 (§ 34) | - | § 19 | II.8 | |
| § 18 | // | 22.25–24.28 (§ 35) | 58.7–64.7 (§ 34) | - | § 19 and 29-31 | II.8-10 | |
| § 18 | // | 24.28–25.5 (§ 35) | 64.7-13 (§ 34) | - | § 30-31 | II.10 | |
| § 19 | // | 25.6-14 (§ 36) | 66.3-10 (§ 35) | *Epitome* Fragment (Funk, *Didascalia et Constitutiones Apostolorum*, II:112) | § 32 | - | Vienna *gr.* 7 |

| Title | *Herm. Com.* 2002 | Latin | Sah/Boh | Arb II | Arb I |
|---|---|---|---|---|---|
| " | § 23.4 | (lac.) | § 47 | § 35 | - |
| **§ 24-25 (Original Placement** | | | | | |
| Concerning Gifts for the Sick | § 29B,1-2 (= § 24) | (lac.) | - | - | § 50 |
| " | § 29B, 3-4 (= § 24) | (lac.) | - | - | § 51 |
| Concerning the Bringing in of the Lamps at the Supper of the Congregation | § 29C,1-9 (= § 25) | (lac.) | - | - | § 52 |
| " | § 29C,10-15 (= § 25) | (lac.) | - | - | (only verse 10) |
| " | § 29C,16 (cp. § 23.4) (= § 26 Botte) | (lac.) | § 47 | § 35 | § 52 |
| **Resume *Herm.Com.*** | | | | | |
| Concerning the Hour of Eating | § 26 | (lac.)75.1-4 | § 48 | § 36 | § 53 |
| That It Is Not Proper for Catechumens to Eat with the Faithful | § 27 | 75.5-9 | § 49 | § 36 | § 54 |
| That It Is Proper to Eat Judiciously and Moderately | § 28 | 75.10–76.3 | § 50 | § 36-37 | § 55 |

| Ethio I | | Ethio II | | ApCons | CH | TD | Other |
|---|---|---|---|---|---|---|---|
| - | - | 25.14-18 (§ 36) | 66.10-14 (§ 35) | - | - | II.13 | |
| **of Chs. 29B and C)** | | | | | | | |
| § 20 | = | [27.2-6 (§ 37)] | [72.6-11 (§ 36)] | - | § 32 (and § 5 and 30) | II.10-11 | |
| § 21 | = | [27.6-9 (§ 37)] | [72.11-14 (§ 36)] | - | " | II.10-11 | |
| § 22 | = | [27.9-26 (§ 37)] | [74.1-15 (§ 36)] | 8.37.3 | " | II.11 | |
| - | - | [27.26–28.10 (§ 37)] | [74.15–76.9 (§ 36)] | - | " | II.11 | |
| § 22 | = | [28.11-14 (§ 37)] | [76.10-13 (§ 36)] | - | - | - | |
| **2002's Order** | | | | | | | |
| § 23 | // | 25.19-24 (§ 37) | 66.15–68.3 (§ 36) | - | § 33 (and §20) | - | |
| § 24 | // | 25.24-29 (§ 37) | 68.4-9 (§ 36) | - | § 33 | II.13 | |
| § 25 | // | 25.29–26.23 (§ 37) | 68.10–70.14 (§ 36) | - | § 33-35 (and § 20 and 31) | II.13 | |

| Title | *Herm. Com.* 2002 | Latin | Sah/Boh | Arb II | Arb I |
|---|---|---|---|---|---|
| That It Is Proper to Eat with Thanksgiving | § 29A*a* | 76.4-6 | § 51 | - | § 56 |
| " | § 29A*b* | - | - | - | - |
| {Addition only in Ethiopic II – Doublet of 28.4b-6} | § 29D | [75.10–76.3] | [§ 50] | [§ 36-37] | - |
| Concerning the Supper of the Widows | § 30A | 76.7-13 | § 52 | § 38 | § 57 |
| {Ethiopic II has moved the Prologue here} | § 30B (= § 1) | [67.31–68.13] | - | - | [§ 30] |
| {Ethiopic II has added here its Baptismal Ritual and Euchologion} | | | | | - |
| Concerning the Fruit That It Is Proper to Bring to the Bishop | § 31 | 76.14-28 | § 53 | § 39 | § 58 |
| The Blessing of Fruits | § 32 | 76.29–77.4 | § 54 | § 39 | § 59 |
| That It Is Not Proper for Anyone to Taste Anything in the Pascha before the Hour When It Is Proper to Eat | § 33 | 77.5-16 | § 55 | § 40 | § 60 |
| That It Is Proper for the Deacons to Assist the Bishop | § 34 | 77.17-23 | § 56 | § 41 | § 61 |
| Concerning the Hour When It Is Proper to Pray | § 35 | 77.24-31 | § 57 | § 42 | § 62 |

| Ethio I | | Ethio II | | ApCons | CH | TD | Other |
|---|---|---|---|---|---|---|---|
| § 26 | // | 26.23-27 (§ 37) | 70.14–72.3 (§ 36) | - | § 35 | - | |
| - | - | 26.27-27.2 (§ 37) | 72.3-5 (§ 36) | - | - | - | |
| - | - | 28.15-25 (§ 38) | 76.14–78.5 (§ 37) | [-] | § 33-35 (and § 20 and 31) | [II.13] | |
| § 27 | // | 28.26–29.4 (§ 39) | 78.6-11 (§ 38) | - | § 35 | - | |
| [Introduction] | = | 29.5-17 (§ 40) | 78.12–80.6 (§ 39) | [8.3.1-2] | [§ 1] | [I.14] | |
| [Texts 9-10] | + | 29.5; 29.17–42.19 (§ 40) | 78.12; 80.7–126.2 (§ 39) | | | | |
| § 28 | = | 42.20–43.2 (§ 40) | 126.3-11 (§ 39) | 8.40.2-4 | § 36 (and § 3c) | II.14, 16 | ex., Barberini gr. 336[143] |
| § 29 | // | 43.2-9 (§ 40) | 126.12–128.2 (§ 39) | - | " | II.16-17 | ex., Barberini gr. 336[144] |
| § 30 | = | 43.10-19 (§ 41) | 128.2-14 (§ 40) | - | § 22 (and § 19e) | II.18, 20 | |
| § 31 | // | 43.20-25 (§ 42) | 128.13-18 (§ 41) | - | § 24 (and § 5) | II.21 | |
| - | - | 43.26–44.4 (§ 43) | 130.1-8 (§ 42) | 8.32.18 | - | - | |

143. Connolly, "An Ancient Prayer in the Mediaeval Euchologia," 132–37.
144. Connolly, 132–37.

| Title | *Herm. Com.* 2002 | Latin | Sah/Boh | Arb II | Arb I |
|---|---|---|---|---|---|
| That It Is Not Proper to Receive the Eucharist Early at the Time It Will Be Offered, before They Taste Anything | § 36 | 77.32-78.2 | § 58 | § 43 | § 63 |
| That It Is Proper to Watch over the Eucharist Diligently | § 37 | 78.3-7 | § 59 | § 44 | § 64 |
| That It Is Not Proper to Spill Anything from the Cup | § 38A | 78.8-14 | § 60 | § 44 | § 65 |
| {Concerning the Sign of the Cross} | § 38B (cp. § 42-43) | 78.15-35 (lac.) | - | - | - |
| {Concerning Deacons and Presbyters} | § 39 | (lac.) | § 60 | § 45 | § 66 |
| Concerning the Places of Burial | § 40 | (lac.) | § 61 | § 46 | § 67 |
| Concerning the Hour When It Is Proper to Pray | § 41 | (lac.)79.1-80.14 | § 62 | § 47 | § 68 |
| {Concerning the Sign of the Cross} | § 42 (cp. 38B.1-4) | 80.14-29 | § 62 | § 47 | § 68 |
| {Conclusion} | § 43.1-3 (cp. 38B.5-6) | 80.30-35 (lac.) | § 62 | § 47 | § 68 |
| " | § 43.4 (cp. 38B) | (lac.) | § 62 | § 47 | § 68 |

| **Ethio I** | | **Ethio II** | | **ApCons** | **CH** | **TD** | **Other** |
|---|---|---|---|---|---|---|---|
| § 32 | // | 44.5-10 (§ 44) | 132.1-6 (§ 43) | - | § 28 (and § 19e) | II.25 | "Ochrid frag-ment"[145] |
| § 33 | // | 44.11-17 (§ 45) | 132.7-14 (§ 44) | - | § 28 (and § 29) | - | |
| § 34 | // | 44.17-27 (§ 45) | 132.14–134.5 (§ 44) | - | § 29 | - | |
| - | - | - | - | - | [(§ 29)] | [II.25] | |
| § 34 | // | 44.28–45.6 (§ 46) | 134.6-13 (§ 45) | - | § 21 and 24 | II.21 | |
| [§ 36] | // | 45.7-11 (§ 47) | 134.14–136.2 (§ 46) | - | § 25 (but not § 24 as in *Herm.Com.* 2002) | II.23 | |
| § 35 | // | 45.12–48.2 (§ 48) | 136.3–144.3 (§ 47) | 8.32.18; 8.34.3-5 | § 25-27 | II.24-25 | 41.9 in Vienna *gr.* 7 |
| § 35 | // | 48.2-15 (§ 48) | 144.3-16 (§ 47) | - | § 29 | - | |
| § 35 | // | 48.15-26 (§ 48) | 144.16–146.10 (§ 47) | - | - | II.25 | |
| [§ 38*b*] | // | 48.26-29 (§ 48) [57.9-11 (§ 52*e*)] | 146.10-12 (§ 47) | - | - | - | |

145. Richard, "Quelques fragments des Pères anténicéens et nicéens," 79.

| Title | *Herm. Com.* 2002 | Latin | Sah/Boh | Arb II | Arb I |
|---|---|---|---|---|---|
| | | | | | Ethiopic I |
| {*Decree of the Apostles* (Acts 15:20; John 19:36)} | | | | | |
| {*Didache* (11.3-5, 7-12; 12.1-5; 13.1, 3-7; 8.1-2)} | | | | | |
| {*Didascalia* (12, cp. Ap-Cons 2.57.2-58.6; 2.59)} | | | | | |
| | [§ 43.4 (cp. 38B)] | [(lac.)] | [§ 62] | [§ 47] | |
| {Ethiopic II has added a citation to ApCons 8.3.1 here} | | | § 63 | § 51 | Included |
| {Ethiopic II has added a citation to ApCons 8.3.2 here} | | | § 63 | § 51 | Included |
| {Parallel section to Ap-Cons 8.4–46.17} | | | § 64-78 | § 52-71 | Included |
| {*Περὶ χαρισμάτων* (Ap-Cons 8.1-2)} | | | § 63 | § 48-51 | Included |
| {Apostles and Disciples[146]} | | | | | |
| {Names of the Months} | | | | | |
| {Baptismal Ritual (BR-AC)} | | | | | |
| {Euchologion (Euch-AC)} | | | | | |

146. The text appears in Latin in another manuscript from Verona: Cod. Veron. LI (49) fol. 156b–157b; see C. H. Turner, "A Primitive Edition of the Apostolic Constitutions and Canons and an Early List of Apostles and Disciples," *Journal of Theological Studies* 15, no. 57 (1913): 63–65.

| **Ethio I** | | **Ethio II** | | **ApCons** | **CH** | **TD** | **Other** |
|---|---|---|---|---|---|---|---|
| **Ordering** | | | | | | | |
| § 37 | = | 54.18-20 (§ 52*b*) | | | | | |
| § 37 | = | 54.20–55.29 (§ 52*c*) | | | | | |
| § 38*a* | = | 55.29–57.9 (§ 52*d*) | | | | | |
| § 38*b* | // | 57.9-11 (§ 52*e*) [48.26-29 (§ 48)] | [146.10-12 (§ 47)] | [-] | [-] | [-] | |
| - | - | 57.11-16 (§ 52*f*) (ApCons 8.3.1) | | | | | |
| - | - | 57.16-25 (§ 52*g*) (ApCons 8.3.2) | | | | | |
| Text 5 | // | 57.26–78.15 (§ 53-72) | | | | | |
| Text 6 | + | [49.1–54.18 (§ 49-52*a*)] | | | | | |
| Text 7 | = | (some manuscripts)[147] | | | | | |
| Text 8 | = | (some manuscripts)[148] | | | | | |
| Text 9 | + | [29.5; 29.17–42.19 (§ 40)] | [78.12; 80.7–126.2 (§ 39)] | | | | |
| Text 10 | + | (only partial correspondence, see Table 2 above) | | | | | |

147. It appears in BNF Éthiopien 181, ff. 125vb-127ra and EMML 3515, ff. 93r-94r; see Bausi, "La *Collezione Aksumita*," 60.

148. It appears in BNF Éthiopien 181, f. 127ra-b; see Bausi, 60.

## 8. Chapters in This Study

In order to study the text topically, this study will begin in Chapter 1 by providing the text of the new Ethiopic witness (Ethiopic I) and the Arabic version of the *Clementine Octateuch* (Arabic I) in English translation and corresponding to the chapters and verses given in *Herm.Com.* 2002. Following the text, Chapter 2 looks at the Prologue and Endings of ApTrad (Prologue: Ch. 1; Endings: Chs. 30B, 42, and 43) in order to posit the original form of these chapters. Chapter 3 looks at orders and ministries in the document. This corresponds roughly to Chs. 2, 3, 7-14, 29B, 34, and 39, though other chapters will also be consulted. Chapter 4 will look at daily prayer and the daily horarium in the document. This will focus primarily on Chs. 18, 29C, 35, 36, 39, and 41. Chapter 5 will take up the question of initiation as described in Chs. 15-21 and 27. Chapter 6 will look at the eucharistic practices outlined in the document, as well as the communal meals and larger meal practices that are described. The Eucharist and communion are described primarily in Chs. 4, 9, 21.25-29 and 31-37, 22, 33, 36–38A; the blessing of foodstuffs connected to the Eucharist in Chs. 5–6 and 21.27-29; firstfruits that are given to the church in Chs. 31–32; and, finally, communal meal practices in Chs. 23–33. Connections to other chapters in ApTrad will also be made. Chapter 7 will address the treatment of the sick (Chs. 5, 14, 29B, and 34) and Christian burial practices (Ch. 40). Chapter 8 looks at the other assorted rituals described in ApTrad. This includes fasting (Chs. 23, 33, and 36), the making of the sign of the cross (Chs. 38B and 42), ritual washings (Chs. 20.5 as well as 41.1, 11-14). This chapter will also look at a number of texts that were added into the document in the version of ApTrad in Ethiopic I that may have a bearing on discussions of ApTrad's development and provenance. This includes a section "Concerning Idols" (§ 37); "Concerning the apostles and prophets, according to the rule of the gospel let them do so" (§ 37); and a text on the organization of the assembly (§ 38*a*). Following this is the Conclusion, which will summarize the results of the study.

# *Chapter 1*

# English Translations of Ethiopic I and Arabic I

*Ethiopic I by Alessandro Bausi*
*Arabic I by Martin Lüstraeten*

Two texts will be presented here for the first time in English. The first column is an English translation of Ethiopic I and the second column is an English translation of Arabic I. The chapters and verses will be given as in *Herm.Com.* 2002. The overall titles of each chapter are also taken from the same commentary, though the specific chapter titles when and as they appear in Ethiopic I and Arabic I will also be given. Each chapter and verse in *Herm.Com.* 2002 will be included here even if absent from both Ethiopic I and Arabic I in order to make it clear to the reader what texts are not in these versions. In some cases, Ethiopic I and Arabic I actually add verses and material not contained in the other witnesses, and which, thus, do not appear in *Herm.Com.* 2002. In such cases, we have introduced new numberings or notations for that material following the conventions of the editors of each text.

Ethiopic I is presented here in English translation from the Ge'ez and Italian edition in Alessandro Bausi, "La nuova versione etiopica della *Traditio apostolica*: Edizione e traduzione preliminare," in *Christianity in Egypt: Literary Production and Intellectual Trends. Studies in Honor of*

*Tito Orlandi*, edited by Paola Buzi and Alberto Camplani, 21–69 (Rome: Institutum Patristicum Augustinianum, 2011). The section numbers (§) of Ethiopic I are included according to Bausi's edition. We thank Alessandro Bausi for preparing this translation from his edition.

The translation of the Arabic version of the *Clementine Octateuch* (Arabic I) is a preliminary translation that was first prepared by Martin Lüstraeten for the *Society of Oriental Liturgy* at The Catholic University of America in Washington, DC, in May 2024. Lüstraeten is preparing a critical edition of Arabic I but has agreed to provide us with his preliminary translation. The section numbers of the Arabic I are included according to Abu-l-Barakat's numbering.[1] Where not included in the text, the titles in [ ] in the Arabic I column are supplied by Abu-l-Barakat. For the signa of manuscripts M1-5,[2] see the section on Arabic I in the introduction to our commentary.

*Signa:*

[/] = missing letters

‡ = a *crux desperationis*, used around a corrupt part of a text

1. See our Introduction, n. 139.
2. M5 has yet to be directly studied and will be excluded from the numbering below.

| Ch./v. | Ethiopic I | Arabic I |
|---|---|---|
| **Ch. 1** | **Prologue** | |
| | **Prelude of the second rule.** | **30. [About the Origin of the Necessary Speech]** |
| 1 | Concerning the word, we have rightly written about the charisms, of what the Lord according to his counsel beforehand granted to man, offering him the image that had erred. | Concerning the origin of the words, we have made because of the gifts that God regarded worthily as a secret from the beginning that he bestows to humankind, presenting to them the heresy which resembles the lie, (he) the creator (by) hand and the Spirit, the extraordinary to movers or the maker of the condition of the places, for the words to those as the ignorance which resembles the heresy on the topics. |
| 2 | And now, having come to the love that is in all the saints, we have arrived at the culminating point of the tradition that is expedient in the churches, | And now, in the love which is for all the saints we get to the summit of faith which is for the catechesis in the church |
| 3 | so that those who have been instructed in the good, respecting the tradition that has been hitherto, after we have adjusted it and once they have come to know it, may become firm | [so that] the educated are steadfast to those who have learned [the tradition which is] till now, that they keep the commandment together with the apostles and learn from that which we have set down, to be steadfast |
| 4 | over the error due to ignorance that has now been found; and in order that those who do not know, | concerning the now found [aspects] of the teaching of the heresy, |
| 5 | granting the Holy Spirit perfect grace to those who believe righteously, may know in what manner those who oversee the church should transmit and observe. | and the learned shall be fellows of the Holy Spirit, without body and with grace, which is without a certain body. They shall persist to believe honestly concerning the commandments. And they should keep the establishment of the organization, which is the church. |

| Ch. | Ethiopic I | Arabic I |
|---|---|---|
| **Ch. 2** | **Concerning Bishops** | |
| | **§1. Concerning the bishop** | **31. Concerning the bishops** |
| 1 | Let the bishop be ordained, being chosen from among all the people, | The hand is to be laid on the bishop according to the words spoken beforehand. He is to be without blame, elected from the people, |
| 2 | who has been appointed and has obtained favor, having the people assembled together with the presbyters and bishops who are present, and let them convene on the Sabbath day, | he, who was named and approved by two presbyters together and by the present bishops. |
| 3 | and all by common consent lay their hands on him, and let the presbyters attend in silence, | And with joy all being at the same place shall lay the hand upon him and [while] the presbyters [are] standing silently. |
| 4 | all keeping silence while they are present, in their hearts praying for the descent of the Spirit | And they shall stand with him, praying in the heart that the Holy Spirit comes down upon the present bishops |
| 5 | and a bishop present, at the request of all, laying his hand on him who is ordained a bishop, let him pray thus saying: | and the one qualified by the assembly shall lay the hand upon the head of him who is being ordained and they shall pray thus: |
| **Ch. 3** | **Prayer for the Ordination of a Bishop** | |
| | | **32. [Prayer and Laying on of the hands on Them]** |
| 1 | "God the Father of our Lord Jesus Christ, the Father of mercies and the Lord of all consolation, who dwells in the highest and sees in the lowest places, who knows all things before they are, | "God, Father of our Lord Jesus Christ, Father of the mercies and Lord of all comfort" and what is next. |
| 2 | you who have given rules to the church by your grace, who have from of old preordained the community of the righteous from Abraham, appointing rulers and priests, not leaving your sanctuary without service, from before the world thou have willed to be given to him with whom you have been pleased: | |

| 3 | even now, pour out the virtue from you, the guiding spirit, which you granted to your beloved Son Jesus Christ, who gave grace to the holy apostles, who consolidated the church in the place of your sanctification, for the glory and unceasing praise of your name. | |
|---|---|---|
| 4 | Grant, you knower of the heart, Father, upon this your servant whom you have chosen for bishop, that he may shepherd the flock of thy holiness, and <exercise the priesthood>[3] for you in purity, serving night and day, continually to propitiate your grace and to offer the offering of the holy church, | |
| 5 | the spirit of the head of the priests, and to find the power to forgive sins according to your commandment, to assign the offices of your rule, and to loosen every bond of wickedness according to the power you have given to the apostles, and to please you in quietness and pure heart, offering unto you a pleasant aroma, | |
| 6 | in your Son Jesus Christ, in whom and with whom to you be glory and power and honor, to the Father and to the Son with the Holy Spirit, in the holy church, now and ever and unto ages of ages. Amen." | |
| **Ch. 4** | **Eucharistic Prayer** | |
| 1 | | |
| 2 | | |

3. Conjectural text: I read *yəkha<n>*, for the transmitted *yəkhal*, "let him be able."

| Ch./v. | Ethiopic I | Arabic I |
|---|---|---|
| 3 | | |
| 4 | | |
| 5 | | |
| 6 | | |
| 7 | | |
| 8 | | |
| 9 | | |
| 10 | | |
| 11 | | |
| 12 | | |
| 13 | | |
| **Ch. 5** | **Concerning the Offering of Oil** | |
| | **§8. Concerning the Offering of Oil** | |
| 1 | If he offers oil like the offering of bread and wine, even if he has not pronounced it entirely, <but> with that effect he gives thanks, saying: | |
| 2 | "As this new oil, may you give health to those who are anointed with it and take of it, from whom you anoint priests, prophets, so may you be powerful to everyone who tastes of it and may you sanctify those who are anointed with it." | |
| **Ch. 6** | **Concerning the Offering of Cheese and Olives** | |
| | **§9. Concerning Cheese and Olives** | |

| 1 | In the same way, cheese or even olives, whoever offers them shall say: | |
|---|---|---|
| 2 | "Sanctify this milk which is curdled, and curdle us too in your love, | |
| 3 | let us not depart from the taste of you; and also this fruit of the olive, which is the image of your <anointing>, which you caused to ooze out of the tree in life for those who hope in you." | |
| 4 | And in every thanksgiving let him say unto thee: "Glory be to the Father, and to the Son, and to the Holy Ghost, in your holy church, now and ever and unto ages of ages. Amen." | |
| **Ch. 7** | **Concerning Presbyters** | |
| | **§2. Concerning the Presbyter** | **33. Concerning the Intercessors [or Presbyters]** |
| 1 | When the presbyter is ordained, the bishop, having laid his hand on his head while the presbyters also touch (him), he shall say according to the formula we said before for bishops, praying, and he shall say thus. | And the presbyter shall have hand laid on him by the bishop. [The bishop] shall lay the hand on his head, and the whole presbytery shall touch him. And he shall speak like what was said before, he shall speak as in the case of the bishop, praying and standing. And he shall lay hand upon the presbyter. |
| 2 | | "God, Father of our Lord Jesus Christ, look upon your servant" and what is next. |
| 3 | | |
| 4 | | |
| 5 | | |

| Ch./v. | Ethiopic I | Arabic I |
|---|---|---|
| **Ch. 8** | **Concerning Deacons** | |
| | **§3. Concerning the Deacon** | **34. Concerning the Deacons** |
| 1 | When the deacon is ordained, elected according to what was said before, in the same way the bishop shall lay his hand, he alone. What we have received as tradition concerning the deacon – that the bishop alone should impose his hand –, | And the deacon, after being elected like as said before [for the bishop], shall stand up, and only the bishop shall lay his hand upon him, [because] he receives the grace of diaconate only. |
| 2 | this is due to the fact that they have not yet been ordained to the priesthood, but, in the service of the bishop, will do what is ordained by him: | The hand of the bishop is laid for the reason alone that the [deacon] is not appointed to the clergy but to the service of the bishop, that he will do what he orders him. |
| 3 | he is therefore not part of the ordained nor of the counsellors; <but> let him give thought and report what is necessary to the bishop; | [The deacon] is not partaker of the clergy but caretaker for what is proper [and] guide to the bishop. |
| 4 | he does not partake of the reception of the spirit of the presbyters, according as the presbyters receive, but of what is entrusted by authority of the bishop: | He is not participant of the presbyteral spirit and he is not offering together with the presbyterate but he is qualified by the bishop who entrusted to him [his tasks]. |
| 5 | for this reason, the bishop alone will create the deacon. | Therefore, a deacon only acts for the bishop. |
| 6 | For the presbyters, let the presbyters together do the imposition, <because> of the sharing and the equal spirit of ordination; | [But for] a presbyter hands are laid on [him] by the presbyters for participation in the clergy, because a presbyter has the one spirit, |
| 7 | the presbyter alone will receive with authority; | because the clergy receives and gives, but has not the authority to appoint a priest. |
| 8 | but as for giving ordination, he has no authority: for this reason, he does not confer ordinations, and with the presbyter he concurs in <consignation> while the bishop ordains. | And therefore the presbyter serves and the bishop appoints. |

| 9 | | **35. Laying on of the Hand on the Deacon** |
|---|---|---|
| 10 | | "God, you who created everything and ordered by the word." |
| 11 | | |
| 12 | | |
| **Ch. 9** | **Concerning Confessors** | |
| | **§7. Concerning Imprisoned Confessors** | **36. Concerning the Confessor**[4] |
| 1 | Confessors, if they are imprisoned for the name of Jesus Christ, let them not receive the ordination of the hand either as deacon or presbyter, since he has the dignity of presbyter for believing. If, however, he is ordained a bishop, they shall receive the ordination of the hand. | And [concerning] he who confesses and got into bonds because of the name, a hand is not to be laid on him for the diaconate or presbyterate, because he has the clerical dignity of a presbyter because of the confession. And if he is appointed as bishop, he has to receive the laying on of the hand. |
| 2 | But if he is a confessor who has not come to court, who has not even been condemned in prison, nor who has been locked up in prison, nor who has been condemned by a sentence, but has thus occasionally been offended by his master, or otherwise harassed under house arrest, for the ordination he has deserved he shall receive the ordination of the hand. | And if there were his words and he has not been handed over to the authority and he was not punished with bonds and he was not shut into prison and he was not condemned by a judicial sentence, but he got into humiliation because of the Lord or under house arrest and he is a confessor, he is thus qualified for the clergy not without receiving the laying on of hand. |
| 3 | The bishop will give thanks as we said before. | And the bishop shall give thanks according to what was said before. |
| 4 | He will not, therefore, necessarily give thanks according to this doctrine, but according to his capacity: | For this the whole form is not necessary, one must rather be aware to thank, but according to the ability of the rest. |

4. Abu-l-Barakat and M1 = 36; M2-4 = no number given.

| Ch./v. | Ethiopic I | Arabic I |
|---|---|---|
| 5 | whoever is able to give a good and honorable thing, well, but if also something inferior, there is nothing to prevent it, and indeed it is a wholesome and upright thing. | And if it is dictated and glorifying and it is possible for the salvation in a not-too-big extent, it is good. [He shall pray] unhindered and honestly. |
| 6[5] | | Not every confessor is chosen for the clergy but the chosen, before he is counted among them, shall have the hand laid upon him. And he is not [able] by himself [to ordain] to service by [his] hand, because there is no one who receives the grace by himself. |
| 7 | | And he shall achieve how he examines with the canon concerning the diaconate and concerning the kiss of the presbyter and concerning the authority of those who buy for themselves an increase in rank. And it is not only women who are qualified to be confessors but also those who have afflictions of the limbs, except for the eyes. And to them is fitting the service of the clergy because of [their confession]. And everything which was recorded through Aba Klementos on the apostles, about their service, about their lives. And hand is laid on with a describing word. The confessor is not to be laid hand on, because he knows this and he is qualified by the big patience or by the huge virtue. And if he is [received] through the hand to diaconal or presbyteral [rank], the hand shall be laid on him and he should be appointed. And as regards the confessor he shall receive this dignity without the laying on of hands, because of [his] confession. And he shall harvest because of this, who negates the order of the Messiah. And he is a nonbeliever. |

5. Note: This verse and the following verse are only in Arabic I.

| Ch. 10 | **Concerning Widows** | |
|---|---|---|
| | **§6. Concerning the Widow** | **37. Concerning the Widows**[6] |
| 1 | The widow is ordained not by the laying on of hands, <but> by that name which has elected her, | If a widow is appointed, a hand shall not be laid [on her] but she is chosen before [by] the name, |
| 2 | if she has let some time pass since the loss of her husband; | [if she is] since a long time without a husband. |
| 3 | but if she has lost her husband a short time ago, let them not believe her. If she is old in age, let them examine her, for that is the time when the passions become senescent; | And if she was left by her husband since her youth, one shall not trust [her]. And especially if she is an old woman, she shall be tested for a time, for the passions enter with age. |
| 4 | let her be ordained by word, being counted with the others, but let her not be ordained by the hand, for she does not communicate;[7] | And she shall be appointed according to the words [above], bound with the rest. And the laying on of hand shall not be given [to her] because she does not offer and does not serve. |
| 5 | let her be <instead> ordained only for the prayer, which is permitted to all. | For the laying on of the hand is for the clergy, it is for service. And as regards the widow, she is concerned with the prayer which she speaks for all. |
| **Ch. 11** | **Concerning a Reader** | |
| | **§5. Concerning the Reader** | **38. Concerning the Reader**[8] |
| | The reader shall be ordained with the first delivery of the book by the bishop and shall not receive the laying on of hands. | The reader shall be appointed in that the bishop first gives him a book and then the hand is laid on him. |

6. Abu-l-Barakat and M1 = 37; M2-4 = 36.
7. Ethiopic: *ʾitəqerrəb*.
8. Abu-l-Barakat and M1 = 38; M2-4 = 37.

| Ch./v. | Ethiopic I | Arabic I |
|---|---|---|
| **Ch. 12** | **Concerning Virgins** | |
| | | **39. Concerning the Virgins**[9] |
| | | The hand shall not be laid on for the virgin, but by the circumstance [alone is she] a virgin. |
| **Ch. 13** | **Concerning a Subdeacon** | |
| | **§4. Concerning the Subdeacon** | **40. Concerning the Subdeacon**[10] |
| | The subdeacon will not receive the laying on of hands, <but> will be appointed after the deacon and will perform the washing[11] for the bishop. | Without laying on of hand, but he is counted [as such] for he follows the deacon. |
| **Ch. 14** | **Concerning the Gift of Healing [and a Presbyter or a Deacon who Travels]** | |
| | **§11. Concerning the Grace of Healing** | **41. [Concerning the Gifts of Healing]**[12] |
| 1 | If there is one who says: The grace of healing in vision I have received, he does not receive the ordination of the hand, for the work itself will show whether he has truly received it. | If one says: "I received through a revelation the gifts of healing," hand shall not be laid on him, for his work will show if he has thus received [the gift of healing]. |

9. Abu-l-Barakat and M1 = 39; M2-4 = 38.
10. Abu-l-Barakat and M1 = 40; M2-4 = 39.
11. Ethiopic: *wayāḫaḍḍəb*.
12. Abu-l-Barakat and M1 = 41; M2-4 = 40.

| | | |
|---|---|---|
| 2[13] | | **42. [Concerning a Presbyter or a Deacon who Travels]**[14] If a presbyter goes on a journey or a deacon moves, then the laying on of hand changes [with them] because they are worthy for the clergy, but not the widow, because of the conscience for the clergy and [risk of] confusion. |
| **Ch. 15** | **Concerning Newcomers to the Faith** | |
| | **§10. Concerning Those who are Initiated for the First Time** | **43. Concerning the Catechumens**[15] |
| 1 | Those who are initiated for the first time to hear the word, before they are admitted among all the people, first they will introduce them for the teaching; | Those coming to hear the words shall enter first, before all the people, [and] they should first approach the teacher |
| 2 | and let them ask about their behavior, for what reason they have been admitted, and let those who admit them be witnesses for them, if they are able to hear the words; | that [the teacher] asks for the reason [that they have come], if they came first for the benefit or for the harm. And one should bear witness for them. And if it is possible for them to speak as well as to hear, |
| 3 | let them examine their lives; and if there is one who has a wife, | one should ask about their life and if he has a wife |
| 4 | and if he is a servant, if his master permits (him); if the servant is a believer, let him testify; if there are no witnesses on his behalf, let him be expelled; | and if he is a slave, and if he is a slave of a believer and his master permits him, he shall hear. And if there is no one bearing witness for him, he is to be rejected. |
| 5 | and if he is a pagan, let him learn to please his lord, that there be no offence | And if he is a heathen, he is to be taught to please his master so that there is no falsity. |

13. Note: this verse is only in Arabic I.
14. Abu-l-Barakat and M1 = 42; M2-4 = 41.
15. Abu-l-Barakat and M1 = 43; M2-4 = 42.

| Ch./v. | Ethiopic I | Arabic I |
|---|---|---|
| 6 | If there is one who has a wife, or if there is a woman who has a husband, let him instruct her or her husband to remain | And if one has a wife or if it is a wife who has a husband, they are to be taught to guard their marriage as man and wife. |
| 7 | and if he is not married, let him learn not to fornicate; if not, let him marry legally, and if not, so remain; | And if one is unmarried, he is to be taught not to fornicate but to marry according to the law or to remain thus. |
| 8 | and if there is one who is possessed with a demon, let him not hear from the master until he is cleansed. | And if someone has a demon, he shall not hear the speech from the saying of the teacher until [the demon] is purged from them. |
| **Ch. 16** | **Concerning Crafts and Professions** | |
| | **§12. Concerning Art and Profession** | **44. Occupations of Those Coming to the Catechesis**[16] |
| 1 | Let them hear about the art and profession of those whom they admit, and let them ask. | They shall ask |
| 2 | If there is a brothel keeper, let him abandon this activity or be expelled. | who is an effeminate with desire [in fornication], and he shall stop or be rejected. |
| 3 | If there is a sculptor or painter, let him be educated, let him not make idols, and if he has refused let him be expelled. | And who is a travelling goldsmith or painter, shall be taught not to make idols and if he does not want to stop, he shall be rejected. |
| 4 | If there is one who performs in the theatres, let him cease, or else be expelled. | Who is famous and who shows himself in sin, he shall stop or be rejected. |
| 5 | If he educates the young, it is good that he should cease, and if he has no other profession, let them be indulgent with him. | And who leads the education of children on the canons shall teach the words of the poets, being busy with the struggle against the canons. And if he teaches lads, it is good, he shall stop or keep doing thus if he does not know anything else. |

16. No number given in M1. Abu-I-Barakat = 44?.

| | | |
|---|---|---|
| 6 | Also, whoever competes with horses and enters the arena, let him cease this activity or else be expelled. | [And someone] taking the reins [has to live] without horsemanship. |
| 7 | A gladiator or a trainer of gladiators, or one who fights with bears, who publicly fights, let him be expelled. | Likewise a fighter going to a fight: He shall stop or he shall be rejected. A swordman or a teacher of swordplay or a hunter or an official, who is in the rank that he does or who hunts or who abuses the congregation shall be rejected. |
| 8 | A priest of idols, or a keeper of idols – that is, one who looks after them – shall cease or be expelled. | A priest of the idols or a watchman of the idols shall stop or be rejected. |
| 9 | A soldier who is in any authority, let him not kill; and even if he has been commanded, let him not immolate, nor swear, nor put wreaths on his head. | A soldier in the authority of force shall not kill. And if he is ordered, he [still] shall not kill. And he shall not offer an animate being, [even if] ordered by a command. And if he is ordered thus, he shall not offer but protect the service, not as ordered, obeying the service of the demons, [but] he shall [live in] pureness and diligence and not quit the military service, growing through the mockery of the idol service so that faith becomes strength for them. |
| 10 | He who executes sentences by the sword, or the governor of a city, or one in purple garb, shall cease, or else be expelled. | An executioner, a ruler of a town wearing purple, shall stop or be rejected.[17] |
| 11 | A catechumen or adult Christian, if he wishes to be enrolled, let him be expelled, because he has wronged the Lord. | A catechumen or a believer, if he wants to become a soldier, is to be rejected [since] they are already fallen from God. |
| 12 | A prostitute, a dissolute or a castrated, if he has given up his business, may be admitted to hearing; | An adulterer or a glutton or one who did what is not possible to be heard of, is an obstacle. He shall be rejected, because he is unclean. |

17. Number 43 appears before this sentence in M2-4.

| Ch./v. | Ethiopic I | Arabic I |
|---|---|---|
| 13a[18] | a statue-maker is to be expelled, because he does not come under scrutiny. | |
| 13b/14[19] | A sorcerer, one who practices spells, an astrologer, {a seer,} an interpreter of dreams, an enchanter, and <one who> makes phylacteries, let him cease, and if not let him be expelled. | Or an augur, a magician, an enchanter or an astrologer or soothsayer or a speaker or a nudist or a maker of amulets – they shall stop or be rejected. |
| 15 | Whosoever's concubine, if the offspring which he gives her be bred and belong to him alone, let her hear, and if not, let her be expelled. | A concubine for someone, if she is his slave and she gives birth and she pleases [him], she alone may hear and if it is not only her, she is to be rejected. |
| 16 | For a man commits murder if he has a concubine, let him cease and marry legally, and if he is not willing, let him be expelled. | A man who has a concubine shall stop and he shall marry according to the law. And if he does not want to, he shall be rejected. |
| 17 | If there is anything we have overlooked, the fact itself will give instruction, for we all have the Holy Spirit within us. | And if there is some [profession] left [that is not described above], those works will inform you, for we all have the Spirit of God. |
| **Ch. 17** | **Concerning the Time of Hearing the Word after the Examination of Crafts and Professions** | |
| | **§13. On the Time of the Hearers** | **45. Concerning the Time and the Expiry[20]** |
| 1 | Let the catechumen be a hearer for three years; | The catechumen shall hear for not less than three years, |

18. Ethiopic I adds here a reference to a statue-maker.

19. In most versions of ApTrad, verse 13 (here labeled 13b) is a separate verse for magicians. In Ethiopic I and Arabic I this has been collapsed into verse 14.

20. M1-4 = 44.

| | | |
|---|---|---|
| 2 | and if he engages in anything and devotes himself continuously, let him not be judged according to time but according to character. | and if he is earnest and persevering with this, he shall not be judged by the time but by the situation. |
| **Ch. 18** | **Concerning the Prayer of Those Who Hear** | |
| | **§14. Concerning the Prayer of the Hearers** | **46. Concerning the Prayer of the Kisses of the Catechumen [and Concerning the Virgin]**[21] |
| 1 | The catechumens, after they have left the teacher, are to pray separately from adult Christians. | If he has finished with the teaching, they shall pray separated from the rest |
| 2 | Women are to stand alone. | and the women shall stand in the church, women believers as well as women catechumens. |
| 3 | The adult Christians with the catechumens shall not exchange the sign of peace, because holy, there is none holy from them. | And after the prayer they do not offer the peace to the women catechumens for they are not sanctified. |
| 4 | Adult Christians shall kiss men with men, and women with women: they shall kiss one another on the mouth. | The sanctified people, believers, [kiss]: men to men and women to women and the man shall not approach the mouth of a woman. |
| 5 | Let all women veil themselves with a headscarf, not soft linen, for it is not a covering; but let the virgin not veil herself because she knows that it manifestly declares her to be a believer. | Every woman shall cover her head with a pallium or with a piece of pure linen, for it is a veil for her. A virgin shall not cover, because of the intention, so that she remains [thus] as a declaration.[22] |

21. M1-4 = 45.
22. Number 46 appears before this sentence in Abu-I-Barakat.

| Ch./v. | Ethiopic I | Arabic I |
|---|---|---|
| **Ch. 19** | **Concerning the Imposition of Hands on Catechumens** | |
| | **§15. Concerning the Laying on of Hands** | **47. Concerning the Laying on of the Hand**[23] |
| 1 | The teacher to the catechumen after he has prayed, having laid his hand on him, let him make him go out; he who teaches, even if he is an adult Christian <. . .>,[24] let him do so. | The teacher shall lay the hand on the catechumens and he shall dismiss them after they have prayed. And likewise, if the teacher prays he shall do so as a layperson. |
| 2 | If there is a catechumen who is arrested for the name <of Christ> and perseveres to receive, do not doubt; and if there is a sudden event and <he died> before receiving his remission, he was baptized with his blood and is a righteous. | Someone who is a catechumen who is arrested for the name and if there is no one found in the land who confirms or who raises in sin, and he is killed, he has received [forgiveness of sins] because of [his] sorrow; he was baptized, absolved in his blood. |
| **Ch. 20** | **Concerning Those Who Are to Receive Baptism** | |
| | **§16. Concerning Those Who are Initiated** | **48. Concerning the Received**[25] |
| 1 | When those who are about to receive have been elected, after you have examined their lives, whether the catechumens have lived well, whether they have honored widows and visited the sick, and whether they have done good works, | The elect are chosen to be prepared, to be examined: Have they lived virtuously as catechumens? Or: Have they honored the widows? Or: Have they visited the sick or have they fulfilled [good] works? |
| 2 | let those who initiate them be witnesses for them, and thus let them hear the gospel. | And the one who brought them bears witness for them so that they shall thus hear the gospel. |

23. Abu-I-Barakat = 47. M1-4 = 46.
24. Perhaps something is missing.
25. Abu-l-Barakat = 48; M1-4 = 47.

| | | |
|---|---|---|
| 3 | During the mornings they shall lay their hands (on them), while they are exorcised, since they have been elected; and before the day approaches, the bishop shall exorcise each one, to be sure whether they have become pure. | And the hand shall be laid on each one of them [from] the day that they were chosen, they shall be exorcised. And at the approaching of the day of exorcism by the bishop for each one of them they shall be cleaned with the faith. |
| 4 | If there is any suspicion, they shall turn them away and shame them, because they have not listened in faith; for a foreign entity cannot dwell in him. | And someone who is defiled shall be forbidden and he shall be blamed, for he has heard without believing, because he has not withstood the stranger. |
| 5 | Let those who are destined to be initiated be instructed to take a bath on the fifth day of the week. | And he shall that when they are elected among those preparing for baptism that they should bathe on Saturday and [when] they [should] abstain. |
| 6 | If there is a menstruating woman, however, they shall turn her away, and she shall be initiated on another day. | And if at that time a woman is menstruating,[26] she shall be set aside and be left for another day. |
| 7 | Those who are to be initiated shall fast on Fridays and Saturdays. On the Sabbath day the bishop, having assembled those who are to be initiated, let him order them to kneel down, | And those who are known to be elect shall fast on Friday and the bishop shall gather them on Saturday, ordering them to kneel down, |
| 8 | and laying his hands on them, exorcise them, saying: "Let every foreign spirit be cast out of him and never return." When he has exorcised, he shall blow, and having marked their foreheads, nostrils, and ears, he shall make them stand up; | and he shall lay the hand upon them, and he shall exorcise them, saying to him: "[Be liberated] from every foreign spirit and he shall not return." And he shall blow, if he exorcised, and he shall seal the forehead, the ears, and the nose, and he shall raise them up. |
| 9 | at night he shall read to them, and they shall comment. | And they shall stay up that night and the [story of] creation[27] shall be read to them, and they shall think about [it] more. |

26. Quite literally "the monthlies" in the Arabic.
27. I.e., the story of Genesis.

| Ch./v. | Ethiopic I | Arabic I |
|---|---|---|
| 10 | There is no other thing that they shall bring, those who are to be initiated, except one loaf each for thanksgiving, for it is fitting, whoever it touches, to offer something at that time. | And they, who are elected by others, shall not receive [communion]. Each one should only [give] thanks. It is right that the elect offer at that time. |
| **Ch. 21** | **Concerning the Tradition of Holy Baptism** | |
| | **§17. On Anointing** | **(48. cont.) Concerning the Matters [of Baptism]**[28] |
| 1 | At the time of the crowing of the cockcrow let him come to the water; | And at cockcrow he shall first pray over the water. |
| 2 | let his water be a water that pours out, or at least running: so be it, if there is no necessity; if he is concerned about any necessity, let him do it with any water. | And the water shall be on a river or at a river. It should be thus except in an emergency. And if it is an emergency it should be water which is not common for the body. |
| 3 | Let them therefore remove their clothes. | They shall undress. |
| 4 | Let them give precedence to the children and baptize them; let those <who are able> to respond, or else one of their relatives or companions, respond; | And they shall baptize the children first. He shall examine those who are able to respond. And if someone is not able, their fathers speak on their behalf or someone from their family. |
| 5 | then the adult men, and then the women, let down their hair and lay aside their ornaments: no one is to have anything with them as they go down into the water. | Then the men and finally the women, the [women] shall loosen their hair and lay aside their gold jewelry so that there is no foreign thing with them in the water. |
| 6 | While they are about to receive the oil for the exorcism, the bishop shall give thanks with a jar, | And [at the hour] it has been set for them [to receive baptism,] they receive the unction with the good fat. And the bishop shall give thanks over a vessel, |
| 7 | and the other [e.g. the other oil], he shall exorcise (it). | and he shall exorcise [oil] in another vessel [as well]. |

28. M1-4 = 48.

| | | |
|---|---|---|
| 8 | Let a deacon take the one exorcised and (place himself) stand(ing) by the presbyter; likewise the other one, of the action of grace [e.g. the oil of thanksgiving], let him stand on the right; and let the presbyter who exorcises it stand on the left. | And as regards the [oil] for exorcism, the deacon shall hold it and he shall stand at another presbyter because of the [oil of] thanksgiving and everyone shall stand. As regards the one who has the water [sic!] of thanksgiving, he shall be to the right. And as regards the one who hast the water [sic!] of exorcism, he shall stand to the left of the presbyter. |
| 9 | Having taken them one by one, let him ask them if they believe. (The initiate) shall say: “I renounce Satan, his work, his ways and his defilement.” | And the presbyter shall ask those grasped [by him] that they show [their decision] saying: “I renounce you, O Satan, and all your works and all your deeds.” |
| 10 | When they have caused him to make his profession, let him be anointed with exorcised oil, pronouncing (the formula) for purification from every foreign spirit; | And if they confessed thus, he anoints with the oil of exorcism saying: “For the change from every evil spirit.” |
| 11 | so, when they have delivered him to the bishop or presbyter, to the one who baptizes him, standing in the water naked, | And in this way, they shall be delivered to the bishop or the presbyter and the baptizand shall stand in the water naked. |
| 12 | let the deacon also go down with him, and when he has gone down into the water, let him who initiates him say: “Do you believe in one almighty God?;” | And likewise the deacon shall go down and he shall do [the service] of the giver in his descent, to the water: “Do you believe in the one God, the almighty?”[29] |
| 13 | And the one who is being initiated shall say: “I believe;” | And the one shall say: “I believe.” |
| 14 | And so, with his hand laid on his head, let him baptize him a first time. | And likewise the question to him and the hand of the giver on his head he shall baptize him one time. |

29. The term “giver” here and in v. 14 is quite odd, but this is what the Arabic dictates. It may also be a reference to the Arabic expression «اعطى أقو اله» = “(to) give one’s testimony,” so that the deacon prompts the baptizand to testify.

| Ch./v. | Ethiopic I | Arabic I |
|---|---|---|
| 15 | Then he shall say: "Do you believe in Christ Jesus, Son of God, who was born of the Holy Spirit and of the Virgin Mary, was crucified under Pontius Pilate, and died and was buried, and rose on the third day alive from the dead, and ascended into heaven, and sits at the right hand of the Father, who shall come to judge the living and the dead?" | Then he shall say: "Do you believe in the one Lord, Jesus Christ, our Lord, the Son of God, who was born from the Holy Spirit and from the Virgin Mary, who was crucified under the direction of Pilate, who died and rose from the dead on the third day alive and who ascended into the heavens and is sitting on the right of the father and that he will judge the living and the dead?" |
| 16 | And when he shall have said: "I believe," he will baptize him a second time. | And he shall say this: "I believe." And he shall baptize a second time. |
| 17 | Again he shall say: "Do you believe in the Holy Spirit, and in the holy church, and in the resurrection of the flesh?." | And he shall also say: "And do you believe in the Holy Spirit [and the] holy church?" |
| 18 | And he that is baptized shall say: "I believe," and so he shall baptize him a third time. | And he shall say: "I believe." And so he shall baptize likewise a third time. |
| | **§18. Concerning the Anointing of the Balm** | |
| 19 | After this, when he has risen, let him be anointed by the presbyter with the balm of thanksgiving, [while anointing], and say: "I [anoint you] [with] the holy [ba]lsam in the name of Jesus Christ." | Then he ascends to be anointed by the presbyter with the perfume of thanksgiving, then the one who anoints him says: "I anoint you with holy perfume in the name of Jesus Christ." |
| 20 | So, after they have each one cleansed themselves, ‡ they shall make them put on their robes, and afterwards he shall enter into the church. | And likewise one after another are anointed and the rest shall dress likewise and enter the church. |
| 21 | The bishop, having laid his hand upon him, shall invoke, saying: "O Lord God, you who have granted to these to receive the remission of sins through the washing of regeneration, grant that they may be filled with the Holy Spirit, sending upon them your | And the bishop shall lay a hand on them and invoke saying thus: "God, as you made these worthy to receive forgiveness of sins through the other generation, make [them] worthy to be filled with the Holy Spirit, sending on them your grace so that they |

| | | |
|---|---|---|
| 21 (cont.) | grace, that they may serve you according to your will. To you glory, Father and Son with the Holy Spirit in the holy church, [and] now and ever, [and] for ever and ever. Amen." | serve you according to your will. Thine is the glory of the Father and the Son and the Holy Spirit in your holy church, now and forever to the ages of ages." |
| 22 | [After] this, [while] pouring out the oil of thanksgiving, having placed it with [his hand] over his head: "I anoint you <with oil> holy in Almighty God and Jesus Christ and the Holy Spirit." | Then, pouring the oil of thanksgiving over his hand and laying his hand on the head he shall also say: "I anoint you with the anointing with the sanctified oil in God, the Father, the almighty, and in Christ Jesus and in the Holy Spirit." |
| 23 | After he has marked his forehead, he shall embrace him and say: "The Lord is with you;" and he who is marked shall answer: "And with your spirit." | And he shall seal his forehead and he shall kiss him and he shall say: "The Lord [be] with you!] And the sealed [one] shall answer: "And with your spirit." |
| 24 | Thus for each one. | Likewise, one after another and the rest. |
| 25 | Therefore, let them pray with all the people; let them not pray with the adult Christians before they have fulfilled all this. | And all the people shall pray together, praying with the believers, except that all that what was said [is not yet carried out]. |
| 26 | When they have prayed and have exchanged the sign of peace <with their mouths>, | Having prayed they shall offer the peace with their mouths. |
| 27 | the deacons shall present the memorial to the bishop; and he shall give thanks of the bread in the image of the body of Christ, and the cup of wine mingled in the image of the blood that was shed for those who believe in him; | And the deacons shall offer the oblation to the bishop, and, likewise, he shall give thanks [over] the bread – because it is a limb of the body of Christ – and the wine is mixed for it is from the blood of Christ that was shed for all the believers. |
| 28 | and milk and honey mingled for the fulfillment of the hope that is of the fathers, for what he said: "He will give a land flowing with milk and honey," that body of Christ has granted, with which the children who believe are brought up, with the taste of his word making the bitterness of the heart savory. | In it milk and honey are mixed for the fulfillment of the promise to the fathers, [for] he said that he gives "a land flowing with milk and honey," and he gave [us] the body of Christ so that the believers like children will be nourished. And the words of sweetness sweeten the bitterness of the heart. |

| Ch./v. | Ethiopic I | Arabic I |
|---|---|---|
| 29 | And water for the offering, the image of the washing, that the inner man also, which is the soul, may receive in this manner as well as the body. | and as a sign the water for the bath so that the inner person, who is the spiritual one, [receives] the same in the soul as the body. |
| 30 | Of all these things, let the bishop give an explanation to those who are initiated. | And the bishop shall give a word to all those receiving. |
| 31 | When he has fractionated the bread and given it to each one, let him say: "Heavenly bread in Christ Jesus," | And if he now gives thanks [over] the bread, he shall give it to each one and say: "Heavenly bread in Christ Jesus." |
| 32 | and let them respond: "Amen." | And the receiver shall respond. |
| 33 | The presbyters then, if there is not enough, let the deacons take the chalices and stand in good order, the chalice of honey first, the chalice of milk second, and the chalice of wine third; | And if the present presbyters are not sufficient for holding the cups, the deacons shall stand in the [following] order: first the water, second the milk, third the wine. |
| 34 | and those who have been initiated shall taste of it, saying [three times] he who [gives it]: "In the Lord the Father Al[mighty];" and he who receives it shall then say: "Amen. Amen. | And for the reception of the three, the one giving it to them says to them: "In God, the Father, the almighty, |
| 35 | And in the body. Amen." "And in the blood. Amen," in the image of the Trinity. | and Christ Jesus |
| 36 | | and the Holy Spirit and the sanctified church." And he shall say: "Amen." |
| 37 | | Thus with everyone. |
| 38 | While this therefore is taking place, let each one endeavor to do his work well, to please the Lord by living righteously, and to devote himself to the church, accomplishing what he has learned and raising himself up to the Lord. | Thus, everyone shall be well-guarded and they shall be eager to do good things, to please God, upright, repentant in the church, doing that which is taught and increased for God. |

| 39 | This therefore is fitting to be given briefly about the washing and the offering, because they have already been admonished before. But concerning the resurrection of the flesh, and concerning everything according to [what is written], | With all this we have already taught once what is fitting and about the baths and all the offerings and what is catechized and about the resurrection of the body and everything as it is written. |
|---|---|---|
| 40 | as far as it is expedient, the bishop shall tell and expound at the time [///] those who are initiated [///] [///] contrast not [know] the gift of the catechumen. This is the white ‡ praise[30] of which John said that in it is found a new name, which no one knows except he who is initiated. | And [about] that which is right to explain so that the bishop shall say to the enlightened what they receive before they receive. And the unbeliever does not know the gift of the believers. This is the white stone, which John speaks about: "The new name is not possible to be known by anyone except the receiver." [Rev 2:17] |
| **Ch. 22** | **Concerning Communion** | |
| | | **(48. cont.)** |
| 1 | On the Sabbath the bishop, if it is possible, with his own hands, while the deacons fractionate [e.g. break the bread], ministers himself to all the people; | If possible, the bishop breaks [the bread] with his own hand on Sunday; the deacons give to all the people |
| 2 | and the presbyters fractionate the bread <baked>; if a deacon offers to a presbyter, let him spread out his garments, and so receive; to the people, he will hand over by hand. | and the presbyterate and all the clergy bread[31] and if the deacons offer to the presbyter [they do this] spreading [their] arms and [thus] the presbyter shall take for himself and to the people they shall give from the hand. |

30. The Ethiopic has *wad(d)āse*, probably for *wəddāse*, "praise," with misreading of the Greek: ψόφος (?) instead of ψῆφος.

31. It might be possible that just one verb was dropped. If it was "ويكسر القساء وكل كهنة خبزا" it would perfectly fit to the other version. But the verb is missing here and since the nouns are determinate and the case endings are not given, it could be accusative ("to give" is rendered with accusative in Arabic) or nominative. As it appears here, "the presbyterate and all the clergy" is the object here. One could also translate as a new sentence as: "And the presbyterate and all the clergy [break/distribute/take] bread and if . . ." But then one has to claim that the verb is missing here and has to give a reason why.

| Ch./v. | Ethiopic I | Arabic I |
|---|---|---|
| 3 | For the other (days), these shall render, once the bishop has ordered (it). | And on the rest of the days, they shall give to the bishop by his command. |
| **Ch. 23** | **Concerning Fasting** | |
| | **§19. On Fasting** | **49. Concerning the Fast** |
| 1 | Let widows and virgins fast often and pray for the holy church. Let presbyters, if they wish, fast. Let the laity fast likewise. | The widows and the virgins shall fast oftentimes, and they shall pray for the church. The presbyters and the laity shall also fast likewise. |
| 2 | The bishop may not fast except when all the people have fasted, | It is not possible that the bishop fasts, except when all the people fast. |
| 3 | because it happens that someone has brought something to offer it, and he may not refuse, because after he has broken the bread he will taste it. | For [if] someone wants to eat what he offers and it is not possible to deny him and he breaks, he must always taste [of it]. |
| 4 | | |
| **Chs. 24/ 25** | **Original Placement of Chs. 29B ( = 24) and 29C ( = 25)** | |
| **Ch. 26** | **Concerning the Hour of Eating** | |
| | **§23. On Lunch** | **53. Concerning Those Being Together and the Eating** |
| 1 | Before everyone drinks, once they have washed themselves, you will give thanks to the chalice; it is fitting that those present should taste and then dine. | Before they drink, they receive a cup of thanksgiving and it is right that those present taste from it this way. |
| 2 | Let the catechumen be given exorcised bread and a chalice each while he offers. | And they shall receive. And one shall give the catechumens bread of exorcism and a cup so that everyone receives. |

| **Ch. 27** | **That It Is Not Proper for Catechumens to Eat with the Faithful** | |
|---|---|---|
| | **§[2]4. On the Catechumen: Let Them Not be Together** | **54. Concerning the Catechumens Together** |
| 1 | The catechumens at the congregational supper shall not sit at table together, | A catechumen shall not be present at the supper on Sunday. |
| 2 | but in all the offering let them remember, <while> offering, who has called him, because for this he has begged that you enter under the roof of his house. | And let the catechumen through the whole offering be mindful of him, who invites him to offer, for the inviter gracefully invites him that they enter under his roof. |
| **Ch. 28** | **That It Is Proper to Eat Judiciously and Moderately** | |
| | **§25. Concerning Rule and Moderation** | **55. Concerning the Superiority of the Order and the Modesty of Those Present** |
| 1 | As you eat and drink, be moderate, not for drunkenness or being an object of derision, so that he who invited you may not criticize you for your unruliness, but that he may pray that it may happen to him that the saints enter in; for "You," he said, "are the salt of the earth." | If they eat and drink, it is not for drunkenness and common and no one shall laugh at you and he who invited you shall not grieve because of the disorder, but he shall pray that he is worthy that the saints enter in his [house], for "you are," he said, "the salt of the earth." |
| 2 | If all together have been offered something to take away, take it; | One should take according to the portion |
| 3 | but if so that all may enjoy it, taste it with moderation, that it may remain; and that he who invited may send food to whom he willed among the saints; and he may rejoice at your coming. | If they receive or taste food, they content themselves with tasting and being moderate and he, who has invited, will bring and send as if it was the food of the saints and a grace in their presence. |
| 4 | While they are enjoying it, those who have been invited shall eat in silence, without quarreling, <but> when the bishop allows something to be asked, answer it, and once the bishop has said the word, everyone in moderation shall keep silent until he asks again. | And the invited shall take, tasting in silence, without words of quarreling. But if one begins to speak, they should listen. [If] the bishop asks, one shall respond, and at the speech of the bishop all shall remain silent until he asks again. |

| Ch./v. | Ethiopic I | Arabic I |
|---|---|---|
| 5 | If any of the faithful are to dine without the bishop, let them take the eulogy [e.g., the blessed bread][32] from the presbyter or otherwise from the deacon, from the hand; so also the catechumen the exorcised; | And if the bishop is not present at the supper of the believers and the presbyter or the deacon is present one shall likewise honestly take with desire everything from the hand of the presbyter or deacon. They shall take the blessed bread from his hand and likewise the catechumens [the bread of] exorcism. |
| 6 | and so also the laity in the same place ‡ shall stand well; but from the laity he may not take the eulogy [e.g., blessed bread].[33] | Likewise, the laity together [shall act] honestly, for a layperson cannot make a blessing. |
| **Ch. 29A** | **That It Is Proper to Eat with Thanksgiving** | |
| | **§26. Concerning Those Who Receive While Giving Thanks** | **56. Concerning the thanksgiving** |
| a | Let each one eat in the name of the Lord, for this is what is fitting for the Lord, that we should be zealous and that even among the Gentiles we should be balanced and sober. | Everyone shall take in the name of God for this is fitting for God so that also the heathens are envious. [Everyone] shall eat and be at the same time vigilant. |
| b[34] | | |
| **Ch. 29B** | **Concerning Gifts for the Sick** | |
| | **§20. On What is Given to the Sick** | **50. Concerning the Gift to Those Who Go Away [the Sick]** |
| 1 | The deacon in a situation of difficulty shall give the signet[35] to the sick as a matter of urgency, if a presbyter is not present, and once | A deacon, if there is an emergency, shall give the seal[36] to the sick and to whom was appointed, except if a presbyter is present. |

32. For more context, see n. 38.
33. For more context, see n. 38.
34. Note: This verse is only in Ethiopic II: "For God rejoices in us . . . become pure."
35. Ethiopic *maʿtab*, for Classical Ethiopic *māʿtab*.
36. The Arabic term here is "خَتْماً/ḫatman," which is the accusative rendering of "خَتْم/ḫatm." It corresponds to the Syriac "ܚܬܡܐ/ḥātmā" or the Greek σφραγίς. It is used here as a liturgical *terminus technicus* and unlike the term "رسم/rasm/ܪܘܫܡܐ/σημεῖον" it usually designates not

| 2 | he has given, as far as it is appropriate, let him take what has been distributed to him, and immediately there let them consume it. | And he shall give also to one to whom it is not appropriate that he takes the significant object, and he shall give thanks for that guest. |
|---|---|---|
| | **§21. Concerning that He Who Has Taken Shall Perform the Service** | **51. Concerning the Taking of the Deacons [or on What One Gives to the Widows]** |
| 3 | He shall give eulogy [e.g., blessed bread][37] promptly. If there is one who has taken, let him bring it to the widows and the sick and to those who {do not} do service for the church; let him bring it on the day, | It is wanted that they give [communion to a widow]. If one takes the service, he shall offer for the widow and for the sick and to those who resist against the church. They shall bring on the same day. |
| 4 | and if he has not brought it, let him bring more of his own the next day, because the poor man's bread is left with him. | And if he has not brought, he shall add for the following day from his own, for with him remained [the portion] for the hungry. |
| **Ch. 29C** | **Concerning the Bringing in of the Lamps at the Supper of the Congregation** | |
| | **§22. On the Introduction of the Lamps** | **52. Concerning the Bringing in [or Lighting] of the Lamps.** |
| 1 | In the supper of the congregation, while the bishop is present, the deacon shall introduce the lamp; | One shall bring in the lamps at supper on Sunday and the bishop is present and it is evening. |
| 2 | and standing among the faithful, while they are present, he shall give thanks. He shall first greet them thus saying: "The Lord with you." | He shall stand in the middle of the present believers, he shall first give thanks, greeting, saying: "The Lord [is] with us!" |
| 3 | And the people shall say: "And with your spirit." | And the congregation shall say: "And with your spirit." |

only the outer act of making a sign on the forehead but a full sacramental act—respectively, what is perceived as one. Louis Leloir went through the works of Ephraem the Syrian and concluded that baptism "is a sign and communicates a seal" ("est une signe et communique un sceau"); cf. Louis Leloir, "Symbolisme dans la Liturgie Syriaque Primitive," in *Le Symbolisme dans le culte des grandes religions: Actes du colloque de Louvain-la-Neuve 4–5 Octobre 1983*, ed. Julien Ries, Homo religiosus, vol. 11 (Leuven: Centre d'Histoire des Religions, 1985), 247–63, here, 255. Thus, the "خَتْم/ḫatm" here is most likely an anointing of the forehead with the sign of the cross, but it might be more than this.

37. For more context, see n. 38.

| Ch./v. | Ethiopic I | Arabic I |
|---|---|---|
| 4 | "We give thanks to the Lord." | "Let us give thanks to the Lord." |
| 5 | "It is a righteous and just thing;" | And they shall say: "Right and just." |
| 6 | and "Lift up your hearts" he will not say this, because it is said in the offering; | And he shall [not?] say: "Lift up your hearts!" for this is at the oblation. |
| 7 | and he will pray: "We give thanks to you, Lord, in your Son Jesus Christ our Lord, through whom you have enlightened us, having revealed to us an incorruptible light. | And to all others this: "We give you thanks, O God, with your Son, Jesus Christ, our Lord, you have enlightened us and revealed to us your perpetual light. |
| 8 | Having completed the length of the day, and come to the beginning of the night, once we were satisfied with the light of the day, which thou have created to our satisfaction, and now, not lacking in the light of the evening, through your grace, we praise you and glorify, | And we have finished the length of the day and come to the beginning of the night, enflamed with the light of the day, which you created for our grace. And now, (since) we do not lack the light of the evening because of your grace we praise you |
| 9 | in your Son Jesus Christ our Lord, in whom to you be glory, power and honor with the Holy Spirit, now and for ever and ever. Amen." | through your Son, Jesus Christ, our Lord, who has, together with you, the glory, the might and the dignity, together with the Holy Spirit, now and for the ages of ages. Amen." |
| 10 | | And all the people shall say: "Amen." |
| 11 | | |
| 12 | | |
| 13 | | |
| 14 | | |
| 15 | | |

| | | |
|---|---|---|
| 16 | Let the faithful who are present at the supper receive from the hand of the bishop a little bread, before they divide their own bread, for this is eulogy [e.g., blessed bread], not rendering of grace [e.g., thanksgiving] like the body.[38] | And at the supper together the present believers shall take from the hand of the bishop a little portion of bread, before they break their own bread, for this is partaking and it is not thanksgiving like the body. |
| **Ch. 29D** | **[Doublet of Ch. 28.4b-6]** | |
| 1 | | |
| 2 | | |
| 3 | | |
| **Ch. 30A** | **Concerning the Supper of the Widows** | |
| | **§27. Concerning the Widow's Meal** | **57. About the Widows** |
| 1 | Let the widows, if there is one who has wished to invite them to lunch, after they have dined, send them away quickly before evening. | If one wants to invite a widow, he shall send her away before evening. |
| 2 | But if he cannot for the ordained clergy who have been invited, once he has given food and wine, let him send (them) away and let them do as they please. | And if it not possible for the invited, he shall give the invited food and wine and send them forth so that they receive as they want. |
| **Ch. 30B** | **[Prologue]** | |
| 1 | | |
| 2 | | |
| 3 | | |

38. The Ethiopic terms used here are *ʾawlogiyā*, loanword from the Greek, "eulogy" [e.g., "blessed bread"], and *ʾakkʷatet*, "thanksgiving, rendering of grace" [e.g., thanksgiving].

| Ch./v. | Ethiopic I | Arabic I |
|---|---|---|
| 4 | | |
| 5 | | |
| **Ch. 31** | **Concerning the Fruit That It Is Proper to Bring to the Bishop** | |
| | **§28. Concerning the Fruit It is Fitting for Them to Offer** | **58. The Fruits for which it is Right to Bring Them** |
| 1 | Let each one give the fruit of the first wheat and hasten to offer (it) to the bishop; | And one should hasten and bring to the bishop the first fruits of the growth, all as donations, |
| 2 | let him offer (it) while he is blessing, and let them name the one who has offered it, saying: | and he, who offers, shall name the offering, blessing, saying: |
| 3 | "Let us give you thanks, O Lord, and present to you the first fruits which you have given us to [receive them] with your pleasure, having given commandment by your word to the earth that it should bear fruit of every kind for the satiety and nourishment of man and for all animals, | "We give thanks to you, O God, and we offer to you the excellent first fruits that you have given to us as examples, that you perfected through your word, when you commanded the earth to send forth every fruit for profiting, gladdening and nourishment of humankind and all animals. |
| 4 | for which we glorify you, O Lord, and for all that you have made fruitful, every creature fruits of every kind, | Therefore, we praise you, O God, and for all that you accomplished for us [and for] all the creation of all kinds of fruit, |
| 5 | through your Son Jesus Christ our Lord, to whom be glory with the Holy Spirit for ever and ever. Amen." | through your Son, Jesus Christ, our Lord, who has the glory with you and the Holy Spirit until the ages. Amen." |
| **Ch. 32** | **The Blessing of Fruits** | |
| | **§29. Blessing of Fruits** | **59. Concerning the Blessing** |

| | | |
|---|---|---|
| 1 | Blessed therefore be the fruits: yelds,[39] the fig, the pomegranate, the olive, the chestnut,[40] the apple, the peach, the cherry, the almond, the sycamore (*saglā*), not the onion, not the garlic, not the watermelon, nor any other vegetable. | The fruits, that are blessed are: wheat, barley, fava bean, lentil, peavine, bean, chickpea, cauliflower, rice, grape, fig, pomegranate, apple, olives, pear, pignolia, citron, peach, almond, mulberry, [but] not onion, not garlic and not watermelon, not pumpkin and not sycamore and nothing from the other vegetables. |
| 2 | Sometimes they will offer flowers, rose flowers, but others will not. | It shall be welcomed to bring rose blossoms, [but] nothing other. |
| 3 | For everything they will deliver, they shall give thanks to the holy Lord as they receive it in his grace. | This is not like everything else which they receive: They shall give thanks to God with his glory if they receive. |
| **Ch. 33** | **That It Is Not Proper for Anyone to Taste Anything in the Pascha before the Hour When It Is Proper to Eat** | |
| | **§30. On Not Eating Anything Before the Proper Time at Pascha** | **60. Concerning That One Does Not Taste Before the Hour of Pascha** |
| 1 | Let fasting not be considered for those in such a condition. | It shall [not] count to the fast on this. |
| 2 | If there is a pregnant woman or a sick person, and he cannot fast the two days, let him fast on the Sabbath day, because of necessity, on bread and water. | Whoever is not able to fast for two days because of the belly or a sickness, shall fast on Saturday because of the emergency, being content with bread and water. |
| 3 | If there is one who is on a ship, and if by some necessity he has missed his day, let him put off his fast which he came to know after Pentecost. | And he who was at sea or in an emergency and did not know this day, is to be taught, and one should give him a fast after Pentecost. |

39. The term *qamḥ* is of uncertain interpretation.

40. The term *kastamen* is not attested elsewhere and its precise meaning cannot be determined. The proposal to interpret it as "chestnut" (cf. e.g., Greek καστανaία, "chestnut-tree," see Geoffrey William Hugo Lampe, *A Patristic Greek Lexicon* [Oxford: Clarendon Press, 1961], 704), albeit not devoid of linguistic difficulties in the Greek-Ethiopic correspondence (one would have expected **qasṭanen*, whereas the exchange *m/n* can be explained with a wrong reading of the Greek), is due to Sever J. Voicu, "Vincenzo e Vito: note sulla *Collezione aksumita*," in Rafał Zarzeczny, ed., *Aethiopia fortitudo ejus. Studi in onore di Monsignor Osvaldo Raineri in occasione del suo 80° compleanno*, Orientalia Christiana Analecta 298 (Rome: Pontificio Istituto Orientale, 2015), 479–92, 488–89.

| Ch./v. | Ethiopic I | Arabic I |
|---|---|---|
| 4 | It is not that he observes the Pascha, because his type has passed, for in the next month it has ceased, and ‡ he has come in to fulfill it once he has known the truth. | For in the law it is written, that he does not keep the Pascha, for it was prescribed to him. He shall come in the month and go away to do so as he knows the truth. |
| **Ch. 34** | **That It Is Proper for the Deacons to Assist the Bishop** | |
| | **§31. That it is Fitting for the Deacons to Serve the Bishop** | **61. Concerning that the Bishop is Eager to [Receive] the Penitents** |
| | Let each one, together with the subdeacons, serve the bishop; and let them tell him about the sick, so that if the bishop wishes, he may visit (them): for truly who is sick is much comforted, if the chief of the priests has remembered him. | And each deacon together with the subdeacons shall attend on the bishop and they shall indicate to him the sick so that the bishop looks out, not to miss anyone. For the sick will be consoled with the commemoration of his high-priest with deeds and a prayer for him. |
| **Ch. 35** | **Concerning the Hour When It Is Proper to Pray** | |
| | | **62. Concerning the Prayer** |
| 1 | | The believers shall pray together at the time of rising, before they begin their work, to the Lord and thus to the work they shall proceed. |
| 2 | | And if there are words of catechesis, he shall honor it and go away to hear the words of God strengthening his soul. And he shall hasten to the church where the spirit dwells. |
| **Ch. 36** | **That It Is Proper to Receive the Eucharist Early at the Time It Will Be Offered, before They Taste Anything** | |
| | **§32. Concerning Receiving the Eucharist Before Anything Else** | **63. Concerning the Thanksgiving Before Everything is Received** |

| | | |
|---|---|---|
| | Let every believer seek to receive the Eucharist before tasting anything; if he receives it with faith, even if there is one who has given him something deadly, after that it will not prevail against him. | And every believer shall try not to taste anything before he receives the Eucharist. For even if something deadly shall be given to the faithful after taking [it,] [the deadly thing] does not harm him. |
| **Ch. 37** | **That It Is Proper to Watch over the Eucharist Diligently** | |
| | **§33. Concerning Keeping the Eucharist Carefully** | **64. Concerning the Care in Conservation of the Eucharist** |
| | Let all take care that those who do not believe do not taste of the Eucharist, neither mice nor pets, and that not even a little of it falls out and is not wasted, for it is the body of Christ, food for the faithful, not to be despised. | Everyone shall take care that an unbeliever does not taste of the Eucharist and [nor] that a fly might infest it and is lost, for it is the body of Christ, it is for the nourishment for the believers and not to be despised. |
| **Ch. 38A** | **That It Is Not Proper to Spill Anything from the Cup** | |
| | **§34. Concerning the Chalice, Let it Not be Poured Out** | **65. Concerning the Chalice, That One Does Not Spill** |
| 1 | Indeed, having been blessed in the name of Christ, you have received like the image of the blood of Christ. | For [the chalice] is blessed in the name of the Lord, one receives it as replacement of the image of the blood of Christ. |
| 2 | Therefore, do not spill any, lest a foreign spirit, as if you had despised him, lick it: you will be guilty of the blood, as if you had despised his price, with which he redeemed you. | Therefore, one shall not spill, so that it will not be despised by a foreign spirit who licks it. And the blood shall be without defect, so that one does not disdain the veneration with which it was bought. |
| **Ch. 38B** | **[Concerning the Sign of the Cross]** | |
| 1 | | |
| 2 | | |
| 3 | | |
| 4 | | |
| 5 | | |
| 6 | | |

| Ch./v. | Ethiopic I | Arabic I |
|---|---|---|
| **Ch. 39** | **[Concerning Deacons and Presbyters]** | |
| | | **66. [On the gathering of the Deacons with the Intercessors (or Presbyters)]**[41] |
| 1 | Let all the deacons with the presbyters assemble where the bishop has ordained, early in the morning, and let the deacons not fail to be present at all times, unless prevented by sickness. | And the deacons shall gather daily with the presbyters where the bishop command them. And the deacons shall not refrain the whole time except for a sickness or an unction or something different. |
| 2 | When they have assembled, let them communicate this to the church and so, after prayer, let each one do what is right. | And they shall gather to hear in the church and they shall teach and they shall pray likewise, so that it is proper that everyone is in harmony. |
| **Ch. 40** | **Concerning the Places of Burial** | |
| | **§36. Concerning Cemeteries** | **67. Concerning the Cemeteries**[42] |
| 1 | Those who are buried in cemeteries, let them not <burden> them, for this is a thing that was created for the poor; only the reward for the laborer who digs and the price of the bricks. | The burial [people] at the cemeteries shall not overcharge the poor, since it is the work of the grave digger with wage, which must not lack, |
| 2 | Who takes care of the place and lives there is to be supported by the bishop, so that there is no burden on those who come. | and of the guard by bounty. And the bishop shall nourish the caretakers and bystanders, so that those who come are not overcharged. |

41. Abu-l-Barakat and M1 = 66; M2-4 = 65.

42. Abu-l-Barakat and M1 = 67; M2-4 = 66.

| Ch. 41 | Concerning the Hour When It Is Proper to Pray | |
|---|---|---|
| | **§35. Concerning Prayer** | **68. Concerning the [Hour of] Prayer**[43] |
| 1 | All the faithful, men and women, at dawn, rising from sleep, before doing anything, let them wash their hands and pray to the Lord, and so go to their work. | Every male believer and female believer shall rise in the morning from the sleep, they shall wash their hands and they shall pray to God before they turn to work. And at work likewise. |
| 2 | If it happens that the word of the homily is celebrated, let him prefer to go: each one will concede to himself all this, to hear the universal word of the Lord. ‡ For he whom you have seen in church, at that time the evil of the day will pass away. Let the God-fearing man therefore consider this a loss, if when they deliver the word of the sermon he is not present, or even when he himself who can read he is present, and the teacher comes. | And if there are words of catechesis they shall honor it and every believer shall be present at those words, according to what is fitting to hear God, for he is present there in the church. They shall remain steadfast for the day or for this he shall be strengthened with the word to be the winner against the gods. It is a loss if the pious is not present and even more so if he can read on his own or if the teacher comes. |
| 3 | Do not let him leave the church while there is the homily, for then is given to him (to whom he) expounds this that ‡ will remain of use to all.[44] While the Spirit grants things that you do not hope for, having heard, you will gain, and your faith will become firm because of what has been said; and in your house say what you have heard: for this everyone will take care in the church, where the Spirit abounds. | And the church shall remain, because it is for the homily which the speaker gives there, so that everyone makes benefit of the speech. And you hear what one hopes that the spirit will give him, benefit without sorrow. The creature shall not revolt against the speeches. And in your house you shall speak [and repeat] the catecheses and everyone should hasten to the church where the Holy Spirit is celebrated. |
| 4 | If there is not a day on which there is homily, let him also in his house read something from the Holy Scripture as far as he can. | And if there was a day, on which no homily was given, you shall pray in your house at every time. Take a holy book and pray, as he knows is sufficient. |

43. Abu-l-Barakat and M1 = 68; M2-4 = 67.
44. This is a literal translation of a passage that appears to be corrupt.

| Ch./v. | Ethiopic I | Arabic I |
|---|---|---|
| 5 | At the time of the third hour, while praying, as you are in your house, glorify the Lord, and if not, pray in your heart, having paid attention to the proper time, | And praying at the third hour if you were in the house. He shall pray the praise of God. At another place, pray in your heart, freeing the time. |
| 6 | because at that hour we received Christ returning: therefore also the Orit [e.g., the Old Testament law (Octateuch)] (has) the rule that they offer the type of the lamb and bread, in the image of the perfect lamb, the shepherd Christ who is the bread of heaven. | For this is the hour before Christ was nailed to the cross. And therefore the law ordered the reception of the lamb and the bread, that they are offered as images for the perfection of the perfect lamb, the shepherd, Christ, and he is the heavenly bread. |
| 7 | Likewise, also at the sixth hour: once Christ was nailed, the day was divided and there was darkness: therefore let prayer be continuous, let the voice of those who pray resemble that of the prophets, while creation acknowledges those who do not believe. | And likewise also at the sixth hour [at which] Christ was hung on the cross, the day was divided and darkness happened. Then he prays, similar to the voice of the one who prayed a lament of the prophets and of the creation about all who passed away.[45] |
| 8 | At the ninth, let prayer be prolonged with glorification, so that we are united in glorifying the soul, while the righteous glorify the Lord who does not lie, who remembered his saints and sent his Word to enlighten them. | And they shall pray at the ninth [hours] in the prayer after the praise so that they praise together with the souls of the righteous, praising God, who does not lie, who has remembered his holy ones and sent his word and he enlightened them. |
| 9 | At that hour, when Christ had been pierced in the side, water and blood gushed forth, and enlightening the rest of the day, brought it to evening. Therefore, you also, as you are about to fall asleep, as you make the beginning of the second day {making it} an image of the Resurrection, | At this hour the side of Christ was opened, and water and blood poured out and the rest of the time he has truly enlightened till the evening. Thus, you also, willing to sleep, shall begin another day, making an image of the resurrection, |

45. This seems to be close to TD II.24.

| | | |
|---|---|---|
| 10 | pray before you rest your body in your bed. | completing it before reclining the body for rest. |
| 11 | Getting up in the middle of the night, washing yourself with water, pray; and if your wife is also with you, both of you. | And at the middle of the night, rise, wash your hands and then pray. And if your husband [is present] he shall pray together [with you]. |
| 12 | But if she is not yet a believer, pray after retiring to another room, and then return to your bed. | And if she [!] is an unbeliever, go apart in another house! |
| 13 | Do not be slothful in praying: he who is bound by marriage is not unclean, for those who have washed themselves have no need to wash themselves, | And do not be lazy with the prayer: He who is bound through marriage shall pray, he is not defiled because he is washed. It is not necessary to [go to] the baths, because they are clean. |
| 14 | for once you have breathed with the sign of the cross, with the dew, with your hand, you have wrapped yourself in the spirit, the body down to the feet,[46] for the grace of the spirit is the coating of a washing, as if it were given from the fountain of a believing heart, sanctifies the one who believes. | And concerning the consignation: One shall breathe out. With the humidity of breath in the hand, one should sign the body [down] to the feet, for it is the gift of the Spirit that sanctifies the legs. The bath shall spring forth from the heart of the believers, he who receives is sanctified if he believes. |
| 15 | Pray promptly at this hour, for even the presbyters who have passed it on to us, so taught, that at this hour all creation rests for the glorification of the Lord: stars, plants, waters, and all the angelic hosts, ministering, at this hour with the souls of the righteous glorify the Lord. | And one should pray at this hour, [it is] a necessity, for the elders who handed it on to us taught us thus, because at this hour all creation is still for God: stars, lights and the water stand [still] and all the armies of angels praise God, serving at that hour, together with the souls of the righteous. |
| 16 | Therefore, it is fitting for those who believe that they should study to pray at this hour, the Lord also being a witness of such a thing. He said: "Behold, great commotion was in the middle of | And because of this, the believers shall be eager to pray at this hour and the Lord said, bearing witness to this: "Behold, there is a voice at midnight saying: 'Behold the bridegroom comes; rise to |

46. One could suspect the presence of a lacuna here.

| Ch./v. | Ethiopic I | Arabic I |
|---|---|---|
| 16 (cont.) | the night, while they were saying: 'The bridegroom will come: arise to receive him,'" and again while he was saying: "Watch out, for you do not know at what hour he will come." | meet him.'" And he shall cling to it, saying: "Watch now, for you do not know at which hour he comes!" |
| 17 | At the hour of the cockcrow, once you get up, so pray, for in that hour the children of Israel denied Our Lord Christ, whom we have known by faith, for the hope of the light of the world, for the resurrection of the dead while we hope for the day. | And at cockcrow stand up likewise, pray, because at that hour of cockcrow the sons of Israel denied Christ, who we know by faith, looking at the eternal light at the resurrection of the dead expecting the day. |
| 18 | As you believers do all this, remembering, admonishing one another, and teaching the catechumens, you will not be tested and will not perish, always remembering Christ. | And you shall fulfill this, the community of believers, remembering each one mutually, you shall teach and you shall counsel the catechumens not to be sad and you will not fall, remembering Christ. |
| **Ch. 42** | **[Concerning the Sign of the Cross]** | |
| | | **(68. cont.) [Concerning the Sign of the Cross]** |
| 1 | Always take care to mark your forehead, because it is a sign of the Passion, against Satan, manifest, and it is evident, if it has been done by his faith, not only so that you may be recognizable to people, <but> you will clothe yourself with the sign as with armor. | And they shall seal the forehead with taught reverence, for this is the sign of the passion. It destroys the devil and it is visible. And you shall do so with faith and visible to humankind only, but known as a shield. |
| 2 | And the adversary, once he has seen the power of the man that is in the heart, made with certainty in the likeness of a washing, shall flee trembling with fear, not from the spitting but from the blowing. | The strength of the spirit, recognized by the adversary, is from your heart and likewise with all signed, visible, putting to flight, without touching, rather this sign is expelling without rest. |
| 3 | This is what Moses showed before, the lamb that is sacrificed at the Pascha, he who shed blood at the table and anointed the doorposts: he therefore made known the faith that is now in us with the perfect lamb. | It was taught by Moses on the lamb of Pascha as sacrifice and he sprinkled blood on the doorposts and the lintel, making visible the faith in the perfect lamb. |

| | | |
|---|---|---|
| 4 | Marking therefore with our hands, our foreheads and eyes, let us keep away from him who plots to bring death. | On the forehead and the eyes they shall seal themselves with the hands, locking out the tempter, so that he decays. |
| **Ch. 43** | **[Conclusion]** | |
| | | **(68. cont.) [Conclusion]** |
| 1 | While with grace and upright faith this is made known, it will give edification in the church and eternal life to all who believe: | And these [things] together with grace and faith received, will be for edification in the church and everlasting life for those who believe. |
| 2 | because by all heeding the apostolic tradition, heresy will not come to mislead any righteous person; | It was ordered that they shall be kept with perfect interest for if all are eager according to the grace of this treatise, then the division of heresy may not harm them. |
| 3 | for heresies have become many in this way: because of you, superiors who have need of the apostolic tradition, who love doctrine and {who love} who give themselves up to their own passions, which desire is not fitting. | And so, they shall aspire [after] the many divisions those who are not appointed for leadership to the coming of the teaching. And they learned the reason of the divisions, they divided but for their own good and they were lazy with what they did not want and what was not fitting. |
| *Additional Texts in Ethiopic I* (*Ch. 43.4 resumes at the end*) | | |
| ***Decree of the Apostles* (Acts 15:20; Jn 19:36)** | **§37. Concerning Idols** [//] [//] and concerning idol[s /] and idolatry, let them beware, for it is demonolatry; abstain from the dead and from blood, and do not break their bones. | |

| Ch. | Ethiopic I | Arabic I |
|---|---|---|
| ***Didache*** **11.3** | **(§37. cont.)** Concerning the apostles and prophets, according to the rule of the gospel let them do so. | |
| **11.4-5** | Every apostle who comes to you shall not stay but a day or two; but if he has desired even the third, and if he has tarried to go, he is a <false> prophet. | |
| **11.7** | Every prophet who speaks in spirit, do not test him or examine him, for not every sin will be forgiven. | |
| **11.8** | Everyone who speaks in the spirit is a prophet, if he behaves in the manner of God: by his manner of conduct, therefore, the false prophet will be known, or the (true) prophet. | |
| **11.9** | Every prophet who sets a table in spirit will not eat of it, otherwise he is a false prophet. | |
| **11.10** | Every prophet who teaches the truth and does not do what he teaches is a false prophet. | |
| **11.11** | Every prophet who is tried in truth, who works (in) the society of people, and acts outside the law, will not be judged with you, for the Lord is his judge: for so did the prophets of old. | |
| **11.12** | Whoever says in spirit: Give me money, or anything else, do not listen to him; if he has said anything else, give it to him: let no one ask. | |
| **12.1** | Whoever comes to you in the name of the Lord, receive him; then, having tested him, you shall know: for you have knowledge: right and left. | |

| | | |
|---|---|---|
| **12.2** | If there are people passing through, help them as much as you can, and they will not stay with you except for two or three days. | |
| **12.3** | If they have desired it and wish to stay with you, if they have a trade let them be in service, and if they <stay in service>, let them not be sustained. | |
| **12.4** | If they have no trade, let them act according to your understanding, that a sluggard may not live with you. | |
| **12.5** | And if he will not do so, he is a seller of Christ: beware of such people. | |
| **13.1** | Whosoever a prophet desires to remain with you, let him have his livelihood. | |
| **13.3** | Therefore, all the first fruits of the winepress, wheat, cattle, and sheep, the first fruits give to the prophets, for they are your <chiefs of the> priests. | |
| **13.4** | And if you have no prophets, give them to the poor. | |
| **13.5** | If you have made bread, after you have taken away the first fruits, give them according to the commandment. | |
| **13.6** | So also, if you have opened a jar of wine or honey, having taken the first fruits, give them to the prophets. | |
| **13.7** | Of money and clothing, taking the first fruits which you have desired, give them according to the commandment of the Lord. | |
| **8.1** | Let not your fast be like that of the hypocrites, for they fast on the second Sabbath and the fifth day. You, on the other hand, fast on Wednesdays and Fridays. | |

| Ch. | Ethiopic I | Arabic I |
| --- | --- | --- |
| **8.2** | And do not pray like the hypocrites, <but> as the Lord commanded in the Gospel. | |
| ***Didascalia* (12, cp. ApCons 2.57.2.-58.6; 2.59)** | **§38[a]. Concerning Prayer**<br>In church, you presbyters and deacons, in every congregation, on Sabbaths, set up the places having been arranged for the brethren with all care and exactitude. If he is found sitting outside the rule, let him be rebuked, for the Lord has made our church like his dwelling place. Just as we see animals without speech, cows, horses, goats and sheep, each of them keeping to his own kind, even if they are awakened and ruminate, they do not separate themselves from one another: so also in the church, let the young people sit on their own, if there is a place; if there is not, let them stand, and the adults keep to themselves; and if they have children, let them look after them. Let the virgins then stand by themselves, and if there is no place, let them stand on account of it before the other women. Those who have children and are married, let them sit on their own; and also ecclesiastical widows and lay widows, on their own. If brothers or sisters have come from the wards, let a deacon, <once has come,> inquire whether she <has a husband>. If they are widows, let them come in, let them each sit in their place; and let the presbyters also sit in their place. If another priest has come from the circumscriptions, let him be received in a place convenient to him. But if someone else or another has come in a secular apparatus, | |

| | | |
|---|---|---|
| | whether men from the region or from the circumscriptions, brothers, you, presbyter, while you are saying the word of the Lord or while you are making them hear or while you are reading, do not show partiality and do not leave your service to show them their seats, <but> remain quiet; and let the brothers receive him. But if there is no place, it is an act of fraternal and charitable love that he should get up and give him his place. And if, while the young men are seated, an elder has risen or an old woman has risen to give him his seat, <you,> deacon, having paid attention to one of the young men who are seated or otherwise of the young women, make them rise, seat that one or the other <who has given up his seat>; and the one whom you have made rise, place her at the door, that the others may be rebuked and yield to those who are older than themselves. Take care to design large churches, and if a poor person comes, from the region or from the districts, and there is no room, you, presbyter, therefore make room for such people wholeheartedly, even if you have to sit on the ground, so that there may be no partiality towards men, but only towards the Lord. | |
| *(Ch. 43.4 Resumes in Ethiopic I)* | | |
| Ch. 43.4 | **§38b.** If there is therefore anything we have overlooked, our brethren, let the Lord reveal it to those to whom it suits, while he governs the holy church in a quiet harbor. | And [if] we left something out, O brothers, God shall show [it] to the just, leading the church into a tranquil harbor. |

# *Chapter 2*

# The Prologue and the Short and Long Endings

## 1. Prologue

Before the discovery of Ethiopic I and Arabic I, the Prologue appeared as Ch. 1 in the Latin version but was located after Ch. 30 (at 30B) in Ethiopic II. The placement of this chapter at the start of Ethiopic I and Arabic I confirms the Latin placement over and against the placement in Ethiopic II. Part of the debate surrounding the authorship of ApTrad has revolved around the use of the phrase "tradition" in Ch. 1.[1] Christoph Markschies had argued that the original Greek text of this chapter did not include the use of the word "tradition."[2] As the *Herm.Com.* 2002 notes:

> The Ethiopic [II] suggests that *ducti*, 'led,' in the Latin is a copyist's error for *docti*, 'taught.' More significantly, where the Latin and Ethiopic have 'the tradition,' the Syriac instead has 'the faith' and [ApCons] has 'the . . . arrangement.' This has led Markschies to argue that the original Greek

1. *Herm.Com.* 2002, 2–4 and 22.

2. Christoph Markschies, "Wer schrieb die sogenannte *Traditio Apostolica*? Neue Beobachtungen und Hypothesen zu einer kaum lösbaren Frage aus der altkirchen Literaturgeschichte," in *Tauffragen und Bekenntnis*, ed. Wolfram Kinzig, Christoph Markschies, and Markus Vinzent (Berlin: De Gruyter, 1999), 25–26.

> word was not παράδοσις, 'tradition,' as is usually assumed, but *διατύπωσις*, 'configuration, arrangement, custom, rule,' as in [ApCons], which could have been translated in the other ways by the various witnesses.[3]

However, the Ethiopic I confirms the use of "tradition" in the Latin version, something Bausi has made explicit.[4] Markschies also argued that

> the interpretation adopted by other scholars (influenced by the word 'first,' πρῶτα, in [ApCons]), that the first sentence refers to an earlier work, or to an earlier part of this work, arguing that the reference is instead intended to be to this work itself and to the various charisms of ministry that it describes, and that 'those things . . . of the word' should be understood as 'those things of the Word [of God],' that is, of Christ.[5]

While this seemed like a reasonable interpretation, it is worth noting that the title in Ethiopic I—there is no title in the Latin—complicates the matter, as well as the fact that χάρισμα clearly underlies the respective text in Ethiopic I.[6] The title in Ethiopic I is "Prelude to the Second Rule."[7] Bausi has suggested this title implies a reference to another work in the Aksumite Collection, namely the *Περὶ χαρισμάτων* (ApCons 8.1-2) [Text 6], and as a result a number of Markschies's conclusions are in need of reconsideration.[8] However, Bausi also acknowledges that this text is displaced after ApTrad in the Aksumite Collection.

The *Canones ecclesiastici*, which contains a number of statutes, particularly for ministers, appears as Text 1 in the Aksumite Collection before Ethiopic I. It is followed by two other texts in that collection: *Alexandrian History* (Text 2) and *Epistle 70* by Cyprian (Text 3). Text 2 does not appear

3. *Herm.Com.* 2002, 22.

4. Alessandro Bausi, "The >so-called *Traditio apostolica*<: Preliminary observations on the new Ethiopic evidence," in *Volksglaube im antiken Christentum*, ed. Theofried Baumeister and Andreas Merkt (Darmstadt: WBG, Wissenschaftliche Buchgesellschaft, 2009), 302n27.

5. *Herm.Com.* 2002, 22–23. See Markschies, "Wer schrieb die sogenannte *Traditio Apostolica*? Neue Beobachtungen und Hypothesen zu einer kaum lösbaren Frage aus der altkirchen Literaturgeschichte," 26–29.

6. Bausi, "The >so-called *Traditio apostolica*<," 302n27.

7. For the difficulties with this title, see Bausi, 299–300.

8. Bausi, 299–300 and 301–3.

in the *Sinodos* (Ethiopic II) and likewise Text 3 only appears in some manuscripts. However, the *Canones ecclesiastici* appear in the Latin version, as well as the *Alexandrian Sinodos* (Sahidic/Bohairic and Arabic II) directly before ApTrad, indicating that the *Alexandrian History* and *Epistle 70* by Cyprian in the Aksumite Collection are likely additions to the traditional circulation of ApTrad. It seems then that the title in Ethiopic I could refer also to the *Canones ecclesiastici*, though it is more likely that Bausi is right that this originally referred to the *Περὶ χαρισμάτων* (ApCons 8.1-2), which has since been transposed in the Aksumite Collection.

Looking at the content of the prologue, it is clear that the text was composed as a result of issues within the community. As the *Herm.Com.* 2002 notes: "[T]he author of this chapter clearly judged that the customs of the church with which he was familiar were under threat as a result of the ignorance of others and so needed recording/transmitting in this document for their preservation."[9] Catechesis is a clear motivating factor of the text, as can be seen in Ch. 1.2, including as the instances of catechesis throughout the document (particularly in Chs. 15–20) as well as references to catechesis in Ch. 21.39-40. But it may not just be ignorance to which the community was under threat. The phrase "fault or error that was recently invented" in Ch. 1.4 suggests that there was a real issue/threat within the community that motivated the need to compile this text. It is not possible to determine what this threat might be—unless one assumes that the text is from third-century Rome—since "the phrase is sufficiently vague that it might refer to almost any dispute in the first few centuries of Christianity, whether known to us or not."[10] Interestingly, the prologue also appears to be addressed to the laity given the way the document is described in Ch. 1.5. If this is the case, this must be a well-educated and literate laity. It is unclear, for instance, why the laity would need so many instructions on the ordination and establishment of ministers, particularly those of the bishop and presbyter. However, much of the material in the respective chapters dealing with their ordinations appears to betray a later date of composition, suggesting that perhaps the audience of the document shifted over time from the laity to ordained clergy. Hints of the lay focus, however, can still be seen in Ch. 4 and Ch. 41, in particular.

9. *Herm.Com.* 2002, 23.
10. *Herm.Com.* 2002, 23.

The prologue also appears to point away from a monarchical episcopate.[11] This would be consistent with Bradshaw's assertion that "the prologue was probably composed sometime in the third century when the oldest materials had first been brought together in a single document."[12]

## 2. Endings—Short and Long

ApTrad has two different endings, a short (Ch. 38B) and a long (Chs. 42 and 43) ending. These endings have a complicated history, but in general they bear similarities to the prologue. As a result, the original form of ApTrad's ending was likely composed at the same time as the prologue.[13] The last few chapters show a significant amount of variation in the different versions of ApTrad and contain the majority of ApTrad's material on daily prayer. Given the complexity of this material, it is best to quote in full the argument in *Herm.Com.* 2002 about the development of these endings:

> There are also some significant differences in order toward the end of the document. In all the versions chap. 35, on the times for prayer, is duplicated as the beginning of chap. 41, a much longer chapter on the same subject, but in addition the Latin includes doublets of chaps. 42 and 43 immediately after chap. 38 (which are designated as chap. 38B in our text). Most scholars have accepted the view advanced by André Wilmart in 1919 that the Latin has conflated two versions of the *Apostolic Tradition* (a shorter one lacking chaps. 39–41 and a longer one that included them), both composed by Hippolytus himself. However, the order of the material in the *Canons of Hippolytus* and the *Testamentum Domini* suggests that they were familiar with a version in which a form of chaps. 39–41 appeared in the place occupied by chaps. 34–35 in the texts known to us.
>
> All these variants can best be explained by the hypothesis of a gradual expansion of the material, with at least four stages: (1) a shorter version lacking chaps. 39–41 altogether; (2) an intermediate version, in which chap. 34 was replaced by an earlier form of what are now chaps. 39 and 40 (which are an adaptation of chap. 34), and chap. 35 was replaced by an earlier form that became the expanded chap. 41—the order apparently

11. *Herm.Com.* 2002, 23.
12. Bradshaw, *Apostolic Tradition*, 14.
13. *Herm.Com.* 2002, 23.

> known to the compilers of the *Canons of Hippolytus* and of the *Testamentum Domini*; (3) a composite version, in which chaps. 34 and 35 were retained and chaps. 39–41 were instead inserted into the shorter version just before the conclusion (chaps. 42–43), thus creating the form underlying the oriental-language texts; and (4) the longer version, represented by the Latin alone, in which the final portion of the composite version (chap. 39 to the end) was appended to the conclusion of the shorter version, resulting in a duplication of chaps. 42 and 43.[14]

*Herm.Com.* 2002 sees Chs. 39–41 as a later addition to the text, with Chs. 39 and 40 expanding on Ch. 35.[15] Stewart also admits that the endings reflect development and argues for a similar line of development. However, he notes that "what is lacking" in the explanation in *Herm. Com.* 2002 "is any explanation of the procedure of replacing chapters, as well as any indication of the time scale in which this took place."[16] The only difference is in regard to Chs. 34/39: "Bradshaw et al. treat the latter chapter as a reworking of the former, whereas . . . they may be seen as entirely distinct on redactional grounds, chapter 39 being new material, as well as chapter 40, deriving from the realignment of the Hippolytean congregation within the Roman church."[17] Ethiopic I raises some questions, in fact, about the *Herm.Com.* 2002's treatment of Ch. 39.

In general, the stages outlined in the *Herm.Com.* 2002 seem to hold up in light of Ethiopic I, though the stages seem to be a little too neat. Support for the later addition of at least Ch. 40 is clear from Ethiopic I, where Ch. 40 divides the first part of the conclusion (Ch. 43.1-3), along with some additional texts—material from the *Decree of the Apostles*, the *Didache*, and the *Didascalia*—from the last part of the conclusion (Ch. 43.4) [see Table 3 in our introduction]. Bausi argues that Ch. 40 has been displaced in Ethiopic I.[18] Regardless, the placement of additional texts within ApTrad's ending (Ch. 43) was likely an attempt to give the material in those three additional texts the same amount of authority as the rest

14. *Herm.Com.* 2002, 16, see also pp. 178, 187, 188–89, 202, 218, and 221.

15. *Herm.Com.* 2002, 16 and 188.

16. Stewart, *On the Apostolic Tradition*, 43. For his discussion of the endings in ApTrad, see p. 45.

17. Stewart, *On the Apostolic Tradition*, 44.

18. Bausi, "The >so-called *Traditio apostolica*<," 298.

of the document, since Ch. 43.4 serves as a final conclusion that admonishes everyone to keep all the previous mentioned teachings (for more on this, see Ch. 8 of our commentary). Ethiopic I also omits Ch. 35, instead including Ch. 41. This provides support that Ch. 35 has been supplanted as in stage 2. However, Ch. 34 is in Ethiopic I. As a result, this witness does not fit neatly into stages 2 or 3 as proposed in the *Herm.Com.* 2002.

TD seems to support the original placement of Chs. 39–41 in the place of Chs. 34 and 35, though the material in Chs. 34 and 35 is largely taken over into TD. CH is a less helpful witness in some regards to the *Herm. Com.* 2002's proposed stages. While CH seems to replace Chs. 34 and 35 with Chs. 39–41, the location of that block of material in CH is in a very different place. The corresponding canons in CH (24–27) are out of place. They have been shifted up in the document and are placed after initiation (CH 19 = ApTrad 21) and before the instructions on the importance of caring for the bread and wine and fasting practices (CH 28 = ApTrad Chs. 36, 37, and 38A). These latter instructions have also been moved up before the discussion of communion more broadly (CH 30 = ApTrad 22). Thus, CH seems to have transposed a number of sections taken over from ApTrad.

Ethiopic I, CH, and TD seem to be witnesses to a number of intermediate forms in what the *Herm.Com.* 2002 describes as stages 2 and 3. Moreover, Arabic I, which abandons a number of sections also complicates neat theories about ApTrad's supposed Greek archetype. This also, it seems, causes some issues with regard to Stewart's theory of the development of the text as well. As a result, there was likely not a single composite version of the text, but rather a mixture of several transitional forms. This would also be in keeping with Meßner's caution against attempting to create a single archetype of the document.[19] Nevertheless, one of these transitional versions appears to have been known to the redactor of the Latin version, which seems to have taken a short version of the text and combined it with one of the longer composite versions to form the Latin text. That transitional version cannot be the same as Ethiopic I because of disparities between the texts. For the same reason, it also cannot be the transitional versions known to CH and TD.

19. Reinhard Messner, "Die Angebliche *Traditio Apostolica*," *Archiv Für Liturgiewissenschaft* 58–59 (2016): 26.

# *Chapter 3*

# Orders and Ministries

The process of ordination and the installation of the various orders in ApTrad is described in several chapters, namely Chs. 2, 3, 7–14, 29B ( = Ch. 24), 34, and 39, though a ministry of "teacher" appears in Chs. 15, 18, 19, and 41.1-3 (in the various versions) and that of a steward in Ch. 40.2. As we will see, the prayers for the ordinations of bishops, presbyters, and deacons in ApTrad creates some confusion because these prayers are not contained in every witness. The rites described in ApTrad are also unique, in many ways, among the ordination rites in the East and West, despite often indirectly or directly influencing later ordination rituals.[1]

## 1. Bishops

### *1.1. Rubrics*

The first chapter to include a reference to ordination is Ch. 2, which contains the instructions for the ordination of the bishop.[2] The instructions in this

1. For overviews of the rites of ordination, see Paul F. Bradshaw, *Ordination Rites of the Ancient Churches of East and West* (New York: Pueblo, 1990); Paul F. Bradshaw, *Rites of Ordination: Their History and Theology* (Collegeville, MN: Liturgical Press, 2013). For an overview of the major order, in particular, in the church orders, and their reception in the Constantinopolitan, Cypriot, West Syrian, Georgian, and Alexandrian tradition, see Heinzgerd Brakmann, "Pseudoapostolische Ordinationsgebete in Apostolischen Kirchen. Beobachtungen Zur Gottesdienstlichen Rezeption Der Traditio Apostolica Und Ihrer Deszendenten," in *Liturgies in East and West: Ecumenical Relevance of Early Liturgical Development. Acts of the International Symposium Vindobonnense I, Vienna, November 17–20, 2007*, ed. Hans-Jürgen Feulner (Vienna: LIT, 2013), 61–98.

2. For a summary, see Bradshaw, *Rites of Ordination*, 59–63.

chapter, particularly in verses 2 and 3, seem to be the result of later revisions to the text. As noted in *Herm.Com.* 2002, the text of verse 2 seems to imply that the mention of other bishops is an afterthought, and that originally the process centered around the presbyters and not bishops. As *Herm.Com.* 2002 points out, these episcopal directives would not be a universally accepted feature until the fourth century when the Council of Nicaea legislated that other bishops should participate in the ordination of a bishop.[3] The awkward note that the presbyters should stand still in verse 3 further implies that this is a recent change.[4] This seems confirmed by CH 2, which focuses less on the role of the bishops in the ordination, and more on the presbyters and assembly. This likely means that here CH is preserving an older reading of the text. However, Stewart has recently argued that CH could be the result of "a redactor familiar with presbyteral ordination of the *episkopos*, faced with a text enforcing episcopal ordination of the *episkopos*, expand[ing] the text in order to embrace the continued involvement of the presbyterate."[5] However, support for the antiquity of CH 2 here can be found in Arabic I, which has:

> 2.1. The hand is to be laid on the bishop according to the words spoken beforehand. He is to be without blame, elected from the people, 2.2. he, who was named and approved by two presbyters together and by the present bishops. 2.3. And with joy all being at the same place shall lay the hand upon him and [while] the presbyters [are] standing silently. 2.4. And they shall stand with him, praying in the heart that the Holy Spirit comes down upon the present bishops 2.5. and the one qualified by the assembly shall lay the hand upon the head of him who is being ordained and they shall pray thus: . . .

In addition to the witness of CH 2 and Arabic I, there may also be another interpretation for the confusion seen here and in ApTrad 7 (more below) concerning the relationship between the presbyters and bishops. Stewart has argued elsewhere that the first Christian communities were based on households each led by an *episkopos*.[6] Outside of their house-

3. *Herm.Com.* 2002, 27. See also Bradshaw, *Ordination Rites of the Ancient Churches of East and West*, 22 and 39; Bradshaw, 51–52. Stewart also seems to see this as a later development; see Stewart, *On the Apostolic Tradition*, 71–73.

4. *Herm.Com.* 2002, 26–27. See also Bradshaw, *Apostolic Tradition*, 15–17.

5. Alistair Stewart, *The Canons of Hippolytus: An English Version, with Introduction and Annotation and an Accompanying Arabic Text* (Macquarie Centre: SCD Press, 2021), 45–46.

6. Alistair Stewart, *The Original Bishops: Office and Order in the First Christian Communities* (Grand Rapids, MI: Baker Academic, 2014).

holds, the *episkopoi* within a city or place were referred to as *presbyteroi kata polin*. While there was no unified local church with a governing council in each city, there was instead a federation of *episkopoi* and elders who were referred to in the collective as *presbyteroi kata polin*. This does not mean, however, that *episkopos* and *presbyteros* are synonyms, despite the fact that their roles had some overlap. It would not be until later that monepiscopacy, or a single bishop leading several Christian communities, emerged, often as late as the third century.

Without adjudicating Stewart's position vis-à-vis the scholarly consensus he proports to seek to overturn, it is worth noting that his work may provide a different way of reading the material in ApTrad, which he, of course, places in Rome. Nevertheless, his statement applies more broadly. He summarizes his position as follows:

> In the ordination rite for an *episkopos* in [ApTrad], it is directed that the people come together with the presbytery and any bishops who are present. These bishops, I may suggest, are other *episkopoi* from Rome, not *monepiskopoi* from other locations. It is directed that one of these *episkopoi* should say the ordination prayer while the *presbyteroi* stand silent. From this I may deduce that here we have mention of a presbytery that clearly is not a gathering of *episkopoi* from within the city, as it is said that one of the *episkopoi* says the ordination prayer, this *episkopos* clearly being distinguished from the presbytery. This presbytery would appear to be a group within the individual Christian community whose *episkopos* is now being appointed. The fact that they are enjoined to be silent is an indication that their role in the ordination of an *episkopos* is being deliberately diminished, as the honor is given to a visiting *episkopos*.[7]

Elsewhere he notes that this itself was also a shift in practice and "the result of a complex redactional history in which handlaying by a single visiting *episkopos* appears to have replaced handlaying by the local congregational presbyters."[8] He finds further support for this in CH 2, which adds that the handlaying is done by "one of the bishops and presbyters." Arabic I's unique addition in Ch. 2.4 "upon the present bishops" may also support this interpretation.

7. Stewart, *The Original Bishops*, 174–75. See also pp. 342–43. This seems to be his position in Stewart, *On the Apostolic Tradition*, 100–102.

8. Stewart, *The Original Bishops*, 242–43.

While Stewart's work has, we believe, placed ApTrad in the wrong time and place, his interpretation is only one possibility among others. Another is that the presbytery referred to in Ch. 2.2 was originally a reference to the local bishops (and elders?) known collectively as the *presbyteroi* or possibly the *presbyteroi kata polin*, and that the rubric to "let one of the bishops present" lay hands on the ordinand is simply the selection of one of the bishops from the presbytery.[9] This seems affirmed by the phrase "from whom let one of the bishops present, being asked by all." An interpretation of this originally being a reference to the collection of bishops as *presbyteroi* or, again, possibly *presbyteroi kata polin*, may even explain the kiss of peace in the text (Ch. 4.1), the act serving as a unique gesture of entrance into the *presbyteroi*.[10] The reference, then, in Ch. 2.2 to "those bishops who are present" and in Ch. 2.3 to the presbytery "stand[ing] by, being still" could be a later expansion with the emergence of the monepiscopacy and the involvement of other monepiscopal bishops in the ordination process.[11] This would subsequently refashion the whole meaning of the chapter and lead to the presbytery to be interpreted not as a collection of bishops, but as the group of congregational presbyters subordinate to the bishop across the city. In this case, the meaning has shifted so radically that CH 2 feels the need to add "one of the bishops and presbyters" to affirm the role of the presbyters, now subordinated to the bishop, in the process.

In any event, the double imposition of hands in the text as it stands is odd, since no other ancient ordination ritual has a double imposition of hands as outlined in ApTrad.[12] This double imposition is either a result of the "fusion of two sets of directives," or, more likely, a revision to the directives as a result of developments in the monepiscopacy.[13] Here Ap-

9. This seems to be Stewart's earlier position as outlined in Alistair Stewart-Sykes, "The Integrity of the Hippolytean Ordination Rites," *Augustinianum* 39 (1999): 112. Against Stewart's position, however, Bradshaw has asserted that the term *presbyteroi kata polin* is questionable since *presbyteroi* in the first- and second-century context is a collective term for bishops; see Paul Bradshaw, "*Presbyteroi* in the First Two Christian Centuries," *Studia Patristica* 106 (2021): 71–76. His comments about a lay consulting group (pp. 75–76) may also explain the reference in ApTrad Ch. 2.1 to the bishop being "chosen by all the people" (Latin), though the other versions have something like "chosen from among all the people" (Ethiopic I).

10. Bradshaw, *Ordination Rites of the Ancient Churches of East and West*, 34–35.

11. Bradshaw, *Apostolic Tradition*, 15–18.

12. Bradshaw, *Ordination Rites of the Ancient Churches of East and West*, 44–46.

13. *Herm.Com.* 2002, 29. See also Bradshaw, *Rites of Ordination*, 61; Bradshaw, *Apostolic Tradition*, 15–18.

Trad is trying to make sense of older forms of community leadership and bring those forms in line with current practice. Following E.C. Ratcliff, Bradshaw has proposed that the original form of this rubric likely read:

> Let him be ordained bishop who has been chosen by all the people, and when he has been named and accepted by all, let the people assemble together with the presbytery on the Lord's day. When all give consent, let the presbytery lay hands on him and let all keep silence, praying in the heart of the descent of the Spirit.[14]

This proposed original form would support any of the explanations given above.

### *1.2. Prayer*

The prayer in Ch. 3 follows directly on the directives in Ch. 2. This prayer is contained in the Latin as well as Ethiopic I and II, but not in the Sahidic or Arabic II versions of ApTrad, which for some reason almost always omit the prayer texts. Its presence in the Latin and Ethiopic I reveals that it was part of the final redaction of the text. The incipit is also present in Arabic I.

This prayer is highly elaborated and developed in its understanding of the office of the bishop (see Table 1 below). As *Herm.Com.* 2002 notes: "The unique character of the prayer in the *Apostolic Tradition*, therefore, suggests that it took its present form in a particularly difficult situation in which the status of the bishop's office and his authority in the local Christian community were under attack from some quarters."[15] This would not be inconsistent with Maxwell Johnson's argument for the inclusion of an ordination prayer in the sacramentary of Sarapion of Thmuis (see below). The prayer, as it stands now, must date from the mid-third century or later. At the same time, there is ancient language in the prayer, suggesting an older date for parts of the text. As a result, Bradshaw has suggested that while the prayer is likely a secondary addition to ApTrad, the prayer itself also has layers.[16] The text in ( ) in the proposed earlier form is considered uncertain by Bradshaw.

14. Bradshaw, *Apostolic Tradition*, 16.

15. *Herm.Com.* 2002, 34.

16. Paul Bradshaw, "The Ordination Prayers in the So-Called *Apostolic Tradition*," *Vigiliae Christianae* 75 (2021): 121–25; Bradshaw, *Apostolic Tradition*, 18–22.

**Table 1: Development of the Bishop's Ordination Prayer**

| **ApTrad Ch. 3 (Latin)**[17] | **Proposed Earlier Form**[18] |
|---|---|
| God and Father of our Lord Jesus Christ, Father of mercies and God of all comfort who dwells on high and looks on that which is lowly, who knows all things before they come to pass, you who gave limits in the church through the word of your grace, foreordaining from the beginning a race of righteous ones [from] Abraham, appointing rulers and priests, and not leaving your holy place without a ministry, from the beginning of the age you were pleased to be given in those whom you chose; now pour forth that power which is from you, of the spirit of leadership that you gave to your beloved Son Jesus Christ, which he gave to the holy apostles, who established the church in every place, your sanctification, for unceasing glory and praise to your name. Bestow, knower of the heart, Father, on this your servant, whom you have chosen for the episcopate, to feed your holy flock and to exercise the high priesthood for you without blame, ministering night and day; unceasingly to propitiate your countenance, and to offer to you the holy gifts of your church; and by the spirit of high priesthood to have power to forgive sins according to your command, to assign lots according to your bidding, also to loose every bond according to the power that you gave to the apostles, and to please you in gentleness and a pure heart, offering to you a sweet-smelling savor; through your Child, Jesus Christ, through whom [be] glory and power and honor to you, Father and Son with the Holy Spirit, {in the holy church,} both now and to the ages of ages. Amen. | God, giving the rules of the church through the word of your grace, having foreordained from the beginning a righteous race from Abraham, having appointed rulers (and priests), pour forth the power from you of the spirit of leadership upon this your servant (whom you have chosen for the episcopate) to shepherd your holy flock (and to offer to you the gifts of your holy church, to give lots according to your bidding,) and to please you in gentleness and a pure heart, offering you a sweet-smelling savour; through your servant Jesus Christ. |

17. { } included from Ethiopic I.
18. Bradshaw, "The Ordination Prayers in the So-Called *Apostolic Tradition*," 125.

This prayer would make its way into other texts like CH 3a, TD I.21, and ApCons (*Epitome* 4.1-4), though it was greatly expanded in the latter two.[19] It is noteworthy, as well, that this text does not have "any explicit reference to prophetic or teaching functions to be exercised by the new bishop, suggesting that such a ministry was not seen as fundamental to the episcopal office in the tradition in which the prayer arose."[20] Stewart has argued that the teaching office of the bishop appears in some circles as early as Acts and the Pastoral Epistles, but more broadly in the third century.[21] Its absence from this prayer could point to an early dating for the prayer. In any event, it provides complications to seeing ApTrad as having emerged primarily out of a school context, at least in the way that Stewart has proposed, since it would be odd if the prayer for the ordination of the bishop of a school did not reference his fundamental teaching role.[22] In any event, this theory could also point away from the Roman context from which Stewart proports ApTrad is derived. Alexandria, with schools like that of Origen, also had a thriving number of schools from which the document could have emerged.[23] But again, the emergence of this text from a school context seems unlikely, especially given the minimized role of the teacher throughout the document (see below).

## 2. Presbyters

Ch. 7 includes the rubrics for the ordination of presbyters.[24] These rubrics (Ch. 7.1) indicate that the bishop is to lay hands on the presbyter, while the presbyters also touch him, and they are to say a prayer that is similar to that given for the bishop in Ch. 3. This seems to indicate that the prayer in Ch. 7.2-5 is not original, something likely confirmed by its presence only in the Latin and Ethiopic II versions of the text, as well as in TD I.30

19. Bradshaw, *Ordination Rites of the Ancient Churches of East and West*, 46–50; Bradshaw, *Rites of Ordination*, 72 and 76.

20. Bradshaw, *Rites of Ordination*, 63.

21. Stewart, *The Original Bishops*, 323–37.

22. Stewart-Sykes, "The Integrity of the Hippolytean Ordination Rites," esp. 114–15; Stewart, *On the Apostolic Tradition*.

23. Stewart, *The Original Bishops*, see, for instance, 335 and 341.

24. For a summary, see Bradshaw, *Rites of Ordination*, 64–67.

(see Table 2 below).[25] It is omitted in Ethiopic I, the Sahidic, and Arabic II versions,[26] though these versions include v. 7.1. Arabic I does maintain the incipit of the prayer. It is worth noting that CH 4 also includes the phrase "one is to pray over him all the prayer of the bishop, except only the name of the bishop." As a result, there is some debate about the original form of this rubric.[27] *Herm.Com.* 2002 argued that originally this rubric referred just to the practice of laying hands on the one being ordained:

> We have suggested earlier that the original form of the rite for the episcopate in chap. 2 may have directed that the presbyters rather than the bishops of neighboring churches should perform the imposition of hands on the candidate. If this were so, then it is possible that the words 'and let him say' were originally absent from the directions here. Thus what was being enjoined was that the imposition of hands on a candidate for the presbyterate should follow the same pattern as for a candidate for the episcopate—all the presbyters touching him. When the practice of presbyters laying hands on a candidate of the episcopate ceased, the interpretation of this instruction would have become problematic. Hence it may have been understood as referring in some way to the prayer, and this reference was eventually clarified by the insertion of 'and let him say' into the Latin text and by recasting the entire end of the sentence in the oriental versions. The author of [CH] was apparently somewhat perplexed by the enigmatic nature of the direction, since he interpreted it to mean that everything in the rite for the episcopate was also to be done in the case of a presbyter, including the same prayer, except that the term 'presbyter' be used instead of 'bishop,' and consequently he simply omitted the entire text of the presbyteral prayer.[28]

Bradshaw has recently reaffirmed this interpretation of the rubric and has suggested that the original form of this rubric was: "And when a presbyter

25. *Herm.Com.* 2002, 55; Stewart, *The Original Bishops*, 172–77; Bradshaw, *Apostolic Tradition*, 35–36.

26. There are some incipits of the presbyterial prayer in the Arabic; see *Herm.Com.* 2002, 55/58.

27. For a summary of the debates, see Stewart-Sykes, "The Integrity of the Hippolytean Ordination Rites," 108–13; *Herm.Com.* 2002, 55; Stewart, *On the Apostolic Tradition*, 98–102.

28. *Herm.Com.* 2002, 55.

is ordained, let the bishop lay the hand on his head, the presbyters also touching him, according to those things that have been said above, as we have said above about the bishop."[29]

This seems to lead *Herm.Com.* 2002 to think that this direction would only apply to the handlaying. But part of the handlaying in ApTrad Ch. 2 is accompanied by the prayer in ApTrad Ch. 3 as indicated in the rubric in Ch. 2.5: "laying [his] hand on him who is being ordained bishop, pray, saying thus . . . " This suggests the laying on of hands with the prayer in Chs. 2 and 3 was implied in the rubric in Ch. 7.1. This is actually the position advanced by Stewart. Stewart has argued that "it is the ordination prayer at [ApTrad Ch. 7] which is the interpolation, and that it is interpolated during the development of [ApTrad] in the third century, whereas the ordination prayer at [ApTrad 3] is original, together with the rubric referring back to it."[30] This would mean that CH 4 preserves an earlier reading of the text. If this is the case, this also provides some support to the proposed earlier form of the prayer for the ordination of a bishop given by Bradshaw since nothing in that proposed earlier form, except the phrase "whom you have chosen for the episcopate," would be inconsistent with a presbyteral office. Stewart has more recently suggested "that not the prayer only but also the introductory rubric" is a later redaction of $^{R}$CN, and "that $^{R}$El made no provision for the appointment of a presbyter."[31] This, however, seems to take things too far, and Stewart's earlier position seems more in keeping with the evidence.

As noted in *Herm.Com.* 2002, the laying on of hands by the presbyters and the bishop is unusual. It is not found in the Roman tradition and is only known independently from ApTrad in the Armenian Rite.[32] Further treatment of the ordination of presbyters is dealt with in Ch. 8.5-8. There it makes it apparent that the presbyters lay hands on the ordinand but this is "on account of the common and like spirit of the clergy." ApTrad then goes on to note that only the bishop can ordain. The explanation "for a presbyter has authority only to receive; he has not authority to give" indicates that there was a tension between the presbyter and bishop. This was likely rooted in a perceived equality between them in some circles.

29. Bradshaw, *Apostolic Tradition*, 35–36.

30. Stewart-Sykes, "The Integrity of the Hippolytean Ordination Rites," 112.

31. Stewart, *On the Apostolic Tradition*, 101.

32. *Herm.Com.* 2002, 58.

Whether this was an addition to the text remains debated, but it seems most likely that it was a latter addition.[33] This seems further affirmed by the less sophisticated form of these verses given in Arabic I.

There are hints elsewhere in the document that there was an equality between bishops and presbyters. In Ch. 7.1 there is a certain equation of presbyter and bishop, given the use of the same prayer text for both. This could easily point to an Egyptian context, as we will see below. This equation is even more apparent in CH 4, which is derived from this chapter.[34] Similarly, in looking at CA, Ewa Wipszycka notes that the text is very clear in equating bishops and presbyters:

> From Canon 10 we learn that in the eyes of God presbyters are equal to bishops as they are responsible for their 'region' in the same way as the bishops are responsible for the city and the regions under their auspices. This is a very important declaration, meaning that we are dealing with such a stage of development of Egyptian Christian communities in which a network of autonomous non-episcopal churches called *katholikai* existed, which were run by the presbyters.[35]

This system of "*katholikai* flourished as early as the second quarter of the fourth century."[36] But of course, these remain distinct offices and so the bishop and presbyter were not quite the same.

The absence of an ordination prayer for the presbyters in some versions of ApTrad, as well as in CH 4, may have parallels in the sacramentary of Sarapion, where it has been persuasively argued that the ordination prayer for deacons (Prayer 12) and the prayer for bishops (Prayer 14) are theologically and literarily distinct from the prayer for the ordination of presbyters (Prayer 13). Prayers 12 and 14 are likely

33. Bradshaw, *Ordination Rites of the Ancient Churches of East and West*, 59–60 and 72. Bradshaw, *Apostolic Tradition*, 40–42.

34. Nathan P. Chase and Maxwell E. Johnson, *The Origins of the Canons of Hippolytus* (Collegeville, MN: Liturgical Press Academic, 2024).

35. Ewa Wipszycka, "A Certain Bishop and a Certain Diocese in Egypt at the Turn of the Fourth and Fifth Centuries: The Testimony of the Canons of Athanasius," *U Schyłku Starożytności: Studia Źródłoznawcze = Late Antiquity: Studies in Source Criticism* 17/18 (2018/2019): 96.

36. Wipszycka, "A Certain Bishop," 96n11.

later than Prayer 13.[37] Perhaps presbyters and bishops were originally ordained in Thmuis—like in an older form of ApTrad and in CH 4—using the same prayer, in this case Prayer 13. There is nothing in Prayer 13 that could not apply to both presbyters and bishops and given that Prayer 13 appears to be an earlier text than Prayers 12 and 14, it could suggest that this was originally the prayer for the bishop too. In fact, "Prayer 13 may well represent a rather early prayer for the presbyterate, a prayer which corresponds to the pre-Nicene presbyteral-episcopal style of church leadership within the Egyptian tradition."[38] This may also explain why Prayers 12 and 14 are closely related, because they were added when distinctions were emerging between the presbyterate and episcopacy in particular. What we may see in comparing Sarapion to ApTrad and CH 3-4 is that both originally used the same ordination prayer for bishops and presbyters.

However, at some point a prayer was added to ApTrad Ch. 7.2-5 (see Table 2 below), as already indicated above.[39] Further support for this prayer's later interpolation into the text is clear from the fact that this prayer and the prayer in Ch. 3 have different theologies of the episcopacy.[40] At the same time, this prayer may also show some signs of antiquity in its use of Num 11:16-17. As a result of this, Bradshaw notes that

> this biblical allusion is hardly ever found in other extant ancient ordination prayers, exception for the *Sacramentary of Sarapion* and those directly dependent on [ApTrad], apparently therefore being an older concept of the presbyterate as a council of advisors to the bishop, chosen from the leading men in the community, that was later superseded by the view that they were his subordinates.[41]

37. Maxwell Johnson, *The Prayers of Sarapion of Thmuis: A Literary, Liturgical, and Theological Analysis*, Orientalia Christiana Analecta 249 (Roma: Pontifico Istituto Orientale, 1995), 92–95 and 148–62.

38. Johnson, *The Prayers of Sarapion*, 153.

39. Bradshaw, "The Ordination Prayers in the So-Called *Apostolic Tradition*," 126–27; Bradshaw, *Apostolic Tradition*, 37–38.

40. Allen Brent, *Hippolytus and the Roman Church in the Third Century: Communities in Tension before the Emergence of a Monarch-Bishop*, Supplements to Vigiliae Christianae 31 (Leiden: E.J. Brill, 1995), 305–6; Stewart-Sykes, "The Integrity of the Hippolytean Ordination Rites," 106–13.

41. Bradshaw, *Apostolic Tradition*, 38.

In this way, there may be some hint of the bishops as forming the collective *presbyteroi* (or *presbyteroi kata polin*) behind this text.

| **Table 2: Development of the Presbyter's Ordination Prayer** | |
|---|---|
| **ApTrad Ch. 7 (Latin)** | **Proposed Earlier Form**[42] |
| God and Father of our Lord Jesus Christ, look upon this your servant and impart the spirit of grace and of counsel of the presbyterate that he may help and guide your people with a pure heart, just as you looked upon the people of your choice and commanded Moses that he should choose presbyters whom you filled with your spirit that you gave to your servant (Numbers 11:16–17). And now, Lord, grant to be preserved unfailingly in us the spirit of your grace and make [us] worthy, that believing in you we may minister in simplicity of heart, praising you through your child, Christ Jesus, through whom to you [be] glory and power, Father and Son with the Holy Spirit, in the holy church, both now and to the ages of ages. Amen. | God, look upon this your servant and impart the spirit of grace and of counsel of the presbyterate that he may help and guide your people with a pure heart, just as you looked upon the people of your choice and commanded Moses that he should choose presbyters whom you filled with your spirit (that you gave to your servant), praising you through your child, Christ Jesus, through whom to you [be] glory and power, in the holy church, both now and to the ages of ages. Amen. |

This prayer would make its way into TD I.30 and ApCons 8.16.2-5, though in both texts it would be greatly expanded.[43]

It is also worth noting the unique form of the doxology in the prayer: "the Holy Spirit, in your holy church, both now and to the ages of ages." This form is rare in the classical anaphoras, only appearing in the Egyptian anaphora of St. Matthew, ApTrad Ch. 4, the Egyptian Sahidic form

42. As proposed in Bradshaw, "The Ordination Prayers in the So-Called *Apostolic Tradition*," 126–27; Bradshaw, *Apostolic Tradition*, 36–37.

43. Bradshaw, *Ordination Rites of the Ancient Churches of East and West*, 60–64; Bradshaw, *Rites of Ordination*, 72–73 and 77.

of St. Basil, Addai and Mari, and Sharar.[44] It also appears in the doxology of an unknown and unnamed anaphora in the *Great Euchologion* from the White Monastery, indicating the continued circulation of this style of doxology in Egypt.[45] Outside of the classical anaphoras, this form of the doxology appears in Euch-AC in the "Prayer for the Papas"[46] and the fraction prayer that accompanies Ethio-AA I.[47] It also appears elsewhere in ApTrad, in particular in ApTrad Chs. 4, 6, and 21.21. This unique form of doxology, which is picked up in a number of Egyptian anaphoras and other liturgical points, may point to the influence of ApTrad on the Egyptian church, in particular.

## 3. Excursus on Provenance

### *3.1. Prayers*

Given the layers of development in Chs. 2 and 3, and also in Ch. 7, determining the provenance of this section of the document is difficult. The prayers in Chs. 3 and 7 are perhaps the least helpful in determining the provenance of the document. As already noted above, they have developed over time, articulate different theologies of the episcopacy, and are the result of later additions, particularly in the case of the prayer in Ch. 7. Nevertheless, scholars like Allen Brent have argued that differences in the theologies of the episcopacy and ministry in these two prayers are attributable to different authors within the Hippolytean school. Brent argues, based on textual and theological parallels, that the prayer in ApTrad Ch. 3 was made by the same author as the *Elenchus* ($^{R}$El), whereas the prayer

44. For a summary and the editions of these sources, see Nathan Chase, *The Anaphoral Tradition in the "Barcelona Papyrus,"* Studia Traditionis Theologiae 53 (Turnhout: Brepols, 2023), 280 and 281.

45. Alois Grillmeier, *Christ in Christian Tradition: Vol. 2, From the Council of Chalcedon (451) to Gregory the Great (590–604); Part 4, The Church of Alexandria with Nubia and Ethiopia after 451*, vol. 2.4 (London: Mowbrays, 1996), 250. For the text of the anaphora, see Emmanuel Lanne, "Le Grand Euchologe du Monastère Blanc," *Patrologia Orientalis* 28, no. 2 (1958): 269–406, §137.20-21.

46. Euch-AC Σ51$^{ra}$-51$^{va}$ (H 86.17–87.8).

47. Emmanuel Fritsch, "New Reflections on the Image of Late Antique and Medieval Ethiopian Liturgy," in *Liturgy's Imagined Past/s: Methodologies and Materials in the Writing of Liturgical History Today*, ed. Teresa Berger (Collegeville, MN: Liturgical Press, 2016), 52.

in ApTrad Ch. 7 was composed by the author of *Contra Noetum* ($^{R}$CN).[48] However, scholars have increasingly noted that this way of attempting to establish authorship of a text is not usually reliable. Moreover, other scholars, like Hanssens, have noted parallels to the form and prayers of the ordination rites for bishops, presbyters, and deacons in the Egyptian context.[49] Hanssens's parallels are to the later Coptic ordination rite, which of course could have been influenced instead by ApTrad.[50] What it does show at the very least is the extent to which ApTrad was received in Egypt. In other words, if it did not emerge from Egypt, it quickly took hold there.

Attempts at establishing the authorship of some of the classical anaphoras reveals the shortcomings of this approach.[51] Cuming's work on the anaphora of St. John Chrysostom continues to outline one of the most influential approaches to authorial attribution in anaphoral studies, and it is largely representative of how authorship has traditionally been determined for any liturgical text. In that article, Cuming highlighted three ways to establish attribution between a liturgical text and an author:[52]

1) Common words and phrases between a liturgy and an author's work

2) The use of stock phrases

3) Assessing stylistic similarities

But more recent scholarship has pointed out issues with Cuming's approach, with both Bradshaw and Juliette Day calling for new understand-

48. Brent, *Hippolytus and the Roman Church in the Third Century*, 302–6. For a summary and analysis, see Stewart-Sykes, "The Integrity of the Hippolytean Ordination Rites," 106–17.

49. Jean Michel Hanssens, *La liturgie d'Hippolyte: Ses documents, son titulaire, ses origines et son charactère*, Orientalia Christiana Analecta 155 (Rome: Pontificium Institutum Orientalium Studiorum, 1959), 384–94.

50. For overviews of the Coptic Rite, see Heinzgerd Brakmann, "Zur Evangeliar-Auflegung bei der Ordination koptischer bischöfe," in *Eulogêma: Studies in Honor of Robert Taft, S.J.*, ed. Ephrem Carr et al. (Rome: Pontificio Ateneo S. Anselmo, 1993), 71–91; Brakmann, "Pseudoapostolische Ordinationsgebete in Apostolischen Kirchen."

51. For more, see Chase, *The Anaphoral Tradition*, 49–51.

52. Juliette Day, *Reading the Liturgy: An Exploration of Texts in Christian Worship* (London: Bloomsbury, 2014), 29.

ings of authorship.[53] Bradshaw, writing about the church orders, explains why authorial attribution for early liturgical texts is problematic:

> Both the individual documents and the various composite collections of the material were subject to a process of emendation and "correction" by successive editors, copyists, and translators. Indeed, most of the church orders are not independent compositions at all, but themselves constitute a further stage of the rewriting of an earlier text in the series.[54]

Day has been even more critical of authorial attribution.[55] She uses SAR as her central example for how new understandings of authorial attribution can reshape our understanding of the text and its creation. While authorship is traditionally established through parallels between an anaphora and an author's other works, this leads to a number of methodological issues. In particular, it "risks a somewhat circular process whereby on the basis of a name appearing in a manuscript, a context and a relationship to other texts bearing the same name are presumed; that context and the other texts then serve to confirm the initial attribution."[56] Stefano Parenti in his study of the anaphora of St. John Chrysostom has similarly noted that "the second of the new 'laws' of comparative liturgy—*Doctrinal development often betrays an individual hand*—should be reconsidered

53. They are not alone; other scholars include Ulrich Volp, Bryan Spinks, and Predrag Bukovec—Ulrich Volp, "Liturgical Authority Reconsidered: Remarks on the Bishop's Role in Pre-Constantinian Worship," in *Prayer and Spirituality in the Early Church: Liturgy and Life (Vol. 3)*, ed. Bronwen Neil, Geoffrey Dunn, and Lawrence Cross (Strathfield: St Pauls, 2003), 189–209; Bryan Spinks, "The Anaphora Attributed to Severus of Antioch: A Note on Its Character and Theology," in *Θυσία Αἰνέσεως: Mélanges Liturgiques Offerts à La Mémoire de l'archevêque Georges Wagner (1930–1993)*, ed. J. Getcha and A. Lossky (Paris: Presses Saint-Serge - Institut de Théologie Orthodoxe, 2005), 345–51; Predrag Bukovec, "Der Einsetzungsbericht: Die Genese des Eucharistischen Hochgebets" (PhD diss., Vienna, Universität Wien, 2016), 562–63; Stefano Parenti, *L'anafora Di Crisostomo*, Jerusalemer Theologisches Forum 36 (Münster: Aschendorff Verlag, 2020), esp. Ch. 3.

54. Paul Bradshaw, "Liturgy and 'Living Literature,'" in *Liturgy in Dialogue: Essays in Memory of Ronald Jasper*, ed. Paul Bradshaw and Bryan Spinks (London: SPCK, 1993), 139.

55. Day, *Reading the Liturgy*, 21–40.

56. Day, 25. Here Day is quoting Johnson, *The Prayers of Sarapion*, 282.

specifying, at least, that the *individual hand* is not necessarily that of the author of the texts used."[57]

In an effort to further clarify our understanding of attribution and authorship, Day turns to the work of Harold Love,[58] who has noted four different kinds of authorship:

> 1) Precursory authorship where a significant amount of material has been taken from previously existing sources, either by influence or direct borrowing.
> 2) Executive authorship which closely resembles the traditional notion of "author"; she is the one who devises, orders, compiles and makes a text ready for publication. This may be achieved by more than one person, although the sole executor carries greater esteem.
> 3) Declarative authorship consists of the process of a text's validation by a named individual whose involvement in its production may be severely limited or non-existent, but who nevertheless influences the contextualization and interpretation of the text. Love includes here the retrospective attribution of authorship to an anonymous text, as well as ghost-writing.
> 4) Revisionary authorship occurs after the creation of a text when it may be polished or corrected, edited or revised by a second author or editor.[59]

Day writes, "[A]uthorship in relation to texts which are based on a preceding oral tradition can only be envisaged as multiple, there cannot be a single creative origin, but instead a creative use of the traditions of structure and language in relation to the specific worshipping context."[60] Since this applies to many of the classical anaphoras and early prayer texts, this complicates our understanding of their authorship. In the age of oral improvisation, in which high levels of stock phrases and the like were used in anaphoral construction, authorship is even more difficult to deduce.[61]

57. "la seconda delle nuove 'leggi' della liturgia comparata—*Doctrinal development often betrays an individual hand*—andrebbe riconsiderata precisando, almeno, che l'*individual hand*, non è necessariamente quella dell'autore dei testi utilizzati." Parenti, *L'anafora Di Crisostomo*, 168. Italics in original. Translation ours.

58. Harold Love, *Attributing Authorship* (Cambridge: Cambridge University Press, 2002).

59. Day, *Reading the Liturgy*, 31.

60. Day, 35.

61. Day, 33. See also the older study by R. P. C. Hanson, "The Liberty of the Bishop to Improvise Prayer in the Eucharist," *Vigiliae Christianae* 15 (1961): 173–76.

At the same time, Day is not willing to abandon the question of authorship, since "it forces us to consider how our texts are created; however, to retain it, 'author' cannot be assigned to an individual . . . it designates the processes which cause a text to come into being."[62] Achim Budde, on the other hand, is much more skeptical. Budde argues in his study of the anaphora of St. Basil that "liturgies do not have an author and do not have an *Urtext*."[63] Day and Budde are correct that an understanding of authorship as multiple and constrained by an oral tradition necessitates new understandings of how these texts were formed. It also requires scholars to reevaluate their approach to authorial attribution, since behind these received texts are oral traditions and a chain of performers, redactors, and copyists.

As a result, one must be careful when placing the prayers in ApTrad Chs. 3 and 7 in the hands of the same authors of *Elenchus* ($^{R}$El) and *Contra Noetum* ($^{R}$CN). The desire to see a common authorship behind these texts and prayers is mostly attributable to Brent and Stewart's presupposition that ApTrad emerged from a third-century Roman context. When this presupposition is removed, the textual and theological parallels become quite vague and inconclusive. Moreover, even if these parallels are granted, they do not definitively indicate that the authors of *Elenchus* ($^{R}$El) and *Contra Noetum* ($^{R}$CN) wrote these prayers, as Brent and Stewart assume, but that a later redactor incorporated their language into the texts.

### *3.2. Rubrics*[64]

Given the inconclusive nature of the prayer texts themselves, it is worth looking at what insights the rubrics may provide vis-à-vis the question of provenance. The question is: Where might the episcopal directives in Ch. 2 have come from? The participation of neighboring bishops in the ordination of bishops in North Africa occurs at an early date.[65] As a result, the recent change in episcopal directives in ApTrad most likely comes from somewhere else. Egypt may be a good place to consider, as Hanssens already had suggested in his comparison of ApTrad with the

62. Day, *Reading the Liturgy*, 39.

63. Achim Budde, "Editing Liturgy—Working with Texts Which Develop in Use," *Studia Patristica* 34 (2006): 5. See also Achim Budde, *Die ägyptische Basilios-Anaphora: Text, Kommentar, Geschichte*, Jerusalemer theologisches Forum, Bd. 7 (Münster: Aschendorff, 2004), 568–77.

64. Adapted from Chase and Johnson, *The Origins of the Canons of Hippolytus*.

65. *Herm.Com.* 2002, 27n14.

later Coptic ordination rite.[66] Like with the prayers, rather than representing an early practice, the rubrics of the Coptic ordination rite could have been influenced instead by ApTrad, but again what this shows is that if the practices described in ApTrad did not emerge from Egypt, they quickly took root there.[67]

What is known about ordinations in the early Egyptian sources has to be pieced together from brief accounts and liturgical prayers like that in the sacramentary of Sarapion of Thmuis as well as the CH 2-4. Other sources that specify the process in more detail, like the CB 46, are thought to be non-Egyptian in origin (more below).[68] In fact, besides CH, CB, and the sacramentary of Sarapion of Thmuis, there is only one other text that may refer to the ordination ritual of a bishop in this period: P.Ryl. Copt. 23, which is from Hermopolis and dated to the fifth/sixth century.[69] CA does not mention ordination at all, though it clearly spells out the expectations of clergy and their roles throughout.

What is clear is that the process leading up to the ordination of a bishop—and the lower clergy—in ApTrad is very similar to what is described in early non-liturgical Egyptian sources.[70] In mid-fourth- and early fifth-century Egypt this process appeared to involve clerical choice, an acclamation of the people, and then ordination.[71] This general process

66. Hanssens, *La liturgie d'Hippolyte*, 376–84.

67. For overviews of the Coptic Rite, see Brakmann, "Zur Evangeliar-Auflegung bei der Ordination koptischer bischöfe"; Brakmann, "Pseudoapostolische Ordinationsgebete in Apostolischen Kirchen."

68. Alberto Camplani and Federico Contardi, "Remarks on the Textual Contribution of the Coptic Codices preserving the Canons of Saint Basil, with Edition of the Ordination Rite for the Bishop (Canon 46)," in *Philologie, herméneutique et histoire des textes entre Orient et Occident: Mélanges en hommage à Sever J. Voicu*, ed. Francesca Prometea Barone, Caroline Macé, and Pablo Alejandro Ubierna (Turnhout: Brepols, 2017), 148–51.

69. For a summary of the text, see Ágnes T. Mihálykó, *The Christian Liturgical Papyri: An Introduction*, Studien und Texte zu Antike und Christentum 114 (Tübingen: Mohr Siebeck, 2019), 24n77, 107, and 260. Sources in Nubia are totally absent; see Heinzgerd Brakmann, "Defunctus adhuc loquitur. Gottesdienst und Gebetsliterature der untergegangenen Kirche in Nubien," *Archiv für Liturgiewissenschaft* 48 (2006): 326–28.

70. For a general overview, see Everett Ferguson, *Early Church at Work and Worship, Volume One: Ministry, Ordination, Covenant, and Canon* (Eugene, OR: Cascade Books, 2013), 86–91, 125–26, and 148–52.

71. Ferguson, 62, 65, and 125–26; Ewa Wipszycka, *The Alexandrian Church: People and Institutions*, The Journal of Juristic Papyrology Supplement 25 (Warsaw: Faculty of Law and Administration of the University of Warsaw, 2015), 127–31.

is confirmed in the earliest liturgical texts, though later texts of the Coptic ordination rite provide much more detail,[72] and there is also evidence for the process in patristic accounts about schismatic communities and their clergy in Egypt.[73]

Concerning the role of the presbyters in the ordination of their bishop, there was a long history in Egypt of presbyters being involved in the ordination of the patriarch of Alexandria, a practice that continued into the fourth century.[74] This may be the result of the close identification between bishops and presbyters in Egypt, which appears already in Origen.[75] In fact, this close identification led to conflicts in Egypt as exhibited by Athanasius's account of a presbyter named Colluthus who was pretending to be a bishop and was ordaining other presbyters.[76] This may explain the rubrics in ApTrad Ch. 8.5-8, which at first seem to give presbyters the ability to ordain presbyters, but then notes that it is only the bishop who ordains (Ch. 8.8). The historical record has also preserved the names of a number of early bishops in Egypt, as well as accounts of the organization of bishops and other clergy—and in some cases their correspondence—in cities like Oxyrhynchus.[77] This evidence can provide some insights into the structure of the Egyptian church in this period.

72. Wipszycka, *Alexandrian Church*, 132–34. For studies of the ordination of the patriarch and bishops, see O. H. E. Khs-Burmester, ed., *The Rites of Consecration of the Patriarch of Alexandria* (Cairo, 1960); O. H. E. Khs-Burmester, ed., *Ordination Rites of the Coptic Church* (Cairo, 1985).

73. Wipszycka, *Alexandrian Church*, 134–46.

74. Ferguson, *Early Church at Work and Worship, Volume One*, 86–91; Bradshaw, *Rites of Ordination*, 51–52; Wipszycka, *Alexandrian Church*, 43–60. Against this consensus, Stewart suggests that these are not presbyters, but rather bishops known collectively as presbyters; see Stewart, *The Original Bishops*, 188–99. He does leave open the possibility that this occurred in the *chora*; see Stewart, 199–201.

75. Bradshaw, *Rites of Ordination*, 43. This much Stewart also shows without having to accept his claims about whether presbyters ordained bishops in Egypt; see Stewart, *The Original Bishops*, 188–201.

76. Ferguson, *Early Church at Work and Worship, Volume One*, 64.

77. See, for example, Klaas Anthony Worp, "A Checklist of Bishops in Byzantine Egypt (A.D. 325–c. 750)," *Zeitschrift Für Papyrologie Und Epigraphik* 100 (1994): 283–318; AnneMarie Luijendijk, *Greetings in the Lord: Early Christians and the Oxyrhynchus Papyri*, Harvard Theological Studies 60 (Cambridge: Harvard University Press, 2008); Wipszycka, *Alexandrian Church*; AnneMarie Luijendijk, "On and Beyond Duty: Christian Clergy at Oxyrhynnchus (c. 250–400)," in *Beyond Priesthood: Religious Entrepreneurs and Innovators*

In any of the above interpretations of the original form of this chapter, it is clear that the bishop was elected by the "presbyters," whether these are part of the collection of bishops known as the *presbyteroi*, *presbyteroi kata polin*, or congregational presbyters subordinate to the bishop.[78] In the case of Alexandria, the evidence

> implies that the presbyters of Alexandria formed an electoral college from whose number the new bishop would be elected, and, moreover, that the electors also ordained the *episkopos* whom they had appointed . . . However, . . . there is no early evidence that individually these persons were known as presbyters within their own churches. I must countenance the possibility that their presbyteral title indicated that they were *presbyteroi kata polin*. We do not know this, but it must be recognized as a possibility. The sources, though ancient, are nonetheless considerably later, and it is entirely possible that they might not realize that presbyters, collectively, might individually be *episkopoi*.[79]

The emergence of the monepiscopacy in Alexandria may have begun with the episcopacy of Julian (c. 178–188), but was clearly established by the third century. This would be consistent with when we might expect some of these shifts to occur in the text.

What is difficult to explain is why, if ApTrad was redacted in Alexandria, it does not mention the role of the patriarch of Alexandria in the ordination of a bishop or even the process by which the patriarch was ordained. More details on the election of the patriarch appear from the fifth century onward.[80] But the earliest references to the ordination of the patriarch or bishop of Alexandria suggest that the bishop of Alexandria was chosen by the college of presbyters,[81] a practice that appears to have ceased by

---

*in the Roman Empire*, ed. R. L. Gordon, Georgia Petridou, and Jörg Rüpke, Religionsgeschichtliche Versuche Und Vorarbeiten 66 (Berlin: Walter De Gruyter, 2017), 103–26.

78. Stewart, *The Original Bishops*, 188–201 and 341.

79. Stewart, 193.

80. Wipszycka, *Alexandrian Church*, 43–60 and 149–69. Stephen Davis, *The Early Coptic Papacy: The Egyptian Church and Its Leadership in Late Antiquity: The Popes of Egypt*, The Popes of Egypt: A History of the Coptic Church and Its Patriarchs 1 (Cairo: American University in Cairo Press, 2017).

81. See n. 74, as well as A. Vilela, *La condition collégiale des prêtres au IIIe siècle* (Paris, 1971), 173–79; T. Vivian, *St. Peter of Alexandria: Bishop and Martyr* (Philadelphia: Fortress Press, 1988), 12–15 and 47–49, and C.W. Griggs, *Early Egyptian Christianity* (Leiden,

the time of Alexander (c. 312).[82] Again, whether this college of presbyters was originally understood as bishops, *presbyteroi kata polin*, or congregational presbyters subordinate to the bishop is not clear. The final redaction of ApTrad, which now distinguishes more clearly the role of the presbyters and gathered bishops (monepiscopal bishops) in the process for the ordination of a bishop, makes it clear that it is now the gathered bishops who are the principal ministers in the ordination. This final redaction of ApTrad seems to have occurred at roughly the same time that the practice of allowing presbyters to ordain the bishop of Alexandria ceased (i.e., by the time of Alexander). In other words, changes were being made to the text of ApTrad's episcopal directives mandating the involvement of other bishops in the ordination process at roughly the same time that Alexandria's process for ordaining her bishop/patriarch was in flux.

This still leaves open the question of why ApTrad, if it was redacted in Alexandria, does not mention the role of the patriarch of Alexandria in the ordination of a bishop outside of the city of Alexandria. In Egypt, unlike other regions, the patriarch participated at an early date in the ordination of every Egyptian bishop, including those in the *chora*. In fact, new evidence has shed light on the growing institutionalization of the church in the *chora* in the mid- to late third century under the leadership of the bishop of Alexandria.[83] Bishop Sotas of Oxyrhynchus, for instance, was ordained by the bishop of Alexandria (Maximus) in the third century, a practice that appears to have been becoming the norm in this period.[84]

By the fourth century, Egyptian bishops were normally ordained in Alexandria as indicated by the Council of Nicaea can. 6 (325 CE). As Wipszycka notes:

> Whenever a bishop died, the local clergy, the notables, the people, and probably also the bishops of the neighbouring dioceses would decide on the choice of a candidate or, if unanimity was not forthcoming, of more

1990), 63–64 and 132–33; Maxwell Johnson, *Liturgy in Early Christian Egypt* (Cambridge: Grove Books Limited, 1995), 37–38.

82. Johnson, *Liturgy in Early Christian Egypt*, 37–38.

83. Ewa Wipszycka, "The Institutional Church," in *Egypt in the Byzantine World, 300–700*, ed. Roger S. Bagnall (Cambridge: Cambridge University Press, 2010), 331–49. See also Wipszycka, *Alexandrian Church*, 60–74.

84. Luijendijk, *Greetings in the Lord*; Luijendijk, "On and Beyond Duty: Christian Clergy at Oxyrhynnchus," 107. See also Wipszycka, "The Institutional Church."

> than one candidate. Delegates would then set out for Alexandria in order to present the candidature(s) to the patriarch, who, however, was not bound in any way and could consecrate somebody else.[85]

A possible exception to this may have occurred in Pentapolis/Cyrenaica (modern Libya) which was part of the Alexandrian Church, but the evidence is very vague. In a letter to the patriarch of Alexandria in the mid-fourth century, Bishop Synesius of Cyrene, metropolitan of Pentapolis, notes the ordination of a Nicene bishop by a single bishop, writing that: "The election was positively unlawful, as I have learned from the older men, inasmuch as he was not consecrated either in Alexandria or by three here, even though the assent to the ordination had been given thence."[86] Wipszycka notes it is not clear if this meant that ordinations could be performed by three local bishops in Pentapolis with the patriarch's consent.[87] It is also worth noting that unlike Egypt, Pentapolis had metropolitans, despite being under the patriarch's jurisdiction.

This also raises the question: why does CH 2 and 3, and the sacramentary of Sarapion of Thmuis for that matter, contain an ordination prayer for a bishop? The inclusion of the process and prayer for the ordination of a bishop in CH may simply be a testament to its derivation from ApTrad and the use of the same prayer for presbyters in CH 4. In other words, this could be a sign of the conservative nature of liturgical sources and the church orders in particular. But this does not explain the inclusion of an ordination prayer in the sacramentary of Sarapion of Thmuis. In analyzing the episcopal ordination prayer in that collection, it is important to note that the ecclesial landscape in fourth-century Thmuis was quite turbulent given the presence of competing bishops. As a result, "[I]t becomes quite tempting to view Prayer 14 as a piece of episcopal propaganda intended to underscore the authority of the bishop as the genuine (γνήσιος) guardian of apostolic tradition against the continued threat of Melitianism."[88] While this does not suggest that Sarapion's prayer is a fiction, it is worth considering if it was included in the collection as a way to bolster the authority of the bishop, rather than provide directions for how to ordain a new bishop.

85. Wipszycka, *Alexandrian Church*, 112–13 and 127–31.

86. Wipszycka, 147. For the whole letter and another treatment, see Wipszycka, 295–98.

87. Wipszycka, 148.

88. Johnson, *The Prayers of Sarapion*, 156.

But it is not just CH and Sarapion that seem to preserve a local treatment of the ordination process of a bishop in a period when episcopal ordinations appear to have occurred in Alexandria. CB, which was known to have circulated in Egypt, contains an ordination ritual in canon 46 that also does not mention the patriarch.[89] Based on this, the ordination rituals described in the text are thought to reflect Syrian rather than Egyptian practice. This, of course, is a bit circular in its reasoning, but the disputed provenance of the document on other grounds makes it dubious that CB reflects native Egyptian practice. Interestingly, CB 46 shows some parallels to the process of ordination in CH 2 and 3; however, CB also appears to be a product of a later date, since it seems to be influenced by ApCons 8.[90]

Later Egyptian practice may help explain the inclusion of an ordination prayer in CH and the sacramentary of Sarapion of Thmuis, though of course one must be cautious when drawing parallels to later practices. Nevertheless, Heinzgerd Brakmann has observed that in the ritual for the installation of a bishop in his local church in later Coptic sources, the ritual included a repetition of the handlaying and consecration prayer.[91] The readings for this ritual (though without a description of the ritual itself) are preserved is P.Ryl.Copt. 60 from the tenth/eleventh century, indicating that some enthronement ritual was used by that time.[92] Earlier fragments of the ritual may be preserved in P.Ryl.Copt. 23 (noted above) and in P.Lond.Copt. I 514, which is from the Fayum and dated to the ninth/tenth century.[93] P.Ryl.Copt. 23 may be an ordination prayer for a bishop or a prayer for his enthronement in his diocese, since it calls the recipient of the prayer the successor of the apostles and includes an epiclesis. Similarly, Ágnes Mihálykó in her description of P.Lond.Copt. I 514, which is "a long litany hailing Victor, the bishop of Arsinoe," notes that this text may have been used on "the enthronement of the bishop,

89. Wipszycka, *Alexandrian Church*, 275.

90. Camplani and Contardi, "Remarks on the Textual Contribution," 148–51.

91. Brakmann, "Zur Evangeliar-Auflegung bei der Ordination koptischer bischöfe," 62–66, esp. 63n36. For more on the early ordination rites in the Egyptian tradition, see Brakmann, "Pseudoapostolische Ordinationsgebete in Apostolischen Kirchen," 86–98.

92. W. E. Crum, *Catalogue of the Coptic Manuscripts in the Collection of the John Rylands Library* (Manchester: University Press, 1909), no. 60.

93. Mihálykó, *The Christian Liturgical Papyri*, 24n77. For later evidence from Nubia, see Brakmann, "Defunctus," 327–28.

or a feast at the return of the bishop to his see after his consecration in Alexandria. Another setting for the litany could be his visit to a monastery, which is a special feast day, witnessed in New York MLM M 575."[94] All of this may point to an earlier practice of enthronement in the Egyptian tradition.

Based on this suggestion, it is possible that the rubrics and prayer in CH 2 and 3, as well as the prayer for the ordination of the bishop in Sarapion's sacramentary (Prayer 14), may have been used for the enthronement of a bishop, or even for sending them to the patriarch in Alexandria. The context for both prayers in CH 2 and 3 and Sarapion's prayerbook are vague enough, though both prayers read as ordination prayers. However, if the consecration prayer, or something like it, was substantially repeated at the enthronement in later sources, this may explain why they are included in CH and the sacramentary of Sarapion. It is worth noting that an enthronement is also implied in CH 4, but an enthronement is not mentioned in CH 2 or 3. It is even possible, whatever its origins, that this ritual came to be seen as an enthronement in the later Egyptian tradition.

It is also possible that the role of the Alexandrian patriarch in the ordinations of bishops in his suffragan sees was not as established or was much more contested at the beginning of the fourth century than the evidence has suggested. If ApTrad did derive from an Egyptian, and specifically Alexandrian, context, this may explain the omission of the patriarch from the directives. While in some places the bishop of Alexandria exerted control over the ordination of bishops already in the third century, like in the case of Bishop Sotas of Oxyrhynchus, perhaps this was not always and everywhere the case, as exhibited by the mid-fourth-century letter of Synesius. At first glance it would, however, seemingly be inconceivable, even in the farthest Egyptian backwaters, for the patriarch to not be involved in some way in an episcopal ordination in Egypt much later than the mid-fourth century. It is unlikely that by the late fourth century any Egyptian center, let alone Alexandria, would receive this text in ApTrad, CH, or any other text for that matter, including Sarapion of Thmuis, and not alter it to reflect the role of the patriarch, even if the text was preserving an archaism. But this appears to be exactly what may have happened. In fact, despite being dated to a slightly later period in Egypt (sixth century), CB was not conformed to this Egyptian practice. Perhaps this speaks to a

94. Mihálykó, *The Christian Liturgical Papyri*, 54n77.

dissenting community in Egypt at this time or a historical archaism. Or, again, perhaps the hold of the bishop of Alexandria over the ordination process in all of Egypt and its suffragan sees was not as strong as suggested by the literary records and took longer to be formalized. But what is clear is that the failure of these documents to mention the patriarch does not at all mitigate against their circulation and use in Egypt.

## 4. Deacons

The following chapter, Ch. 8, concerns the ordination of the deacons, but is more about the ordination and function of presbyters, especially in verses 5-8 (see above).[95] Ch. 8.1 seems to suggest that the process of choosing a deacon is through "election to office by the people" and by the laying on of hands.[96]

The prayer for deacons (Ch. 8.9-12) is only found in the Latin and Ethiopic II versions of ApTrad, as well as TD I.38 (see Table 3 below). A totally different prayer appears in CH 5. Interestingly, the prayer for the ordination of deacons is not in Ethiopic I. The incipit of the prayer is given in Arabic I. In fact, the prayer for the ordination of the deacon is only partially contained in the Latin given the lacuna in the text. It is very possible, based on the witness of Ethiopic I, that like with the prayer for the presbyter, the prayer for the deacon is a later addition to ApTrad. As *Herm.Com.* 2002 notes, likely only the first sentence in verse 1 is original, the rest being later expansions, likely in the fourth century.[97] The prayer as found in verses 10-11 in the Latin and Ethiopic II versions shares some similarities to the ordination prayers in Chs. 3 and 7, which may further confirm a common structure behind these prayers.

Eric Segelberg noted that this prayer is the tightest of all three ordination prayers but also follows a structure similar to the other two. He argues that the deacon's prayer, then, was likely composed as a whole, but one which is modeled on the bishop's prayer.[98] Originally, there was probably simply a common handlaying prayer that was used, like with the bishops and presbyters (see above). This appears to be at the core of the Ch. 8

95. For a summary, see Bradshaw, *Rites of Ordination*, 67–68.

96. *Herm.Com.* 2002, 64–65.

97. *Herm.Com.* 2002, 64.

98. Eric Segelberg, "The Ordination Prayers in Hippolytus," *Studia Patristica* 13 (1975): 405–6.

before the additions were made likely in light of controversies over the relationship between bishops, presbyters, and deacons.[99] The following is the text and a reconstruction of the prayer for the ordination of a deacon:

| **Table 3: Development of the Deacon's Ordination Prayer** | |
|---|---|
| **ApTrad 8 (Latin/Ethiopic II)** | **Proposed Earlier Form**[100] |
| *Latin:* God, who created all things and ordered [them] by [your] word, Father of our Lord Jesus Christ, whom you sent to serve your will and manifest to us your desire, give the Holy Spirit of grace and caring and diligence to this your servant, whom you have chosen \|to serve for\|[101] your church and to offer *Ethiopic II:* in your Holy of Holies that which is offered to you by your ordained high priest to the glory of your name so that he may acquire, having served without blame in a pure way of life, the great levels of ordination and your honor and may glorify you through your Son Jesus Christ our Lord, in whom you have glory and power and praise with the Holy Spirit, now and always and forever. Amen. | God, who created all things and ordered [them] by [your] word, give the spirit of grace and diligence[102] to this your servant, whom you have chosen \|to serve for\|[103] your church, that ministering without blame in a pure way of life, \| he may be counted worthy of this high and exalted office\|[104] and may glorify you through your Son Jesus Christ, in whom you have glory and power and praise,[105] now and always and forever. Amen. |

99. *Herm.Com.* 2002, 64.

100. Based on Bradshaw, "The Ordination Prayers in the So-Called *Apostolic Tradition*," 128–29; Bradshaw, *Apostolic* Tradition, 42–43.

101. Ethiopic II: "to be a deacon in"

102. Following Ethiopic II here. Latin: "caring and diligence"

103. Following the Latin here. Ethiopic II: "to be a deacon in"

104. Following TD I.38 here. Ethiopic II: "the great levels of ordination and your honor"

105. Following TD I.38 here. Ethiopic II: "power and praise with the Holy Spirit, now . . ."

Outside of ApTrad, this prayer is only received in TD I.38, where it is also expanded.[106]

## 5. Directives for Other Orders and Ministries

### *5.1. Confessors*

Ch. 9 deals with confessors and their ordination. Unlike early Christian writers (e.g., Tertullian and Cyprian), this chapter allows confessors to be admitted to the clergy without having to receive the imposition of the hands, unless they are to become a bishop. However, in Arabic I, two further verses are added (Ch. 9.6-7) that preclude a confessor from being made part of the clergy without the imposition of hands and prevent them from ordaining others:

> Not every confessor is chosen for the clergy but the chosen, before he is counted among them, shall have the hand laid upon him. And he is not [able] by himself [to ordain] to service by [his] hand, because there is no one who receives the grace by himself.

This verse then talks about how those who buy ranks and who are women and those who are disabled (except for the eyes) can be among the ranks of confessors and they can be counted among the clergy. The remainder of the verse then goes on to specify that the confessor receives the rank of clergy by honor of his/her confession, but becomes a member of the diaconate or presbytery through the imposition of hands.

In North Africa, the confessors were extremely influential, and their role caused issues with the rites of initiation and penance in Cyprian's time.[107] As *Herm.Com.* 2002 notes, the evidence from North Africa, in particular Tertullian and Cyprian, makes it clear that confessors were ordained to the presbyterate and were not automatically presbyters by

106. Bradshaw, *Ordination Rites of the Ancient Churches of East and West*, 74; Bradshaw, *Rites of Ordination*, 77.

107. J. Patout Burns, "On Rebaptism: Social Organization in the Third Century Church," *Journal of Early Christian Studies* 1 (1993): 367–403. See also Kimberly Hope Belcher, Nathan Chase, and Alexander Turpin, *One Baptism—One Church? A History and Theology of the Reception of Baptized Christians* (Collegeville, MN: Liturgical Press Academic, 2024), Ch. 2.

virtue of their status as confessors.[108] This may, however, be a response to practices in North Africa. In any event, it appears to point away from a North African context.

### 5.2. Widows

Ch. 10 concerns the widows and makes it clear that they do not receive the laying on of hands because they do not have an ordination for service in the Eucharist. This part of the document can help in its dating, since "the order of widows declined during the fourth century, being replaced to some extent by the order of deaconesses, who are not mentioned in the *Apostolic Tradition.*"[109] *Herm.Com.* 2002 point outs that it is very probable that the clear comment that the widows do not fulfill a liturgical function is evidence that in some places they were doing just that.[110] The distinction that widows are not to be ordained is consistent with the way the church orders and closely related documents, like CA, talk about the clergy (bishops, stewards, priests, and deacons) being charged with the care of widows.[111]

ApTrad Ch. 10.1-3 is largely carried over into ApCons 8.25.1-3, CH 9, and TD I.40, though each of these adds its own material. TD even adds a prayer. While CH 9 expands the role of the widows, it is significant in that it maintains that prayer is the primary ministry of widows, as seen also in ApTrad Ch. 10.5.

### 5.3. Readers

Ch. 11 has the appointment of readers, who do not have hands laid on them except in Arabic I, where hands are laid on them. Hanssens argued that the order of reader before subdeacon, unlike the Roman sources, was indicative of Alexandrian origin.[112] Interesting, in Ethiopic I, the reader is mentioned between the subdeacon and widows. The ordering of the

108. *Herm.Com.* 2002, 67. See also Allen Brent, "Cyprian and the Question of *Ordinatio per Confessionem*," *Studia Patristica* 36 (2001): 323–37.

109. *Herm.Com.* 2002, 71.

110. *Herm.Com.* 2002, 71.

111. Canon 16 (Arabic), Wilhelm Riedel and W. E. Crum, *The Canons of Athanasius of Alexandria: The Arabic and Coptic Versions* (London: Williams and Norgate, 1904), 26–28; Canon 61 (Arabic and Coptic), Ibid., 40–41 and 126–29; Canon 70 (Arabic and Coptic), Ibid., 44–47 and 133–35; and Canon 84 (Arabic), Ibid., 51.

112. Hanssens, *La liturgie d'Hippolyte*, 371–76. *Herm.Com.* 2002, 74–75.

ministers here may be a sign of changing importance, since confessors are listed last.

The instructions in ApTrad, CH 7, CB 48 (Arabic), TD I.45, and *Epitome* 13 make it clear that hands are not to be laid on the reader; rather, the gospel book is to be given to them. The *Epitome* 13 and CH 7 are close to ApTrad, while TD I.45 expands its instructions considerably and also includes a prayer. The handing over of the gospel book rather than a handlaying is not, however, what is seen in ApCons 8.22, where there is an imposition of hands on the reader.[113] Here Arabic I and ApCons 8.22 must be showing signs of development.

This office is unknown in the West, except in some Gallican sources which are dependent on the *Statuta Ecclesiae Antiqua*, which is itself dependent on ApTrad.[114] The reader, at least in CB 97 (Arabic) and CA 78 (Arabic and Coptic), focused particularly on psalmody, but they could, according to CA 78, also recite non-biblical texts that were still considered "catholic" works.[115] Interestingly, according to CA 58 (Arabic and Coptic), the reader also could fulfill a teaching function in the church.[116] This may help explain the "teachers" who are described in ApTrad, but are not given an official office in the text (see below).

### *5.4. Virgins*

Ch. 12 concerns virgins, and in the extant versions it is clear that hands are not laid on them. This passage has been omitted from Ethiopic I, which may be explained by the fact that a prayer for the laying on of hands for a virgin appears in Euch-AC. It is also quite different from what appears in ApCons 8.24, CH 7, and TD I.46. The question is whether this chapter is original to ApTrad.[117] In its incorporation of the making of female virgins in ApTrad 12, CH 7 applies this to both men and women, as does TD I.46. However, TD makes it clear, following ApTrad 12, that a laying on of hands is not used to set aside those who wish to be virgins, while the

113. Ewa Wipszycka, "Les ordres mineurs dans l'Église d'Egypte du IVe au VIIIe siècle," *The Journal of Juristic Papyrology* 23 (1993): 195–96; *Herm.Com.* 2002, 74–75.

114. *Herm.Com.* 2002, 75.

115. Wipszycka, "Les ordres mineurs dans l'Église d'Egypte du IVe au VIIIe siècle," 196–97.

116. Wipszycka, 197.

117. Bradshaw, *Apostolic Tradition*, 47–48.

text of CH 7 is more ambiguous and seems to suggest that a laying on of hands can be offered for ascetics (i.e., for virginity alone) after maturity has been reached. This text in CH has often been treated as a reference to ordination, likely to the subdiaconate, given the switch to "he" in the canon.[118] Interestingly, however, in the slightly later Euch-AC there is a prayer for the laying on of hands of virgins (explicitly stated as male and female in the text) and nuns.[119] This seems to be closely related to the practice described here in CH, and represents a different practice than that outlined in TD. It is also worth noting that in BR-AC, virgins are given the task of helping with baptism during the pre-baptismal anointing: "If (it is) a man, (he shall be anointed) by one who ministers (= a deacon) or by one who is a priest; but if (it is) a woman, by a believer who has been a virgin from an early age."[120] This suggests that the role of the virgin, at least in the Egyptian context, appears to have some limited liturgical function.

### *5.5. Subdeacons*

Ch. 13 concerns subdeacons, who are not to have hands placed on them either. Ethiopic I includes a phrase not found in the other sources, mainly that the subdeacon is "to carry out the washing [Ethiopic: *wayāḫaḍḍəb*] for the bishop." This washing is implied to be baptism. Nowhere else is the subdeacon tasked with carrying out baptisms, and Stewart notes that this may not be what is implied here by "washing."[121] Interestingly, this may parallel somewhat the role of virgins in the baptismal process in BR-AC, noted above. In ApCons 8.21, the subdeacon is to care for the vessels, something paralleled in CB 97 (Arabic), which notes they can take care of the chalice. ApCons 8.2.11 and CA 11 (Arabic and Coptic),

118. Paul F. Bradshaw, ed., *The Canons of Hippolytus*, Alcuin/Grow Liturgical Study 2 (Bramcote: Grove Books, 1987), 15.

119. Euch-AC, Σ57[va]. There may also be some connection here to P.Bal. I 30 though the content of that material is difficult to judge; see Ágnes T. Mihálykó, "Writing the Christian Liturgy in Egypt (3rd to 9th Century)" (PhD diss., University of Oslo, 2016), 267–78.

120. "Wenn (es) ein Mann (ist), (soll er gesalbt werden) von einem, der dient (= einem Diakonen) oder auch von einem, der Priester ist; wenn (es) aber ein Weib (ist), von einer Gläubi- gen, welche von jeher Jungfrau war." Alessandro Bausi, "The *Baptismal Ritual* in the Earliest Ethiopic Canonical Liturgical Collection," in *»Neugeboren aus Wasser und Heiligem Geist« Kölner Kolloquium zur Initiatio Christiana*, ed. Heinzgerd Brakmann, Tinatin Chronz, and Claudia Sode (Münster: Aschendorff Verlag, 2020), 71.17-20. Translation ours.

121. Stewart, *On the Apostolic Tradition*, 112.

also note that the subdeacons function as doorkeepers.[122] They may also have assisted in some way with the eucharistic bread, as evidenced by CA 34 (Arabic). The directives on the subdeacon are expanded in CH 7 and TD I.44. Here ApCons is very different.

### *5.6. Healer*

The final order given its own chapter in ApTrad is that of the healer in Ch. 14. What we appear to have here is a tension in the text between healers who have traditionally healed apart from the clergy, and the desire to locate the charism of the healers within the work of the clergy themselves.[123] Here we likely see resistance against an older group of healers who were often thought of as ministers. This is consistent with the larger tension in the third and fourth centuries between charismatic ministries and those that were institutionalized. However, as noted in Ch. 7 of our commentary, there were disputes from the fourth century onward, especially in the Egyptian church, between magical and ecclesial healings. Furthermore, in this period a clear distinction was drawn between the oils and waters used for healing in magical and ecclesial circles. These healing oils and waters were especially prominent in Christian and non-Christian healing and pilgrimage centers. In fact, there was often little difference between healing and pilgrimage centers in the early Christian context. This tension is likely behind the form of this chapter in ApTrad. In addition, Stewart notes that this may be discussing healing from a vision:

> Healing however might be received through revelation and visions received at incubations in the shrines of saints, in which the saint would visit the sick person in a dream or vision and effect healing, and so it is possible that the translators into Sahidic and Ethiopic, as well as the redactor of *Apostolic Constitutions* 8, all understood the statement here to be discussing the claim that somebody had received healing, or the means of healing, in or through a vision or revelation.[124]

122. Wipszycka, "Les ordres mineurs dans l'Église d'Egypte du IVe au VIIIe siècle," 191–92.

123. *Herm.Com.* 2002, 80.

124. Stewart, *On the Apostolic Tradition*, 115. See also Johan Leemans et al., eds., *"Let Us Die That We May Live": Greek Homilies on Christian Martyrs from Asia Minor, Palestine, and Syria (c. AD 350–AD 450)* (New York: Routledge, 2003), 173.

In *Herm.Com.* 2002's ordering of the chapters in ApTrad, the gift of healing appears after the discussion of the subdeacon, but in Ethiopic I, it appears after the offering of oil, cheese, and olives, and the directive on newcomers to the faith, and before the section on crafts and professions. Its location in Ethiopic I is unusual. Bradshaw suggests that its location in Ethiopic I is "probably the result of a scribal error of having accidentally skipped over the chapter and needing to insert it later."[125]

There may, however, be some logic to its placement in Ethiopic I. Magicians and non-Christian healers were viewed by Christians like Shenoute of Atripe as demonic. Shenoute, for instance, in a sermon (Acephalous Work A14), derided those who went to these magicians: "If it is the oracles of demons that are of profit to you, and enchanters and sorcerers and all the other things of this type that do lawless things, indeed, go to their feet so that you will receive a curse on the earth. But if it is the house of God which is of profit to you, the Church, indeed, go there."[126] A reference to demons actually concludes the previous chapter in ApTrad Ch. 15: "And if there is one who has a demon, let him not hear the word of the teacher until he is purified." Perhaps in the community using ApTrad, "demonic" healers were particularly problematic. Furthermore, the material in ApTrad Ch. 16 is a logical extension of this, especially with its references to "magician[s]" (Ch. 16.13) as well as "astrologer[s]," "wizard[s]," and phylactery makers (Ch. 16.14).

In his analysis of Ch. 16, Bradshaw rightly notes that the "length [of this chapter] suggests it might have been a separate source before later being incorporated into the church order" and that "there is little internal logic to the sequence of the chapter, which might mean that it gradually expanded over time."[127] It could be that prohibitions against these magical professions is at the core of this chapter. But it is also not odd that treatments of "hearers" would follow on a discussion of healers. Christian healing and pilgrimage centers were places for both healing and initiation. In fact, healing rituals and initiation were both viewed as sources

125. Bradshaw, *Apostolic Tradition*, 48.

126. Translation taken from Korshi Dosoo, "Healing Traditions in Coptic Magical Texts," *Trends in Classics* 13 (2021): 51–52. For more information, see Stephen Emmel, *Shenoute's Literary Corpus*, 2 vols., Corpus Scriptorum Christianorum Orientalium; Subsidia, v. 599-600. t. 111-112 (Leuven: Peeters, 2004), II:692–93. For more, see Ch. 7 of our commentary.

127. Bradshaw, *Apostolic Tradition*, 52.

of spiritual and physical healing.[128] Roman martyr accounts from the fifth and sixth centuries also talk about baptism in association with the martyrs and their churches as a source of spiritual *and* physical healing.[129] There was an ecclesiological connection, too, between baptism and healing rituals at the pilgrimage shrines: the success of healing rituals often depended on the invoker belonging by baptism to the correct ecclesial group. Béatrice Caseau, for instance, notes that

> Miracle stories report the conversion of heretics to the faith of the sanctuary, and the conversion of pagans, Jews and Samaritans to the Christian faith. . . . In regions where churches changed religious affiliation, from a Chalcedonian to Miaphysite creed for example, pilgrims continued to visit the saints, whether or not they agreed with the theological affiliation of the clergy, who took these visits as a means of converting the pilgrims to their creed. . . . Miracle stories also justify failure in receiving healing from the saints, sometimes precisely on account of a sick person's heretical or pagan inclination.[130]

At pilgrimage centers, baptism, reconciliation, and changes in ecclesial identity were ritualized, as was healing.[131]

But there is another reason to suggest that the placement of healers in this location may have been intentional. In Ethiopic I, the chapters on the offering of oil, cheese, and olives have been displaced as a result of the omission of Ch. 4.[132] Oil was a key part of the healing in the ancient world (see Ch. 7 of our commentary). There would have been a desire to keep Chs. 5 and 6 together, but the placement of healers after this material,

128. This appears already in the early New Testament; see Maxwell Johnson, *The Rites of Christian Initiation: Their Evolution and Interpretation* (Collegeville, MN: Liturgical Press, 2007), esp. Ch. 1; Robin Margaret Jensen, *Baptismal Imagery in Early Christianity: Ritual, Visual, and Theological Dimensions* (Grand Rapids, MI: Baker Academic, 2012), esp. Ch. 1.

129. Stefan Heid, "Die Taufe in Rom nach den frühen römischen Märtyrerlegenden," *Rivista di archeologia cristiana* 89 (2013): 217–52.

130. Béatrice Caseau, "Ordinary Objects in Christian Healing Sanctuaries," in *Objects in Context, Objects in Use: Material Spatiality in Late Antiquity*, ed. Luke Lavan, Ellen Swift, and Toon Putzeys, Late Antique Archaeology 5 (Leiden: Brill, 2007), 642.

131. For more, see Nathan Chase, "Breaking Down the 'Golden Age' of Initiation: Baptism in Monasteries, Pilgrimage Centers, and Cemeteries in the Nile Valley," in *Proceedings from the Liturgies of the Church of Alexandria: From Late Antique Origins to the Medieval Heritage* (Washington, DC: The Catholic University of America Press, forthcoming).

132. Bradshaw, *Apostolic Tradition*, 33–35.

as well as the directives on newcomers to the faith, might have been in order to place them in close proximity to the uses of oil outlined in Ch. 5.

### *5.7. Additional Material Added in Arabic I*

In Arabic I there is an addition after Ch. 14.1 concerning a presbyter going on a journey or a deacon moving (Ch. 14.2). Reference is also made to the movement of widows. This additional material in many ways parallels what can be seen in CH 9a, though CH 9a is expanded and includes more information on widows taken from the section on widows in ApTrad. Arabic I could, alongside CH 9a, be attesting to the antiquity of this material in ApTrad. Since the movement of clergy was prohibited by Nicaea canons 15 and 16, this may point to an early date for this material, that may have been excised in later versions to align with Nicaea.

### *5.8. Teacher*

While not included specifically in the grouping of offices treated in ApTrad, it is clear that there was some sort of teaching minister in the community using the text. A reference to a teacher appears in Chs. 15, 18, 19, and 41.1-3 (in the various versions). In ApTrad Ch. 19.1, it is stated that the teacher can be a cleric or a laic. It is clear that this once was a distinct ministry in the church that appears to have been gradually taken over by the clergy.[133] It is possible that the vague references to teachers in ApTrad are the result of edits made to the document to minimize this ministry in light of tensions between bishops (or other clergy) and teachers. Such tensions were well known in the second and third centuries.[134] However, it seems that if the tensions were substantial, all references to teachers would have been omitted from the document. Instead, a teaching function is still referenced, and can be performed by clergy or laity. Interestingly, this includes—even for lay teachers—the ability to lay hands on the catechumens (Ch. 19.1). An explanation for the omission of this as an official office in the church may be explained by reference to CA. CA notes that one of the functions of the reader was to teach (see above). It is unclear if the reader would have been considered clergy or laity. The

133. *Herm.Com.* 2002, 84, 102, 189–90, and 206–7. See also Stewart, *On the Apostolic Tradition*, 118, 126–27, and 198.

134. Stewart-Sykes, "The Integrity of the Hippolytean Ordination Rites," esp. 114–15; Stewart, *The Original Bishops*, 323–37. See also Wipszycka, *Alexandrian Church*, 70–72.

presence of teachers in churches is also witnessed to by GCN 14.2.[135] This seems to indicate that a teaching office was particularly significant in the Egyptian context.

### *5.9. Steward(?)*

ApTrad Ch. 40.2 mentions a cemetery steward who is under the patronage of the bishop. This is the only possible reference to a steward in ApTrad and it is quite vague. However, the steward will emerge as an important office in the middle of the fourth century.[136] The office of steward appears, for instance, in derivatives of ApTrad, like CH 25a: "Concerning [the Appointment of] the Steward of the Sick by the Bishop, and Concerning the Times of Prayer. The steward is the one who has care of the sick. The bishop is to support them—even the vessel of clay necessary for the sick, the bishop is to give it to the steward." This is an adaptation of ApTrad Ch. 34, which concerns how deacons and subdeacons are called to help the bishop in supporting the sick. This chapter may also be rooted in secular patronage practices like the *amicitia*, and it was almost certainly an attempt to bolster the authority of the bishop.[137] But CH's treatment of the institution of the steward for the sick is also an adaptation of ApTrad Ch. 40.2. There are parallels in CH 25 to CA canon 80 (Arabic).[138] It is clear, for instance, in CA that the steward (or bishop) distributed the firstfruits and offerings given within the context of the Eucharist (Arabic and Coptic canon 63) to the clergy and for church use, as well as being distributed to the poor, widows, and sick (Arabic canons: 3, 14–16, 61, 65, 69, and 82; Coptic canons: 47, 61, 62, 65, and 87).[139] Whether we have

135. Alistair Stewart, ed., *The Gnomai of the Council of Nicea (CC 0021): Critical Text with Translation, Introduction and Commentary*, Texts from Christian Late Antiquity 35 (Piscataway, NJ: Gorgias Press, 2015), 79.

136. Wipszycka, *Alexandrian Church*, 111, 114, 199, and 256–58.

137. Stewart, *On the Apostolic Tradition*, 190.

138. Bradshaw, *The Canons of Hippolytus*, 27. See also Stewart, *The Canons of Hippolytus*, 60. Here Stewart means canon 80. Canon 80 is only partially extant in the Coptic. References to a "steward" also appear in CA canons 61 (Arabic and Coptic), 81 (Arabic and Coptic), 89 (Arabic and Coptic), and 90 (Arabic, not extant in Coptic); see Riedel and Crum, *The Canons of Athanasius of Alexandria: The Arabic and Coptic Versions.*

139. Riedel and Crum, *The Canons of Athanasius of Alexandria: The Arabic and Coptic Versions.*

here in ApTrad a glimmer of the later office of steward, which like that of teacher could also be performed by clerics, is unclear.

## 6. Institution through Handlaying, or Not

Throughout the document, it is clear that only some orders or offices were established through the laying on of hands, while others were not (see Table 4 below):

| Table 4: Handlaying in Ordination? | |
|---|---|
| Bishop | Yes |
| Presbyter | Yes |
| Deacon | Yes |
| Subdeacon | |
| Reader | Only in Arabic I |
| Widow | |
| Confessors | Only for episcopal ordination |
| Healers | |
| Virgin | |
| Teacher | |
| Steward(?) | |

Confessors only had hands laid on them if they were ordained to the episcopate. This ritual of handlaying creates a clear differentiation among the various orders and offices. The bishop, presbyters, and deacons are of a special set of orders that are ordained by the laying on of hands, whereas the other orders and offices—subdeacon, reader, widow, confessors, healers, and virgins—are not. At the same time, ApTrad Ch. 23 mentions presbyters and bishops, as well as virgins and widows, but only then mentions the laity. It would seem that the rest of these ministries are either classified as laity—even the deacons, though they have hands laid on them—or the redactor simply has not bothered to make the document consistent.

A comparison of all the ordination prayers with handlaying also reveals a simple prayer structure underlying the laying on of hands:[140]

- Invocation[141]
- Request for the Spirit
- Mention of service
- Doxology

This is further confirmed by a turn to the other location in the text that includes a prayer for the laying on of hands, the post-baptismal handlaying in Ch. 21.21 (Latin):[142]

> Lord God, who have made them worthy to receive the forgiveness of sins through the laver of regeneration of the Holy Spirit, send on them your grace, that they may serve you according to your will; for to you is glory, Father and Son with the Holy Spirit in the holy church, both now and to the ages of ages. Amen.

These requests will include a filling of the Holy Spirit in the Boharic, Arabic I and II, and Ethiopic II versions. Regardless, we see a similar handlaying prayer pattern. Likely, then, these prayers were once much simpler and followed the pattern outlined above. This can shed insights on the likely original form of those prayers, and largely confirms the proposed earlier versions put forward above.

## 7. Sequence of Orders and Ministerial Function

These orders—with the exception of teachers and possibly a steward—are presented in at least three different sequences in the various versions of ApTrad (see Table 5 below). Because of the lacuna in the Latin version, it is not possible to know which sequence the Latin followed after the treatment of deacons and what material it may have had:

140. Segelberg, "The Ordination Prayers in Hippolytus," 405–6.

141. Bradshaw has argued that this invocation was standardized to "God, Father of our Lord Jesus Christ," at some point in ApTrad's redactional history; see Bradshaw, "The Ordination Prayers in the So-Called *Apostolic Tradition*," 121, 126, and 128.

142. Segelberg, "The Ordination Prayers in Hippolytus," 406.

**Table 5: Sequence of Orders in the Various Witnesses**

| **Latin** | **Sequence 1** | **Sequence 2** | | | **Sequence 3** | **Other Witnesses** | | |
|---|---|---|---|---|---|---|---|---|
| | **Ethiopic I** | **Ethiopic II** | **Arabic I** | **Arabic II** | **Sahidic** | **ApCons** | **CH** | **TD** |
| Bishop | Bishop | Bishop | Bishop | Bishop | Bishop | Bishop | Bishop | Bishop |
| Presbyter | Presbyter | Presbyter | Presbyter | Presbyter | Presbyter | Presbyter | Presbyter | Presbyter |
| Deacon | Deacon | Deacon | Deacon | Deacon | Deacon | Deacon | Deacon | Deacon |
| (lac.) | Subdeacon | Confessor | Confessor | Confessor | Confessor | Subdeacon | Confessor | Confessor |
| (lac.) | Reader | Widow | Widow | Widow | Reader | Reader | Reader | Widow |
| (lac.) | Widow | Reader | Reader | Reader | Subdeacon | Confessor | Subdeacon | Subdeacon |
| (lac.) | Confessor | Virgin | Virgin | Virgin | Widow | Virgin | Celibacy | Reader |
| (lac.) | Healer | Subdeacon | Subdeacon | Subdeacon | Virgin | Widow | Healer | Virgin |
| (lac.) | | Healer | Healer | Healer | Healer | Healer | Widow | Healer |

*Herm.Com.* 2002 argued that Ethiopic II and Arabic II (to which we can now add Arabic I) likely preserved the original sequence, especially based on TD. It argued that the placement of the reader after the subdeacon in TD is the result of fourth-century developments. This is also how it appears in Ethiopic I. *Herm.Com.* 2002 argues that the Sahidic grouped the women's orders together after the ecclesiastic offices. CH follows similar tendencies but subordinates the order of virgins—now termed simply as celibacy—and the office of healer to the office of the subdeacon. ApCons is also more hierarchical.[143] What all of these versions show is changing perceptions and understandings of the various orders while the clerical orders are increasing in importance.

Ethiopic I creates some further confusion with regard to the original arrangement of this section. Like the Sahidic, ApCons, and TD, the subdeacon proceeds the reader. Ethiopic I also seems to have made the healer and confessor the lowest of the orders. Interestingly, the order of virgin is not included at all. All of this seems to betray a later stage of development in Ethiopic I, especially since the office of virgin appears elsewhere in the Aksumite Collection in BR-AC and Euch-AC.

Most of the functions of these offices and ministries are not described in these chapters, but rather throughout ApTrad. The following table (Table 6) summarizes the various functions of these orders and ministries:

**Table 6: Functions of These Orders**

| Order | Role | Chapter in ApTrad |
|---|---|---|
| Bishop | Ordain bishops | 2 |
| | Celebrate the Eucharist | 4 |
| | Ordain presbyters | 7 |
| | Ordain deacons | 8 |
| | Lay hands on confessors | 9 |
| | Appoint readers | 11 |
| | Exorcise catechumens | 20 |

143. *Herm.Com.* 2002, 15.

| **Table 6: Functions of These Orders** (cont.) | | |
|---|---|---|
| Bishop (cont.) | Pray with catechumens | 20 |
| | Pray over oils in baptism | 21 |
| | Baptize | 21 |
| | Lay hands on the baptized | 21 |
| | Perform the post-baptismal anointing | 21 |
| | Perform the post-baptismal signing | 21 |
| | Distribute eucharistic bread | 21/22 |
| | Fast when all the faithful fast | 23 |
| | Bless food | 28 |
| | Lead evening prayer | 29C |
| | Offer and say psalms over the cup at evening prayer and distribute bread | 29C |
| | Bless new fruits | 31 |
| | Visit the sick | 34 |
| | Watch over cemeteries | 40 |
| Presbyters (or Elders—41.15) | Be present at bishop's ordination | 2 |
| | Celebrate the Eucharist | 4 |
| | Lay hands in ordination of presbyters | 8 |
| | Help with the blessed oils | 21 |
| | Lead the renunciation during baptism | 21 |
| | Perform the pre-baptismal anointing | 21 |
| | Baptize | 21 |
| | Perform the post-baptismal anointing | 21 |
| | Distribute the chalice | 21 |
| | Distribute eucharistic bread | 22 |

| **Table 6: Functions of These Orders** (cont.) | | |
|---|---|---|
| Presbyters (cont.) | Fast | 23 |
| | Bless food | 28 |
| | Sign/seal the sick | 29B |
| | Bring Eucharist to the sick | 29B |
| | Say psalms over the mixed cup at evening prayer | 29C |
| | Attend daily gathering with prayer | 39 |
| | Instruct the faithful on prayer | 41 |
| Deacon | Assist with the celebration of the Eucharist | 4 |
| | Assist with blessed oils | 21 |
| | Assist with baptism | 21 |
| | Distribute the chalice | 21 |
| | Break the eucharistic bread | 22 |
| | Bless food | 28 |
| | Sign/seal the sick | 29B |
| | Distribute the Eucharist to the sick | 29B |
| | Carry in the light during evening prayer | 29C |
| | Hold mixed cup and say psalms over it at evening prayer | 29C |
| | Assist the bishop | 34 |
| | Visit the sick and inform the bishop | 34 |
| | Attend daily gathering with prayer | 39 |
| Subdeacon | Help the deacons | 13 |
| | Help with baptism | 13 (Ethiopic I only) |
| | Assist the bishop | 34 |
| | Visit the sick and inform the bishop | 34 |

| **Table 6: Functions of These Orders** (cont.) | | |
|---|---|---|
| Widow | Pray | 10/23 |
| | Fast | 23 |
| | Have a communal meal | 30A |
| Virgin | Pray | 23 |
| | Fast | 23 |
| | Say psalms at evening prayer | 29C |
| Reader | Read | 11 |
| Confessor | *No defined role* | 9 |
| Healer | Heal | 14 |
| Teacher (lay or cleric) | Interrogate newcomers | 15 |
| | Instruct catechumens | 18 |
| | Pray and lay hands on catechumens | 19 |
| | Give daily instruction | 41 |
| Steward(?) | Take care of cemeteries | 40.2 |

## 8. Conclusion

The possible dating and provenance of the offices and ministries in ApTrad is difficult to establish in light of the layers of composition and edits in the text. In general, the final redaction of the ministerial sections of the text seems to suggest a late third- or early fourth-century context, especially given the continued role of presbyters in the ordination process of the bishop. While the monepiscopacy had been established by the time of the final redaction of the text, it is possible that the instructions in the text have their roots in an earlier period in which a more federated style of ecclesial leadership predominated. The prayers are also almost certainly compositions that have evolved over time. While the original core of the episcopal, presbyteral, and diaconal prayers may date to before the third century or earlier, the final redactions of these prayers also seem to belong to the early fourth century. There are still tensions in the text between the three foundational orders of ministry—bishop, presbyter, and deacon—as well as other ministries, particularly the confessors, healers, and teachers. This may also point to an earlier period.

As far as provenance is concerned, there is nothing that is particularly unique to any region. The inclusion of the reader, though, is strongly indicative of an Eastern context, since this ministry was not known in the West, except in those documents influenced by ApTrad. What makes determining provenance even more difficult is that the instructions and prayers in ApTrad are taken over in other church orders from different regions, including CH (Egypt), TD (Syria, but early circulation in Egypt), and ApCons (Syria), as well as CB, which was from Syria but also circulated in Egypt. Nevertheless, we can say a few things about provenance:

- A school context—Roman or Alexandrian—is hard to sustain for the final redaction of the text given the watered-down role of the teacher in the text.
- There is nothing that supports a Roman, or even Western, provenance for the text.
- There are a few indications that point away from a North African context:
  - The recent change in the episcopal directives to incorporate neighboring bishops.
  - The allowance for confessors to be considered presbyters by virtue of their status and without ordination.
- There are a number of parallels here to an Egyptian context, but there are also some challenges to an Egyptian provenance.
  - The role of the patriarch is not defined in the text, but this might, as argued above, be explained away as a result of an underdevelopment in the authority of the patriarch and is not inconsistent with other documents from Egypt at this time or even later.
  - The "minor orders" in the document also do not perfectly align with the Egyptian sources; however, the Egyptian sources themselves are not consistent in the number of minor orders and their ordering.[144] CA canon 10 (Arabic), for instance, gives the following offices in this order: bishops, presbyters, deacons, subdeacons, readers, cantors, and doorkeepers.[145] CB includes deaconesses and

144. Perhaps the most thorough study to date on the minor orders in the Egyptian tradition was conducted by Ewa Wipszycka, "Les ordres mineurs dans l'Église d'Egypte du IVe au VIIIe siècle."

145. Riedel and Crum, *The Canons of Athanasius of Alexandria: The Arabic and Coptic Versions*, 20.

> the sacramentary of Sarapion of Thmuis does not include doorkeepers and cantors, but includes an office of "translator."[146] The absence of cantors and doorkeepers in ApTrad and CH as well may indicate that they were only just forming in this period.[147] At the same time, both ApTrad and the Egyptian sources lack any mention of acolytes or exorcists, as well as deaconesses.[148]

In general, the ministerial material in ApTrad is difficult to decipher, especially with regard to the dating of the layers in the instructions and prayers. What is clear is that that the ministerial chapters of the document have been thoroughly reworked over time, but they also appear to have been frozen before some of the significant developments of the fourth century. There are a number of indications that this has happened. The first is the lack of any clear editing in light of the instructions surrounding episcopal ordination put forward by the Council of Nicaea. But there is still a tension apparent in the text between presbyters and bishops. While the final redaction of the text relegates presbyters to a subordinate position under bishops, this seems to have been a recent development. If the final redaction emerged from an Egyptian context, it predates the clear emergence of patriarchal authority in Egypt. The lack of attention to the patriarch is, in fact, the largest challenge to Egyptian provenance. It also continues to hold on to older, likely bygone, ministries like that of the confessor and widow, whose ministries decline in the fourth century. It also predates the establishment, it seems, of the clear role of a steward. Finally, there is also the curious omission of teachers in this part of the text that reveals disjunctures with the rest of the document that are not easily explained. Given all this, it seems that the text was frozen in the early fourth century, and Egypt remains the most likely location for its final redaction. In fact, with the exception of the lack of reference to the patriarch, which we have noted is also the case in a number of Egyptian texts on ordination into the sixth century, there is no reason to see anywhere but Egypt as the place for ApTrad's final redaction.

146. Wipszycka, "Les ordres mineurs dans l'Église d'Egypte du IVe au VIIIe siècle," 188.

147. Wipszycka, 205–10.

148. Wipszycka, 189–90; Bradshaw, *Ordination Rites of the Ancient Churches of East and West*, 83–84.

# Chapter 4

# The *Daily Horarium*[1]

## 1. Introduction

The daily horarium in ApTrad has been studied systematically by only a handful of scholars, most notably Paul Bradshaw,[2] L. Edward Phillips,[3] Alistair Stewart,[4] and *Herm.Com.* 2002.[5] Most studies of ApTrad's horarium predate Ethiopic I's discovery and publication. The current form of the horarium in ApTrad likely reflects the context of lay ascetical movements in Egypt in the third or early fourth century, before the distinction

1. Adapted and updated from Nathan Chase, "Another Look at the 'Daily Office' in the Apostolic Tradition," *Studia Liturgica* 49 (2019): 5–25.

2. Paul Bradshaw, "Prayer Morning, Noon, Evening, and Midnight—an Apostolic Custom?," *Studia Liturgica* 13:1 (1979): 57–62; Paul Bradshaw, *Daily Prayer in the Early Church: A Study of the Origin and Early Development of the Divine Office* (London: Alcuin Club/SPCK, 1981), Ch. 3.

3. L. Edward Phillips, "Daily Prayer in the 'Apostolic Tradition' of Hippolytus," *The Journal of Theological Studies* 40:2 (1989): 389–400; "The Early Christian Prayer Offices: Origin and Development," *Liturgy* 16:1 (2000): 42–51.

4. Alistair Stewart-Sykes, "Prayer Five Times in the Day and at Midnight: Two Apostolic Customs!," *Studia Liturgica* 33 (2003): 1–19; Stewart, *On the Apostolic Tradition* (Crestwood, NY: St. Vladimir's Seminary Press, 2015).

5. *Herm.Com.* 2002, see in particular the commentary on Ch. 41.

between the so-called cathedral and monastic offices developed.[6] The daily cursus of prayer in ApTrad is described in several chapters, namely Chs. 18, 29C, 35, 36, 39, and 41. By closely analyzing these chapters, a daily horarium can be seen in ApTrad. It will also become clear that Chs. 18, 35, 39, and the first part of 41 (vv. 1-4) are referring to the same morning service.

### *1.1. Ch. 18*

The first chapter to include a reference to daily or regular prayer is Ch. 18. This chapter contains directives for a morning instructional service with prayer embedded in a section on the formation of the catechumens that runs from Ch. 15 to Ch. 21. Already, hints of a regular service for catechumens can be found in Ch. 15.[7] The Sahidic, Arabic I and II, and Ethiopic I and II of Ch. 18 all note that "when the teacher has finished instructing, let the catechumens pray by themselves separated from the faithful." Nothing between Chs. 15 and 21 gives any indication of whether this was a daily or weekly service, though the parallel text in CH 18 notes that this instruction occurs "each day."[8] The corresponding text in TD II.4

6. This distinction was first established by Anton Baumstark—see *Comparative Liturgy* (London: Mowbray, 1958), 111ff. It was then clarified by Juan Mateos—see "The Origins of the Divine Office," *Worship* 41:8 (1967): 477–85. The monastic and cathedral distinction has recently been questioned by some scholars; see George Guiver, *Company of Voices: Daily Prayer and the People of God* (London: SPCK, 1998), here 53; Byron Stuhlman, "The Morning Offices of the Byzantine Rite: Mateos Revisited," *Studia Liturgica* 19 (1989): 162–78; Paul Bradshaw, "Cathedral vs. Monastery: The Only Alternatives for the Liturgy of the Hours?," in *Time and Community. In Honor of Thomas Julian Talley*, ed. J. Neil Alexander (Washington, DC: Pastoral Press, 1990); Peter Knowles, "A Renaissance in the Study of Byzantine Liturgy?," *Worship* 68 (1994): 232–41; Paul Bradshaw, "Cathedral and Monastic: What's in a Name?," *Worship* 77 (2003): 341–53; Gregory W. Woolfenden, *Daily Liturgical Prayer: Origins and Theology* (Burlington, VT: Ashgate, 2004); Robert Taft, "Cathedral vs. Monastic Liturgy in the Christian East: Vindicating a Distinction," *Bolletina della Badia Greca di Grottaferrata* series 3, 62 (2005): 173–219; Stig Simeon R. Frøyshov, "The Cathedral-Monastic Distinction Revisited Part I: Was Egyptian Desert Liturgy a Pure Monastic Office?," *Studia Liturgica* 37 (2007): 198–216; Paul Bradshaw, *Two Ways of Praying* (Maryville, TN: OSL Publications, 2008).

7. Chs. 15.1 and 8 both suggest that the service outlined in this chapter occurs at a regular instruction of the word. This is similar to the language found in 18, 35, 39, and 41, likely suggesting that these are all the same service.

8. *Herm.Com.* 2002, 101.

also gives no indications. The GCN also seem to know of a daily service like that outlined by ApTrad (GCN 2:1-4, and possibly 8:11-14, 14:2, and 15:5).[9] This mid-fourth-century text, likely from Egypt and with ties to CH and ApTrad, is directed toward well-off, literate lay Christians, as well as ascetics.[10] This appears to be in keeping with at least the original intent of ApTrad as a whole (see Ch. 2 of our commentary).

This service in Ch. 18 may parallel the services of the word found in early Christian circles. Morning assemblies were known throughout the ancient world. Tertullian may have known of a word service, especially at the ninth hour.[11] From Origen's sermons it is clear that he also knew of a daily catechetical service.[12] A morning assembly also appears in Egeria (381–384 CE), who is a witness to the fact that "the faithful continued to attend the daily *catechesis*, which lasted for three hours after the morning office."[13] Ambrose of Milan (d. 397 CE) also expected Christians to go to church every morning to hear the Gospel.[14] Caesarius of Arles (d. 542 CE), too, appears to have known of a morning service with scripture readings and a sermon.[15] Whether the more catechetical services witnessed to by Egeria and perhaps others were the same as a morning service is unclear. But what we see is the widespread gathering of Christians in morning assemblies for prayer and/or instruction.

9. GCN 2:1 says: "Somebody who wishes to be obedient to God pays attention to his commandments (ἐντολή). Such a person hurries daily to the church (ἐκκλησία)"—Alistair Stewart, ed., *The Gnomai of the Council of Nicea (CC 0021): Critical Text with Translation, Introduction and Commentary*, Texts from Christian Late Antiquity 35 (Piscataway, NJ: Gorgias Press, 2015), 33. See also Appendix 2.

10. Stewart, *The Gnomai of the Council of Nicaea*, "Introduction."

11. Tertullian, *De Ieiun.*, 10; *De Cult. Fem.* 2.11. Bradshaw, *Daily Prayer in the Early Church*, 67–71, here 67–68. A word service in the evening seems to have continued in later sources as well; see Bradshaw, *Daily Prayer in the Early Church*, 90–92—Egeria, *Peregrinatio* 27.5-7; Epiphanius, *Adversus Haereses 3, De Fide* 22–23; and John Chrysostom. For Chrysostom, see Rolf Zerfass, *Die Schriftlesung im Kathedraloffizium Jerusalems* (Münster Westfalen: Aschendorffsche Verlagsbuchhandlung, 1968), 133f; Gabriele Winkler, "Der geschichtliche Hintergrund der Präsanktifikatenvesper," OC 56 (1972): 184–206.

12. Bradshaw, *Daily Prayer in the Early Church*, 70. Origen, *Hom. in Jes. Nav.* 4.1; *Hom. in Gen.* 10.3

13. Bradshaw, 90–91. Egeria, *Peregrinatio* 46.1–47.2

14. Bradshaw, 112. Ambrose, *Expos. in Ps. 118, sermo* 19.32.

15. Bradshaw, 121–22. Caesarius, *Serm.* 72; 76.3; 86.5; 188.6; 196.2; 212.6.

### *1.2. Ch. 29C ( = Ch. 25)*

The next possible instance of daily prayer occurs in Ch. 29C ( = Ch. 25), another part of the core material in ApTrad. It is contained only in Ethiopic I and II, as well as Arabic I. In its current form, Ch. 29C is an evening lamp-lighting service with a meal. This text can be found in Ethiopic I and Arabic I before Ch. 26, confirming the suggestion in *Herm. Com.* 2002 that this is likely the original location of this chapter.[16] Scholars have suggested that this chapter might originally have been a eucharistic meal that has since been adapted into an evening service (see Ch. 6 of our commentary).[17] Interestingly, Ethiopic I and Arabic I are missing the material that *Herm.Com.* 2002 sees as the result of subsequent expansion (29C.10-15, though Arabic I contains v. 10).[18] While this missing section contains many of Ch. 29C's eucharistic hints, Ethiopic I and Arabic I still preserve the note in 29C.16 that "for this is eulogy [e.g., blessed bread], not rendering of grace [e.g., thanksgiving] like the body" (Ethiopic I). In other words, "this is not the Eucharist," suggesting that at one time at least part of it was (see Ch. 6 of our commentary).

In many ways, the placement of chapter 29C in a section on meal practices (Chs. 22, 23, 26, 27, 28, 29A, 33) also confirms its eucharistic connotations. In its original placement before Ch. 26, Ch. 29C was also followed by directions for the blessings of a number of objects (Chs. 29D, 31, 32), as well as directions for how to deal with catechumens (Ch. 29D), the sick and widows (Chs. 29B, 30A, 33, 34). All of this mirrors the tradition of including prayers for the blessing of objects, catechumens, the sick, and widows, after the anaphora within early prayer collections.[19] Thus, it is difficult to determine whether this material belongs properly to the divine office, the Eucharist or both. Likely it was originally a Eucharist.

16. *Herm.Com.* 2002, 141, 156–60. See also Bradshaw, *Apostolic Tradition*, 88.

17. *Herm.Com.* 2002, 158–60.

18. Meßner sees this text as having fallen out of the original—see Reinhard Messner, "Die Angebliche *Traditio Apostolica*," *Archiv Für Liturgiewissenschaft* 58–59 (2016): 34. There they are listed as sections 4–8. Bradshaw, however, disagrees with this assessment; see Bradshaw, *Apostolic Tradition*, 88–89.

19. See especially the Barcelona Papyrus and the Euchologion of Sarapion of Thmuis. The blessing of fruits in association with the meal, also mirrors what can be seen in Chs. 5 and 6 following the anaphora found in Ch. 4 in some versions of ApTrad.

It is also not clear if Ch. 29C represents a daily or weekly practice, but it was probably weekly.

### *1.3. Ch. 35*

The next reference to daily prayer is found in Ch. 35. This chapter is from the core material of ApTrad, and it instructs the faithful to pray to God as soon as they rise and before going to work. Further mention is made of a catechetical service, and the faithful are instructed to go to the church if this service occurs. *Herm.Com.* 2002 interprets the passage as suggesting that the catechetical service takes priority over prayer at rising: "preference is to be given to the communal meetings rather than to the private prayer at home."[20] But this does not appear to be the case. Ch. 35 does not seem to suggest that the catechetical service substitutes for prayer at rising, but rather directs the faithful to go to the catechetical service *before work* if there is catechesis.

The Latin version of ApTrad reads: "Let the faithful, as soon as they have woken and rise, before they touch their work, pray to God and so hasten to their work. And if there is any instruction by word, let him give preference to this. "[21] The catechetical service is an *addition* to prayer at rising if it occurs. Preference is given to the catechetical service over *work*, not prayer at rising. The corresponding passage in ApCons 8.32.18,[22] as well as passages found in the GCN (2:3, 6:5, 15:5, and Ostrakon C. 8123),[23] support this reading, and Chs. 18 and 39 in ApTrad appear to reference the same service.[24] These chapters come from different sets of directives, but the redactor(s) has attempted to reconcile these two sets of material into a single morning instructional service in ApTrad. Stewart also suggests this may point to a philosophical school context, though

20. *Herm.Com.* 2002, 178; Phillips, "Daily Prayer in the 'Apostolic Tradition' of Hippolytus," 392.

21. *Herm.Com.* 2002, 178.

22. "Let every faithful man and woman rising early in the morning, before they undertake their work, wash themselves and pray. But if there is a word of catechesis, *let them honor the word of godly living over work*"—*Herm.Com.* 2002, 179.

23. GCN 2:3 reads: "Hurry to church (ἐκκλησία) first of all and afterwards to your work (τέχνη) so that God may bless the work of your hands"—see Stewart, *The Gnomai of the Council of Nicaea*, 33.

24. See *Herm.Com.* 2002, 178–79.

also noting it may point to a broader catechetical/instructional context as noted by the parallels to GCN.[25]

The material in this chapter is largely duplicated in Ch. 41, which is likely why it was omitted from Ethiopic I (but interestingly not Arabic I).[26]

### *1.4. Ch. 36*

The following chapter, Ch. 36, should also be included since it specifies either frequent or daily reception of the Eucharist before eating (see also Ch. 6 of our commentary). This chapter, along with Ch. 35, may derive from an independent set of instructional material:

> There is some thematic connection between receiving the Eucharist in the morning referred to in this chapter and the morning prayer and assembly for instruction referred to in chap. 35. On the other hand, these chapters may owe their position in the church order not to any similarity of theme to what precedes but rather to a resemblance in the opening words to the beginning of chap. 35: "Let the faithful . . . " (plural)/ "Let every faithful person . . . " It is even possible that these chapters were once part of an independent list of such instructions, from which they were extracted to form an addition to an older version of the *Apostolic Tradition* with 35 as its final chapter.[27]

Of course, Ethiopic I complicates this theory, since it does not contain Ch. 35. This means that in Ethiopic I, Chs. 36, 37, and 38A, are a continuation of the material found in Chs. 22–34. This may further bolster arguments that Ch. 29C, and the meal practices that surround it, were originally understood as a eucharistic celebration. Regardless, in Chs. 36, 37, and 38A, it is unclear when the reception of the Eucharist was intended, and whether that occurred frequently or even daily.[28]

25. Stewart, *On the Apostolic Tradition*, 191.

26. Bradshaw, *Apostolic Tradition*, 99–100 and 106.

27. *Herm.Com.* 2002, 180.

28. For more on the reception of communion in the early church, see Robert Taft, "The Frequency of the Celebration of the Eucharist Throughout History," in *Between Memory and Hope*, ed. Maxwell Johnson (Collegeville, MN: Liturgical Press, 2000), 77–96. See also Nathan Chase, "Reprising the Evidence for the Origins of Daily Eucharistic Celebrations,"

### *1.5. Ch. 39*

The next chapter that references daily prayer is Ch. 39. This text mirrors that found in Ch. 18, as well as Ch. 35; however, it is thought to be a later addition to ApTrad. Ch. 39 mentions a daily gathering of deacons, presbyters, and sometimes bishops, the purpose of which is to teach. Ethiopic I does not mention that this gathering takes place every day, but all the other sources do, including the corresponding text in Arabic I and CH 21.[29] Interestingly, Ethiopic I notes that this is "early in the morning," just like the directives found in Chs. 18 and 35, again suggesting that Chs. 18, 35, and 39 (and later 41) are referring to the same service.

*Herm.Com.* 2002 identifies these gatherings with those described in Chs. 18 and 19,[30] while Stewart connects them with Chs. 35 and 41.[31] *Herm.Com.* 2002, as well as Stewart appear to be correct. The structure in this chapter parallels that found in Ch. 18—"gathering, teaching, praying, going off to work"—and also contains the reference to prayer coming before work that is also found in Chs. 35 and 41.[32] Ch. 39's remark that after they gather for catechesis the faithful should go to work, serves as further proof that in Chs. 35 and 41, catechesis does not substitute for prayer in the morning but is an addition to it if such a service occurs. When this happens, the service should occur between prayer and work. Additionally, a comparison of Chs. 18–19, 35, and 41 suggests that Ch. 39 may be correcting the practice of allowing "teachers," and not clerics, to lead these services (see Ch. 3 of our commentary). This may in turn suggest that this chapter is later than Chs. 18 and 19.[33] Given the similarities, this chapter strongly suggests that Chs. 18, 35, 39, and 41 are all directions for the same morning service.

---

presented *in absentia* at "Fractio panis," a symposium at Pusey House, Oxford, England, August 2024. To be published in the series "Studia Traditionis Theologiae" by Brepols.

29. Sahidic ApTrad says: "And (δέ) let the deacons (διάκονος) and the presbyters (πρεσβύτερος) *gather daily* in the place where the bishop (ἐπίσκοπος) will command them"; and *Canons of Hippolytus* says: "The presbyters are to assemble *each day* at the church . . . "—see *Herm.Com.* 2002, 188–89.

30. *Herm.Com.* 2002, 189.

31. Stewart, *On the Apostolic Tradition*, 198.

32. *Herm.Com.* 2002, 190.

33. *Herm.Com.* 2002, 189–90.

The corresponding text in CH 21a not only mirrors the descriptions of the catechetical services found in Chs. 18, 35, 39, and 41 in ApTrad, but includes a reference to this prayer occurring at cockcrow. While Ch. 18 in ApTrad specifies no time for its service, Ch. 35 suggests it is early in the morning, between when the faithful arise and before they go to work. The same is the case in Ch. 41.1. Ch. 39 of Ethiopic I also mentions that this service is conducted "early in the morning." *Herm.Com.* 2002 argues that

> Canons of Hippolytus 21 places this morning gathering earlier still, at cockcrow, and changes the public catechetical nature of the meeting into a public prayer service, similar in order to the morning office of the Egyptian monks described by John Cassian. The catechetical origin of the chapter is retained, however, in the inclusion of the reading of Scripture lessons in the order of service, usually absent from fourth-century prayer offices outside Egypt.[34]

But if Chs. 18, 35, 39, and 41 in ApTrad are all referring to the same service, then CH 21a is not changing anything, since together with Chs. 18, 35, 39, and 41 of ApTrad, it attests to a service of prayer and instruction. This is even affirmed in Sahidic ApTrad 41.2, which says: "But (δέ) if it happens that there is catechesis (κατήχησις) of the Word of God, let each one choose to go to that place . . . for (γάρ) having prayed in the church."[35] Also, with its reference to prayer and instruction at cockcrow, CH 21a mirrors Ch. 41.17-18 of ApTrad, and further suggests (see below) that this is not an additional hour of prayer, but part of the same early morning prayer and catechesis found in Chs. 18, 35, 39, and 41.1-4.

### *1.6. Ch. 41*

Directly following Ch. 39 in Ethiopic I is Ch. 41. Ch. 41 is by far the most developed section on daily prayer in ApTrad. It begins in vv. 1-4 with a parallel to Ch. 35 with prayer upon rising and a reference to a catechetical service, but is an expansion of Ch. 35 as indicated, especially, by "the mixture of the third person plural, third person singular, and second

34. *Herm.Com.* 2002, 190.
35. *Herm.Com.* 2002, 194.

person singular" addresses at the start of the chapter.[36] If there is not catechesis, Ch. 41 calls for the private reading of "holy books." A similar practice can be found in the GCN (6:5 and 10:3).[37] A number of early sources call for the reading of scripture at home:[38] Origen recommends reading the scriptures at home, even daily;[39] Melito of Sardis is said to have given scriptural texts to a layperson;[40] and Clement of Alexandria mentions daily reading from texts.[41] So too does Caesarius.[42] However, Stewart also notes that this might refer to a common library in the church/community complex, since books were expensive.[43]

As with Ch. 35, Ch. 41.1-4 envisions prayer upon rising followed by a communal catechetical service if there is one. Again, the catechetical service does not substitute for prayer at rising. In fact, that Ch. 41.1-4 calls for the reading of a holy book at home if there is no catechesis further confirms that here, and in Ch. 35, ApTrad calls for prayer at rising every day.

Ch. 41 then continues with a treatment of prayer at the third, sixth, and ninth hours, using scriptural rationales. The third hour (41.5-6) is tied to Christ being nailed on the cross, as well as shewbread and the slaughter of the sheep. The sixth hour (41.7) is tied to Christ hanging on the cross, which brought darkness to the world. The ninth hour (41.8-9) is tied to the piercing of Christ's side and his resurrection. Following this is prayer at bedtime (41.10) and in the middle of the night (41.11-16). The latter is described using baptismal imagery and the stillness of creation which calls all to praise God. Mention is also made of the bridegroom. Prayer at

36. Bradshaw, *Apostolic Tradition*, 106–7.

37. Stewart, *The Gnomai of the Council of Nicaea*.

38. These have helpfully been pointed out by Sarah Gaffino Mœri, Sophie Gällnö, Noemi Poget, and Paul Schubert, eds., *Les papyrus de Genève. Vol. 4: Nos 147–205: textes littéraires, semi-littéraires et documentaires* (Genève, 2010), 46. The private use of Christian books was likely confined to a small and rather elite group of Christians—see Harry Gamble, *Books and Readers in the Early Church: A History of Early Christian Texts* (New Haven: Yale University Press, 1995), esp. Ch. 1.

39. Origen, *Hom. in Gen.* 10.1; 11.3; 12.5; *Hom. in Ex.* 12.2; *Hom. in Num.* 2.1.

40. See Eusebius, *Historia Ecclesiastica* 4.26.12-14.

41. Clement, *Paed.* 2.10.96; *Strom.* 7.7.49.

42. Caesarius, *Sermon* 196.2.

43. Stewart, *On the Apostolic Tradition*, 202–3 and 205.

cockcrow follows and is tied to the denial of Christ by the sons of Israel. After this, ApTrad calls the faithful to follow the patterns of prayer laid out in the document in order to properly teach the catechumens (Ch. 41.17-18).

Ch. 41.17-18 ties prayer at cockcrow to the teaching of the catechumens, and in so doing parallels what is seen in Chs. 35 and 39, as well as the beginning of Ch. 41.1-5. Given the similarities to other sections in ApTrad, and to CH 21a, it seems that the redactor of this section of ApTrad was not envisioning another prayer hour at cockcrow that was separate from the prayer at rising and the catechesis found in Ch. 41.1-5. Rather, the redactor was repeating the prayer at rising in order to give an allegorical interpretation to this prayer. Stewart has defended this interpretation of the material, noting that Ch. 41.17-18 supplements the material in Ch. 41.1-5 "with the result that there is duplication, but no additional hour of prayer."[44] Bradshaw, however, disagrees with this, claiming that it is an additional hour of prayer that has been later added.[45] Nevertheless, CH 27 likewise parallels Ch. 41.17-18 in ApTrad, but is very clearly a summation of the daily prayer cycle outlined in Ch. 41.1-16 and the corresponding texts in CH,[46] supporting this interpretation of ApTrad 41.

## 2. Summary of ApTrad's Horarium

Thus, a study of ApTrad reveals a daily (or regular) cycle of prayer that emerges from the various directives that have been combined to form ApTrad (Table 1 below):

44. Stewart, *On the Apostolic Tradition*, 208.

45. Bradshaw, *Apostolic Tradition*, 113.

46. CH 27 reads: "At the time when the cock crows, *again* it is a time when there are prayers in the churches, for the Lord says, 'Watch, for you do not know at what time the master comes, in the evening, or in the middle of the night, or at cockcrow, or in the morning,' that is to say that we must remember God at each hour. And when one is lying on his bed, he must pray to God in his heart . . . "—see *Herm.Com.* 2002, 200–3. Earlier in CH 27, mention was already made of prayer at church; this is again mentioned at the end of 27: "Let us do that and instruct one another with the catechumens . . . " This suggests that the daily prayer cycle has been given in full and is being restarted again.

**Table 1: Daily Cycle of Prayer in ApTrad**

| **Chs. 18/19** | **Ch. 29C (= Ch. 25)** | **Ch. 35** | **Chs. 36-38** | **Ch. 39** | **Ch. 41** |
|---|---|---|---|---|---|
| | | Prayer at rising . . . | | | Prayer at rising/ cockcrow . . . |
| Morning prayer with catechesis | | . . . sometimes followed by catechesis | | Catechesis early in the morning | . . . followed by catechesis or private reading |
| | | | Morning Communion (possibly at third hour) | | |
| | | | | | Third hour |
| | | | | | Sixth hour |
| | | | | | Ninth hour |
| | Eucharistic meal / Evening Prayer | | | | |
| | | | | | Prayer before bed |
| | | | | | Prayer in the night |

It seems that Chs. 18, 19, 35, 39, and 41 all refer to the same service of catechesis in the morning. This service is either a frequent or daily occurrence. Prayer at rising is attested to in both Chs. 35 and 41. The meal with the lighting of the lamps in Ch. 29C was likely originally a eucharistic meal. This was probably a weekly occurrence, not part of an individual's daily horarium, since it is not included within the horarium outlined in Ch. 41. In fact, the only communal service mentioned in Ch. 41 is the service of catechesis also found in Chs. 18, 19, 35, and 39. Similarly, the reception of the Eucharist in the morning found in Chs. 36–38 is not incorporated into the horarium outlined in Ch. 41. This suggests that the reception of the Eucharist was either part of one of these prayer times or was unaffiliated with the horarium outlined by ApTrad. If it was part of one's daily horarium, the third hour, with its reference to Jesus as the bread of life, may have been the time.

## 3. Peeling Back the Layers

*Herm.Com.* 2002 argues that the original text of the horarium in ApTrad was Ch. 35, to which three expansions have been made to create the text found in Ch. 41 (see Ch. 2 of our commentary for more). The first expansion was of the third, sixth, and ninth hours, as well as prayer at night. Prayers at bedtime and cockcrow were then added, likely separately. The morning prayer/catechetical instruction in Ch. 35 was expanded to form the opening of Ch. 41; this could have occurred at any time.[47] There is no reason to question this line of development, though we disagree that the mention of prayer at cockcrow is a reference to a separate hour. An analysis of ApTrad indicates that multiple celebrated traditions have been merged to form the daily horarium outlined in the document. However, the complexities of the various chapters of ApTrad suggest that it likely was not celebrated as written. CH seems to be an attempt to sort through and make sense of the daily and weekly prayer practices in ApTrad in order to create a usable horarium. This suggests that the horarium in CH was actually celebrated.

47. *Herm.Com.* 2002, 202.

## 4. The Tradition(s) Behind ApTrad and the Final Shape of ApTrad's Horarium

Scholarly attention to the horarium in ApTrad has focused primarily on Ch. 41 and its connection to earlier patterns of prayer.[48] Walker, for instance, has argued that the creator of ApTrad "used St. Mark's account of the passion not only in the wording of the incidents but also because Mark is the sole Evangelist to mention the third hour in the crucifixion narrative."[49] This sets this document apart from Origen, Tertullian, and Cyprian, who all use Daniel 6:10 as the controlling narrative for their horaria.[50] Interestingly, however, Cyprian also refers to the passion when discussing the sixth and ninth hours.[51] Tertullian references the passion in discussion of the ninth hour on station days, but in his discussion of daily prayer ties the ninth hour to Acts 3:1, where Peter and John go up to the Temple.[52]

But while ApTrad follows the Marcan narrative, "[ApTrad] does not merely rely on the Marcan chronology."[53] In ApTrad the third hour also uses eucharistic imagery of the shewbread and the morning sacrifice of the lambs.[54] As noted above, this may in fact provide the morning context for the daily reception of the Eucharist outlined in Chs. 36–38A. The sixth hour makes reference to Christ's prayer on the cross, which "made all creation dark for the unbelieving Jews." This is a rather peculiar reference, and, as Phillips notes, "if the author of [ApTrad] used a source,

48. An horarium worth noting, but which is very different from ApTrad, is the *Testament of Adam*, which is possibly dated to the third century. For a summary, see Teresa Berger, " 'All You Have Created Rightly Gives You Praise': Re-Thinking Liturgical Studies, Re-Rooting Worship in Creation," *Ex Fonte - Journal of Ecumenical Studies in Liturgy* 1 (2022): 13–20.

49. Joan Hazelden Walker, "Terce, Sext and None. An Apostolic Custom?," in *Studia Patristica* 5 (Leuven: Peeters, 1962), 210–11.

50. *Herm.Com.* 2002, 214–15; Phillips, "The Early Christian Prayer Offices," 47. Origen, *De or.* 12.2; Tertullian, *De or.* 25; Cyprian, *De dom. orat.* 34–35.

51. Bradshaw, *Daily Prayer in the Early Church*, 55. Walker, "Terce, Sext and None. An Apostolic Custom?," 208. Cyprian, *De dom. orat.* 34.

52. Bradshaw, *Daily Prayer in the Early Church*, 55 and 67–68. Walker, however, believes that both sext and none show signs of Christ's Passion—see Walker, "Terce, Sext and None. An Apostolic Custom?," 207. Mateos, "The Origins of the Divine Office," 479.

53. Phillips, "Daily Prayer in the 'Apostolic Tradition' of Hippolytus," 393.

54. Phillips, 393–94.

it appears to have been lost."[55] The ninth hour also uses more than just the crucifixion as its controlling narrative; it plays with imagery of light, evening, resurrection, and the new day.

Phillips has argued that the third and ninth hours parallel one another and that "they are meant to parallel the morning and evening sacrifice of the temple and, consequently, are intended to be the times for morning and evening prayer in [ApTrad]."[56] Phillips thinks that this is probable since the prayer at rising is more instructional, and there is no mention of evening prayer anywhere else in the document, given that Ch. 29C is likely a weekly service.[57] However, he is wrong in seeing the prayer at rising as more instructional in nature. As argued above, the prayer at rising is actually a separate, albeit private, hour before communal catechesis, or a private meditation on "holy books." While Robert Taft also agrees that this service is instructional in nature and not "matins,"[58] it is crucial to note that even the catechetical gathering includes prayer. This can be seen in the treatment of this service in Ch. 18 (which has catechesis followed by prayer), Ch. 39 (which has teaching and prayer), and the Sahidic version of Ch. 41 (which has prayer included with the instructions about catechesis).[59] Nevertheless, Phillips argues that

> in [ApTrad,] the third, sixth, and ninth hours serve as morning, noon, and evening prayer, rather than providing a pattern of 'little' hours of terce, sext, and none. This hypothesis offers support to J.H. Walker's thesis that terce, sext, and none form the earliest Christian horarium, but it goes further than Walker in identifying the third and ninth hours with morning and evening prayer. This hypothesis also suggests a further link between [ApTrad] and Alexandrian sources.[60]

Phillips further believes that this helps to explain the discrepancies in Cyprian and Tertullian about which daily prayer hours were more an-

55. Phillips, 394.
56. Phillips, 395.
57. Phillips, 395.
58. Robert Taft, *The Liturgy of the Hours in East and West: The Origins of the Divine Office and Its Meaning for Today* (Collegeville, MN: Liturgical Press, 1986), 26.
59. Even *Herm.Com.* 2002, 178, affirms this: "for having prayed in the church . . . "
60. Phillips, "Daily Prayer in the 'Apostolic Tradition' of Hippolytus," 395–96.

cient.[61] Based on Phillips's work, Bradshaw has now nuanced his own theory and has suggested that

> while for some early Christian communities the three times of daily prayer may have been morning, noon, and evening, for others they may well have been the third, sixth, and ninth hours instead, and that these two parallel traditions eventually coalesced to form the fivefold pattern of prayer in the morning, at the third, sixth (= noon), and ninth hours, and in the evening (together with prayer in the night) found in some third-century sources.[62]

Despite this theory, Bradshaw and Phillips have to account for the addition of prayers at bedtime and cockcrow in ApTrad. Concerning the prayer at cockcrow, Bradshaw has noted that

> prayer at cockcrow is unknown elsewhere at such an early date, and when it does make its first appearance in some fourth-century monastic rules, it is usually as an alternative to midnight prayer and not as an additional time as it is here. Therefore at least this element is very probably a later addition to the document.[63]

Phillips also notes that in CH, the prayer at cockcrow "is not an hour of private prayer, but a gathering in the church. All in all, the differences are so striking that it is difficult to be sure that [CH] is relying on [ApTrad]

61. Phillips, 399. The prayers at terce, sext, and none were, for Tertullian, prescribed in the New Testament "as if by law," and those at morning and evening were "obligatory prayers which are due without any command."—see Bradshaw, "Prayer Morning, Noon, Evening, and Midnight—an Apostolic Custom?," 59. For the full text, see Tertullian, *De or.* 25. For Cyprian, however, prayer at the third, sixth, and ninth hours is considered the older practice, with morning and evening prayer having recently been added. See Cyprian, *De dom. orat.* 34–35, where in 34 he talks about the antiquity of prayer at the third, sixth, and ninth hours, and at the start of Ch. 35 mentions that the number of hours has "increased beyond those observed for prayer of old" to include morning and evening prayer—Stewart-Sykes, *Tertullian, Cyprian, and Origen: On the Lord's Prayer*, Popular Patristics Series 29 (Yonkers, NY: St Vladimir's Seminary Press, 2004), 91. This, however, contradicts Tertullian. Thus, Bradshaw notes that Cyprian must be confused—see Bradshaw, "Prayer Morning, Noon, Evening, and Midnight—an Apostolic Custom?," 59.

62. *Herm.Com.* 2002, 213–14; Bradshaw, *Search for the Origins of Christian Worship* (Oxford: Oxford University Press, 2002), 190–91.

63. Bradshaw, *Daily Prayer in the Early Church*, 54–55; *Herm.Com.* 2002, 213.

at this point."[64] However, as noted above, this section in CH 27 appears to represent a summary of why we pray the daily horarium. So while the text may be a later addition to ApTrad, it does not represent an additional prayer time. Phillips has also noted that prayer at bedtime in ApTrad must be a later addition.[65] Stewart has argued instead that this is a reference to evening prayer.[66] Phillips, however, appears to be correct here—prayer at bedtime does seem to be a later addition to the text and not a reference to evening prayer.

Stewart has argued for a different line of development in ApTrad's horarium:

> ApTrad is the first appearance outside of Africa of a cycle of daily prayer that is found commonly in later centuries, with prayer in the morning and evening supplemented by prayer three times in the day, and prayer at midnight added. It should be noted that this understanding of the text is in accordance with the recognition that the final appearance of prayer at cock-crow is a duplication of the first appearance of morning prayer and that the prayer before going to bed is prayer in the evening. This pattern probably derives from the conflation of two ancient but independent patterns of prayer, both rooted in Judaism, one of which consisted of prayer in the morning, afternoon and evening, the other of which involved the offering of prayer at dawn, midday, and dusk. The prayers at the third and ninth hours were originally morning and evening prayers tied to the offering of sacrifice in the Temple, and are more prominent here than the prayers at rising and retiring.[67]

Against Stewart's line of thinking, Robert Taft has observed that there is no case within early Christian sources of a pattern of morning and evening prayer alone.[68] In taking a slightly different approach, Taft believes that in ApTrad we can see the following structure (Table 2 below):[69]

64. Phillips, "Daily Prayer in the 'Apostolic Tradition' of Hippolytus," 398.
65. Phillips, 395.
66. Stewart, *On the Apostolic Tradition*, 206–7.
67. Stewart, 209–10.
68. Taft, *The Liturgy of the Hours in East and West*, 21.
69. Taft, 25–26.

| Table 2: Private vs. Communal Prayer | |
|---|---|
| Private Prayer | Common Assemblies |
| on rising<br>third, sixth, ninth hours<br>on retiring<br>at midnight<br>at cockcrow | morning instruction<br>evening agape |

Taft is likely incorrect in seeing cockcrow as a separate hour of prayer, and, it seems, in seeing the evening agape as a daily occurrence.[70]

What then is the shape of the daily horarium in ApTrad, and how did it develop? It appears that the following is the shape of daily prayer in ApTrad:

- Prayer at rising/cockcrow
- A communal catechesis and prayer, or a private reading of "holy books"
- [Possibly a morning reception of the Eucharist, perhaps in conjunction with prayer at the third hour]
- Prayer at the third hour
- Prayer at the sixth hour
- Prayer at the ninth hour
- [A weekly(?) Eucharist/Evening Prayer]
- Prayer before bed
- Prayer in the middle of the night

If this is in fact the structure of daily prayer behind ApTrad, it appears that what we see in ApTrad is a slightly later development from that seen in Egyptian sources (like Origen and Clement[71]), as well as North

70. *Herm.Com.* 2002, 210n54.

71. Origen knew of a custom of praying three times a day; see Origen, *De Oratione* 12.2. Walker has suggested this was at the third, sixth, and ninth hours, while Bradshaw had earlier suggested morning, noon, and evening, together with prayer at night. Phillips

African sources (like Tertullian and Cyprian[72]). In fact, ApTrad seems to differ from Origen and Clement—if their prayers at morning, noon, and evening do correspond to the third, sixth, and ninth hours, as Phillips and Bradshaw suggest—in adding prayers at rising and bedtime. Like ApTrad, Origen also knows of a morning catechesis (see above). ApTrad differs from Tertullian in containing a morning catechesis (see above), but is also similar to Tertullian and Cyprian in containing prayer at the third, sixth, and ninth hours, alongside prayer at rising (morning) and going to bed (evening). Thus, it seems that the *Herm.Com.* 2002's assessment[73] is probably the most accurate: in ApTrad we see the merging of one tradition of prayer at morning, noon, evening, and midnight, and another of prayer at the third, sixth, and ninth hours, as well as midnight.

## 5. Use

ApTrad's horarium is addressed primarily towards the laity within an ecclesiastical setting. In fact, the audience for ApTrad's horarium parallels closely the audience for the GCN, which was for well-off, literate, lay and ascetical Christians, or perhaps it parallels an early form of the confraternities of Christians, sometimes known as *philoponoi* or *spoudaioi*, that begin to appear in Egypt at the end of the fourth century.[74]

---

has favored the identification of these hours with the third, sixth, and ninth hours, a point which Bradshaw concedes. Taft had earlier sided against this view, and Stewart has been critical of it as well—see Walker, "Terce, Sext and None. An Apostolic Custom?," 209; Bradshaw, "Prayer Morning, Noon, Evening, and Midnight—an Apostolic Custom?," 57–58; Phillips, "Daily Prayer in the 'Apostolic Tradition' of Hippolytus," 395–96; Taft, *The Liturgy of the Hours in East and West*, 17; *Herm.Com.* 2002, Ch. 41; Bradshaw, *The Search for the Origins of Christian Worship*, 176; Stewart, "Prayer Five Times in the Day and at Midnight," 12. Clement of Alexandria also knows of prayer "at the third, sixth, and ninth hours, besides at morning, evening and night prayer"—see Mateos, "The Origins of the Divine Office," 478; Taft, *The Liturgy of the Hours in East and West*, 14. Bradshaw argues that the third and ninth hours were later additions—see Bradshaw, "Prayer Morning, Noon, Evening, and Midnight—an Apostolic Custom?," 58

72. See n. 61.

73. See n. 62.

74. Ewa Wipszycka, "Les confreries dans la vie religieuse de l'Egypte chretienne," in *Proceedings of the Twelfth International Congress of Papyrology*, American Studies in Papyrology 7 (Toronto: A.M. Hakkert Ltd., 1970), 511–25; Frank R. Trombley, *Hellenic Religion and Christianization c. 370–529 (Vol. 2)* (Boston: Brill, 2001), vol. 2, Ch. 5; Edward

Nonetheless, the morning instructional prayer contains a number of what are traditionally considered monastic parallels. Combined with the catechetical tradition found in the GCN, the morning catechetical service (and ApTrad as a whole), may represent an early tradition prior to, or just after, a divide in lay and monastic spiritual formation, when the distinctions between laity and monastics were just emerging.

The morning instructional prayer found in ApTrad may then represent a movement towards the common synaxes in the morning and evening in what are later termed the cathedral and monastic forms before these traditions diverged.[75] If so, ApTrad represents a time when only morning prayer was a communal prayer.[76] In many ways, ApTrad appears as a lay form of what is seen around the same time, or slightly later, in the Pachomian tradition. There, morning prayer is the communal and more dominant liturgy, with evening prayer being held in the individual households.

## 6. Provenance

The structure of the horarium in ApTrad is close to Tertullian and Cyprian in North Africa, who have prayer at morning, terce, sext, none, evening, and midnight. North Africa could be the source of ApTrad's horarium, or perhaps the location of one of the traditions that forms the basis for

---

Jay Watts, *City and School in Late Antique Athens and Alexandria*, The Transformation of the Classical Heritage 41 (Berkeley: University of California Press, 2006), esp. Ch. 8: Alexandrian Schools of the Fifth Century; Alberto Camplani, "The Transmission of Early Christian Memories in Late Antiquity: The Editorial Activity of Laymen and Philoponoi," in *Between Personal and Institutional Religion: Self, Doctrine, and Practice in Late Antique Eastern Christianity*, ed. Brouria Bitton-Ashkelony and Lorenzo Perrone (Turnhout: Brepols, 2013), 129–54. Similar confraternities emerged in Syria in the fourth century and these confraternities may even be tied to the Bodmer Library; see Arthur Vööbus, *History of Asceticism in the Syrian Orient*, vol. 2, CSCO 184 (Louvain: Secrétariat du CorpusSCO, 1958), I: 97–103; II: 331–42; Cristiano Berolli, "Tracce di ascetismo in ὁ δεσπọ́[τ]ης πρὸς τοὺς πά̣[σχο]ντας," *Adamantius* 21 (2015): 136–43.

75. Taft and Phillips have both suggested this—see Taft, *The Liturgy of the Hours in East and West*, 26; L. Edward Phillips, "Daily Prayer in the 'Apostolic Tradition' of Hippolytus," 399.

76. This would not be unlike the account of Pliny the Younger, who notes that Christians gather in the morning for prayer—see Andrew McGowan, *Ancient Christian Worship: Early Church Practices in Social, Historical, and Theological Perspective* (Grand Rapids, MI: Baker Academic, 2014), 188.

ApTrad's conflated horarium. But there are also strong indications that ApTrad is Egyptian, at least in its current formulation. The morning catechesis suggests a connection to contemporary or later monastic practices like those seen in the Pachomian sources and the GCN.[77] In fact, if the GCN are Egyptian,[78] the parallels to ApTrad's horarium strongly suggest an Egyptian origin (or at least final composition) for the daily prayer practices in ApTrad as well. The usage of scripture at morning catechesis is also a typical Egyptian feature, though it can be seen outside of Egypt as well. There are also connections between ApTrad's horarium and Origen in the identification of the shewbread with the Eucharist.[79] The reference to prayer at cockcrow, which we have argued above, along with Stewart, is a duplication of the prayer at rising, and which in Ethiopic I is noted as "early in the morning," has Egyptian monastic parallels.[80] This may again suggest that ApTrad represents a tradition just before, or just after, the split between what scholars now term the monastic and cathedral morning offices. If the latter, ApTrad's horarium is a very early witness to monastic influence on a lay/cathedral text, and perhaps provides a lay corollary to the urban monastic form. Regardless, it further muddies the sharp distinctions often drawn between the cathedral and monastic forms.

It is also worth noting that there are some parallels in Euch-AC with the material given in Ch. 18 and 19 in ApTrad. Ch. 18 addresses a morning assembly with catechesis and prayer, something that, as noted above, is repeated in Chs. 35, 39, and 41. Ch. 19 directly follows Ch. 18 and references the morning prayer in Ch. 18 by noting the teacher and the imposition of hands after prayer. It precedes Ch. 20, which addresses the examination of catechumens and even mentions that every morning they are to have hands laid on them. Whether the reference to a daily hand-laying is part of the original core or not,[81] it clearly links the initiatory material in Chs. 20–21 to the instructions in Ch. 19. But as a result, it also situates these catechumenal handlayings in the context of the morning assembly in Ch. 18 (and by extension Chs. 35, 39, and 41.1-4). A very

77. Monastic influence appears even more pronounced in CH 21, where the communal service from ApTrad Ch. 39 now occurs at cockcrow—see *Herm.Com.* 2002, 190.

78. Stewart, *The Gnomai of the Council of Nicaea*, 7–11.

79. *Herm.Com.* 2002, 208.

80. *Herm.Com.* 2002, 213.

81. Bradshaw, *Apostolic Tradition*, 64–65.

similar pattern occurs in Euch-AC (see Table 2 in our Introduction). That text begins with morning prayer ($\Sigma 46^{rb}$-$46^{vb}$), followed by a number of independent intercessions ($\Sigma 46^{vb}$-$51^{vb}$) that include a prayer with handlaying for the catechumens, and then leads into the baptismal ritual in the text, which begins at $\Sigma 51^{va}$ and continues to either $\Sigma 54^{vb}$ or possibly $\Sigma 54^{rb}$ depending on whether the "Prayer of the oil for the new ones. Entrance of the catechumens to the sick" and "Prayer of the exorcism of the water" are part of the initiatory rituals. It seems that this whole set of material in Euch-AC may be a remnant of an early form of morning prayer, which included scripture readings and prayers along with the handlaying on the catechumens. If so, this shows how much ApTrad influenced the Egyptian church and through it the Ethiopian at an early date.

## 7. Dating

In all, the majority of the horarium in ApTrad has parallels in early Christian sources. It appears that in ApTrad's horarium we see a form of daily prayer contemporaneous with, or slightly after, Tertullian, Cyprian, Origen, and Clement. If after, it likely represents in its current form an Egyptian tradition before or around the same time as Pachomius. In fact, it appears that ApTrad may represent a lay horarium that stands at the head of a growing split between the cathedral and monastic prayer, and lay and monastic spiritual formation more generally.

# Chapter 5

# Christian Initiation

The materials on Christian initiation in ApTrad Chs. 15–21 begin an entirely new section of the document and describe the ritual process of Christian initiation from a presentation, preliminary examination of motives and life, and enrollment of "newcomers" into the catechumenate (Ch. 15), to various prohibited occupations for both catechumens and fully initiated Christians (Ch. 16), to the duration of the catechumenate as well as other rites during the catechumenal process (Chs. 17-20), all the way to the rites themselves (Ch. 21.1-26) and their culmination in the baptismal Eucharist (Ch. 21.27-29 and 31-37). This is followed by some concluding materials (Ch. 21.30 and 38-40). Each will be treated here, with the exception of the postbaptismal reception of communion, which will be treated in Ch. 6 below. Since the lacuna in the Latin version continues until the beginning of the second baptismal interrogation in Ch. 21.15 the lacuna in the Latin version continues, the earliest available *witnesses* for the content of these chapters are now Ethiopic I and Arabic I. In a manner similar to Bradshaw's recent commentary,[1] our comments here similarly summarize and expand the section on Christian initiation from *Herm.Com.* 2002, although we do not use the Latin text from Ch. 21.15 on since there is no reason to grant the Latin any kind of normativity over Ethiopic I at this point.[2]

1. Bradshaw, *Apostolic Tradition.*
2. *Herm.Com.* 2002, 82–135.

## 1. Ch. 15. Concerning Those to Be Baptized Who Come for the First Time

Rites of enrollment in the catechumenate and preliminary examinations of "newcomers" to the faith (Ch. 15.1-3) have no *explicit* parallels within early Christian *liturgical* sources prior to the second half of the fourth century.[3] The existence of similar practices, however, *may* be discernable from, or assumed on the basis of, other genres of Christian literature prior to that time period. The proto-church order *Didache* refers to prebaptismal catechesis (*Didache* 1-6) and fasting for one or two days prior to baptism (*Didache* 7),[4] and in his *First Apology*, Justin Martyr makes a passing reference to such a process when he writes that "as many as are persuaded and believe that these things which we teach and describe are true, and undertake to live accordingly, are taught by us to pray and ask God, while fasting, for the forgiveness of their sins; and we pray and fast accordingly."[5] But the closest explicit parallel to entrance into the catechumenate and examinations of those seeking to enter is not provided until the middle of the third century by Origen of Alexandria in his *Contra Celsum*:

> But as far as they can, Christians previously examine the souls of those who want to hear them, and test them individually beforehand; when before entering the community the hearers seem to have devoted themselves sufficiently to the desire to live a good life, then they introduce them. They privately appoint one class consisting of recent beginners who are receiving elementary introduction and have not yet received the sign that they have been purified, and another class of those who, as far as they are able, make it their set purpose to desire nothing other than those things of which Christians approve. Among the latter class some are appointed to inquire into the lives and conduct of those who want to join the community in order that they may prevent those who indulge in secret sins

3. Cf. the prebaptismal and mystagogical catecheses attributed to Cyril of Jerusalem in *Saint Cyril of Jerusalem: Lectures on the Christian Sacraments: Greek Original and English Translation*, text, translation, and introduction by Maxwell E. Johnson (Yonkers: St. Vladimir's Seminary Press, 2027), as well as Edward Yarnold, *Cyril of Jerusalem* (London: Routledge, 2000).

4. DBL, 1–2.

5. *Apology* 1, 61; translation from DBL, 3.

from coming to their common gathering; those who do not do this they whole-heartedly receive and make them better every day.[6]

In ApCons 8.32.2 (bishop or presbyter), CH 10 (deacon), and TD II.1, the "teacher" from Ethiopic I and Arabic I has been clericalized, a shift easily explained as reflecting an overall fourth-century context in which such clericalization was increasing.[7]

Concerns about whether slaves might become catechumens, questions about the permission of their masters to do so or not, and about the marital status of catechumens in general (Ch. 15.4-7) are also not clearly reflected in literature outside of the extant versions and derivative documents of ApTrad. At the same time, despite the limited attention given to these questions in the CH 19b, there is nothing in the versions or derivative documents that is inconsistent with the general Christian attitude toward slavery itself in the first three centuries of the common era:

> Christian writers from the second century onward . . . accepted . . . slaves as members of the Church, and they urged masters to treat slaves well. They recommended mutual respect between master and slave, and they hoped that masters would try to convert their non-Christian slaves. But repeatedly Christians told slaves to honor their masters and accept their lot. Although from the fourth century onward there was a practice called *manumissio in ecclesia*, a legal act by which a master freed a slave in church, no evidence indicates that this encouraged masters to free their slaves. In fact, its main importance lay in the recognition it gained for the Church's role in civic affairs. . . . Christians also recognized the rights of slaves in marriage. Pope Callistus I (217–222), an ex-slave, went beyond the prevailing Roman civil code and recognized the validity of marriages between a male slave and a free woman.[8]

6. *Contra Celsum* III.51; trans. Henry Chadwick, *Origen: Contra Celsum* (Oxford: Oxford University Press, 1953), 163.

7. On this, see Paul Bradshaw, *Liturgical Presidency in the Early Church* (Bramcote: Grove Books, 1983), 15–20. See also Ch. 3.

8. J. F. Kelly, *The World of the Early Christians* (Collegeville, MN: Liturgical Press, 1997), 144–45. See also R. Grant, *From Augustus to Constantine: The Thrust of the Christian Movement into the Roman World* (New York: Harper & Row, 1970), 269–70. Among early Christian writers who make some reference to slavery see Ignatius of Antioch, *Polyc* 4.3; Athenagoras, *Leg.* 35, 1; the *Shepherd of Hermas*; Eusebius, *Historia ecclesiastica* 5.1,14;

Of possible relevance in the above quotation is the well-known conflict between Callistus and Hippolytus of Rome over the question of marriages between free women and male slaves. For Hippolytus, this permission constituted one of the grounds for his charge of severe moral laxity against Callistus and within his heretical "sect" at Rome.[9] Nevertheless, there is nothing in the versions or derivative documents which would permit us to conclude that this particular conflict played any role in the development of ApTrad or is to be interpreted as reflected in the directions provided in this section. Even the parallel reference to slavery in ApCons 8.32.5-6, it is to be noted, is not concerned with marriage relationships between free women and male slaves but simply with the marriage relationship among slaves themselves.

There is nothing in ApTrad Ch. 15 that would either contradict or be inconsistent with the traditional assumption of an early third-century date for the document. Such consistency, however, proves nothing about the date, authorship, or provenance of this chapter. Rather, the only thing that can be concluded with any degree of certainty is that it *may* reflect an overall third-century context. Even so, questions about the relationship between Christianity and slavery continued well into the late fourth century and beyond,[10] and, as such, there is also nothing here that would not be highly consistent with an overall *fourth*-century context as well.

## 2. Ch. 16. Concerning the Craft and the Profession

The initial examination of the lives and motives of those seeking entrance into the catechumenate continues in Ch. 16 by providing a catalog of prohibited occupations which would bar someone from admission into the catechumenal process. These prohibited occupations are linked together throughout the chapter by the recurring literary refrain, "let him cease or be rejected." The versions and derivative documents show considerable

---

and Tertullian, *Apol.* 7.3. ApCons 4.9.2 *does* recommend the emancipation of slaves, but such a recommendation does not appear within the parallel materials here, and, for that matter, appears to be limited to the context of persecution. For a discussion of slavery in, at least, the New Testament world of the first century CE see D. Martin, *Slavery as Salvation: The Metaphor of Slavery in Pauline Christianity* (New Haven and London: Yale University Press, 1990).

9. See Hippolytus, *The Refutation of All Heresies* VII, in ANF, 131.

10. Cf. Augustine, *City of God* XIX.15.

variation in this chapter as to the catalog of prohibited occupations, the order of their appearance in this catalog, and, occasionally, their interpretation. General parallels to the prohibited occupations in Ch. 16 and derivative documents have often been noted in the writings of Tertullian, especially *De Idolotria* (ca. 211) and *De Spectaculis* (ca. 197–202),[11] although they have seldom, if ever, been documented in detail. Parallels here also appear in the later CA 41 and 71–75 (Arabic and Coptic) in reference to different groups of people with whom Christians should not interact.[12]

While Tertullian himself never produced a "list" of prohibited occupations in relationship to those seeking to enter the catechumenate, the various occupations listed in Ch. 16 certainly reflect the kinds of ethical, moral, and social concerns that Tertullian had in mind for those who already were Christians or were seeking to become Christians in the Church of his day. As such, much of Ch. 16 is certainly consistent with an early third-century context, at least in North Africa, but only because that's where we find this to be documented.

References to lust and fornication, in parallel to the prohibition against "brothels" and "brothel keepers" (Ch. 16.2), appear in prebaptismal catechesis as early as *Didache* 3:2. Similarly, Tertullian speaks of Christians being unable to engage in or manage brothels in *De idolatria* XI.

> *Didache* 3:2: My child, do not be a person given to passion, because passion leads to fornication; nor should you be given to obscene speech or to bold gazes, for from all of these [actions] flow acts of adultery.[13]
>
> Tertullian, *De idolotria* XI: In that I am interdicted from fornication, I furnish nothing of help or connivance to others for that purpose; in that I have separated myself from stews, I acknowledge that I cannot exercise the trade of pandering, or keep that kind of places for my neighbour's behoof.[14]

With regard to "idols" and "idol makers" (16.3) Tertullian makes several references:

11. Cf. G. J. Cuming, *Hippolytus: A Text for Students*, 2nd ed., GLS 8 (Nottingham: Grove Books, 1998), 15n16.

12. Wilhelm Riedel and W. E. Crum, *The Canons of Athanasius of Alexandria: The Arabic and Coptic Versions* (London: Williams and Norgate, 1904), Arabic: 34 and 47–48; and Coptic: 118 and 135–36.

13. K. Niederwimmer, *The Didache*, Hermeneia (Minneapolis: Fortress Press, 1998), 94.

14. ANF, III, 67.

> Tertullian, *De idolotria* V: We will certainly take more pains in answering the excuses of artificers of [idols], who ought never to be admitted into the house of God, if any have knowledge of that Discipline.[15]

> Tertullian, *De idolotria* VI: If no law of God had prohibited idols to be made by us; if no voice of the Holy Spirit uttered general menace no less against the makers than the worshippers of idols: from our sacrament itself we would draw our interpretation that arts of that kind are opposed to the faith. For how have we *renounced* the devil and his angels, if we *make* them? What divorce have we declared from them, I say not *with* whom, but *dependent on* whom, we live? . . . Can you have denied with the tongue what with the hand you confess? unmake by word what by deed you make? preach one God, you who make so many? preach the true God, you who make false ones?[16]

> Tertullian, *De idolotria* VII: A whole day the zeal of faith will direct its pleadings to this quarter: bewailing that a Christian should come from idols into the Church; should come from an adversary work-shop into the house of God; should raise to God the Father hands which are the mothers of idols; should pray to God with the hands which, out of doors, are prayed to in opposition to God; should apply to the Lord's body those hands which confer bodies on demons. . . . Idol artificers are chosen even into the ecclesiastical order. . . . Now let the saying, 'If thy hand make thee do evil, amputate it,' see to it whether it were uttered by way of similitude *merely*. What hands more to be amputated than those in which scandal is done to the Lord's body?[17]

The reference to actors and to the theatre (Ch. 16.4) appears in Ethiopic I (but not Arabic I). Prior to the publication of Ethiopic I by Bausi our knowledge of this prohibition was based on the Sahidic version with parallels in CH 11, ApCons 8:32.7-13, and TD II.2. But an early parallel also appears in Tertullian's *De spectaculis:*

> Tertullian, *De spectaculis* XVII: Are we not . . . enjoined to put away from us all immodesty? On this ground, again, we are excluded from the theatre, which is immodesty's own peculiar abode, where nothing is in repute but

15. ANF, III, 63.
16. ANF, III, 64.
17. ANF, III, 64.

what elsewhere is disreputable. So the best path to the highest favour of its god is the vileness which the Atellan gesticulates, which the buffoon in women's clothes exhibits, destroying all natural modesty, so that they blush more readily at home than at the play, which finally is done from his childhood on the person of the pantomine, *that he may become an actor*. The very harlots, too, victims of the public lust, are brought upon the stage, their misery increased as being there in the presence of their own sex, from whom alone they are wont to hide themselves: they are paraded publicly before every age and every rank—their abode, their gains, their praises, are set forth, and that even in the hearing of those who should not hear such things. . . . You have the theatre forbidden . . . in the forbidding of immodesty. If . . . we despise the teaching of secular literature as being foolishness in God's eyes, our duty is plain enough in regard to those spectacles, which from this source derive the tragic or comic play. If tragedies and comedies are the bloody and wanton, the impious and licentious inventors of crimes and lusts, it is not good even that there should be any calling to remembrance the atrocious or the vile. What you reject in deed, you are not to bid welcome to in word.[18]

Reference to "one who attends the circus" appears in neither Ethiopic I nor Arabic I but does appear in Ethiopic II and Arabic II. That it may be early is suggested by its parallel in Tertullian's writings:

Tertullian, *De spectaculis* VIII: I shall break with my Maker, that is, by going to the Capitol or the temple of Serapis to sacrifice or adore, as I shall also do by going as a spectator to the circus and the theatre. The places in themselves do not contaminate, but what is done in them; from this even the places themselves, we maintain, become defiled. The polluted things pollute us. It is on this account that we set before you to whom places of the kind are dedicated, that we may prove the things which are done in them to belong to the idol-patrons to whom the very places are sacred.[19]

Similarly, the prohibition against teachers of classical literature in Ch. 16.5 is particularly strong in Tertullian:

18. ANF, III, 86–87.
19. ANF, III, 83.

> Tertullian, *De idolotria* X: Moreover, we must inquire likewise touching schoolmasters; nor only of them, but also all other professors of literature. Nay, on the contrary, we must not doubt that they are in affinity with manifold idolatry: *first*, in that it is necessary for them to preach the gods of the nations, to express their names, genealogies, honourable distinctions, all and singular; and *further*, to observe the solemnities and festivals of the same, as of them by whose means they compute their revenues. . . . Learning literature is allowable for believers, rather than teaching; for the principle of learning and of teaching is different. If a believer teach literature, while he is teaching doubtless he commends, while he delivers he affirms, while he recalls he bears testimony to, the praises of idols interspersed therein. . . . Inquire whether he who catechizes about idols commit idolatry. But when a believer *learns* these things, if he is already capable of understanding what idolatry is, he neither receives nor allows them; much more if he is not yet capable. Or, when he *begins* to understand, it behooves him first to understand what he has previously learned, that is, touching God and the faith. Therefore he will reject those things, and will not receive them; and will be as safe as one who from one who knows it not, knowingly *accepts* poison, but does not *drink* it. To *him* necessity is attributed as an excuse, because he has no other way to learn. Moreover, the not *teaching* literature is as much easier than the not *learning*, as it is easier, too, for the pupil not to attend, than for the master not to frequent, the rest of the defilements incident to the schools from public and scholastic solemnities.[20]

With regard to this, Tertullian is certainly more rigorist than is ApTrad, which states that the teacher "keep doing thus if he does not know anything else" (Arabic I). Both CH 12 and TD II.2 also make this concession as well, with CH adding that the schoolmaster is to reveal "if he reveals at all times to those he teaches and confesses that what the Gentiles call gods are demons, and says before them every day there is no divinity except the Father, the Son, and the Holy Spirit." Such leniency in the versions and derivative documents at this point may suggest development on this issue after the time of Tertullian himself or, alternatively, it may merely be nothing other than a concession made for pastoral reasons.

Until the publication of Ethiopic I and Arabic I, the prohibition against "charioteers," or "taking the reins" (Arabic I) or "competes with horses

20. ANF, III, 66–67.

and enters the games" (Ethiopic I) in Ch. 16.6 appeared in only the Sahidic translation, ApCons 8.32.7-13, and TD II.2. It also receives special treatment in Tertullian:

> Tertullian, *De spectaculis* IX: . . . if Trochilus the Argive is maker of the first chariot, he dedicated that work of his to Juno. If Romulus first exhibited the four-horse chariot at Rome, he too, I think, has a place given him among idols, at least if he and Quirinus are the same. But as chariots had such inventors, the charioteers were naturally dressed, too, in the colours of idolatry; for at first these were only two, namely white and red,—the former sacred to the winter with its glistening snows, the latter sacred to the summer with its ruddy sun: but afterwards, in the progress of luxury as well as of superstition, red was dedicated by some to Mars, and white by others to the Zephyrs, while green was given to Mother Earth, or spring, and azure to the sky and sea, or autumn. But as idolatry of every kind is condemned by God, that form of it surely shares the condemnation which is offered to the elements of nature.[21]

Alistair Stewart has argued that this reference to charioteers points to a Roman origin for ApTrad, since "this sport did not extend beyond Rome until the end of the second century, and even then was restricted to large urban centers."[22] How this proves a Roman origin, however, is baffling since charioteers and chariot racing are well documented not only for Rome but for ancient Egypt and Greece, even in Greece as an Olympic sport.[23] If there is little reason to doubt the antiquity of this reference, it is possible that its absence from Arabic II and Ethiopic II has to do with the lack of charioteers in their respective communities at the time of their later translations.

Gladiators and teachers of gladiators (Ch. 16.7), as well as all other occupations associated with the gladiatorial games (e.g., fighting with bears and public combat), are already condemned by Tertullian:

> Tertullian, *De idolotria* XI: So, too, the interdiction of murder shows me that a trainer of gladiators also is to be excluded from the Church; nor will

21. ANF, III, 83.

22. Stewart, *On the Apostolic Tradition*, 121.

23. Cf. *Chariots in Ancient Egypt: The Tano Chariot, A Case Study*, ed. André J. Veldmeijer and Salima Ikram (Havertown, PA: Sidestone Press, 2018).

anyone fail to be the means of doing what he subministers to another to do. Behold, here is a more kindred fore-judgment: if a purveyor of the public victims come over to the faith, will you permit him to remain permanently in that trade? or if one who is already a believer shall have undertaken that business, will you think that he is to retained in the Church?[24]

Tertullian, *De spectaculis* XII: It remains for us to examine the 'spectacle' most noted of all, and in highest favour. It is called a dutiful service (*munus*), from its being an office, for it bears the name of '*officium*' as well as '*munus*.' The ancients thought that in this solemnity they rendered offices to the dead; at a later period, with a cruelty more refined, they somewhat modified its character. For formerly, in the belief that the souls of the departed were appeased by human blood, they were in the habit of buying captives or slaves of wicked disposition, and immolating them in their funeral obsequies. Afterward they thought good to throw the veil of pleasure over their iniquity. Those, therefore, whom they had provided for the combat, and then trained in arms as best they could, only that they might learn to die, they, on the funeral day, killed at the places of sepulture. They alleviated death by murders. Such is the origin of the 'Munus.' But by degrees their refinement came up to their cruelty; for these human beasts could not find pleasure exquisite enough, save in the spectacle of men torn to pieces by wild beasts. Offerings to propitiate the dead then were regarded as belonging to the class of funeral sacrifices; and these are idolatry: for idolatry, in fact, is a sort of homage to the departed; the one as well as the other is a service to dead men. Moreover, demons have abode in the images of the dead. To refer also to the matter of names, though this sort of exhibition has passed from honours of the dead to honours of the living, I mean, to quaestorships and magistracies—to priestly offices of different kinds; yet since idolatry still cleaves to the dignity's name, whatever is done in its name partakes of its impurity.[25]

Tertullian, *De spectaculis* XIX: . . . gladiators not chargeable with crime are offered in sale for the games, that they may become the victims of the public pleasure. Even in the case of those who are judicially condemned to the amphitheater, what a monstrous thing it is, that, in undergoing their punishment, they, from some less serious delinquency, advance to the criminality of manslayers![26]

24. ANF, III, 67.
25. ANF, III, 85.
26. ANF, III, 87.

Although "idols" and "idol makers" in Ch. 16.3 are condemned by Tertullian elsewhere, the following appears have some relationship to the prohibition against the "priest" or "custodian" of idols in Ch. 16.8:

> Tertullian, *De idolotria* XV: Let . . . them who have no light, light their lamps daily; let them over whom the fires of hell are imminent, affix to their posts laurels doomed presently to burn: to them the testimonies of darkness and the omens of their penalties are suitable. *You* are a light of the world, and a tree ever green. If you have renounced temples, make not your own gate a temple. I have said too little. If you have renounced stews, clothe not your own house with the appearance of a new brothel.[27]

On soldiers and killing (in Ch. 16.9 and 11), whether during warfare or in administering capital punishment, the witness of Tertullian is generally consistent again with both Ethiopic I and Arabic I.

> Tertullian, *De corona* XI: . . . we must first inquire whether warfare is proper at all for Christians. What sense is there in discussing the merely accidental, when that on which it rests is to be condemned? Do we believe it lawful for a human *oath* to be superadded to one divine, for a man to come under promise to another master after Christ . . . ? Shall it be held lawful to make an occupation of the sword, when the Lord proclaims that he who uses the sword shall perish by the sword? And shall the son of peace take part in the battle when it does not become him even to sue at law? And shall he apply the chain, and the prison, and the torture, and the punishment, who is not the avenger even of his own wrongs? Shall he, forsooth, either keep watch-service for others more than for Christ, or shall he do it on the Lord's day, when he does not even do it for Christ Himself? And shall he keep guard before the temples which he has renounced? And shall he take a meal where the apostle has forbidden him? And shall he diligently protect by night those whom in the day-time he has put to flight by his exorcisms, leaning and resting on the spear the while with which Christ's side was pierced? . . . .
>
> Of course, if faith comes later, and finds any preoccupied with military service, their case is different . . . ; yet, at the same time, when a man has become a believer, and faith has been sealed, there must be either an immediate abandonment of it, which has been the course with many; or all

27. ANF, III, 71.

sorts of quibbling will have to be resorted to in order to avoid offending God, and that is not allowed even outside of military service; or, last of all, for God, the fate must be endured which a citizen-faith has been no less ready to accept. Neither does military service hold out escape from punishment of sins, or exemption from martyrdom. Nowhere does the Christian change his character.[28]

Tertullian, *De idolotria* XIX: . . . now inquiry is made about this point, whether a believer may turn himself unto military service, and whether the military may be admitted unto the faith, even the rank and file, or each inferior grade, to whom there is no necessity for taking part in sacrifices or capital punishments. There is no agreement between the divine and the human sacrament, the standard of Christ and the standard of the devil, the camp of light and the camp of darkness. One soul cannot be due to two *masters*—God and Caesar.[29]

Ethiopic I and Arabic I, however, permit soldiers to enter into the catechumenate if they refrain from killing and from offering sacrifice, even when ordered to do so by a superior. And because Ethiopic I (followed by the Sahidic version) also refers in Ch. 16.9 to the military oath ("nor let him swear"), a direction paralleled in the CH 13 ("they are not to pronounce a bad word"), and the wearing of military wreaths or crowns, Ethiopic I appears to be the more primitive of the versions here.[30] Certainly Tertullian's reference in *De Idolatria* XIX that "there is no agreement between the divine and the human sacrament" parallels this prohibition, although Tertullian also notes that even the silent acceptance of a military crown, without speaking the words of the oath, is itself an idolatrous response for Christians.[31]

28. ANF, III, 99–100.

29. ANF, III, 73.

30. See Cuming, *Hippolytus*, 16.

31. See *De Corona* 12, in ANF, III, 101. See also *De Corona* 1 (ANF, III, 93) for Tertullian's praise of a Christian soldier who refused to accept the crown and so suffered its consequences in martyrdom. See also Eoin de Bhaldraithe, "Early Christian Features Preserved in Western Monasticism," in A. Kreider, ed., *Christendom: The Experience of the West*, vol. 1: *The Origins of Christendom in the West* (Edinburgh: T & T Clark, forthcoming), 15–18. On the question of military service and early Christianity, see Alan Kreider, "Military Service in the Church Orders," *Journal of Religious Ethics* 31 (2003): 415–42; J. Helgeland, "Christians and the Roman Army: AD 173–337," *Church History* 43 (1974):

The prohibition against admitting rulers into the catechumenate (Ch. 16.10), including parallel reference to "garb . . . and apparatus of office," closely related to idolatry connected to the various ruling offices, also appears in Tertullian:

> Tertullian, *De idolotria* XVII:. . . let us grant that it is possible for any one to succeed in moving, in whatsoever office, under the mere *name* of the office, neither sacrificing nor lending his authority to sacrifices; not farming out victims; not assigning to others the care of temples; not looking after their tributes; not giving spectacles at his own or the public charge, or presiding over the giving them; making proclamations or edict for no solemnity; not even taking oaths; moreover (what comes under the head of *power*), neither sitting in judgement on any one's life or character, for you might bear with his judging about *money*; neither condemning nor fore-condemning; binding no one—if it is credible that all this is possible.[32]

> Tertullian, *De idolotria* XVIII: But we must now treat of the garb only and apparatus of office. There is a dress proper to every one, as well as for daily use as for office and dignity. That famous purple, therefore, and the gold as an ornament of the neck, were, among the Egyptians and Babylonians, ensigns of dignity, in the same way as bordered, or striped, or palm-embroidered togas, and the golden wreaths of provincial priests, are now; but not on the same terms. For they used only to be conferred, under the name of *honour* . . . but *not* on the understanding that that garb should be tied to *priesthoods* also, or *to any idol-ceremonies*. For if *that* were the case, of course men of such holiness and constancy would

149–63; idem, "Christians and the Roman Army from Marcus Aurelius to Constantine," in H. Termporini and W. Haase, eds., *Aufstieg und Niedergang der Römischen Welt*, II (Berlin/New York: Walter de Gruyter, 1979), 724–834; idem, R. Daly and J. Patout Burns, *Christians and the Military: The Early Experience* (Philadelphia: Fortress Press, 1985); L. J. Swift, "War and the Christian Conscience 1: The Early Years," in H. Temporini and W. Haase, eds., *Aufstieg und Niedergang der Römischen Welt*, 835–68; idem, *The Early Fathers on War and Military Service*, Message of the Fathers of the Church, 19 (Collegeville, MN: Michael Glazier, 1983); D. Hunter, "A Decade of Research on Early Christians and Military Service," *Religious Studies Review* 18.2 (1992): 87–94; idem, "The Christian Church and the Roman Army in the First Three Centuries," in M. Miller and B. Gingerich, eds., *The Church's Peace Witness* (Grand Rapids, MI: Eerdmans, 1994), 161–81; and J. M. Hornus, *It Is Not Lawful for Me to Fight: Early Christian Attitudes toward War, Violence and the State* (Scottdale, PA: Herald, 1980).

32. ANF, III, 72.

have refused the defiled dresses . . . But the purple, or other ensigns of dignitaries and powers, dedicated from the beginning to idolatry engrafted on the dignity and the powers, carry the spot of their own profanation; since, moreover, bordered and striped togas, and broad-barred ones, are put even on idols themselves; and *fasces* also, and rods, are borne before them; and deservedly, for demons are the magistrates of this world; they bear the *fasces* and the purples, the ensigns of one college. What end, then, will you advance if you use the garb indeed, but administer not the functions of it? In things unclean, none can appear clean. If you put on a tunic defiled in itself, it perhaps may not be defiled through you; but you, through it, will be unable to be clean. . . .

If you have forsworn 'the devil's pomp,' know that whatever there you touch is idolatry. Let even this fact help to remind you that all the powers and dignities of this world are not only alien to, but enemies of, God; that through them punishments have been determined against God's servants; through them, too, penalties for the impious are ignored. But 'both your birth and your substance are troublesome to you in resisting idolatry.' For avoiding it, remedies cannot be lacking; since, even if they be lacking, there remains that one by which you will be made a happier magistrate, not in the earth, but in the heavens.[33]

While it is difficult to know if the other versions are concerned with the cessation of wearing the purple of office or with the office itself, certainly the reference to the one "raised to the authority of prefect or the magistracy" in CH 13, who is instructed to "put on the righteousness of the Gospel," reflects a changed situation in which it was possible to conceive of a "Christian" ruler. Ethiopic I is unique among all of the versions in specifying the prohibition against execution by the sword but it is undoubtedly parallel to references to the sword or power of the sword in other versions.

Prohibitions against diviners, astrologers, and magicians, with the exception of the "one who makes phylacteries" (Arabic I has "amulets") in Ch. 16.12-14 appear as early as *Didache* 3:4, as well as in Tertullian:

*Didache* 3:4: My child, do not practice augury, because this leads to idolatry; nor should you be an enchanter, or an astrologer, or a person who performs purificatory rituals; you should not even want to see <or hear> such things, for from all of these [activities] idolatry is spawned.[34]

33. ANF, III, 72–73.

34. Niederwimmer, *The Didache*, 94.

> Tertullian, *De idolotria* IX: Both [Simon Magus] and that other magician, who was with Sergius Paulus, (since he began opposing himself to the same apostles) was mulcted with loss of eyes. The same fate, I believe, would astrologers, too, have met, if any had fallen in the way of the apostles. But yet, when magic is punished, of which astrology is a species, of course the species is condemned in the genus. After the Gospel, you will nowhere find either sophists, Chaldeans, enchanters, diviners, or magicians, except as clearly punished. . . . You know nothing, astrologer, if you know not that you should be a Christian. If you did know it, you ought to have known this also, that you should have nothing more to do with that profession of yours which, of itself, fore-chants the climacterics of others, and might instruct you of its own danger. There is no part nor lot for you in that system of yours. He cannot hope for the kingdom of the heavens, whose finger or wand abuses the heaven.[35]

With regard to prohibiting the one who makes phylacteries in Ethiopic I, Bradshaw is undoubtedly correct in concluding that "such a person would be working for Jewish masters"[36] and this would be seen as problematic.

The statements against concubines and men with concubines (Ch. 16.15-16) are not reflected in literature outside of the versions and derivative documents of ApTrad, although the practice of concubinage is well attested in the ancient Greco-Roman world.[37] Since various concerns about marriage appear at the end of Ch. 15 above, and so seem out of place here, Bradshaw suggests that Ch. 16.15 may have originally served as the conclusion to Ch. 15 and hence be older than the prohibitions of Ch. 16.[38] But even if that could be proven, the fact remains that there is nothing in Ch. 16, especially given the parallels in Tertullian and the *Didache,* that would be inconsistent with a third-century or even earlier date. Even the reference to all having the Holy Spirit with regard to making possible decisions (see 1 Cor. 7:40) about further prohibitions in the conclusion to this section (Ch. 16.17) is also paralleled in Tertullian's writings.

35. ANF, III, 66.

36. Bradshaw, *Apostolic Tradition*, 55.

37. Cf. Peter Brown, *The Body and Society: Men, Women and Sexual Renunciation in Early Christianity* (New York: Columbia University Press, 1988).

38. Bradshaw, *Apostolic Tradition*, 55.

> Tertullian, *De virginibus velandis* I: . . . the reason why the Lord sent the Paraclete was, that, since human mediocrity was unable to take in all things at once, discipline should, little by little, be directed, and ordained, and carried on to perfection, by the Vicar of the Lord, the Holy Spirit. . . . What, then, is the Paraclete's administrative office but this: the direction of discipline, the revelation of the Scriptures, the re-formation of the intellect, the advancement toward 'better things'?[39]

> Tertullian, *De exhortatione castitatis* IV: It is true that believers . . . 'have the Spirit of God;' but not all believers are apostles. . . . For apostles have the Holy Spirit properly, who have him fully, in the operations of prophecy, and the efficacy of (healing) virtues, and the evidences of tongues; not partially, as all others have. Thus he [Paul] attached the Holy Spirit's authority to that form (of advice) to which he willed us rather to attend; and forthwith it became not an *advice* of the Holy Spirit, but, in consideration of His majesty, a *precept*.[40]

The numerous parallels in the writings of Tertullian throughout Ch. 16, however, should not be taken as some kind of proof of either the dating or North African provenance or redaction of ApTrad in general. Rather, as noted above, Tertullian is the one who, together with the *Didache*, in part, provides us with comparative documentary evidence of early Christian attitudes toward who should or should not be admitted to the catechumenate and baptism, without repentance and change. The fact of the matter is that we lack any other documentary evidence elsewhere for this, from either East or West, and so cannot say any more than that Ch. 16 has numerous parallels with the writings of Tertullian.

## 3. Ch. 17. On the Time of the Hearers

The reference to a three-year catechumenate in Ch. 17.1, together with all derivative documents, but with the notable exception of CH 11, have led many to assume that the catechumenate in early Christianity was universally three years in length. In support of this, scholars have often pointed to a three-year tree-planting allegory in Clement of Alexandria as an early Alexandrian parallel in this context:

39. ANF, IV, 27.
40. ANF, IV, 53.

> Clement of Alexandria, *Strom.* II. 18: And it [the Law] does not allow imperfect fruit to be plucked from immature trees, but *after three years*, in the fourth year; dedicating the first-fruits to God after the tree has maintained maturity. This type of husbandry may serve as a mode of instruction, teaching that we must cut the growth of sins, and the useless weeds of the mind that spring up round the vital fruit, till the shoot of faith is perfected and becomes strong. For in the fourth year, *since there is need of time to him that is being solidly catechized*, the four virtues are consecrated to God, the third alone being already joined to the fourth, the person of the Lord.[41]

It is not clear, however, if Clement is actually referring to a prebaptismal catechumenal period, to the length of philosophical and theological training given at his famous catechetical school in Alexandria, or to something else altogether.[42] Nevertheless, Alistair Stewart suggests that it was original to ApTrad and "is comparable to the length of time spent before admission to philosophical schools"[43] and, hence, could point to the school context of Hippolytus's community at Rome. Reference to a three-year probationary period appears in Peter of Alexandria's *Canons* but therein it is related not to preparation for baptism but to the duration of penance for penitent apostates:

> Peter of Alexandria, *Canon* 1: for they did not come to this of their own will, but were betrayed by the frailty of the flesh; for they show in their bodies the marks of Jesus, and some are now, *for the third year*, bewailing their fault: it is sufficient, I say, that from the time of their submissive approach, other forty days should be enjoined upon them, to keep them in remembrance of these things.[44]

Basil of Caesarea makes a similar requirement of a three-year abstinence from the Eucharist for a "soldier with unclean hands."[45] The Jewish historian

41. ANF, II, 368 [emphases added].

42. See P. Bradshaw, "Baptismal Practice in the Alexandrian Tradition, Eastern or Western?," in idem., ed., *Essays in Early Eastern Initiation* (Bramcote: Grove Books, 1988), 10. See also Nathan Chase, "Rites Belonging to the Period of the Catechumenate," in *A Pastoral and Theological Commentary on the* Order of Christian Initiation of Adults, ed. Victoria M. Tufano, 65–79 (Chicago: Liturgical Training Publications, 2024).

43. Stewart, *On the Apostolic Tradition*, 124.

44. ANF, VI, 269 [emphasis added].

45. Letter 188.13; NPNF II, 228.

Josephus in his *Jewish War* 2.8.7 describes a three-year period of preparation for Jews seeking to join the Essenes, a suggestive reference in light of the parallels James Vanderkam has noted between Essene practice and the Christian community described at Pentecost in Acts 2, where three thousand are baptized.[46] And in a tenth-century "letter of Macarius, Bishop of Memphis" it is said that "in the first generation" catechumens were taught "for three years" and then baptized, but according to Bradshaw, this reference is much too late to give it any credence.[47] At the same time, there is a reference to a three-*month* catechumenate in the mid-third-century Syrian *Pseudo-Clementine Recognitions:*

> *Pseudo-Clementine Recognitions* 3:67: When he had given them these and such like precepts, he made proclamation to the people, saying: 'Since I have resolved to stay three months with you, if any one desires it, let him be baptized; that stripped of his former evils, he may for the future, in consequence of his own conduct, become heir of heavenly blessings, as a reward for his good actions. Whosoever will, then, let him come to Zacchaeus and give his name to him, and let him hear from him the mysteries of the kingdom of heaven. Let him attend to frequent fastings, and approve himself in all things, that at the end of these *three months* he may be baptized on the day of the festival.'[48]

Outside of these documents the only clear parallel statement about such a lengthy catechumenal period in the early Church is Canon 42 of the early fourth-century Council of Elvira (ca. 305), which specifies a *two-year* general catechumenate:

46. See James C. Vanderkam, "Covenant and Pentecost," *Calvin Theological Journal* 37 (2002): 239–54; and Maxwell E. Johnson, "Tertullian's '*Diem baptismo sollemniorem*' Revisited: A Tentative Hypothesis on Baptism at Pentecost," in M. E. Johnson and L. E. Phillips, eds., *Studia Liturgica Diversa: Essays in Honor of Paul F. Bradshaw* (Portland: Pastoral Press, 2004), 31–44.

47. See Louis Villecourt, "La lettre de Macaire, evêque de Memphis, sur la liturgie antique du chrême et du baptême à Alexandrie," *Le Muséon* 36 (1923): 33–46, here at 34, cited by Paul F. Bradshaw, "Fourth Century Baptismal Practice: A Reevaluation of the Evidence," *Explorations in Christian Initiation from the East: In Honor of Maxwell E. Johnson*, ed. Stefanos Alexopoulos, Nathan Chase, and Anna Petrin, Eastern Catholic Studies and Texts (Washington, DC: The Catholic University of America Press, forthcoming).

48. ANF, VIII, 132 [emphasis added].

> The Council of Elvira, *Canon* 42: It was agreed that those who come to the beginning of faith, if they are of good behaviour, may be admitted to the grace of baptism after *two years*: except when under the compulsion of sickness reason requires earlier support for the man in danger or asking for grace.[49]

Michel Dujarier interpreted this canon as indicative of a reduction or "relaxation of discipline" in relation to both Clement and Ch. 17.1. But the fact of the matter, as Dujarier himself notes, is that this same council mandates that serious faults could prolong the catechumenate to *three years* (Canon 4), five years (Canon 73), or even to the end of one's life (Canon 73).[50] Similarly, as Dujarier again notes,[51] the Council of Nicaea also sought to ensure that a period of adequate preparation for baptism be provided in order to guarantee that the transition from pagan to Christian life not be as abrupt as apparently it had been previously. Canon II of Nicaea is especially concerned here about those who, "instructed but a little while, are straightway brought to the spiritual laver, and as soon as they have been baptized are advanced to the episcopate or the presbyterate."[52]

Other references to the length of prebaptismal catechesis tend to suggest that this period was three *weeks* in duration within several places in the early Church (Rome, Jerusalem, Syria). What is not known, however, is whether this three-week period constituted the total length of prebaptismal preparation or was merely the final period immediately preceding baptism.[53]

Since the earliest derivative document of ApTrad, CH 11, refers to only a *forty-day* prebaptismal preparation period, the question is raised about the precise original contents of Ch. 17.1. That is, it is quite possible that the reference to a three-year catechumenate in Ch. 17.1 belongs more appropriately to a fourth-, rather than third-, century context,

49. DBL, 223 [emphasis added].

50. M. Dujarier, *A History of the Catechumenate* (New York: Sadlier, 1979), 69.

51. Dujarier, *A History of the Catechumenate*, 69.

52. NPNF, second series, XIV, 10.

53. On this, see Maxwell E. Johnson, "From Three Weeks to Forty Days: Baptismal Preparation and the Origins of Lent," LWSS, 118–36; and idem., "Preparation for Pascha? Lent in Christian Antiquity," in P. Bradshaw and L. Hoffman, eds., *Two Liturgical Traditions*, vol. 6: *Passover and Easter: The Symbolic Structuring of Sacred Seasons* (Notre Dame: University of Notre Dame Press, 1999), 36–54.

where a concern for the length of baptismal preparation is clearly being expressed elsewhere in the Church. Like the canons of the Council of Elvira themselves, this reference in Ch. 17.1—for which no undisputed third-century corroboration is available—may best be interpreted as a parallel attempt to ensure adequate catechumenal preparation in the early fourth century. If so, this reference may be an addition to the text and with this, the traditional assumption that the pre-Nicene Church knew a general catechumenate of three years would fall to the wayside.

This, of course, cannot be concluded with certainty. The lack of clear third-century corroborating evidence and the fact that, again, our earliest derived document does not have this particular reference, may suggest that Ch. 17.1 originally contained only a reference to the "time of catechesis" in general without specifying *any* particular length. If so, the forty days in CH 12, and the references to "three years" elsewhere, reflect either local adaptations or the changes brought about by a later historical context. At the same time, however, with regard to questions of the provenance of ApTrad in general, it is worth noting that references to three-year periods—although, apart from Clement, associated with penance—are generally *Egyptian*, a point that has not been noted before in scholarship and may provide some cumulative evidence in support of the thesis of Jean Michel Hanssens that ApTrad had an Egyptian, possibly Alexandrian, origin. And, if, as we have argued elsewhere,[54] the CH are also Egyptian in origin, then reference therein to a "forty-day catechumenate" may simply reflect an alternative, especially local, Egyptian pattern and tradition.

## 4. Ch. 18. Concerning the Prayer of the Hearers

As noted in Ch. 4 of this commentary, this prayer in ApTrad Ch. 18 is referring to the same morning service as that given in Chs. 35, 39, and the first part of 41 (vv. 1-4). More on that service appears in our earlier chapter. A parallel to liturgical assemblies being segregated according to sex and status in Ch. 18.1-2 appears in the mid-third-century Syrian *Didascalia Apostolorum*:

54. Nathan P. Chase and Maxwell E. Johnson, *The Origins of the Canons of Hippolytus* (Collegeville, MN: Liturgical Press Academic, 2024).

> *Didascalia Apostolorum* 12: For thus it should be, that in the most easterly part of the house the presbyters sit with the bishops, and next the lay men, and then the women; so that when you stand up to pray, the leaders may stand first, and after them the lay men, and then the women too. . . . The young girls should also sit separately, or if there is no room, they should stand up behind the women. Young women who are married and have children should stand separately, and elderly women and widows should sit separately.[55]

This text is, of course, present in Ethiopic I. Segregation by gender at public events was common not in Judaism but in the Greco-Roman world within a variety of settings and is reflected in Christian liturgical assemblies.[56]

References to prayer being concluded by the kiss of peace (Ch. 18.3-4) appear as early as Justin Martyr's *First Apology* and Tertullian's *De oratione*:

> Justin Martyr, *Apology* I.65: At the conclusion of prayers we greet one another with a kiss.[57]

> Tertullian, *De oratione* XVIII: What prayer is complete if divorced from the 'holy kiss'?[58]

The kiss of peace concluding several liturgical rites in early Christianity was reserved to the baptized alone for the simple reason that this kiss was a literal exchange of the "breath" or "spirit" (*pneuma*) received in baptism.[59] In *De oratione* XVIII, Tertullian further refers to this kiss as

55. S. Brock and M. Vasey, eds., *The Liturgical Portions of the Didascalia* (Bramcote: Grove Books, 1982), 15–16.

56. See Ross S. Kraemer, *Her Share of the Blessings: Women's Religions among Pagans, Jews, and Christians in the Greco-Roman World* (New York: Oxford University Press, 1992), 106–7, 126; and idem, "Jewish Women and Women's Judaism(s) at the Beginning of Christianity," in idem and Mary Rose D'Angelo, eds., *Women & Christian Origins* (New York: Oxford University Press, 1999), 64–65.

57. T. Finn, ed., *Early Christian Baptism and the Catechumenate: Italy, North Africa, and Egypt* (Collegeville, MN: Liturgical Press, 1992), 40.

58. ANF, III, 686.

59. See L. Edward Phillips, *The Ritual Kiss in Early Christian Worship*, Alcuin/GROW Joint Liturgical Studies 36 (Cambridge: Grove Books, 1996); and Nathan Chase, "Kiss," in *Brill Encyclopedia of Early Christianity*, ed. David G. Hunter, Paul J. J. van Geest, Bert Jan Lietaert Peerbolte (Boston: Brill, 2022).

the "seal of prayer." While there appears to be no evidence in any other sources for the kiss being segregated by gender, Ethiopic I and Arabic I, together with the Oriental versions and derivative documents, are all insistent on this.

The reference to the necessity of veiling or full head coverings for women (Ch. 18.5) has some parallel in Tertullian's *De virginibus velandis*:

> Tertullian, *De virginibus velandis* XVII: But we admonish you, too, *women* of the second (degree of) modesty, who have fallen into wedlock, not to outgrow so far the discipline of the veil, not even in a moment of an hour, as, because you cannot *refuse* it, to take some other means to *nullify* it, by going neither covered nor bare. For some, with their turbans and woolen bands, do not *veil* their head, but bind it up; protected, indeed, in front, but, where the head properly lies, bare. *Others are to a certain extent covered over the region of the brain with linen coifs of small dimensions* [emphasis added]—I suppose for fear of pressing the head—and not reaching quite to the ears. If they are so weak in their hearing as not to be able to hear through a covering, I pity them. Let them know that the whole head constitutes 'the *woman*.' Its limits and boundaries reach as far as the place where the robe begins. The region of the veil is co-extensive with the space covered by the hair when unbound; in order that the necks too may be encircled.[60]

Both Ethiopic I and Arabic I make an exception for virgins not covering their heads either because they are obviously believers (Ethiopic I) or clearly virgins (Arabic I). While the rationale as to how this supposedly reveals their faith is not given, Ethiopic I and Arabic I are clearly reflecting the common cultural context in which virgins were not generally veiled.[61]

## 5. Ch. 19: Concerning the Imposition of the Hand

While TD II.5 specifies that the "teacher" should be a bishop or presbyter, Ethiopic I and Arabic I, together with all of the Oriental versions

60. ANF, IV, 37.

61. See Brown, *The Body and Society*, 80. See also Mary Rose D'Angelo, "Veils, Virgins and the Tongues of Men and Angels: Women's Heads as Sexual Members in Ancient Christianity," in Howard E. Schwartz and Wendy Doniger, eds., *Off with Her Head! The Denial of Women's Identity in Myth, Religion, and Culture* (Berkeley: University of California Press, 1995), 131–64.

and derivative documents, with the exception of CH 18, which does not specify status, reflect an earlier time period before the clericalization of this position and the need for only an ordained "teacher" to lay hands on the catechumens at their dismissal.[62] Further, if an early third-century date for ApTrad as a whole is correct, then Ch. 19.1 constitutes our sole witness in the first three centuries of the common era to this liturgical rite of handlaying and dismissal of catechumens. All other witnesses to this practice belong to the late fourth century (e.g., ApCons 8.6.1–9.11 in the context of dismissals of various categories of people in the eucharistic liturgy,[63] and in the *Pilgrimage of Egeria* within the context not only of prebaptismal catechesis itself but within a variety of liturgical occasions).[64]

The lack of early corroborating references, of course, does *not* mean that Ch. 19.1 does *not* belong to the early third century or that what we see in fourth-century documents does not reflect a consistent evolution in relationship with what came before. But it does suggest that considerable caution needs to be exercised here with regard to drawing firm conclusions from Ch. 19.1 about early third-century liturgical practice.

References to baptism by martyrdom or blood (Ch. 19.2) do occur in *some* third-century documents. In *De baptismo* 16, Tertullian refers to a "baptism by blood," but it is by no means clear here whether martyrdom is intended at all:

> Tertullian, *De baptismo* 16: As a matter of fact, we do have a second baptism; it too is once-for-all, that of blood, about which our Lord says, 'I have a baptism to be baptized with,' after he had already been baptized. As John had written, he had come by water and blood, so that he would be washed by water and glorified by blood. Likewise, by water he called us and by blood elected us. These two baptisms gushed forth from the wound in his pierced side, because those who believed in his blood were washed by water, and those who had washed in the water would need also [to be

62. See Ch. 3. For a summary of the use of the imposition of hands in the catechumenal rites, see Chase, "Rites Belonging to the Period of the Catechumenate," 65–79.

63. See *Apostolic Constitutions* 8, 6.1–9.11, in M. Metzger, *Les Constitutions Apostoliques*, III (Paris: Editions du Cerf, 1985), 150–67.

64. See Anne McGowan and Paul F. Bradshaw, *The Pilgrimage of Egeria: A New Translation of the* Itenerarium Egeriae *with Introduction and Commentary*, Alcuin Club Collection 93 (Collegeville, MN: Liturgical Press Academic, 2018), 149–57.

> washed] in blood. This second baptism replaces the baptism of water, when the latter has not been received, and it restores what has been lost.[65]

More obviously parallel to Ch. 19.2 than this ambiguous reference is the description of the death of Saturus and Perpetua in the famous *Passion of St. Perpetua*, sometimes ascribed to Tertullian himself:

> And immediately at the conclusion of the exhibition he was thrown to the leopard; and with one bite of his he was bathed with such a quantity of blood, that the people shouted out to him as he was returning, the testimony of his second baptism, 'Saved and washed, saved and washed.'[66]

Another reference comes from the middle of the third century in the context of the Decian persecution. Cyprian of Carthage writes that:

> [Catechumens who suffer martyrdom before they have received Baptism with water] are not deprived of the Sacrament of Baptism. Rather, they are baptized with the most glorious and greatest *Baptism of blood*, concerning which the Lord said that He had another Baptism with which He Himself was to be baptized.[67]

In a similar way Origen of Alexandria writes in his *Exhortation to Martyrdom*, 30:

> Let us remember also the sins that we have committed, and that except by baptism it is not possible to obtain remission (*aphesin*) of sins. . . . We are given, however, the *baptism of martyrdom*.[68]

While this reference in Ch. 19.1 is certainly consistent with the interpretation of baptism as martyrdom or in blood as it existed in the early and mid-third-century churches, including Alexandria, it tells us nothing really about the date or provenance of ApTrad in general. All versions and

65. English translation from Finn, *Early Christian Baptism and the Catechumenate*, 126.

66. *The Passion of Perpetua* 21.2. See also 18.3. ANF, III, 705.

67. *Letter* 73.22 [emphasis added].

68. ACW, 19, 171 [emphasis added]. See also Origen, *On Leviticus, hom. 2*, in P. F. Palmer, *Sources of Christian Theology: Sacraments and Forgiveness* (London: Westminster, 1959), 35–36.

derivative documents, with the exception of ApCons 8, from the fourth century on continue to include this reference even in a time period when martyrdom was no longer perceived as a possibility or threat.

## 6. Ch. 20: Concerning Those Who Are Initiated

Chs. 20 and 21 describe and interpret the rites of Christian initiation as a whole from election to baptism all the way to the first communion of the neophytes. There are several issues to be addressed here, especially with regard to origins and provenance.

Ch. 20.1-4 provides for an "election" and examination of candidates for baptism and inaugurates an unspecified period of final baptismal preparation including a ritual of daily exorcism. The rite begins with an examination of the lifestyles of the catechumens, testified to by those who would eventually be called sponsors or godparents, as to whether during the catechumenate they lived "virtuously, if they honored the widows, and if they did good works" (Ethiopic I). Because Ch. 20 makes a distinction between these two periods of catechumenal instruction—a three-year general catechumenate in Ch. 17 and an *election* for baptism here—this section has been commonly viewed as the first historical reference to two categories of "catechumens" in early Christianity: (1) catechumens or "hearers" themselves; and (2) after election, what various traditions refer to as the *electi* (Rome), *competentes* (in the non-Roman West), and *photizomenoi* (East). These particular terms for the final stage of preparation for baptism are well known only from the fourth century and beyond.

Unique to Egypt was also a shorter period of catechesis of forty days. However, this period, at least according to the CH 12, as well as BR- and Euch-AC, was rather strenuous. The catechumenate included an enrollment and intense examinations throughout. In fact, these examinations appear to be a key part of the Egyptian liturgical sources.[69] Catechumens

69. BR-AC, for instance, says: "So they enter into baptism. They are to give their names and then their lives are to be examined to see whether they are prepared for baptism, whether they have read the scriptures and whether they have learned the psalms. And so whoever it is should vouch for the one who is to be baptized, and so he should vouch for himself, knowing that he will give an account for him on the Day of Judgement. The prayer after the examination should then follow as follows." Translation ours. Alessandro Bausi, "The *Baptismal Ritual* in the Earliest Ethiopic Canonical Liturgical Collection," in

were expected to go to regular (if not daily) instruction and prayer, as well as visit widows and the sick. They could also participate, to a limited extent, in communal meals (CH 20).[70]

Against the commonly accepted theory that in the early Church catechumens were universally and regularly dismissed from the Liturgy of the Word *after* the reading of the Gospel and homily, recent scholarship has suggested that Ch. 20.2 may witness to an earlier tradition of withholding the reading of the Gospel itself from them until some kind of profession of faith and repentance had been made by them.[71] In fact, catechumens were actually not dismissed from the worship space, as is clear from Ch. 20.2, and elsewhere in ApTrad.[72] The following parallels may be indicative that such a practice was once the case:

> *Didascalia Apostolorum* 10: ii.39: " . . . when the heathen desire and promise to repent, saying, 'We believe,' we receive them into the congregation so that they may hear the word, but do not receive them into communion until they receive the seal and are fully initiated."[73]
>
> *The First Council of Orange,* Canon 18: "It was agreed that the Gospel shall be read to catechumens in all churches in our provinces."[74]
>
> *Ordo Romanus XI* (*Before* the reading of the Gospel): "They are admonished by the deacon thus: *Let the catechumens retire. Let anyone who is a catechumen retire. Let all catechumens go outside.*"[75]

---

*»Neugeboren aus Wasser und Heiligem Geist« Kölner Kolloquium zur Initiatio Christiana*, ed. Heinzgerd Brakmann, Tinatin Chronz, and Claudia Sode (Münster: Aschendorff Verlag, 2020), 65.3-10. German: "So treten sie in die Taufe. Sie sollen die Namen (an-) geben und darauf soll ihr Leben geprüft werden, ob ihr Gerüstetsein auf die Taufe (da) ist, ob sie die Schriften gelesen haben und ob sie die Psalmen gelernt haben. Und also soll, wer immer es sei, sich verbürgen für den, der getauft wird, und also soll er sich verbürgen, indem er weiß, daß er am Tage des Gerichtes um seinetwillen Rechenschaft ablegen wird. Es soll dann also das Gebet nach der Prüfung folgendermaßen folgen." See also Ethio-MC in Excursus below.

70. Maxwell Johnson, *Liturgy in Early Christian Egypt* (Cambridge: Grove Books, 1995), 10.

71. On this, see Paul F. Bradshaw, "The Gospel and the Catechumenate in the Third Century," *Journal of Theological Studies* 50 (1999): 143–52.

72. Stewart, *On the Apostolic Tradition*, 129.

73. Brock and Vasey, *Didascalia*, 12.

74. DBL, 228.

75. *Ordo Romanus* XI, 29; DBL, 198.

> *Gelasian Sacramentary* XXXIV: "The Exposition of the Gospels to the Elect at the Opening of the Ears: . . . . Beloved children, we shall open to you now the gospels, that is, the story of the divine life."[76]

Together with these, the absence of Gospel readings from the prebaptismal catechesis of Cyril of Jerusalem and the list of catechetical readings from the *Armenian Lectionary*,[77] what is known of the content of prebaptismal catechesis in the sermons of Ambrose of Milan, and the fact that in the West Syrian tradition (cf. John Chrysostom) some kind of interval may once have existed between the renunciation of Satan (*apotaxis*) and the especially "Syrian" act of adherence to Christ (*syntaxis*), may provide cumulative evidence of *an* early tradition of forming catechumens in the moral and ethical life of Christianity *before* "opening" to them more specific aspects of the Christian faith flowing from the Gospels. Alternatively, of course, there is also the possibility that this "reading of the Gospel" to the elect may have some correlation to what has been suggested for the early Alexandrian tradition was a "secret Gospel" read only to the initiated.[78]

There is great variation among the versions and derivative documents with regard to this period of final preparation and daily "exorcism." While Ethiopic I, Arabic I, the Sahidic, Arabic II, and TD II.6 refer now to daily *exorcism*, Ethiopic II refers only to daily *instruction* and the CH 19b to *neither*. Similarly, while Ethiopic I, Arabic I, the Sahidic version and TD II.6 all refer to the "bishop" himself "exorcising" the elect at some point close to the day of baptism, Arabic II and Ethiopic II do *not* refer to an episcopal exorcism at all but have the bishop "gain a solemn assurance" (Arabic II) or "bind every one of them [the candidates] by an oath" (Ethiopic II). Again, the CH 19b at this point would seem to closely parallel Arabic II and Ethiopic II in merely having the bishop ask several questions of the candidate after reading the Gospel over them.[79]

76. *Gelasian Sacramentary* XXXIV, in DBL, 172. According to OR XI, this "Exposition" was to take place at the third scrutiny.

77. See C. Renoux, *Le Codex armenien Jérusalm* 121 II (Turnhout, 1971), 239–55.

78. On this, see Morton Smith, *Clement of Alexandria and a Secret Gospel of Mark* (Cambridge: Harvard University Press, 1973); Thomas Talley, *The Origins of the Liturgical Year*, 2nd emended ed., (Collegeville, MN: Pueblo, 1991), 194ff.; and Paul F. Bradshaw and Maxwell E. Johnson, *The Origins of Feasts, Fasts, and Seasons in Early Christianity*, Alcuin Club Collections 86 (Collegeville, MN: Liturgical Press, 2011), 101ff.

79. For texts of the various editions here see *Herm.Com.* 2002, 104–5.

Further, while some references to prebaptismal exorcism do appear, especially within Gnostic literature of the first three centuries,[80] as well as in Cyprian,[81] explicit references to *daily* exorcism in the context of final baptismal preparation occur *only* in Eastern (West Syrian and Syro-Palestinian)—but not Western—liturgical sources of the fourth century, and are only known in Rome from Pope Siricius's *Letter to Himerius* 3:[82]

> Cyril of Jerusalem, *Cat.* 1. 5,6: Come regularly to the exorcism; attend the catechism regularly and remember what you are told. . . . Be regular at the meetings, not only now, when you are to give an account of your regularity to the clergy, but also after you have received the grace.[83]
>
> Egeria, *Peregrinatio* 46.1: For the custom here is such that those who come to baptism during those forty days in which there is fasting are first exorcized by the clergy early, as soon as the morning dismissal from the Anastasis has been done.[84]
>
> John Chrysostom, *Baptismal Homily* II.12: Since you are on the threshold of the time when you are to receive these great gifts, I must now teach you, as far as I can, the meaning of each of the rites, so that you may go from here with knowledge and a more assured faith. So you need to know why it is that after the daily instruction we send you off to hear the words of the exorcists.[85]

80. See E. A. Leeper, "From Alexandria to Rome: The Valentinian Connection to the Incorporation of Exorcism as a Prebaptismal Rite," in *Vigiliae Christianae* 44 (1990): 6–24, who argues that rites of prebaptismal exorcism in Rome come directly from Valentinian Gnostic rituals of initiation.

81. Cyprian, *Letter 69, To Magnus*, 15: "This is being carried out even today that through exorcists, by means of the human voice and the divine power, the devil is lashed out and burned out and tortured and, although he says often that he is going out and leaving the man of God, yet he deceives in what he has said and does what was first done through Pharoah with the same lying of obstinacy and of fraud." Finn, *Early Christian Baptism and the Catechumenate*, 136.

82. For a summary, see Nathan Chase, "Rites Belonging to the Period of the Catechumenate." See also *Herm.Com.* 2002, 109; Stewart, *On the Apostolic Tradition*, 130.

83. Text cited in AIRI, 11.

84. McGowan and Bradshaw, *The Pilgrimage of Egeria*, 189.

85. Text cited in AIRI, 162.

Thus, this reference in Ch. 20.3, appearing in Ethiopic I, Arabic I, Arabic II, and the Sahidic translation, then, may reflect a later development and be an addition to an earlier text. Bradshaw, in fact, underlines this reference in Ethiopic I as belonging to a such a development of episcopal rites, the second stratum in the document.[86] In this context, since scholars have wanted to argue that the document is third-century *Roman* in origin and content, it is important to note that the later Western liturgical documents we possess (e.g., Augustine and the Roman sacramentaries and *ordines*) seem to know nothing of a *daily* exorcism, and instead relate the exorcisms of the *electi* to the (three or seven) solemn scrutinies of the Lenten period. If Rome or North Africa *ever* had a practice of *daily* exorcism of *electi* we certainly know nothing about it. In this regard, the omission of this reference in Ethiopic II and CH 19b-c may indicate that the version of ApTrad at their disposal also did not yet contain it, or, alternatively, these two documents are merely reflecting the *single*, non-exorcistic "scrutiny," assumed to have been a characteristic of the early Alexandrian liturgical tradition.[87]

Closely related here, Ch. 20.3-4 refers to what would come to be called the "scrutinies," i.e., the solemn public examinations of the candidates at various intervals throughout the final period of baptismal preparation.[88] It is well known that these scrutinies, originally three in number within the *Roman* liturgical tradition and taking place on the third, fourth, and fifth Sundays in Lent (later expanded to seven and shifted to weekdays), were to become highly exorcistic in character.[89] Significantly, however, apart from the process of daily exorcism, Ch. 20.3 contains only *one* such

86. Bradshaw, *Apostolic Tradition*, 63.

87. On this, see Paul F. Bradshaw, "Baptismal Practice in Alexandria: Eastern or Western?," in idem., ed., *Essays on Early Eastern Initiation*, Alcuin/GROW Liturgical Study 8 (Bramcote/Nottingham: Grove Books, 1988), 10–12; idem., "Fourth Century Baptismal Practice: A Reevaluation of the Evidence"; and Johnson, *Liturgy in Early Christian Egypt*, 10.

88. For a summary, see Nathan Chase, "Rites Belonging to the Period of the Catechumenate."

89. See the *Sacramentarium Gelasianum* XXVI–XXVII in L. C. Mohlberg, ed., *Liber Sacramentorum Romanae Aeclesiae ordinis anni circuli* (Rome: Herder, 1960), 32–33 and 36–37; *Ordo Romanus XI*, 81, in Michel Andrieu, ed., *Les Ordines Romani*, vol. 2 (Louvain: Spicilegium Sacrum Lovaniense, 1948), 442; Maxwell Johnson, *The Rites of Christian Initiation: Their Evolution and Interpretation*, rev. and exp. ed. (Collegeville,

solemn scrutiny and tells us nothing about when during the final preparation process it was to take place (other than near to baptism). Further, since the Sahidic, Arabic II, and TD II.6 all place this scrutiny within an overall exorcistic context (i.e., the daily exorcisms of the candidates and the fact that the bishop is not simply to examine but to exorcise), may suggest that both Ethiopic II and CH 19c reflect here an earlier tradition before references to *daily exorcism* or to an exorcistic scrutiny rite by the bishop were added. Both Ethiopic II and the CH 19c contain a scrutiny which is clearly an examination alone.

It is also quite likely that within an even earlier stage in the evolution of the document there was no reference to the bishop at all at this point in the text and that this entire section dealing with daily exorcism and an episcopal exorcism is a later addition. That is, up to this point in the document, references to the bishop in the process of Christian initiation have been few and far between. While bishops, presbyters, or deacons have been referred to in *some* of the versions or derivative documents in relationship to teaching or blessing, it has been the catechumens or candidates themselves who have functioned as the subjects of the various directives. From this point on, however, rubrical directions concerning the various roles of the ordained ministers in Christian initiation—bishops, presbyters, and deacons—will appear with greater frequency and the versions will now alternate between more general directives concerning Christian initiation and specific directives regarding the ministers. In fact, Jean-Paul Bouhot suggested that the rites of initiation in Chs. 20–21 reflected various strata of development: an earlier *Roman* document focusing on the role of the bishop; and an "African" interpolation beginning with "at the time fixed for baptism" in Ch. 21.6 focusing on the roles of presbyters and deacons, and continuing throughout the remainder of Ch. 21.[90] While we agree here on the presence of strata in the document, we follow *Herm.Com.* 2002 and Bradshaw in holding that

MN: Pueblo, 1999), 164ff.; and Aidan Kavanagh, *The Shape of Baptism* (New York: Pueblo, 1978), 57–60, 67.

90. See J.-P Bouhot, *La confirmation, sacrement de la communion ecclésiale* (Lyon, 1968), 38–45. See also R. Cabié, "L'ordo de l'Initiation chrétienne dans la 'Tradition apostolique' d'Hippolyte de Rome," in *Mens concordet voci, pour Mgr. A. G. Martimort* (Paris, 1983), 543–58.

the earliest layer was not that of the bishop, but a simple rite without specifying any ministers, similar to that appearing in *Didache* 7 and Justin Martyr's *First Apology* 65. The second stratum would be that of adding those materials peculiar to bishops (no earlier than the third century), and the third specifying roles for deacons and presbyters, especially when they presided in the absence of bishops.[91]

The concluding phrase in this opening section of Ch. 20.4—"for a foreign entity cannot dwell in him" (Ethiopic I), "since it is never possible to hide the stranger" (Sahidic), "because he has not withstood the stranger" (Arabic I), "because it is never possible that an outsider should be baptized" (Arabic II), or "because it is not proper to baptise an utter alien" (Ethiopic II)—poses a difficulty in trying to discern the stranger or alien. According to both Geoffrey Cuming and Bernard Botte, the original Greek word translated here as stranger, outsider, or alien was "almost certainly '*allotrios*,' which was used of the Devil."[92] If so, it is not the seemingly impossible situation of a baptismal *candidate* being at this point in the catechumenal process a stranger, *outsider*, or *alien*. Rather, the episcopal exorcism (at least in the Sahidic) is concerned with revealing or determining whether or not the power of the demonic stranger, outsider, or *alien* has been overcome.[93]

Ch. 20.5-10 now shifts to immediate preparation for baptism, including prebaptismal bathing on Thursday, the two-day fast, and the day and time for the rites. The reference in Ch. 20.5 to a washing is consistent with North African practice as seen in Augustine, *Ep.* 54.10.[94]

Apart from the versions and derivative documents, there are no parallels in other liturgical sources in support of the prohibition against the baptism of menstruating women in Ch. 20.6. According to R. Werblowsky, there is also no precedent for such a prohibition in Rabbinic Judaism, where menstruation did not appear to constitute an obstacle in the

91. See *Herm.Com.* 2002, 108; and Bradshaw, *Apostolic Tradition*, 63–64.

92. Bernard Botte, *La Tradition apostolique de saint Hippolyte: Essai de reconstitution* (1963; 5th ed. with addenda by Albert Gerhards; Liturgiewissenschaftliche Quellen und Forschungen 39; Munster: Aschendorff, 1989), 34n6, henceforth Botte, *La Tradition*; Cuming, *Hippolytus*, 17.

93. See also below, Ch. 21.5.

94. Stewart, *On the Apostolic Tradition*, 131.

baptism of female proselytes.[95] Early Christianity, of course, did inherit from Leviticus (see especially Lev 15) the notion of ritual impurity or pollution resulting from menstruation and sexual emissions, but, according to the very limited evidence, this was related to eucharistic reception and not to baptism. So, Dionysius of Alexandria (248–265 CE), for example, states that "menstruous women ought not to come to the Holy Table, or touch the Holy of Holies, nor to churches, but pray elsewhere."[96] Such prohibitions would continue through the early medieval period.[97] But this was by no means a universal position. *Didascalia Apostolorum* 6.21, in fact, argues strongly that neither menstruation nor any kind of sexual emission constitutes ritual impurity or serves as an impediment to eucharistic reception.

With regard to this verse, Werblowsky conjectures "that the menstruous woman is *e definitione* still in the grip of the demonic powers," but he offers no evidence in support of seeing a relationship between menstruation and the demonic.[98] The simplest explanation is that this prohibition against baptizing menstruous women is a baptismal extension and application of the inherited notion of ritual impurity encountered elsewhere in relationship to the Eucharist.

*Didache* 7:4, the *First Apology* 61 of Justin Martyr, and Tertullian's *De baptismo* are clear already that some kind of fast was part of baptism's immediate preparation:

> *Didache* 7:4: Before the baptism, let the person baptizing and the person being baptized—and others who are able—fast; tell the one being baptized to fast one or two [days] before.[99]

> Justin Martyr, *First Apology*, 61: As many as are persuaded and believe that those things which we teach and describe are true, and undertake to live accordingly, are taught to pray and ask God, while fasting, for the forgiveness of their sins; and we pray and fast with them.[100]

95. R. Werblowsky, "On the Baptismal Rite According to St. Hippolytus," *Studia Patristica* 64, 2 (1957): 97.

96. Dionysius of Alexandria, *Canon* 2; NPNF, second series, XIV, 600.

97. Brown, *The Body and Society*, 433–34 and 145–46.

98. Werblowsky, "On the Baptismal Rite," 97.

99. Niederwimmer, *The Didache*, 125.

100. DBL, 2.

> Tertullian, *De Baptismo*, 20: Those who are at the point of entering upon baptism ought to pray, with frequent prayers, fastings, bendings of the knee, and all-night vigils, along with the confession of all their sins, so as to make a copy of the baptism of John.[101]

Indeed, all that this section does is to specify the particular days for the immediate preparatory fast, for other elements, and for the time of baptism itself.

The reference to two days of fasting in Ch. 20.6-9 "on the day of preparation and the Sabbath" (Ethiopic I) or "Friday" (Arabic II and Ethiopic II) in Ch. 20.6 and the immediate prebaptismal rites of exorcism (verses 7-8) taking place "on the Sabbath" (Ethiopic I) or "Saturday" (Arabic I and II, as well as Ethiopic II) have led to the common assumption that the all-night vigil referred to in verse 9 took place between Saturday night and cockcrow (see Ch. 21.1) on *Sunday* morning. Hence, the pattern of ApTrad here is merely the equivalent to what later Roman evidence reports as the ritual pattern of bathing on Maundy Thursday, fasting on Good Friday, immediate preparation for baptism taking place on Holy Saturday morning, and the rites themselves being celebrated during the Paschal Vigil between Holy Saturday night and Easter Sunday morning. Gregory Dix, for example, added the subtitle, "Friday and Saturday in Holy Week" before Ch. 20.7, with the additional subtitle "The Paschal Vigil" before Ch. 20.9.[102] But the text does not say this! It is worth noting that Arabic I adds an interesting addition to Ch. 20.9: "And they shall stay up that night and the [story of] creation shall be read to them." It is not clear, however, what to make of this addition.

Thanks to Gregory Dix and Bernard Botte, and followed today by Alistair Stewart, it has been traditionally assumed that Holy Week and Paschal baptism are what is being referred to here. TD II.8 ("in the forty days of Pascha," and the candidates being "exorcized until the middle of the night [on] Saturday") can be taken in support of this interpretation. The reference to the candidates "*eating*" after their Thursday bath in the CH

101. DBL, 9.

102. Gregory Dix, *Apostolike Paradosis: The Treatise on the Apostolic Tradition of St. Hippolytus of Rome* (New York: Macmillan, 1937; 2nd ed. with preface and corrections by Henry Chadwick, London: SPCK, 1968; reprinted Ridgefield, CT: Morehouse, 1992), 32, henceforth Dix, *The Apostolic Tradition*.

19b, however, would appear to directly contradict Paschal baptism since it would mean breaking the Paschal fast on the Thursday of Holy Week. Similarly, the versions themselves are not clear in this context as to which days are intended. Ethiopic II, for example, makes no reference to *any* vigil taking place and the references to the "Sabbath" or "Saturday" in all three versions (Ethiopic I, Arabic I, and Ethiopic II) need not be interpreted as indicating Saturday *morning* for the immediate rites of final baptismal preparation. That is, depending upon how *Sabbath* is to be interpreted, it remains possible that the Friday fast is to be followed immediately by these rites at the *beginning* of the Sabbath, namely, after *sundown* on Friday. If so, the vigil referred to in verse 9 would be a Friday to Saturday, *not* Saturday to Sunday, vigil.[103] While Ch 21.1 will make it clear that baptism itself is to take place at "cockcrow" after an all-night vigil, the fact that the text does not indicate this as *Easter*, or necessarily even *Sunday*, may be a sign of antiquity. In his *Commentary on Daniel,* Hippolytus of Rome *does* make a clear association between baptism and Easter:

> On that day [the Pasch] the bath is prepared in the Garden for those who are burning and the Church . . . is presented to God as a pure bride; and faith and charity, like her [Susanna's] companions, prepare the oil and the unguents for those being washed. What are the unguents but the commandments of the Word? What is the oil but the power of the Holy Spirit, with which, like perfume, believers are anointed after the bath?[104]

Paschal baptism is likewise becoming a preference for the North African tradition in the early third century, as witnessed to by Tertullian:

> Tertullian, *De Baptismo*, 19: The Passover offers the day of most solemnity for baptism, when our Lord's passion, into which we are baptized, was completed. . . . After that, Pentecost is a most joyful time for conferring baptisms, when also the resurrection of the Lord was frequently made known to the disciples and the grace of the Holy Spirit. . . . However,

103. See Jean Michel Hanssens, *La liturgie d'Hippolyte: Ses documents, son titulaire, ses origines et son charactère*, Orientalia Christiana Analecta 155 (Rome: Pontificium Institutum Orientalium Studiorum, 1959), 448–51.

104. SC 14, 100. English translation by Bradshaw, "'*Diem baptismo sollemniorem*,'" 138.

every day is the Lord's day: any hour, any season, is suitable for baptism. If there is a difference of solemnity, there is no difference in the grace.[105]

If, therefore, ApTrad is the result of *Hippolytan* authorship, the absence of any reference to Easter initiation in this text is strange. And, since Pascha is a topic dealt with in Ch. 33, it would be logical to assume that *if* Easter Baptism was the practice intended here there would be *some* indication of it in the extant versions. But there is not. The reference to these things taking place "in the forty days of Pascha" in the TD II.8 cannot be taken as evidence against this for the simple reason that by the time of the TD both the forty-day Lent and Paschal baptism are clearly established in the East.[106] And, as noted above, the reference to the candidates "eating" after their Thursday bath in the CH 19b would directly contradict Paschal baptism since it would mean breaking the Paschal fast on the Thursday of Holy Week.

Furthermore, the reference to a *Friday* fast before baptism need refer to nothing other than baptismal candidates joining in the traditional weekly fast days, a tradition as old as *Didache* 8:1. With the absence of any explicit reference to *Easter* baptism in this section, the most logical assumption, as Raniero Cantalamessa notes, is that this section is referring to a structure and process that would have been followed *whenever* baptisms were celebrated.[107]

Because Egypt apparently knew a baptismal rite which was celebrated on the *sixth day* of the sixth week of a forty-day prebaptismal period of fasting and preparation, which was not paschal in orientation or character,[108] J. M. Hanssens concluded that this section of ApTrad, with its possible Friday to Saturday baptismal vigil, was not Roman but Alexandrian in origin.[109] If Hanssens's hypothesis on the Alexandrian origins of this document has not been widely accepted by scholars, his

105. Bradshaw, "'*Diem baptismo sollemniorem*,'" 138–39.

106. On the development of Paschal baptism in early Christianity, see Bradshaw, "'*Diem baptismo sollemniorem*,'" 137–47.

107. See R. Cantalamessa, *Ostern in der alten Kirche* (Bern, 1981), 79.

108. See Talley, *The Origins of the Liturgical Year*, 163–224; and Bradshaw and Johnson, *The Origins of Feasts, Fasts, and Seasons in Early Christianity*.

109. Hanssens, *La liturgie d'Hippolyte*, 450–51.

caveat against making assumptions about the text based on later Roman practice, especially with regard to the particular days of the week in question, still merits strong consideration. Nowhere in Chs. 15–21 is it ever indicated that Paschal baptism is the practice intended in ApTrad. And, thanks to Ch. 20.6-9, it is also not clear if the baptismal rites themselves were to take place even on a Sunday at all.

The exorcism and other rites performed by the bishop at the Sabbath or Saturday gathering in Ch. 20.8-9 do not find any explicit parallels in other Christian literature from the first three centuries. Episcopal ceremonies equivalent to these (i.e., a final exorcism of the *electi* and *apertio* or *ephatha* rites) on Holy Saturday morning are known from Ambrose of Milan in the late fourth century as well as from later Roman practice.[110] And, the rite of breathing (insufflation) upon the faces of the candidates and the signing of their foreheads, ears, and noses (viewed by Bradshaw as a later addition) by the bishop[111] has often been interpreted as an *apertio* or *ephatha*.[112] Its close association with the exorcism immediately preceding it suggests, alternatively, that it is to be seen here as more of a "closing" of the senses to evil than as an "opening" of them for the reception of catechesis. The phrase "that they flee from them and not return to them ever again" may refer to an actual liturgical formula of exorcism.[113] The rubrical directions in Ethiopic II, where the bishop is only to lay hands on the *electi* and breathe on them, appear less developed than in the Sahidic or Arabic II, where, like Ethiopic I and Arabic I, both insufflation and signing of the foreheads, ears, and nostrils, in addition to a handlaying, are present. It is quite possible here that Ethiopic II reflects an earlier form of the text.

The baptismal vigil referred to in Ch. 20.9 would certainly be consistent with the Paschal Vigil. Easter, however, was not the only occasion for common public vigils in Christian antiquity and it should not automatically be assumed that this is what is intended here. The evidence for vigils other than the Paschal Vigil may be sparse for the first three centuries of the Christian era, but it is not completely absent (e.g., Tertullian, *Ad uxorem* 2.4; Pontius, *De vita et passione Cypriani* 15; and Canon 35 of

110. See Ambrose, *De Sacramentis* I.2.

111. Bradshaw, *Apostolic Tradition*, 67–68.

112. See AIRI, 16.

113. See Cuming, *Hippolytus*, 17. Cuming refers here to Mark 9:25 as a possible biblical source for this formula.

the Council of Elvira). Later evidence indicates that, together with the Paschal Vigil itself, vigils on other feasts (e.g., Pentecost and Epiphany), Sundays, at the tombs of martyrs, and on other occasions were common and widespread.[114]

The practice of the faithful presenting their offerings or oblations at the Eucharist in Ch. 20.10 is well attested in early Christian literature,[115] although apart from the versions and derivative documents there are no explicit parallels to the newly baptized doing so, except as we will see in the Egyptian sources. That the practice did exist in some places at the baptismal Eucharist, however, is certainly indicated by Ambrose's refusal to allow it at Milan. There, the newly baptized were not permitted to offer oblations at the Eucharist until the following Sunday.[116] The admonition against bringing anything else with them at this point—except for the "except one loaf each for thanksgiving" in Ethiopic I, or "that which each one will bring in for the Eucharist" in the Sahidic—is underscored again in the next section (see Ch. 21.5 below) where women are instructed to lay aside their jewelry before being baptized.

However, the differences between the Ethiopic I and Sahidic here allow for the possibility that more than just "bread" may be allowed to be supplied according to the text. What may be implied is the bringing in of things needed for the baptismal and eucharistic celebrations, of which more than just a loaf would be required. The bringing in of some sort of offering—oil, water, bread—was actually a common practice in the Egyptian initiatory tradition. Sarapion Prayers 5, 6, and 17 describe the bringing of oil and water to the church, the last of which is a prayer for the sick.[117] Additionally, BR-AC describe the bringing of bread, oil, and water to the church during Lent, clearly in connection with the initiatory rituals.[118]

114. On vigils in Christian antiquity see Robert Taft, *The Liturgy of the Hours in East and West: The Origins of the Divine Office and Its Meaning for Today* (Collegeville, MN: Liturgical Press, 1986), 165–77.

115. See Irenaeus, *Adv.Haer.*, IV.xxviii.2; Tertullian, *De Corona*, 4; and Cyprian, *de Op. et Eleemos*, 15.

116. See Ambrose, *In Ps. 118 Expos.*, Prologue 2, as cited in AIRI, 39–40.

117. Maxwell Johnson, *The Prayers of Sarapion of Thmuis: A Literary, Liturgical, and Theological Analysis*, Orientalia Christiana Analecta 249 (Rome: Pontifico Istituto Orientale, 1995), 52/53 and 62/63.

118. Bausi, "The *Baptismal Ritual*," 65.22-37 and 67.1-7.

Nubian archaeological evidence at Banganarti may also point to this practice.[119] There are two churches at Banganarti: (1) the Lower Church, which was built in roughly three phases from the sixth/seventh to the eleventh centuries, and (2) the Upper Church, which was built in the eleventh century. The extant fonts are from the Lower Church, the first of which is dated to the sixth/seventh century and was recessed in the floor. A second font was constructed sometime either in the first half of the eighth century or after 836 CE.[120] While there is not much more evidence that Banganarti can provide, other than its function as a place for baptisms and eventually pilgrimage, it is worth noting that there were many *amphorae,* some dated from the sixth/seventh century, found throughout the Lower Church and apparently placed there during the construction of the Upper Church in the eleventh century. What makes this odd, as Bogdan Żurawski notes, is that "these ceramics had to have been stored somewhere for at least three hundred years before they were thrown into the [Lower Church] interior. . . . Among the ceramics collected, complete and nearly complete examples were found; an indication that the material had to have been deposited somewhere nearby, most probably outside the church, and then swept into its interior."[121] Żurawski has argued these fragments were associated with either the baptismal service—specifically the consecration of the font, the process of consecrating the church, church festivals, or even philanthropic activity.[122]

119. For more on the archeological work done at Banganarti, see Bogdan Żurawski, *St. Raphael Church I at Banganarti Mid-Sixth to Mid-Eleventh Century: An Introduction to the Site and the Epoch*, African Reports, 10.2012 (Gdańsk: Muzeum Archeologiczne w Gdańsku, 2012); Bogdan Żurawski, *Kings and Pilgrims: St Raphael Church II at Banganarti, Mid-Eleventh to Mid-Eighteenth Century*, Banganarti 2 (Warszawa: Wydawnictwo Neriton: Instytut Kultur Śródziemnomorskich i Orientalnych Polskiej Akademii Nauk, 2014). See also *Baptisteries of the Early Christian World*, ed. Robin Jensen, Nathan Dennis, and Nathan Chase (Turnhout: Brill, forthcoming), Cat. #X.2.5.

120. Later a second square/rectangle font was added, but the older font was still usable. That font was about 1 m square and raised above the ground. Żurawski notes at one point that "the upper tank was installed . . . no earlier than the first half of the eighth century," but elsewhere attributes its construction to Phase 3 of the Lower Church, which is dated after 836; see Żurawski, *St. Raphael Church I at Banganarti Mid-Sixth to Mid-Eleventh Century*, 149n25, 167n178, and 171.

121. Żurawski, *St. Raphael Church I*, 184.

122. Żurawski, 182–86.

There are some issues with these vessels being connected to the baptismal rite. As noted in the chapter "Region X: Eastern North Africa and Nilotic Lands (Egypt, Eritrea, Ethiopia, Sudan)" in *Baptisteries of the Early Christian World*:

> Żurawski's assertions for the excessive pottery sherds appear plausible. Yet, his curious reference to Coptic consecration rites, which calls for breaking the pottery vessels used in both the consecration of a font or church, seems less likely. According to the Coptic consecration rite attributed to Severus ibn al-Muqaffaʿ, the tenth-century bishop of al-Ashmunīn, only seven amphorae were used in the consecration rite and that the broken pieces were distributed to the congregation. Furthermore, Horner's fourteenth-century account of Coptic consecration rites does not specify the number of amphorae used nor the pottery sherds' distribution.[123]

However, the Egyptian liturgical evidence above does provide some support to Żurawski's interpretation. These jars could very well be associated with these rituals, which in turn appear to have some connection to the rites of initiation. Banganarti may provide material evidence for the water rituals described in *Sarapion* and BR-AC.

At the same time, as we will see in Ch. 21.1, these jars may have also been used simply for filling up or administering the rites of initiation. Many vessels would have needed to be used to carry water for the baptismal ritual in baptisteries that did not have regular water inflows and outflows.[124] This would have been even more so the case in fonts with a sand floor, like at Banganarti, or those fonts that could not hold water. Thus, each catechumen would need water poured over them from a jar.

123. Nathan Chase, Mary Farag, and Arsany Paul, "Region X: Eastern North Africa and Nilotic Lands (Egypt, Eritrea, Ethiopia, Sudan)," in *Baptisteries of the Early Christian World*, ed. Robin Jensen, Nathan Dennis, and Nathan Chase (Turnhout: Brill, forthcoming). See also George Horner, *The Service for the Consecration of a Church and Altar according to the Coptic Rite* (London: Harrison and Sons, 1902), 29 (Arabic)/30 (English); Julius Assfalg, *Die ordnung des priestertums* (Cairo: Publications du Centre d'Etudes Orientales de la Custodie Franciscaine de Terre-Sainte, 1955), 48–49 (Arabic)/125–27 (German).

124. Robin Jensen, "Chapter 1: Baptism and Baptisteries in Early Christianity," in *Baptisteries of the Early Christian World*, ed. Robin Jensen, Nathan Dennis, and Nathan Chase (Turnhout: Brill, forthcoming).

## 7. Ch. 21. On Baptism

The title of Ch. 21 in Arabic I, "Concerning the matters of baptism," as also in all of the Oriental versions, is much clearer and more descriptive of the contents of this chapter than is Ethiopic I's title, which refers inexplicably to "anointing" alone. Bradshaw notes that the reference to baptism taking place at "cockcrow," roughly 3:00 AM, has no particular significance since it would have been natural to conclude a nocturnal vigil at this third division or watch of the night.[125] The one exception here is in TD, in which no reference to time of day is made when baptism is to occur other than at night, presumably at the Easter Vigil.

With the exception of Ethiopic I, which has no reference to a blessing of water, all other versions agree that the water for baptism to be prayed over at cockcrow in Ch. 21.1 is water either flowing into or collected in a "pool" (κολυμβήθρα, Sahidic), "font" (Arabic II), "place of baptism," or "baptistry" (Ethiopic II), reflecting, undoubtedly, a shift from running or living water to baptismal "fonts."[126] Here again, the logistics mentioned above with regard to Banganarti may indicate that vessels filled with water were brought in for the initiatory rituals. The derivative documents, however, contain no equivalent terms and state clearly that the baptismal water is to be "water from a river, running and pure, prepared and sanctified" (CH 19c) or, simply, water "pure and flowing" (TD II.8), and suggest with Ethiopic I a similarity to *Didache* 7.1-3:

> *Didache* 7:1-3: As for baptism, baptize in this way: Having said all this beforehand, baptize in the name of the Father and of the Son and of the Holy Spirit, in running water. If you . . . do not have running water, however, baptize in another kind of water; if you cannot [do so] in cold [water], then [do so] in warm [water]. But if you have neither, pour water on the head thrice in the name of Father and Son and Holy Spirit.[127]

Kurt Niederwimmer has also drawn attention to the parallels here between *Didache* and ApTrad Ch. 21 in this context.[128] And, although prayer

125. Bradshaw, *Apostolic Tradition*, 69.

126. For a summary, see Jensen, "Chapter 1: Baptism and Baptisteries in Early Christianity."

127. Niederwimmer, *The Didache*, 125.

128. See Niederwimmer, 128–29.

over the baptismal water (Ch. 21.2-3) has third-century parallels in Tertullian (*De baptismo* 4),[129] Cyprian of Carthage (*Ep.70.1*),[130] and the *Syrian Acts of the Apostles*,[131] the absence of references to such a prayer in Ethiopic I and TD II.8 may well indicate, with both *Didache* 7 and Justin Martyr (*1 Apology 65)*, a sign of antiquity. That is, there is no need to bless water that is already alive with spirit and life. Only later would this come to be seen as a necessity. Thus, Stewart might be correct that likely there was originally no blessing of water, since the Latin is lacuna here and Ethiopic I does not mention a blessing.[132]

The remainder of this "introductory" section (Ch. 21.4-5) provides a rather complete description of the order in which the candidates are to be baptized, first, "children" (Ethiopic I and Arabic I), second "grown men," and, finally, "the women." Although, apart from the derivative documents, there is no exact parallel to this baptismal "order" anywhere else; the practice of infant initiation is attested for the third century also in Tertullian,[133] Cyprian,[134] and Origen of Alexandria.[135] It is important to note, however, that these children or those "who cannot answer for themselves" here are not necessarily infants but could well include children from infancy all the way to the age of seven years (i.e., the ancient Roman interpretation of "*infantes*"). Even after attaining the age of seven in Roman society, and until puberty, children were limited as to their legal

129. Tertullian, *De Baptismo*, 4: "Therefore, in consequence of that ancient original privilege, all waters, when God is invoked, acquire the sacred significance of conveying sanctity: for at once the Spirit comes down from heaven and stays upon the waters, sanctifying them from within himself, and when thus sanctified they absorb the power of sanctifying. . . . Thus when the waters have in some sense acquired healing power by an angel's intervention, the spirit is in those waters corporally washed, while the flesh is in those same waters spiritually cleansed." DBL, 7.

130. Cyprian, *Letter 70, To Januarius,* 1: "It is required then that the water should first be cleansed and sanctified by the priest, that it may wash away by its baptism the sins of the man that is baptized." DBL, 11.

131. For texts, see DBL, 15–22.

132. Stewart, *On the Apostolic Tradition*, 136–37 and 143–44.

133. *De baptismo,* 18; DBL, 8–9.

134. *Epistle* 64, ANF V, 354. See also David Holeton, *Infant Communion—Then and Now*, Grove Liturgical Study 27 (Bramcote: Grove Books, 1981).

135. *Homilies on Leviticus* 8.3, as cited by J. Quasten, *Patrology*, vol. 2 (London: Westminster, 1964), 83.

rights to conduct their own affairs and, if not under the direct authority of their fathers (the *paterfamilias*), they were often placed under the system of tutelage. A similar parallel with betrothal and marriage laws and customs in the ancient Roman world wherein marriages themselves were often arranged by the *paterfamilias* may also be operative here.[136] Mary Rose D'Angelo has suggested that women would have been baptized last in this order because "It was not expected that [women] would be aroused by seeing the men baptized,"[137] something that could not be assumed of men watching naked women being baptized.

The phrase "loosening all the hair and laying aside their jewelry" (Ch. 21.5) is attested in all the versions and documents. According to Dix, consistent with his interpretation that the baptismal rite in ApTrad is derived from Jewish proselyte baptismal practice, this loosening of the hair and laying aside of jewelry was "a custom directly drawn from Jewish lustrations."[138] It has been argued by others that in the ancient world knotted hair was frequently viewed as a dwelling place for demons and evil spirits and so its loosening is be interpreted in an exorcistic or anti-demonic manner.[139] "But it also suggests," writes R. J. Z. Werblowsky:

> the Rabbinic rules for the monthly lustration of women after the menses. Loosening the hair (and even washing and combing it) is enjoined by the Talmud and all later rituals as necessary before immersion. . . . The Talmud gives as one of the reasons for this ordinance (ascribed to Ezra

136. See S. Dixon, *The Roman Family* (Baltimore: Johns Hopkins University Press, 1992), 64–65, 105–6, and 117–18; and J. E. Evans, *Law and Family in Late Antiquity: The Emperor Constantine's Marriage Legislation* (Oxford: Clarendon Press, 1995), 140ff. Our thanks to Professor Blake Leyerle of the University of Notre Dame for directing us to these references.

137. D'Angelo, "Veils, Virgins, and the Tongues of Men and Angels," 158n6.

138. Dix, *The Apostolic Tradition*, m. On the difficulties concerning the origins of Jewish proselyte baptism, see A. Collins, "The Origin of Christian Baptism," in LWSS, 35–57.

139. See F. Gavin, "Rabbinic Parallels in Early Church Orders," *Hebrew Union College Annual* 6 (1929): 57–67; and W. C. van Unnik, "Les Chevaux défaits des femmes baptisés: un rite de baptême dans l'Ordre ecclésiastique d'Hippolyte," *Vigiliae Christianae* 1 (1947): 77–100.

and therefore, perhaps, a tradition of some standing) the fear that 'a knot may have formed itself in the hair,' thereby impeding the access of water.[140]

Hence, whatever its origins or explicit relationship to Jewish proselyte baptism may be, the loosening of the hair may simply have been an attempt "to ensure that all the hair got wet."[141] Some kind of exorcistic or anti-demonic context, however, may be implied in the phrase in Ch. 21.5 "no one is to have anything with them as they go down into the water" (Ethiopic I), or "let nothing foreign down into the water with them" (Sahidic). The Greek word ἀλλότριον, i.e., "a foreign or alien object," appearing here in the Sahidic version, may suggest that the jewelry to be laid aside before baptism is not simply jewelry but an object such as an amulet or charm, which was interpreted as being "in the power of the Devil,"[142] which was dealt with in ApTrad 20 above. It is also worth noting that in the Egyptian context, CA 44 (Arabic and Coptic) has an interesting parallel to ApTrad Ch. 21.5: "No priest shall suffer his wife to adorn herself with gold or silver or precious stones or with antimony or anklets or head-dresses or costly stuffs; for this guise is not for the children of the church" (Arabic).[143] SD talks also about no jewelry in the worship space in VIII.4.[144]

As a concluding note here, with the exception of the mention of the "bishop" in the TD II.8, none of the versions or CH 19 assigns any baptismal roles to any specific ministers in this context. Hence, it would not be unreasonable to conjecture, then, that at one stage in the development of Ch. 21.1-5, before the addition of cockcrow, the development of fonts, and an initial blessing of the water, something very much like Ethiopic I would have constituted the original core of the initiation rites up to the baptismal plunge, with clear and distinct parallels to both *Didache 7* and Justin Martyr's *1 Apol. 65*.

140. Werblowsky, "On the Baptismal Rite," 99.

141. Cuming, *Hippolytus*, 18.

142. Cuming, 18. See also Cuming, 17, and Ch. 20.8 above.

143. Riedel and Crum, *The Canons of Athanasius of Alexandria: The Arabic and Coptic Versions*, 34. For the Coptic, see 119.

144. H. Hyvernat, "Le Syntagma Doctrinae," in *Studia Patristica: Études d'ancienne Littérature Chrétienne*, ed. Pierre Batiffol (Paris: Leroux, 1890), 153–54.

After having provided rather complete baptismal instructions in ApTrad Ch. 21.1-5, the versions and derivative documents of ApTrad Ch. 21.6-10 now seem to begin anew with specific instructions including: (1) the initiatory roles of bishops, presbyters, and deacons in the consecration of the two baptismal oils (the "oil of thanksgiving" and that of "exorcism") and other places in the rite, reflecting both what Bradshaw refers to as stages two and three in the development of ApTrad; (2) the renunciation of Satan and a profession of faith; (3) the prebaptismal (exorcistic) anointing; and (4) entry into the baptismal waters. All of this is quite distinct from what has come immediately before in the document and, in the process, even duplicates some of what has already been said there (e.g., references to the time fixed for baptism [although cockcrow itself is not mentioned], another prebaptismal exorcism, and the nakedness of the candidates).

Tertullian refers both to a consecration or blessing of the baptismal waters (*De Baptismo* 4) and to a renunciation of Satan before baptism, but there is no evidence before the mid- to late fourth century (e.g., in Sarapion of Thmuis,[145] Cyril of Jerusalem,[146] and John Chrysostom[147])

145. *The Prayers of Sarapion of Thmuis*, 15: "We anoint with this oil those who approach this divine rebirth, imploring that our Lord Christ Jesus may work in it and reveal healing and strength-producing power through this oil, and may heal their soul, body, spirit from every sign of sin and lawlessness or satanic taint . . . And, when they have been molded again through this oil and purified through the bath and renewed in the Spirit, they will be strong enough to conquer against other opposing works and deceits of this life which come near them." Johnson, *The Prayers of Sarapion of Thmuis*, 63.

146. Cyril of Jerusalem, *Mystagogical Catechesis* 2.3: "Then, when ye were stripped, ye were anointed with exorcized oil from the very hairs of your head to your feet, and were made partakers of the good olive tree, Jesus Christ." DBL, 29.

147. John Chrysostom, *Baptismal Homilies*, 3.27: "Hence, God anoints your countenance and stamps thereon the sign of the cross. In this way does God hold in check all the frenzy of the Evil One; for the devil will not dare to look upon such a sight. Just as if he had beheld the rays of the sun and had leaped away, so will his eyes be blinded by the sight of your face and he will depart; for through the chrism the cross is stamped upon you. The chrism is a mixture of olive oil and unguent; the unguent is for the bride, the oil is for the athlete. And that you may again know that it is not a man but God himself who anoints you by the hand of the priest, listen to St Paul when he says: *It is God who is warrant for us and for you in Christ, who has anointed us.* After he anoints all your limbs with this ointment, you will be secure and able to hold the serpent in check; you will suffer no harm." DBL, 37.

of the use of "exorcised oil" for a prebaptismal exorcism. Similarly, prayers, or references to prayers, for the *consecration* of baptismal oils are known to us only from a variety of relatively early (mid-third century) and later *Eastern* liturgical sources but not—except for a passing reference in Cyprian to the consecration of oils at the Eucharist (*Letter 70, to Januarius*, 2)—from any available sources in the West. For that matter, there is no early *Western* evidence anywhere to corroborate the presence of a prebaptismal *anointing* at all prior to the witness of Ambrose of Milan, where it *does* appear immediately *before* the renunciation itself.[148] In the Syrian East, however, such an anointing—but *pneumatic* and *messianic* rather than exorcistic in orientation—is attested much earlier.[149] Contemporary scholarship has argued that a prebaptismal anointing in the Egyptian liturgical tradition was, originally, also non-exorcistic in nature and became an exorcism only in the context of the fourth century, when a postbaptismal anointing in relationship to the gift of the Holy Spirit was imported and introduced into Egypt from elsewhere.[150]

### *7.1. The Blessing of the Oils (vv. 6-8)*

The question of the oils used in the document is worth further consideration at this point. This is because the language differs between the various versions, and it is not entirely clear, either, how the oils themselves are blessed/consecrated. The following (see Table 1 below) are the descriptions of the oils in ApTrad and its derivatives:

148. See Ambrose, *De Sacramentis* I.5.

149. On this, see G. Winkler, "The Original Meaning of the Prebaptismal Anointing and Its Implications," *Worship* 52 (1978): 24–45; see also, idem., *Das armenische Initiationsrituale*, Orientalia Christiana Analecta 217 (Rome: Pontificio Istituto Orientale, 1982).

150. See G. Kretschmar, "Beiträge zur Geschichte der Liturgie, insbesondere der Taufliturgie, in Ägypten," *Jahrbuch für Liturgik und Hymnologie* 8 (1963): 1–54; Bradshaw, "Baptismal Practice in the Alexandrian Tradition, Eastern or Western?"; Johnson, *Liturgy in Early Christian Egypt*, 7–16.

**Table 1: The Oils in ApTrad and Its Derivatives**

| | ApTrad | | | | | | CH 19 | TD II.8-9 |
|---|---|---|---|---|---|---|---|---|
| | **Latin** | **Ethiopic I** | **Sahidic/ Bohairic** | **Arabic I** | **Arabic II** | **Ethiopic II** | | |
| Pre-bapt. (blessed in v. 7, used in v. 10) | (text lost) | Oil for exorcism ("exorcized" but also "thanks" given over it) | Oil of exorcism | Oil of exorcism | Oil of exorcism | Oil of exorcism | Oil of exorcism | Oil of exorcism |
| Post-bapt. 1 (blessed in v. 6, used in v. 19) | Sanctified oil | The other oil = the "action of grace," also "exorcized" [e.g. balm of thanks-giving; Oil of thanksgiving] | Oil of thanksgiving | Oil of the good fat (e.g., Oil of thanks-giving) | Oil of thanksgiving | Oil of exorcism | Oil of thanksgiving | Oil of anointing (thanks-giving is given over it) |
| Post-bapt. 2 (blessed in v. 6, used in v. 22) | Sanctified oil | Oil of thanksgiving | Oil of thanksgiving | Oil of thanksgiving | Oil of thanksgiving | Oil of exorcism | Oil of anointing | Oil of anointing (thanks-giving is given over it) |

In every version of ApTrad and its derivatives, except Ethiopic I, it is clear that the postbaptismal anointing oil is blessed in v. 6; this is then followed by the blessing of the prebaptismal anointing exorcistic oil in v. 7. The confusion really lies with Ethiopic I, but also the lack of terminological specificity in Ethiopic II and CH 19c. The text of Ethiopic I is particularly confusing:

> While they are about to receive the oil for the exorcism, the bishop shall give thanks with a jar, and the other [e.g., the other oil], he shall exorcise (it). Let a deacon take the one exorcised and (place himself) stand(ing) by the presbyter; likewise the other one, of the action of grace [e.g., the oil of thanksgiving], let him stand on the right; and let the presbyter who exorcises it stand on the left.

This seems to imply an oil for the exorcism that the bishop gives thanks over, and another oil that will be exorcized. The second oil seems to be the one the deacon takes, now also referred to as exorcized and the first oil becomes the action of grace (or oil of thanksgiving) that a presbyter also exorcizes! What this seems to suggest is a strong confusion in Ethiopic I about the oils. This only gets sorted out in the administration of the rite, where the oil of exorcism is clearly used for the prebaptismal anointing (v. 10) and the oil of thanksgiving (= balm of thanksgiving) for the postbaptismal anointings (vs. 19 and 22). In this way, Ethiopic I is distinct here from the other versions of ApTrad. See Arabic I here:

> And [at the hour] it has been set for them [to receive baptism,] they receive the unction with the good fat. And the bishop shall give thanks over a vessel. And he shall exorcize [oil] in another vessel [as well]. And as regards the [oil] for exorcism, the deacon shall hold it and he shall stand at another presbyter because of the [oil of] thanksgiving and everyone shall stand.

In this case, the "unction with the good fat" appears to be the "oil of thanksgiving," since the bishop "gives thanks over" it, and the second oil is the oil of exorcism, which he "exorcize[s]." Ethiopic I appears to have the order and the oils confused. This confusion makes its way also into Ethiopic II, where term "oil of exorcism" is used throughout the text! CH 19c also uses two different names for the postbaptismal oils, either "oil of thanksgiving" or "oil of anointing." All of this likely suggests that Ethiopic

I is the first to try to distinguish between these oils and that Ethiopic II and CH 19c are also pointing to an older reading where a single oil was used. This would be consistent with our understanding of the development of the pre- and postbaptismal anointings in the Syrian and Egyptian traditions.[151] Additionally, what is somewhat confusing, however, is that Arabic I adds something else entirely: "As regards the one who has the water [sic!] of thanksgiving, he shall be to the right. And as regards the one who has the water [sic!] of exorcism, he shall stand to the left of the presbyter." Perhaps this was just a confusion of oil and water, but it is intriguing nonetheless. It could also be a sign of initiates bringing water for their baptism.

Support for an early confusion of the oils may also be seen in the later Egyptian sources (see Table 2 below):

**Table 2: Oil in Later Egyptian Sources**

| | **SAR** | **BR-AC** | **CB** | **Arabic TD II.B** | **CR** |
|---|---|---|---|---|---|
| Pre-bapt. | Oil[152] | Oil | Oil of exorcism | Oil of exorcism | Oil of gladness of the oil of exorcism[153] |
| Post-bapt. 1 | Chrism | Chrism | Chrism | Chrism | Chrism |
| Post-bapt. 2 | | [Oil for sick] | | | |

In these sources we also see some intriguing connections. SAR and BR-AC both refer to the prebaptismal oil of anointing simply as "oil," perhaps again a testament to the confusion or lack of distinction between the oil of exorcism and thanksgiving in some versions of ApTrad (Ethiopic I and II, respectively), though the prebaptismal anointing is clearly using chrism. Perhaps more intriguing is the use of the name "oil of gladness

151. See above, n. 150.

152. This was likely the oil of anointing as seen by parallels to the later Ethiopian version of ApTrad; see Johnson, *The Prayer of Sarapion of Thmuis*, 140.

153. Bradshaw, "Baptismal Practice in the Alexandrian Tradition, Eastern or Western?," 13.

of the oil of exorcism" in CR, which appears to be pointing to a similar confusion in terminology as that contained in Ethiopic I.

Finally, it is worth noting that nowhere in Ch. 21 does ApTrad actually describe the blessing of the oils. Stewart argues that Ch. 5 may have been a baptismal oil;[154] however, it seems that the oil described there is really a multi-use oil, and it could have been used for the oil of the sick and the rites of initiation as Stewart also seems to acknowledge. This actually seems to also be the case in the oil of the sick in BR-AC (see Excursus below). This would actually not be surprising since (as will be noted in Ch. 7 below) distinctions between the function of oils in the early sources are not entirely clear. This is the only prayer for the oil in ApTrad, despite there being two oils mentioned for the rites of initiation in Ch. 21.6-7, 10, 19, and 22. That Ch. 5 is a blessing of the oil and does not contain any exorcistic connotations may suggest that this prayer was used for the "oil of thanksgiving," which may point to the "oil of exorcism" being a more recent addition. This may again explain some of the confusion in Ethiopic II concerning the oil.[155]

### *7.2. The Renunciation or Apotaxis and Prebaptismal Anointing (vv. 9-11)*

The renunciation of Satan ("I renounce you, Satan, and all your works, all your service, and all your contamination") and, presumably, some kind of profession (Ethiopic I) follows. This in turn is followed by an anointing with exorcised oil, with some kind of formula of exorcism, "pronouncing (the formula) for purification from every foreign spirit" (Ethiopic I) or "for the change from every evil spirit" (Arabic I). The reference to the orientation of the candidates (i.e., facing west) for this renunciation appears only in the CH 19c and the TD II.8, where it is followed by a *syntaxis*, or act of adherence, to Christ facing East (to be considered in the next section of our commentary). This specific orientation in CH 19c and TD II.8 undoubtedly reflects the developing shape of the initiation rites in the fourth century. No parallels to orientation exist before that time period.[156]

154. Stewart, *On the Apostolic Tradition*, 91–92.

155. *Herm.Com.* 2002, 124.

156. The first witness to a change of orientation in the rite of renunciation, if not CH itself, is Cyril of Jerusalem, *Mystagogical Catechesis* 1.4 and 1.9. It also appears in BR-AC; see Bausi, "The *Baptismal Ritual*," 67.8-12 (West) and 67.19-20 (East).

All extant versions and derivative documents agree to a single declaratory rather than interrogatory renunciation of Satan, with slight variation in wording (Table 3 below):

**Table 3: Declaratory Renunciation**

| Ethiopic I | Arabic I | Sahidic | Arabic II | Ethiopic II | CH 19c | TD II.8 |
|---|---|---|---|---|---|---|
| I renounce you, Satan, and all your works and all your contamination | I renounce you, O Satan, and all your works and all your deeds | I renounce you, Satan, with all your service and all your works. | I renounce you Satan, and all your service and all your *unclean* works. | I renounce you, Satan, and all your *angels* and your every *impure* work. | I renounce you, Satan, and all your service. | I renounce you, Satan, and all your service, and your *theaters, and your pleasures*, and all your works. |

Ethiopic II is repeated almost verbatim in BR- and Euch-AC (see Excursus below): "I curse you, Satan, and all your evil angels and all your work and all your idols and all your orders and so turn him to the east."[157]

According to J. M. Hanssens, these *declaratory* formulas find their closest parallels in later Alexandrian, Syrian, and Armenian liturgical sources, but not in Roman, North African, or Byzantine documents, where the renunciation is generally formulated in a three-fold (or even five-fold) interrogative style.[158] Consistent with his hypothesis that ApTrad is of Alexandrian origins, Hanssens concluded that the form of the renunciation in the Oriental versions and derivative documents shows no correspondence to Roman or other Western liturgies and that it must, therefore, reflect an Alexandrian context.[159] Hanssens was correct that the extant versions do not correspond with what is known of the rite of renunciation in later Western liturgical sources. And an Alexandrian or Egyptian context for Ethiopic I and II, Arabic I and II, and the Sahidic as well as CH 19c would not be surprising, especially since, according to Bausi, Ethiopic I is translated from an Alexandrian Greek manuscript. However, it is far from certain that this is an exclusively Egyptian feature.[160]

We do not know exactly when Western rites began to formulate the renunciation in an interrogative manner, although it is already present in Ambrose of Milan's *De Sacramentis I.5*. Our earliest Western witness to a rite of renunciation is Tertullian, who does not indicate the manner in which this rite was performed, but simply describes it, saying:

> *De Corona*, 3: In short, to begin with baptism, when on the point of coming to the water we then and there, as also somewhat earlier in church under the bishop's control [*sub antistitis manu* ] affirm that we renounce the devil and his pomp and his angels.[161]
>
> *De Spectaculis,* 4: . . . we bear public testimony that we have renounced the devil, his retinue, and his works.[162]

157. "Ich verfluche dich, Satan, und alle deine bösen Engel und all dein Werk und alle deine Götzen und all deine Truppe und so wende du ihn nach Osten." Bausi, "The *Baptismal Ritual*," 67.19-21. Translation ours. See also Euch-AC (Σ52$^{ra}$-52$^{rb}$).

158. For the pertinent liturgical sources, see Hanssens, *La liturgie d'Hippolyte*, 452–56.

159. Hanssens, 456.

160. See *Herm.Com.* 2002, 130–32.

161. DBL, 9–10.

162. DBL, 9.

> *De anima,* 35: Now the compact you have made respecting him [the devil] is to renounce him, and his pomp, and his angels.[163]

The wording and location of an exorcistic pre-baptismal anointing show no major variations among the versions. Because of its location immediately *after* the renunciation (and profession in Ethiopic I), however, Hanssens again concluded that the rite in the extant versions does not reflect Roman liturgical usage, where the prebaptismal anointing is located *before* the renunciation, but rather Egyptian use.[164] As we will see, this is more or less affirmed in the early Egyptian evidence as well (see Excursus below). While this may be true of the Roman initiation rites within the eighth-century *Sacramentarium Gelasianum*, the lack of early *Roman* liturgical sources might not permit this conclusion. But there is nothing to contradict it! Other early Western sources (e.g., Ambrosian, Gallican, and Mozarabic) are consistent with the *Gelasianum* in locating this anointing *before* the renunciation, described by Ambrose of Milan himself, like Chrysostom, as an athlete preparing for combat. Whether Alexandrian or not, the renunciation of Satan and prebaptismal anointing in Ch. 21 are consistent with an *Eastern*, rather than Western, location in the rite, and hence, may call into question its meaning as being originally exorcistic.[165]

### 7.3. The Profession of Faith and Water Bath (vv. 12-18)

Immediately following the renunciation or *apotaxis,* and right before the baptismal candidate is delivered to the baptizer, the Oriental versions, together with CH 19c and TD II.8 (see Table 4 below) have introduced here an east-facing *syntaxis*, that is, an Act of Adherence to Christ or to the Holy Trinity, usually regarded as a Syrian characteristic of the fourth century. This *syntaxis* consists of rather complete, declaratory (Sahidic) or interrogative (Arabic II and Ethiopic II) creedal formulas corresponding, presumably, to the first baptismal immersion. Dix viewed these formulas as an interpolation,[166] and Botte saw this section as having been "pro-

163. ANF, III, 216.

164. See Hanssens, *La liturgie d'Hippolyte*, 452.

165. Traces of this may be seen in Prayer 15 of Sarapion. See also *Mystatogical Catechesis II.3,* ascribed to Cyril of Jerusalem, where the pre-baptismal anointing shows both "christic" and exorcistic elements.

166. Dix, *The Apostolic Tradition*, 35.

foundly altered."[167] With reference made in these formulas to "three in one substance, one divinity" (Sahidic), "Trinity, co-equal, one divinity" (Arabic II), and "the Trinity whose divinity is equal" (Ethiopic II), the contents of these formulas have been obviously and decidedly influenced by post-Nicene, orthodox, trinitarian theology.

**Table 4: CH and TD**

| CH 19c | TD II.8 |
| --- | --- |
| Before going down into the water, his face towards the east and standing near the water, he says this after having received the oil of exorcism: "I believe, and I submit myself to you and to all your service, O Father, Son, and Holy Spirit." | And also let him say ([the bishop] turning him [the baptizand] toward the east), "I submit to you, Father, Son, and Holy Spirit, from whom all nature quakes and trembles. Grant that I may do all your wishes, without fault." |

It is important to note, however, that the first baptismal immersion itself in both CH 19c and TD II.8, as in Ethiopic I and Arabic I, is accompanied not by a similar formula but by the simple interrogation, "Do you believe in God the Father Almighty?" Such might certainly suggest that a Syrian-type *syntaxis* as viewed by Dix is indeed an interpolation or addition into a text which began at this point, originally, with the first of a three-fold trinitarian invocation.[168] At the same time, following what appears to have been the first immersion in relationship to that creedal formula already, the odd rubric in the Oriental versions directing a three-fold confession and immersion, followed in verses 15-18 by only *two* creedal interrogations regarding Christ and the Holy Spirit, suggests that in those versions the first baptismal interrogation has been reworked considerably from what it would have been. Hence, what appears to be taking place at this point in the Oriental versions and derivative texts is the further evolution of declaratory creeds recited by the candidate as a *redditio symboli* in either declarative or interrogatory form, before the administration of baptism itself along with its accompanying interrogations, or, as in the case of the

167. Botte, *La Tradition*, 49.
168. See Dix, *The Apostolic Tradition*, 35.

CH 19c, interrogations and baptismal formula (e.g., "I baptize you . . ."). As such, it is clearly Ethiopic I and Arabic I which are the clearest witnesses to what the earlier shape of the text probably was.

With special regard to Egypt, Stewart has argued that the Egyptian tradition originally contained not baptismal interrogations at all but a five-fold creedal declaration consistent with the Oriental versions, CH 19c, and the later CR declaratory profession or *syntaxis*:

> I believe in one God, God the Father Almighty, and his Only-Begotten Son, Jesus Christ our Lord, and the holy lifegiving Spirit, and the resurrection of the flesh, and the one only catholic apostolic Church. Amen.[169]

While according to Stewart there is no evidence here of interrogations, as the following demonstrates, in both Arabic II and Ethiopic II this "creed" is framed precisely as an *interrogation* (see Table 5 below).

| **Table 5: Interrogatory Creed** | | |
|---|---|---|
| **Sahidic** | **Arabic II** | **Ethiopic II** |
| I believe in God, the Father, the Almighty, | Do you believe in one God, the Father, the Almighty, | Do you believe in the one God, the Father, the Lord of all, |
| and his only begotten Son, Jesus Christ our Lord and Savior | and his only Son, Jesus Christ our Lord and Savior, | and in his only Son, Jesus Christ our Lord and our Savior, |
| with his Holy Spirit, the giver of life to everything | and his Holy Spirit, who gives life to the whole creation, | and the Holy Spirit, the one who gives life to all creation, |
| Three in one substance, one divinity, one Lordship, one kingdom, one faith, one baptism, in the holy catholic church, which lives forever. Amen. | The Trinity, coequal, one divinity, one Lordship, one kingdom, one faith, one baptism, in the catholic church [and] everlasting life? Amen. | The Trinity whose divinity is equal, and one Lord and one faith and one baptism in the holy catholic church and the life everlasting? Amen. |

169. DBL, 135.

When the obvious post-Nicene trinitarian theology and the quotation from Ephesians 4:5 are removed from the above formulae, it is striking how similar these are to what appears in the current CR. These versions, then, may well point us back to an earlier form of the baptismal interrogations that became expanded by the text of the developing Apostles' Creed. Such is confirmed even for Egypt by the absence of this syntaxis in favor of the three creedal questions in Ethiopic I and Arabic I.[170] In fact, a similar text with interrogations appears also in BR-AC:

> Belief in the Trinity: And I believe in you, Father of Jesus Christ, and in your only Son Jesus Christ our Lord, and in the Holy Spirit and in the resurrection of the flesh and in the holy one catholic apostolic church. And he should be asked three times: Do you believe? And three times he says: I believe.[171]

This text is also the same as that in Euch-AC (Σ52$^{rb}$).

By omitting the obvious post-Nicene language in these formulas, we are left with short statements which, if not exact, provide some parallels to early brief creedal statements known from the second-century *Epistula Apostolorum* and the later *Deir Balyzeh papyrus* (sixth/seventh century) (see Table 6 below):

170. The presence of a five-fold *syntaxis* in the Oriental versions and CH was viewed by Hanssens as evidence of Alexandrian rather than Roman origins of ApTrad. See Hanssens, *La liturgie d'Hippolyte*, 457–61. In light of Ethiopic I and Arabic I, however, the *syntaxis* appears to be later in the Egyptian tradition. This does not mean, however, that this *syntaxis* in interrogatory form is not early.

171. "Glaube an die Dreieinigkeit: Und ich glaube an dich, Vater Jesu Christi, und an deinen einzigen Sohn Jesus Christus, unsern Herrn, und an den heiligen Geist und an die Auferstehung des Fleisches und an die heilige eine katholische apostolische Kirche. Und dreimal soll man ihn fragen: Glaubst du? Und dreimal sagt er: Ich glaube." Bausi, "The *Baptismal Ritual*," 67.25-31. Translation ours.

**Table 6: Creedal Statements**

| ***Epistula Apostolorum***[172] | **Deir Balyzeh Papyrus**[173] | **Sahidic** | **BR-AC** | **CR** |
|---|---|---|---|---|
| . . . in (the Father) the ruler of the universe, | I believe in God the Father almighty, | I believe in God, the Father, the Almighty, | I believe in you, Father of Jesus Christ | I believe in one God, God the Father Almighty, |
| and in Jesus Christ (our Redeemer) | and in His only-begotten Son our Lord Jesus Christ, | and his only begotten Son, Jesus Christ our Lord and Savior | and in your only Son Jesus Christ our Lord, | and his Only-Begotten Son, Jesus Christ our Lord, |
| and in the Holy Spirit (the Paraclete) | and in the Holy Spirit, | with his Holy Spirit, | and in the Holy Spirit | and the holy lifegiving Spirit, |
| | | the giver of life to everything, | | |
| | and in the resurrection of the flesh | | and in the resurrection of the flesh | and the resurrection of the flesh, |

172. J. N. D. Kelly, *Early Christian Creeds*, 3rd ed. (Essex, 1972), 82.

173. Kelly, *Early Christian Creeds*, 94. Critical edition in Jürgen Hammerstaedt, *Griechische Anaphorenfragmente aus Ägypten und* Nubien, Abhandlungen der Nordrhein-Westfälischen Akademie der Wissenschaften (Opladen: VS Verlag für Sozialwissenschaften, 2013), 171–86.

| | | three in one substance, one divinity, one Lord-ship, one kingdom, one faith, one baptism, | | |
|---|---|---|---|---|
| and in the holy Church, | in the holy catholic Church. | in the holy catholic Church, | and in the holy one catholic apostolic church. | and the one only catholic apostolic Church. |
| and in the forgiveness of sins. | | | | |
| | | which lives forever. Amen. | | Amen. |

While the creed in the *Deir Balyzeh papyrus* has often been viewed as preserving even a second-century creedal tradition from *Rome*, a primitive skeleton creed from which the later texts of the specifically Roman or Apostles' Creed would evolve,[174] Stewart is careful not to assume that the context in *Deir Balyzeh* is originally baptismal. Nevertheless, he says that:

> The fact that the Sahidic translator of *Traditio apostolica* employs it in his reconstruction of the first baptismal question implies that it is in current liturgical use. Moreover, the very simplicity of the form in Deir Balyzeh, as in the Coptic rite, is an indication of antiquity. As such we may reasonably suggest that it is a relic of an ancient creed in liturgical use, and possibly that it had originated as a brief statement of the *regula fidei*, and had come into liturgical use through that route. Evidence for this, in turn, is found in the letter of Alexander of Alexandria to Alexander of Constantinople, in which, towards the conclusion of the letter Alexander proclaims his own faith, which he claims as that of the apostolic church, a confession which, as Lanne shows, may be grouped under the same five headings, namely belief in each of the three persons of the Godhead, the church, and the resurrection.[175]

This is not, however, a new position in the history of liturgical scholarship on Egyptian baptism. Paul Bradshaw, in his 1988 "Baptismal Practice in the Alexandrian Tradition," while certainly holding to a change from an interrogatory to a declaratory creedal formula, states:

> This interrogatory form of the baptismal confession of faith *did not last long* in the Alexandrian tradition, but was replaced by a declaratory form with a fivefold shape. Emmanuel Lanne has recently presented evidence

174. See Kelly, *Early Christian Creeds*, 122. On the development of Creeds see L. H. Westra, *The Apostles' Creed: Origin, History, and Some Early Commentaries*, Instrumenta Patristica et Mediaevalia, 43 (Turnhout: Brepols, 2002); and W. Kinzig, C. Markschies, and M. Vinzent, eds., *Tauffragen und Bekenntnis. Studien zur sogenannten "'Traditio Apostolica'" zu den "Interrogationes de fide" und zum "Römischen Glaubensbekenntnis"* (Berlin: Walter de Bruyter, 1999).

175. Alistair Stewart-Skyes, "The Early Alexandrian Baptismal Creed: Declaratory, Interrogatory . . . or Both?," *Questions liturgiques* 95 (2014): 246. See also Alistair Stewart, *Two Early Egyptian Liturgical Papyri: The Deir Balyzeh Papyrus and the Barcelona Papyrus with Appendices Containing Comparative Material*, Joint Liturgical Studies 70 (Norwich: Hymns Ancient and Modern, 2010), 17–21.

> for the existence from early times of a fivefold creedal affirmation in the Alexandrian tradition, and whilst none of this proves that such a form was used in a baptismal context at an early date, it does suggest that, when the change was made, such a creedal form was already an established feature in that ecclesiastical tradition, and it may have been already in use for some time in baptismal practice in Egyptian dioceses outside Alexandria.[176]

It should also be noted that it is unclear in all the versions and derivative documents of ApTrad as to who it is that hands over the candidate to the baptizer, or who it is that actually administers baptism itself. If in Ethiopic I and Arabic I, the Oriental versions, and TD II.8 it is a deacon who accompanies the candidate into the baptismal waters and asks the interrogations, in CH 19c it is a presbyter. But in all the versions of ApTrad and the TD the identity or ecclesiastical order of the baptizer is not indicated. Rather, instead of designating any minister in particular, the versions of ApTrad and TD revert stylistically here to the use of the third-person hortatory subjunctive either in reference to the baptizer ("let him who baptizes . . . "), to the candidate ("let him be baptized"), or to both. Such stylistic changes in the various texts may suggest again that at some point prior to the development of rubrics about bishops, presbyters, and deacons, ApTrad itself was non-specific in this context.

Baptism administered with three interrogations as in Ch. 21.15-18 ("Do you believe? . . . I believe") is a well-known characteristic of early and later Western baptismal rites (cf. Tertullian, *De corona* 3, *Adversus Praxean* 26, and *De spectaculis* 4;[177] Cyprian of Carthage, *Letter to Januarius* 70.2;[178] Ambrose of Milan, *De Sacramentis* 2.20;[179] and the *Sacramentarium Gelasianum*[180]). In *De Sacramentis* 2.20 we read:

> You were asked: "Do you believe in God the Father almighty?" You replied: "I believe", and you were immersed: that is, buried. You were asked for a second time: "Do you believe in our Lord Jesus Christ and in his cross?"

176. Bradshaw, "Baptismal Practice in the Alexandrian Tradition, Eastern or Western?," 14 [emphasis added].

177. DBL, 9–11.

178. DBL, 12–13.

179. DBL, 179.

180. DBL, 212–43.

> You replied: "I believe" and you were immersed: which means that you were buried with Christ. For one who is buried with Christ rises again with Christ. You were asked a third time: "Do you believe also in the Holy Spirit?" You replied: "I believe", and you were immersed a third time, so that the threefold confession might absolve the manifold lapses of the past.[181]

And in the Roman rite, as late as the eighth-century manuscript of the *Sacramentarium Gelasianum*, the baptismal interrogations themselves are also formulated in a manner similar to that of Ambrose:

> Do you believe in God the Father Almighty? R. I believe.
>
> And do you believe in Jesus Christ his only Son our Lord,
> who was born and suffered? R. I believe.
>
> And do you believe in the Holy Spirit; the holy Church; the
> remission of sins; the resurrection of the flesh? R. I believe.[182]

While Stewart views these texts as abbreviations of a fuller recitation of the Creed in a *redditio symboli* earlier in the rite, the work of Kinzig has argued for the antiquity of the form of the baptismal interrogation in the *Gelasianum*, and claims that the "creed" of the Latin version of ApTrad can be no older than the Roman Creed itself. Hence, he concludes that the Latin version itself represents an updating to correspond to the form of the Roman Creed available at the time the Verona translation was made.[183] Similarly, Markus Vinzent notes that the oldest evidence for the Apostles' and Roman Creeds is the, above noted, Letter of Marcellus of Ancyra to Julius of Rome in 340/341 CE. That is, the oldest evidence is not to be found in the text of ApTrad because what appears there in the Latin version is not, in his opinion, from the early third century but, rather, is a reconstructed text in which "the Verona fragment has been changed by the insertion

181. DBL, 179.

182. DBL, 242.

183. M. Vinzent, "Die Entstehung des 'Römischen Glaubensbekenntnis," in *Tauffragen und Bekenntnis*, 189. At the end of his study Vinzent points to the irony that the Apostles' and Roman Creeds are thus actually Eastern in origin but they were accepted in the West and not in the East. See 408–9. If Hanssens may not have been correct about the Alexandrian origins of these creeds, his insight that these creeds did not have a Western origin is vindicated by Vinzent's study.

of the Roman custom."[184] And while Westra is critical of the approach of Kingzig and Vincent in his work on the Apostles' Creed, he too notes that ApTrad reflects "the wording of a number of *later* variants of the Creed."[185]

Such an interrogatory form of baptism is also a characteristic of early Egyptian baptismal liturgy and may well be reflected in Origen's *Homilies on Numbers*, a letter from Dionysius of Alexandria, Athanasius, the *De trinitate* of Didymus the Blind, Cyril of Alexandria, and Mystagogical Catechesis II.4, attributed to Cyril of Jerusalem,[186] a position strongly challenged by Stewart, who argues instead that the earliest Egyptian creed was a five-fold declaration.[187] In response to Stewart, the claim has been made that there are too many examples of interrogation in Egypt for baptism by interrogation to be discounted.[188] In fact, the five-fold creedal declaration or syntaxis could have been originally an interrogation as appears in Arabic II and Ethiopic II, apart from the post-Nicene additions. As Bradshaw has recently noted, current scholarship has "open[ed] the door to the possibility that the original core of the baptismal rite in the *Apostolic Tradition* came from Egypt rather than North Africa."[189]

184. Vinzent, "Die Entstehung des 'Römischen Glaubensbekenntnis," 93–94.

185. Westra, *The Apostles' Creed*, 68 [emphasis added].

186. On the possible Egyptian connection to the Jerusalem Mystagogical Catecheses, see Juliette Day, *The Baptismal Liturgy of Jerusalem: Fourth- and Fifth-Century Evidence from Palestine, Syria and Egypt,* Liturgy, Worship and Society (Burlington, VT: Ashgate, 2007); Anna Petrin, *The Egyptian Connection: Egyptian Elements in the Liturgy of Jerusalem Revisited* (University of Notre Dame, PhD diss., 2018); *Lectures on the Christian Sacraments: The Procatechesis and the Mystagogical Catecheses Ascribed to St. Cyril of Jerusalem*, text, translation, and introduction by Maxwell E. Johnson, Popular Patristic Series 57 (Yonkers: St. Vladimir Seminary Press, 2017); and Maxwell E. Johnson, "The Anaphora in *Mystagogical Catechesis V* attributed to St Cyril of Jerusalem and the Anaphora of St James," *Interdisciplinary Symposium: The Liturgy of St James, Origins, Contexts, and Receptions in East and West*, Regensburg, Germany: University of Regensburg, June 8, 2022, in Studies in Eastern Christian Liturgies series (Münster: Aschendorff, 2024).

187. See Maxwell E. Johnson, "Interrogatory Creedal *Formulae* in Early Egyptian Baptismal Rites: A Reassessment of the Evidence," *Questions liturgiques* 101 (2021): 75–93.

188. See Maxwell E. Johnson, "Interrogatory Creedal *Formulae* in Early Egyptian Baptismal Rites: A Reassessment of the Evidence," *Questions Liturgiques* 101 (2021): 75–93.

189. Bradshaw, "Fourth-Century Egyptian Baptismal Practice: A Reevaluation of the Evidence," in *Explorations in Christian Initiation from the East: In Honor of Maxwell E. Johnson*, ed. Stefanos Alexopoulos, Nathan Chase, and Anna Petrin, Eastern Catholic Studies and Texts (Washington, DC: The Catholic University of America Press, forthcoming).

The creedal formulas (Ch. 21.15-18) in the Oriental versions, in relationship to Ethiopic I and Arabic I, the Latin version, CH 19c, and, with the addition of the christological phrase "who came from the Father, who, pre-existing, is with the Father" in the second interrogation in TD II.8, reflect considerable, especially christological, expansion at this point. Because of close parallels between the baptismal interrogations in the Latin version and the later available versions of what is called the Roman creed, a creed known to us in Greek from a letter of Marcellus of Ancyra to Julius of Rome in 340/341 CE and in Latin from a commentary by Rufinus of Aquileia in ca. 404 CE, scholars have often assumed that ApTrad is to be dated ca. 215 CE, and have often taken the Latin version as evidence that such a creed was in existence already as a fixed formula by the end of the second century at Rome.[190] The one notable exception to this was Hanssens. Because of what appears to be a uniquely non-Western phrasing of "*Christum* Iesum" (Χριστὸν Ἰησοῦν), "*qui natus est de Spiritu sancto ex Maria virgine*," and the addition of the word "*vivus*" to "*et resurrexit die tertia [vivus ] a mortuis,*" Hanssens held, on the basis of parallels in Egyptian patristic authors primarily, that such terminology could only indicate Alexandrian origins.[191] While Hanssens was correct to underscore the Eastern origins of the Western Apostles' or Roman Creed, parallels to, at least, "*Christum* Iesum" and "***qui natus est de Spiritu sancto* ex *Maria virgine*,**" do appear in some manuscripts of early Latin creedal formulas recounted in various *Acta* of the martyrs.[192] Even Hippolyus of Rome himself cites a parallel to "*Christum Iesum*" in his statement in *Contra Noetus* 8 that "A man . . . is compelled to acknowledge *God the Father Almighty*, and *Christ Jesus* the *Son* of God, who, being God, became man . . . and the Holy Spirit; and that these three are one."[193]

While scholars have and continue to take the Verona Latin as normative, picking up the Latin version where the lacuna ends, this appeal is based undoubtedly on the hypothesis that ApTrad is Western. But in light of Ethiopic I and Arabic I, basing scholarship on the normativity of the

190. Cf. Kelly, *Early Christian Creeds*, 126ff.

191. Hanssens, *La liturgie d'Hippolyte*, 463–70.

192. See W. Kinzig, "'. . . *natum et passum* etc.' Zur Geschichte der Tauffragen in der lateinischen Kirche bis zu Luther," in *Tauffragen und Bekenntnis*, 128–32.

193. ANF, V, 226 [emphasis added].

Verona Latin is no longer necessary. Ethiopic I, for example, shows the same Creed in question-and-answer form as the Latin in approximately the same fifth-century context (see Table 7):

| **Table 7: Latin and Ethiopic I** | |
|---|---|
| **Latin** | **Ethiopic I** |
| [lacuna] | Do you believe in one almighty God? |
| Do you believe in **Christ Jesus, the Son of God**, who was born by the Holy Spirit **from** the Virgin Mary and crucified under Pontius Pilate, **and died and was buried** and rose on the third day **alive from the dead**, and ascended into heaven and sits on the right hand of the Father, and will come to judge the living and the dead? | Do you believe in **Christ Jesus, Son of God**, who was born of the Holy Spirit and **of the** Virgin Mary, was crucified under Pontius Pilate, **and died and was buried**, and rose on the third day **alive from the dead**, and ascended into heaven, and sits at the right hand of the Father, who shall come to judge the living and the dead? |
| Do you believe in the Holy Spirit and the holy church and the resurrection of the flesh? | Do you believe in the Holy Spirit, and in the holy church, and in the resurrection of the flesh? |

Apart from "in" the holy church and the first question overall, together with its reference to *one* God, which parallels Arabic I and what has been called the *syntaxis* in all Oriental versions of ApTrad,[194] Ethiopic I is clearly identical to the Verona Latin. Hence, taking Ethiopic I and Arabic I into account, there is no need to accept uncritically the theory of Zinzent and Kinzig that "the Verona fragment has been changed by the insertion of the Roman custom." From wherever it might have come originally, it was already there in Greek in the fifth-century Alexandrian manuscript from which Ethiopic I was translated.

Further, Vinzent and Kinzig have made a compelling case that a "creed" was not known in the Roman Church until the creed of the staunch anti-Arian associate of Athanasius, Marcellus of Ancyra, which was borrowed

194. *Herm.Com.* 2002, 114.

by Rome after ca. 340 CE.[195] Marcellus's Creed, with obvious parallels to both ApTrad and the later Apostles' Creed, is as follows:

πιστεύω οὖν είς θεὸν παντοκράτορα,

καὶ είς **Χριστὸν Ἰησοῦν,**
τὸν υἱὸν αὑτοῦ
τὸν μονογενης
τὸν κύριον ἡμῶν,
τὸν γεννηθέντα **ἐκ** πνεύματος ἁγίου,
καὶ Μαρίας τῆς παρθένου,[196]

τὸν ἐπὶ Ποντίοθ Πιλάτου σταυρωθέντα

**καὶ ταφέντα,**
καὶ τῇ τρίτῃ ἡμέρα
ἀναστάντα **ἐκ τῶν νεκρῶν,**
ἀναβάντα εἰς τοὺς οὐρανοὺς
καὶ καθήμενον ἐν δεζιας τοῦ πατρός

ὃ ἔρχεται κρίνειν ζῶντας καὶ νεκρούς
καὶ είς τὸ ἅγιον πνεῦμα
ἅγιαν ἐκκλησίαν
ἄφεσιν ἀμαρτιῶν
σαρκός ἀνάστασιν
Ζωὴν ἀιώνιον[197]

If current scholarship as represented by Kinzig and Vinzent is correct, the most that can be concluded is that the baptismal interrogations of the *fifth-century* Verona Latin version reflect *a* version of the *Roman* Creed in a way similar to how it was known in the middle of the *fourth* century (Marcellus) and at the at the beginning of the *fifth* (Rufinus). But it tells nothing certain about its shape in the early third century. Of course, since the creedal interrogations in CH 19c, the earliest derivative document of ApTrad, reflect a rather similar form it can be concluded safely that whatever the original Greek text may have contained, it included some expansion of the specifically christological section of the Creed. Some christological "expansions" are known to us already from the writings of

195. *Herm.Com.* 2002, 114–19.

196. The phrase καὶ Μαρίας τῆς παρθένου is in the genitive and so corresponds to **ἐκ** just as πνεύματος ἁγίου does.

197. Kinzig, "' . . . *natum et passum* etc.,'" 93–94.

Justin Martyr[198] and Irenaeus,[199] and it was only inevitable that these would find a place in the continuing development of the baptismal interrogations.

Nevertheless, if the *explicit* formulation of the baptismal interrogations in Ethiopic I, Arabic I, and the Latin are read as reflecting liturgical and creedal development consistent with a date beyond the early third century, then one must be content with not knowing the original contents of the three interrogations prior to the CH 19c. If Kinzig is correct in his assessment of the antiquity of the interrogatory formulas in the *Gelasianum*, however, it would not be unreasonable to conclude that a simple form such as that once existed at this point also in ApTrad. But even if so, the replacement of such short interrogations with a more complete creedal text, as appears already in Ethiopic I, Arabic I, and the Latin, was not a pattern followed by any liturgical rite in subsequent history. Complete creeds, whether that of Nicaea-Constantinople or the "Apostles," were delivered at the *traditio symboli* and returned by the candidates at the *redditio symboli* at some point prior to baptism itself during the final stages of the catechumenate. But, at least in the West, baptismal interrogations themselves were to remain in an immediate prebaptismal context in approximately the same form they are found in the *Gelasianum*. In fact, with the exception of some medieval liturgical texts (e.g., the *Sacramentary of Gellone*[200]), it is not until the post-Vatican II reforms of the Roman rites for Christian initiation in 1969 (infants) and 1972 (adults) that the complete text of the Apostles' Creed came to function interrogatively in place of the formula from the *Gelasianum*, due largely to the supposition that the Latin version of ApTrad was authentically and originally *Roman*.

Finally, whatever the shape of the baptismal interrogations may have been in the "original" Greek text, the relative absence of any explicit references to *particular* ministers (bishop, presbyter, or deacon) of baptism at the point of baptism itself may well reflect an earlier version of the document before a later assignment of initiatory roles to specific ordained ministers. If so, this section may have followed immediately after what was suggested

198. Justin Martyr, *First Apology*, 61: "they are then washed . . . in the water in the Name of the Father and Lord God of all things, and of our Saviour Jesus Christ, and of the Holy Spirit. . . . And he that is being enlightened is washed . . . in the Name of Jesus Christ who was crucified under Pontius Pilate, and in the Name of the Holy Spirit, which through the prophets foretold all things concerning Jesus." DBL, 3.

199. See *Epideixis* 3 and 7, and *Adv. haer.* 1, 10,1; 3,1,2; 3,4,2; and 3,16,6.

200. See Kinzig, "' . . . *natum et passum* etc.,'" 170.

above to be an earlier version of the immediate preparation for baptism in Ch. 20.5-10 and the opening instructions for baptism in Ch. 21.1-5.

### *7.4. The Postbaptismal Rites (vv. 19-24)*

The conferral of baptism is followed immediately in Ch 21.19-24, first, by an anointing with the oil of thanksgiving (with "balsam" in Ethiopian I and with "oil of exorcism" in Ethiopic II, an issue addressed above) by a presbyter, and, second, by a handlaying with prayer and subsequent anointing by the bishop. This implies the following shape for the postbaptismal rites:

- The newly baptized are anointed with the blessed oil by the presbyter (Ch. 21.19)
- The neophytes dress and go into the church (Ch. 21.20)
- The bishop lays hands on them in a prayer for grace (Ch. 21.21)
- The neophytes are anointed with the blessed oil by the bishop via a handlaying (Ch. 21.22)
- The neophytes are signed on their foreheads (Ch. 21.23)

While Bradshaw holds that the presbyteral anointing witnesses to a later development when a presbyter alone would baptize in the absence of a bishop,[201] the fact is that a postbaptismal anointing, whether by a bishop or presbyter, first appearing in Tertullian (*De baptismo* 7-8; *De res. carn.* 8)[202] and Cyprian of Carthage (*Ep.* 70.2; 73.9; 74.5),[203] enjoys a long history in

201. Bradshaw, *Apostolic Tradition*.

202. Tertullian, *De Baptismo*, 7: "After that we come up from the washing and are anointed with the blessed unction, following that ancient practice by which, ever since Aaron was anointed by Moses, there was a custom of anointing them for priesthood with oil out of a horn. That is why [the high priest] is called a Christ, from 'chrism' which is [the Greek for] 'anointing': and from this also our Lord obtained his title, though it had become a spiritual anointing, in that he was anointed with the Spirit by God the Father." DBL, 8; and *De Resurrectione Carnis*, 8: "The flesh is washed that the soul may be made spotless; the flesh is anointed that the soul may be consecrated: the flesh is signed [with the cross] that the soul too may be protected: the flesh is overshadowed by the imposition of the hand that the soul also may be illumined by the Spirit." DBL, 10.

203. Cyprian, *Letter 70, To Januarius*, 2: "It is also necessary that he who is baptized should be anointed: so that having received the chrism, that is the anointing, he may be anointed of God and have in him the grace of Christ." DBL, 11.

both East and West as a constitutive liturgical element, becoming in the East especially related to the gift and "seal" of the Holy Spirit in Christian initiation. At the same time, Hippolytus of Rome himself, in his *Commentary on Daniel* (1.16.23) testifies to what may have been a pneumatic-oriented postbaptismal anointing at Rome in the same time period.[204] Rather than dating the anointing to a later period, then, it is probably the case that the *reservation* of this anointing to a presbyter, in the absence of the bishop or not, is what constitutes a development here, though the double postbaptismal anointing will be taken up more below.

As to the theology of this presbyteral anointing, consistent with the early North African witnesses, but not Hippolytus himself, the anointing ("I anoint you with holy oil in the name of Jesus Christ," or "Father, Son, and Holy Spirit" in CH 19c) is "christic" or "trinitarian" in orientation and, given its location in the rite immediately after baptism, may have been a full-body anointing, although elsewhere it appears to have been only of the head.

A postbaptismal episcopal handlaying prayer (Ch. 21.21) has early parallels again both with Tertullian and Cyprian. Tertullian in *De Baptismo*, 8 writes:

> Next follows the imposition of the hand in benediction, inviting and welcoming the Holy Spirit . . . But this too is involved in that ancient sacred act in which Jacob blessed his grandsons, Joseph's sons, Ephraim and Manasseh, by placing his hands interchanged upon their heads, turned transversely upon themselves in such a manner as to make the shape of Christ, and at that early date to prefigure the blessing that was to be in Christ.[205]

And he continues in *De Resurrectione Carnis*, 8:

> The flesh is washed that the soul may be made spotless; the flesh is anointed that the soul may be consecrated: the flesh is signed [with the cross] that the soul too may be protected: the flesh is overshadowed by the imposition of the hand that the soul also may be illumined by the Spirit.[206]

204. See ANF, vol. 5, 18, 192.
205. DBL, 8
206. DBL, 10.

Similarly, Cyprian provides an even closer parallel to ApTrad Ch. 21.21 in stating in *Letter 73, To Januarius*, 9:

> They who are baptized in the church are brought to the prelates of the church, and by our prayers and by the imposition of the hand obtain the Holy Spirit, and are perfected with the Lord's seal [*signaculo dominico*].[207]

And further in *Letter 74, To Pompeius* 5, he says:

> If they attribute the efficacy of baptism to the majesty of the name, so that anyone who is baptized in the name of Jesus Christ, wherever it may take place and however it may be performed, is held to be renewed and sanctified, why is not the hand also laid on him after baptism in the name of the same Christ so that he may receive the Holy Spirit, why does not the same majesty of the same name avail in the imposition of the hand which avails, as they maintain, in the sanctification of baptism?[208] (DBL, 11–12)

Of all the versions and relevant derivative documents, however, the Verona Latin alone makes no reference to the Holy Spirit in this prayer by the bishop but to the invocation of grace alone and this has triggered a long debate on whether the Latin is corrupt here and whether the language about the bestowal of the Holy Spirit in the Oriental versions, including now both Ethiopic I and Arabic I, is to be preferred. Dix, for example, was so convinced of the corrupt nature of the Latin at this point that, while normally following the Latin version throughout his edition, he based his English translation of *this* prayer upon the Oriental versions and entitled the entire section with the anachronistic term "Confirmation."[209] Along similar lines, Botte suggested that a line referring to the gift of the Holy Spirit in this prayer had been left out here from either the Latin version or the Greek original.[210]

The scholarly evaluation of the Latin, however, has changed since the work of both Dix and Botte. G.W.H Lampe, for example, noted that there are no grammatical problems with the Latin at this point and that the text

207. DBL, 12.

208. DBL, 13.

209. Dix, *The Apostolic Tradition*, 38.

210. Botte, *La Tradition*, 53.

as it stands translates quite clearly.[211] It is the Latin that Geoffrey Cuming translated in his edition.[212] Aidan Kavanagh also argued strongly for the reliability of the Latin, saying:

> While it is true that translations of AT in other languages such as Arabic and Ethiopic render the "Lord God" prayer as an epiclesis of the Holy Spirit, these texts are very much later than the Verona Latin version, which was done c. 350; the Arabic and Ethiopic versions date from the thirteenth century, over nine centuries later. The probability is strong that these later translations represent a development of AT on this matter which was unknown when the document was written and the Verona translation was made. . . . The text of the "Lord God" prayer in the Verona translation clearly associates the Holy Spirit with *baptism*, the "bath of regeneration of the Holy Spirit," in complete harmony with Titus 3.5 and John 3.5. AT is not alone in this. Later Western baptismal allusions make similar associations.[213]

The scholarly consensus today is that the Verona Latin reflects an earlier period than the Oriental versions, which have become expanded by an epiclesis of the Holy Spirit in the bishop's handlaying prayer at some point during the fourth century.[214] The fourth century in general was an era in which various postbaptismal rites throughout the Christian world were added to rites that did not have them and the rites which were added—most often, at least in the East, a single postbaptismal chrismation—were those associated with the conferral of the gift or seal of the Holy Spirit.[215] In the West this developed as well but there the pneumatic focus became attached not specifically to an *anointing* but to the episcopal handlaying prayer, though this was not immediate even in Rome.[216] Since the years between the Councils of Nicea I (325) and Constantinople I (381) were years of intense pneumatological debate and doctrinal dispute

211. See G. W. H. Lampe, *The Seal of the Spirit* (London: SPCK, 1967), 138–41.

212. Cuming, *Hippolytus*, 20.

213. Aidan Kavanagh, *Confirmation: Origins and Reform* (New York: Pueblo, 1988), 47.

214. See *Herm.Com.* 2002, 127ff.; and Bradshaw, *Apostolic Tradition*, 77–78.

215. On this development, see G. Winkler, "The Original Meaning of the Prebaptismal Anointing and Its Implications," *Worship* 52 (1978): 24–45 (= LWSS, 58–81).

216. Nathan Chase, "Anointings with Oil and Handlaying in the Early Church: Early Ritual Cognates?," presented at the conference on "Öl in der frühen Liturgie: Verwendung und Deutung," Regensburg, Germany, February 9, 2024.

and consensus regarding the Holy Spirit, such ritual development may be seen as a perfectly logical development. And, that the Holy Spirit became increasingly connected to a postbaptismal handlaying with prayer in the fourth-century West, and that this was closely connected as well to the particular ministry of bishops, is witnessed to by Jerome (342–420 CE), secretary to Pope Damasus at Rome from 382 to 385 CE, in his *Altercation of a Luciferian with an Orthodox*. In the role of an orthodox Christian responding to Luciferian challenges, Jerome writes:

> I agree that it is the Church's custom that when people are baptized by presbyters and deacons far from the major cities the bishop hurries round to lay his hand on them for the invocation of the Holy Spirit. . . . If at this point you ask why anyone baptized in the Church only receives the Holy Spirit by the hands of the bishop, while we assert that it is given in true baptism, learn that the source of this custom is that the Holy Spirit descended on the Apostles after our Lord's Ascension. We learn the same practice in many places, more to the honour of the ministry than for the principle of necessity. Otherwise, if the Holy Spirit only came down in answer to the bishop's prayers, one may single out those who were baptized by presbyters and deacons in farms or villages or in remote places and have fallen asleep before they were discovered by the bishop.[217]

Such a pattern of anointing followed by a handlaying prayer for the gift of the Spirit is a common pattern elsewhere in the non-Roman West, where nothing equivalent to the episcopal anointing after the handlaying prayer occurs.[218]

At the same time, it must be noted that contrary to Kavanagh's assertion about the medieval dating of Ethiopic II and Arabic II his argument falls to the wayside since Ethiopic I ("grant that they may be filled with the Holy Spirit") and Arabic I ("make them worthy to be filled with the Holy Spirit") already contain Holy Spirit language from the same time period as the Verona Latin manuscript. It is here especially that we disagree with the current scholarly consensus. Whether the Verona Latin represents an

217. G. Jeanes, *The Origins of the Roman Rite*, Alcuin/GROW Liturgical Study 20 (Bramcote: Grove Books, 1991), 19–20. For other Western sources in Gaul and Spain, see Johnson, *The Rites of Christian Initiation*, 179–84; and DBL, 205–8.

218. See Johnson, *The Rites of Christian Initiation*, 185ff.; and DBL, 140ff.

earlier text or a scribal error in removing Holy Spirit language matters little, and too much has been made of this in the history of scholarship. That is, contrary to Kavanagh and most scholars, there is, in fact, no explicit *epiclesis* of the Holy Spirit in *any* of the versions of ApTrad. The only epiclesis there is for grace! Even where the Holy Spirit is expressly mentioned, the handlaying prayer asks for grace and not the Holy Spirit, though CH 19c asks for "the pledge of your kingdom," after assuming that the "Holy Spirit" of "you pour your Holy Spirit on them" is what is received in rebirth.[219] Ethiopic I may provide here an exception in asking "that they may be filled with the Holy Spirit," but the very means by which this happens is by "sending upon them your grace," and so even here there is no Spirit-epiclesis. Further, what appears to be the driving force for this handlaying prayer in all the versions (not just the Latin) is Titus 3:5 ("he saved us . . . according to his mercy, through the water of rebirth and renewal by the Holy Spirit") and John 3:5 ("Very truly, I tell you, no one can enter the kingdom of God without being born of water and Spirit"). The handlaying prayer thus reflects this theology in closely associating the Holy Spirit with baptism, i.e., the water bath.

Further development of this type of handlaying prayer, of course, would evolve into an explicit epiclesis of the Holy Spirit, whether Titus 3:5 and John 3:5 were invoked or not. For instance, in the Egyptian tradition, BR- and Euch-AC identify the handlaying as the moment of the bestowal of the Holy Spirit.[220] The text of BR-AC reads:

> Eternal God, who rules over all things, Father of the Lord Jesus Christ, who has born again your male and female servants of water and of the Spirit through the washing of rebirth, who has graciously granted the forgiveness

219. See Geoffrey Cuming, "The Post-Baptismal Prayer in *Apostolic Tradition*: Further Considerations," *Journal of Theological Studies* 39 (1988): 117–19.

220. For more on this prayer's reception, see Nathan Chase, "Further Reflections on the Post-Baptismal Anointing and Handlaying in the Egyptian Tradition," in *Explorations in Christian Initiation from the East*, ed. Stefanos Alexopoulos, Nathan Chase, and Anna Adams Petrin, Eastern Catholic Studies and Texts (Washington, DC: The Catholic University of America Press, forthcoming); Heinzgerd Brakmann, "ⲂⲀⲠⲦⲒⲤⲘⲀ ⲀⲒⲚⲈⲤⲈⲰⲤ: Ordines und Orationen kirchlicher Eingliederung in Alexandrien und Ägypten," in *»Neugeboren aus Wasser und Heiligem Geist« Kölner Kolloquium zur Initiatio Christiana*, ed. Heinzgerd Brakmann, Tinatin Chronz, and Claudia Sode (Münster: Aschendorff Verlag, 2020), 110, 133, and 191.

> of sins, send upon them from yourself the Holy Spirit, the Counselor, as through you your only Son Jesus Christ promised, when they were born again of water and of the Spirit, that through this he may grant them to enter the kingdom of heaven according to the holy, unfailing hope, in the name and power of the Lord Jesus Christ, through whom to you with him and with the Holy Spirit be praise and glory and power, now and for all generations, for the time to come, for ever and ever. Amen.[221]

Similarly, the current postbaptismal handlaying prayer and prayer after clothing in the CR, for example, read as though they are an update and expansion of Ethiopic I and Arabic I, although grace now appears in relationship to "sonship."

> *Postbaptismal handlaying prayer:* Mayest thou be blessed with the blessing of the heavenly ones, and the blessing of the angels. May the Lord Jesus Christ bless thee: and in his name (*here shall breathe in the face of him that has been baptized and say*), receive the Holy Spirit and be a purified vessel; through Jesus Christ our Lord, whose is the glory, with his good Father and the Holy Spirit, now and ever.
>
> *Prayer after clothing:* Master, Lord God Almighty, who alone are eternal, the Father of our Lord and our God and our Saviour Jesus Christ; who commanded that your servants should be born through the laver of the new birth, and has bestowed upon them forgiveness of their sins and the garment of incorruption and the grace of sonship. Now again, O our Master, send down upon them the grace of your Holy Spirit the Paraclete; make them partakers of life eternal and immortality, in order that, according as your Only-Begotten Son, our Lord and our God and our Saviour Jesus Christ promised, being born again by water and spirit, they may

221. German: "Ewiger Gott, der du alles beherrschest, Vater des Herrn Jesu Christi, der du deine Knechte und deine Mägde wiedergeboren hast aus Wasser und aus Geist durch das Bad der Wiedergeburt, der du gnädig gewährt hast Vergebung der Sünde, sende von dir her über sie den heiligen Geist, den Tröster, wie durch dich, dein einzelner Sohn Jesus Christus versprach, indem sie neu geboren aus Wasser und aus Geist waren, damit er ihnen dadurch zuerteile, daß sie eingehen in das Reich der Himmel gemäß der heiligen nicht trügenden Hoffnung im Namen und in der Kraft des Herrn Jesu Christi, durch den dir mit ihm und mit dem heiligen Geist (ist) Lob und Preis und Macht vor der Ewigkeit und jetzt und für die Geschlechter der Geschlechter für die Zukunft für die Ewigkeit der Ewigkeit. Amen." Bausi, "The *Baptismal Ritual*," 75.13–77.10. Translation ours.

> be able to enter into the kingdom of heaven. Through the Name and the power and the grace of your Only-Begotten Son Jesus Christ our Lord. Through whom . . .[222]

The prayer after clothing in the CR is really an adaptation of the original postbaptismal handlaying prayer in BR-AC given above.[223]

In the West, however, apart from references to handlaying and the gift of the Holy Spirit in various places, liturgical-textual references are later. In fact, our earliest liturgical reference is in the eighth-century manuscript of the *Sacramentarium Gelasianum*, Vat. Reg. 316, which reads:

> God almighty, Father of our Lord Jesus Christ, who granted regeneration to your servants by water and the Holy Spirit, and who have given them forgiveness of all their sins, send on them, Lord, your Holy Spirit the Paraclete, and give them the Spirit of wisdom and understanding, the Spirit of counsel and might, the Spirit of knowledge and godliness, fill them with the Spirit of the fear of God, in the name of our Lord Jesus Christ, with whom you live and reign, God forever with the Holy Spirit for ever and ever. Amen.[224]

But again, this Western prayer for the seven-fold gift of the Spirit, apart from the opening, is not what ApTrad in any of its versions says. Further, Ambrose of Milan, in his description of the "Spiritual Seal" in *De Sacramentis* III. 8-9, may also be referring to a similar postbaptismal handlaying prayer in use at Milan, saying:

> The spiritual sealing follows. You have heard about this in the reading today. For after the ceremonies of the font, it still remains to bring the whole to perfect fulfillment. This happens when the Holy Spirit is infused at the priest's invocation: 'the Spirit of wisdom and understanding, the Spirit of counsel and strength, the Spirit of knowledge and piety, the Spirit of holy fear.' These might be called the seven 'virtues' of the Spirit.[225]

222. DBL, 138–39.
223. Chase, "Further Reflections."
224. DBL, 235.
225. AIRI, 124–25.

But it is by no means certain if this is the case or what ritual act or gesture may have accompanied this "seal."[226] Furthermore, this kind of development is not seen in the various versions of ApTrad, although reference to the Holy Spirit in all versions, with the exception of the Verona Latin, could easily suggest further development. But building a case on the Verona Latin, especially now given the availability of Ethiopic I and Arabic I, seems to us unwarranted as a methodological principle. None of the extant versions actually separate the gift of the Spirit from baptism by seeking a separate conferral via the handlaying prayer.

It is also worth noting that the doxology of this prayer in ApTrad Ch. 21.21—"the Holy Spirit, in your holy church, both now and to the ages of ages"—is somewhat unique, though it appears in ApTrad Chs. 4, 6, and 7. However, this doxology does have a long reception in Egypt, where it appears as a doxology in an unknown and unnamed anaphora in the *Great Euchologion* from the White Monastery, as well as some other anaphoras and prayers, indicating the continued circulation of this style of doxology in Egypt.[227] At the very least, this indicates the long reception of ApTrad in the Egyptian tradition.

The anointing by the bishop at the conclusion of the handlaying prayer in Ch. 21.22—with the exception of Ethiopic II, which again repeats the error of using "exorcised oil"—is consistent across the versions employing not a pneumatic but trinitarian formula: "I anoint you <with oil> holy

226. Because Ambrose claims to be following the liturgical practices of Rome closely, it is quite possible that he is referring here to the kind of pneumatic handlaying prayer that does appear in the later *Sacramentarium Gelasianum* and that he is actually our first witness to late-fourth century Roman postbaptismal practice in this context. In any event, his "spiritual seal" is not clearly an anointing and one might well speculate as to whether the Roman rite knew a second postbaptismal anointing in this time period. See Maxwell Johnson, "The Postchrismational Structure of *Apostolic Tradition* 21, the Witness of Ambrose of Milan, and a Tentative Hypothesis Regarding the Current Reform of Confirmation in the Roman Rite," *Worship* 70, no. 1 (1996): 16–34; and Pamela Jackson, "The Meaning of 'Spiritale Signaculum' in the Mystagogy of Ambrose of Milan," *Ecclesia Orans* VII (Rome, 1990), 77–94.

227. Alois Grillmeier, *Christ in Christian Tradition: Vol. 2, From the Council of Chalcedon (451) to Gregory the Great (590–604); Part 4, The Church of Alexandria with Nubia and Ethiopia after 451*, vol. 2.4 (London: Mowbrays, 1996), 250. For the text of the anaphora, see Emmanuel Lanne, "Le Grand Euchologe du Monastère Blanc," *Patrologia Orientalis* 28, no. 2 (1958): 269–406, §137.20-21. For a full list of parallels, see pp. 110–11.

in Almighty God and Jesus Christ and the Holy Spirit" (Ethiopic I). One of the most interesting parts of this text for our purposes is 21.22-23, which appears to fuse and even condense the anointing and handlaying[228]—Latin: "Afterward, pouring the sanctified oil from [his] hand and placing [it] on the head, let him say . . ."; Ethiopic I: "[After] this, [while] pouring out the oil of thanksgiving, having placed it with [his hand] over his head . . ."; and most explicitly in the Bohairic: "And he pours oil of thanksgiving (εὐχαριστία) on his hand and lays his hand on his head . . ." This condensation or fusion of the ritual gestures is further confirmed in TD II.9, which has: "Similarly also as he pours out the oil, when he places a hand on his head let him say . . ."[229] This seems to suggest a blending of the two ritual gestures—anointing and handlaying, though it does not necessarily indicate which came first.

The combined anointing–handlaying in Ch. 21.22 is then followed in Ch. 21.23 by a signing on the forehead. A signing on the forehead, as can also be seen with Tertullian and Cyprian, is a ritual gesture that is frequently coupled with both anointings and handlayings. The text of ApTrad Ch. 21.23 leaves it ambiguous as to whether the signing accompanies the combined anointing-handlaying in Ch. 21.22, or whether it is a separate ritual gesture. *Herm.Com.* 2002 even suggests that this could be indicative of a handlaying with consignation that has since also become an anointing. In fact, the North African evidence "provides a clear parallel to what may have been the case in an earlier version of ApTrad. In other

228. Condensation is the process by which ritual patterns and symbols are combined and abbreviated to form a ritual. Fusion is a related phenomenon in which ritual components are brought together in a way that allows for the meaning of each component to combine in order to generate new connections and meanings, but the ritual components are not reduced. With ritual fusion, the ritual gestures remain distinct, but share a common meaning. For more, see Chase, "Anointings with Oil and Handlaying in the Early Church"; Nathan Chase, "Anointings with Oil and Handlayings in the Early Eastern Church: Further Evidence for These Gestures as Early Ritual Cognates," forthcoming in *Studia Liturgica*.

229. Grant Sperry-White, *The Testamentum Domini: A Text for Students, with Introduction, Translation, and Notes* (Nottingham: Grove Books, 1991), 29. For a more recent overview of the sources, dating, and provenance, see Martin Lüstraeten, "Edition und Übersetzung der Euchologie der Eucharistiefeier der Redaktion 'M' des arabischen *Testamentum Domini* (I.23-I.28)," *Ex Fonte – Journal of Ecumenical Studies in Liturgy* 2 (2023): 65–179.

words, prior to [the] composition of the Latin version, the postbaptismal episcopal rites added to the core rite in chap. 21 may have consisted simply of a handlaying prayer and consignation."[230] Interestingly, CH 19c does not mention the laying on of hands in conjunction with the episcopal anointing as in ApTrad Ch. 21.22, but it will note that the episcopal anointing is done via a signing: "Next, he signs their forehead with the oil of anointing." Here we may be seeing some ritual condensation or this may simply further suggest that the consignation in ApTrad Ch. 21.23 was done with the anointing in Ch. 21.22. It may also, as we will see, point to CH 19c preserving an earlier form. In any event, TD II.9 also follows ApTrad closely here.[231] It seems that this consignation in ApTrad is a continuation of the handlaying–anointing in Ch. 21.22.

Turning back to CH, in one manuscript of CH 19c, the bishop merely *signs* the forehead of the neophyte with "the sign of charity" and no reference is made to either anointing or oil: "Next he signs their forehead with the sign of charity and gives them the kiss, saying, 'The Lord be with you.' And those who have been baptized also say, 'And with your spirit.' He does this to each of the baptized."[232] Hanssens argued that the reading of this manuscript was to be preferred as providing the best and, thus, original reading at this point in ApTrad, and as we will see below there are reasons to hold this view.[233] If Hanssens was correct, it would mean that, at some stage, Ch. 21.21-22 may have had a structure of prayer with imposition of hands and some kind of "signing" by the bishop after the postbaptismal anointing, but this episcopal "signing" had not yet become a second postbaptismal *anointing*. While Hanssens's assessment may be correct, he himself failed to provide any concrete evidence that this was the case.

Nevertheless, one should not automatically rule out his hypothesis altogether. It is worth noting that in ApTrad Ch. 21.19, the first anointing is done by the presbyter—"I anoint you with holy oil in the name of Jesus

230. *Herm.Com.* 2002, 133.

231. Sperry-White, *The Testamentum Domini: A Text for Students*, 29.

232. DBL, 131–32.

233. J. M. Hanssens, "L'édition critique des Canons d'Hippolyte," *Orientalia Christiana Periodica* 32 (1966): 542–43. See also Paul Bradshaw, *The Canons of Hippolytus*, Alcuin/GROW Liturgical Study 2 (Bramcote: Grove Books, 1987), 24. It has been suggested that this "sign of charity" was originally the baptismal kiss but, at least here, it appears to be a separate act from the kiss which immediately follows.

Christ"—while the second anointing in Ch. 21.22 is done by the bishop—"I anoint you with holy oil in God the Father Almighty and Christ Jesus and the Holy Spirit." The administration of the first anointing is not described, while that of the second is on the forehead. In CH 19c, the first anointing is a full-body anointing done by the presbyter with the formula: "I anoint you in the name of the Father, of the Son, and of the Holy Spirit"; however, the second anointing is done by the bishop on the forehead and unlike ApTrad Ch. 21.22 lacks a formula. Furthermore, the formula used for the presbyteral anointing, which is now a full body anointing, is the formula given in ApTrad for the second episcopal anointing. This will actually be retained in the later CR (see Excursus below).

All of this clearly indicates some development in either CH or ApTrad.[234] The episcopal anointing in ApTrad Ch. 21.22 either: 1) quickly fell out of use in CH 19c or was greatly minimized; or 2) the episcopal anointing in ApTrad Ch. 21.22 was a recent addition to ApTrad and CH 19c actually preserves an older form. The first possiblity is supported by the fact that one version of CH 19c omits it (as Hanssens has observed), and the fact that CH 19c combines the full-body anointing of the presbyteral anointing—this full-body anointing possibly being the only indication of a local Egyptian tradition, since ApTrad does not indicate the way of anointing—with the formula of the episcopal anointing, and concludes by giving the episcopal anointing a passing glance.[235] The second possibility, that the episcopal anointing was a recent addition to ApTrad, is again possibly supported by the manuscript of CH 19c that omits the anointing, as well as the fact that, again, all the other versions of CH 19c have a mixture of the full-body presbyteral anointing with the episcopal anointing formula. However, further support for this latter possibility is the omission of a reference to the handlaying along with the episcopal anointing in CH 19c. This would seem to suggest that a single postbaptismal anointing followed by a handlaying was the original core of the ritual in CH 19c before an episcopal anointing came to be added. In other words, CH 19c seems to point to an earlier time when there was not a duplication of the postbaptismal anointings.

234. Bradshaw, *The Canons of Hippolytus*, 24.

235. Bradshaw, 24.

Internal evidence also seems to point to developments in ApTrad's postbaptismal rites. ApTrad Ch. 21.21-23 are especially convoluted, and interestingly begin after a change in venue into the church. This suggests a quite natural break in the text. How to read the texts in ApTrad Ch. 21.21-23 is complex. It seems, as noted above, that there was a handlaying done by the bishop that would come to include an anointing (v. 22) and likely that was done through a consignation (v. 23). That the relationship between vv. 22 and 23 is not entirely clear also points to some developments. ApTrad appears to be adding on here rather than preserving an earlier form, especially in comparision to CH 19c. In any event, a case can be made that CH 19c may actually be hinting at an earlier read of the text that included a single postbaptismal anointing done by either the presbyter or the bishop, followed by a handlaying prayer. This likely possibility is significant when looking at the later Egyptian rites of initiation.

In fact, a single postbaptismal anointing and handlaying is precisely what is seen in BR- and Euch-AC, though there the handlaying precedes the anointing according to the rubrics, despite the fact that the handlaying is actually given second in the text (see Excursus below). There is some clear disruption in the postbaptismal rites at this point in BR- and Euch-AC, and it cannot be discounted that originally the pattern was handlaying—anointing even if the reverse is how the text indicates the gestures should be administered.[236] In the later Egyptian rites, like CB and Arb-TD.B, there is only a single postbaptismal anointing, though in those sources too there are indications that the postbaptismal anointing was once followed by a handlaying as well.[237] And, in fact, the CR has no signing or anointing or even kiss by the bishop (or presbyter) after the handlaying prayer but has a similar structure of postbaptismal anointing with chrism and handlaying prayer, both of which by this point are highly pneumatic in emphasis. Such may speak once again in favor of the Egyptian origins of not only CH[238] but of ApTrad itself. This will be treated more in the Excursus below.

In fact, a *second* postbaptismal, episcopal anointing such as this within liturgical *texts* of Christian initiation rites has no parallel prior to the

236. See Chase, "Further Reflections"; Brakmann, "ⲃⲁⲡⲧⲓⲥⲙⲁ ⲁⲓⲛⲉⲥⲉⲱⲥ," 145–94.

237. See Chase, "Further Reflections."

238. See our study, Chase and Johnson, *The Origins of the Canons of Hippolytus*.

eighth-century *Sacramentarium Gelasianum*, where the formula is not pneumatic but christic: "the sign of Christ unto life eternal."[239] And, depending upon how one interprets the *Spiritual Seal* in the Milanese baptismal rites described in the *De Sacramentis* of Ambrose of Milan,[240] the earliest reference to this episcopal anointing is the famous fifth-century letter of Pope Innocent I to Decentius of Gubbio (416 CE), in which Innocent not only appears to be aware of a pneumatic handlaying prayer,[241] but boldly asserts the following:

> About the signing of the newly baptized: it is quite clear that no one may perform it except the bishop. For although presbyters are priests (*sacerdotes*), they do not have the highest degree of the priesthood (*pontificatus*). It is not only the custom of the Church which demonstrated that the signing and the gift of the Holy Spirit is restricted to bishops (*pontifices*), but the passage in the Acts of the Apostles which declares that Peter and John were sent to give the Holy Spirit to those already baptized. For when presbyters baptize, whether in the absence of a bishop or in his presence, they may anoint the baptized with chrism (provided that it is consecrated by the bishop) but they do not sign the forehead with this same oil. That is reserved to the bishops when they give the Spirit, the Paraclete.[242]

That an episcopal handlaying and prayer followed by some kind of "signing," rather than anointing, however, was part of the structure of the post-baptismal rites in mid-third-century North Africa *may* be corroborated by the witness of Cyprian. In *Letter 73, To Januarius*, 9, Cyprian writes that "They who are baptized in the church are brought to the prelates of the church, and by our prayers and by the imposition of the hand obtain the Holy Spirit, and are perfected with the Lord's seal [*signaculo dominico*]."[243] Although it is difficult to tell whether Cyprian intends to say that this perfecting "with the Lord's seal" is the consequence of the imposition of the hand and prayer or a subsequent ritual gesture *after* the imposition and

239. DBL, 235.

240. See above. See also DBL, 181.

241. Though this has recently been challenged by Chase, "Anointings with Oil and Handlaying in the Early Church."

242. Martin Connell, *Church and Worship in Fifth-Century Rome: The Letter of Pope Innocent I to Decentius of Gubbio*, JLS 52 (Cambridge: Grove Books, 2002), 44–45.

243. DBL, 11.

prayer, scholars have tended here to favor the latter interpretation.[244] If this is correct it provides a clear parallel to what may well have been the case in an earlier version of ApTrad possibly represented by CH 19c. In other words, prior to the postbaptismal episcopal rites added to the core rite, Ch. 21 may have consisted simply of a postbaptismal anointing (later reserved to presbyters), a handlaying prayer primarily for grace, and some kind of consignation (kiss?). That this later "signing" would be connected eventually to an anointing is no surprise, at least in the context of fourth-century liturgical development, where many churches throughout the world now received pneumatic postbaptismal anointings into their initiation rites or a new pneumatic interpretation of those anointings already existing.[245]

### *7.5. Prayer of the Faithful (vv. 25-26)*

The description of the initiation rites concludes rather abruptly in Ch. 21.25-26 with the newly baptized joining now for the first time in the prayers of the faithful and, after those prayers, offering what all versions refer to as "peace with the mouth," a reference to sharing the kiss of peace. Such undoubtedly reflects a very early stage in the document's development and shows a remarkable degree of consistency with Justin Martyr's description of what took place immediately after baptism in the mid-second century:

> *First Apology*, 65: After thus baptizing the one who has believed and given his assent, we escort him to the place where are assembled those whom we call brethren, to offer up sincere prayers in common for ourselves, for the baptized person, and for all other persons wherever they may be, in order that, since we have found the truth, we may be deemed fit through our actions to be esteemed as good citizens and observers of the law, and thus attain eternal salvation. At the conclusion of prayers we greet one another with a kiss.[246]

### *7.6. Conclusion (vv. 30 and 38-40)*

Amid the discussion of the baptismal Eucharist, there are a few verses that seek to wrap up the section on initiation (v 30 and 38-40). Most of this

244. See Frank Quinn, "Confirmation Reconsidered: Rite and Meaning," in LWSS, 223f. As noted above, similar problems are encountered in attempting to interpret what gestures may have been associated with the conferring of the "Spiritual Seal" in the writings of Ambrose of Milan.

245. See Johnson, *The Rites of Christian Initiation*, 137–57 and 159–200.

246. DBL, 3.

section is dedicated to the bishop providing proper formation to those who have just been initiated (vv. 30 and 39-40). However, part of the section repeats the call to live a good life (v. 38). Finally, it is worth noting the absence of the Lord's Prayer anywhere in the initiatory materials, something that is rather odd for the rites of initiation in this period.[247]

## 8. Excursus on Egyptian Parallels

### *8.1. Introduction to the Egyptian Sources*

Turning to explicit Egyptian connections, there are only two sources that definitively attest to the rites of initiation in fourth-century Egypt, both contemporary with ApTrad, and neither coming from Alexandria (for more information on each source, see our Introduction):[248] CH and the sacramentary of Sarapion of Thmuis. Two other possible sources, however, are the Baptismal Ritual (BR-AC) and Euchologion (Euch-AC) in the Aksumite Collection, which may attest to practices as early as the fourth century in Alexandria. Other sources worth including are the CB—Canons 101-106; Arb-TD.B; and the initiatory rituals of the modern CR. More work is needed on the medieval Coptic manuscripts, but the CR appears to follow the earliest Bohairic sources.[249] The Ethiopian Mystagogical Catechesis (Ethio-MC), copied from a Greek exemplar in Alexandria in the fifth century, will be mentioned in passing.

*Reconstructing Alexandria's Initiatory Rites (BR- and Euch-AC)?*

It is worth beginning by outlining the initiatory rites in BR-AC and Euch-AC, which attest to the first form of initiation rites in Egypt not directly derived from ApTrad (henceforth BR-/Euch-AC). Significantly, they were also included in the Aksumite Collection alongside the material in ApTrad Chs. 20-21, perhaps as an updated set of rites of initiation. For ease of comparison, and to provide an outline of the initiatory rites as described in BR-AC and Euch-AC, the following table (Table 8 below) outlines the rites in the BR- and Euch-AC according to the ordering of the material in Euch-AC. Citations for the Euch-AC use the folio number and those for

247. Stewart, *On the Apostolic Tradition*, 157.

248. Cf. Brakmann, "ⲃⲁⲡⲧⲓⲥⲙⲁ ⲁⲓⲛⲉⲥⲉⲱⲥ"; Johnson, *The Rites of Christian Initiation*, 148–53 and 154.

249. See n. 116 in our Introduction.

the BR-AC are taken from the German translation by Bausi.[250] In a few cases, prayers from elsewhere in the Euch-AC will also be referenced in the table below in their ritual sequence in order to provide the fullest possible description of the initiatory rituals according to both documents. The consistency between the documents suggests that a common structure can be seen behind these initiatory rites, and it is this common structure that will be compared to the other sources under consideration in Table 9 below.

**Table 8: Comparison of Euch-AC and BR-AC**

| Euch-AC | | BR-AC |
|---|---|---|
| | *Rites of the Catechumenate* | |
| | | Enrollment and examination (65.1–10) |
| Prayer for those who are enrolled (Σ50$^{va}$–51$^{ra}$)[251] | ≠ | Prayer for those who are enrolled (65.11–21) |
| Prayer of exorcism for the catechumens (Σ48$^{vb}$–49$^{ra}$) | | |
| Prayer for the laying on of hands on the catechumens (Σ49$^{ra}$)[252] | | |
| | | Prayer of exorcism for those who bring bread, water, or oil (65.22–37)[253] |
| | | Anointing with oil (67.1–7) |
| | | Dismissal of the catechumens during liturgies (81.8–25) |

250. Bausi, "The *Baptismal Ritual*."

251. From the independent intercessions in Euch-AC. Parallels in H 30.5–21; D 82.6–84.2.

252. From the independent intercessions in Euch-AC. Parallels in H 36.13–23; D 102.14–104.6.

253. The prayer in BR-AC may be a remnant of a prayer for the catechumens. A similar set of prayers appears in Sarapion's sacramentary, see Prayers 5 and 6, as well as 17 (Johnson, *The Prayers of Sarapion of Thmuis*; Ágnes T. Mihálykó, "Healing in Christian Liturgy in Late Antique Egypt: Sources and Perspectives," Trends in *Classics* 13 [2021]: 176–79).

| *Prebaptismal Rites* | | |
|---|---|---|
| Blessing of the Water (Σ51$^{vb}$–52$^{ra}$)[254] | ≠ | [Blessing of the Water (73.5–75.8)][255] |
| Prayer of the Prebaptismal Oil (Σ52$^{ra}$) | ≠ | [Prayer of the Prebaptismal Oil (69.23–71.11)][256] |
| Anathematization [*apotaxis*] (Σ52$^{ra}$–52$^{rb}$) | ≈ | Anathematization [*apotaxis*] (67.8–21) |
| Profession of faith [*syntaxis*] (Σ52$^{rb}$) | = | Profession of faith [*syntaxis*] (67.22–31) |
| | | Confession for adults, children, and those who are unwell and mute (67.32–69.5) |
| Laying on of hands (Σ52$^{rb}$–52$^{va}$)[257] | ≈ | Laying on of hands (69.6–22) |
| | | *Prayer of the Prebaptismal Oil (69.23–71.11) |
| Full-body anointing with prayer (Σ52$^{va}$–52$^{vb}$)[258] | = | Full-body anointing with prayer (71.11–31) |
| | | **Blessing of the Water (73.5–75.8) |

254. Another prayer for the exorcism of water appears in Σ54$^{rb}$ (H 32.3-11; D 90.1-8), though it is not clear what this prayer was for. Its form suggests multiple uses.

255. Located in BR-AC at ** below in table.

256. Located in BR-AC at * below in table.

257. The prayer in Euch-AC Σ52$^{rb}$-52$^{va}$ is different from H 36.13-23, which is the prayer used in this location in H. H 36.13-23 is actually used earlier in Euch-AC for the prayer for the laying on of hands on the catechumens (Σ49$^{ra}$) (see n. 252). This prayer on Σ52$^{rb}$-52$^{va}$ of Euch-AC is, however, very similar to the second half of the prayer in H 38.25–39.6 and D 112.10–114.2—the same prayer in BR-AC 68.6-16. The prayer in H 38.25–39.6 and D 112.10–114.2 shares similarities in the first part of its prayer to H 36.13-23 and in the second part of its prayer to the prayer for the imposition of hands in Σ52$^{rb}$-52$^{va}$ of Euch-AC. All of this points to the complex reception of these prayers.

258. See also n. 257. The anointing formula also appears in P. Ryl. III.471, see Theodore De Bruyn, "P. Ryl. III.471: A Baptismal Anointing Formula Used as an Amulet," *The Journal of Theological Studies* 57 (2006): 94–109.

| **Table 8: Comparison of Euch-AC and BR-AC** (cont.) | | |
|---|---|---|
| | *Baptism* | |
| Descent into font ($\Sigma 52^{vb}$) | = | Descent into font (73.1–2; 75.9–10) |
| Baptism with trinitarian formula ($\Sigma 52^{vb}$–$53^{ra}$) | ≈ | Baptism with trinitarian formula (75.11–14) |
| | | Baptism of the sick (75.20–26) |
| | *Postbaptismal Rites* | |
| Ascent from the font ($\Sigma 53^{ra}$) | ≠ | Ascent from the font (75.15–19) |
| | | Clothing (75.27) |
| Laying on of hands ($\Sigma 53^{vb}$) [displaced in the text[259]] | ≈ | Laying on of hands (75.27–77.10)[260] |
| Prayer for the chrism ($\Sigma 53^{ra}$–$53^{va}$) | ≠ | Prayer for the chrism (77.11–79.17) |
| | | Anointing of the forehead and chest (79.17–25) |
| Prayer of oil for the new ones. Entrance of the catechumens to the sick ($\Sigma 53^{vb}$–$54^{ra}$)[261] | ≈ | Anointing for those who are sick (79.26–81.7) |
| | | Communion with milk and honey (81.26–83.19) |
| | | Laying on of hands with concluding prayer for baptized (83.20–33) |

*Signa:*
*= denotes the same text*
*≠ denotes different texts*
*≈ denotes similar texts*

259. This prayer actually comes at the end of the text, but a rubric says that it comes before the prayer for the chrism.

260. This prayer is the same as the one in Euch-AC, except that it contains the phrase, "as through him, your only Son Jesus Christ, you promised, in that they were born again of water and of the Spirit." Translation ours. German: "wie durch dich, dein einzelner Sohn Jesus Christus versprach, indem sie neu geboren aus Wasser und aus Geist waren." See also n. 257.

261. H 33.25–34.10; D 94.15–96.7. This prayer may not belong to the baptismal rites.

On the whole, BR-AC and Euch-AC together fill in missing material from the other, providing us with a combined rite of initiation in the fifth/sixth century—or possibly even earlier—that will be used as the basis for our comparison to ApTrad below. Whether it is representative of Alexandrian tradition remains to be seen, but will be taken up below.

The key differences between BR- and Euch-AC are the way BR-AC provides more information about the catechumenate and the treatment of the sick. However, there are some discrepancies over the location of the blessing of the water and the prebaptismal anointing oil. The text also presupposes episcopal involvement as normative; however, there are also indications that the rite has been adapted to a context where the bishop is not always present (see below). This would not be entirely surprising since we know from other liturgical sources that the celebration of the rites of initiation by commissioned presbyters in non-emergency contexts likely began in the late fourth or early fifth century in Egypt, and was clearly established by the sixth century.[262] This was likely in part the result of a shift to infant baptism, which is already clear in writings of Shenoute of Atripe (c. 348–465).[263] Similarly, this coincided with a shift away from the celebration of baptism at specific times in the liturgical year.[264]

### *8.2. Comparing ApTrad and the Egyptian Rites of Initiation*

Having established the combined testament of BR-AC and Euch-AC (BR-/Euch-AC), it is now worth turning to the Egyptian rites of initiation and their relationship to ApTrad. The following is a structural comparison of the rites (see Table 9 below):

262. Brakmann, "ⲃⲁⲡⲧⲓⲥⲙⲁ ⲁⲓⲛⲉⲥⲉⲱⲥ," 115–16.

263. Hugo Lundhaug, "Baptism in the Monasteries of Upper Egypt: The Pachomian Corpus and the Writings of Shenoute," in *Ablution, Initiation, and Baptism in Early Judaism, Graeco-Roman Religion, and Early Christianity*, ed. David Hellholm et al. (Berlin: Walter de Gruyter, 2011), 1372.

264. Brakmann, "ⲃⲁⲡⲧⲓⲥⲙⲁ ⲁⲓⲛⲉⲥⲉⲱⲥ," 139–41.

**Table 9: Structural Comparison of ApTrad's Rites of Initiation to the Egyptian Sources**

| **ApTrad** | **CH** | **Sacramentary of Sarapion**[265] | **Combined rites from BR- and Euch-AC**[266] | **CB** | **Arb-TD.B** | **CR** |
|---|---|---|---|---|---|---|
| *Catechumenate* | *Catechumenate* | *Catechumenate* | *Catechumenate* | *Catechumenate*[267] | *Catechumenate* | *Catechumenate/ Prebaptismal Rites*[268] |
| -Entrance[269]<br>-3 year catechumenate[271]<br>-Examination of life, regular moral teaching and instruction[273] | -Entrance<br>-40 day catechumenate[272]<br>-Examination of life, regular moral teaching and instruction | | -Enrollment[270]<br><br>-Examination of life | | | |

265. The prayers in Sarapion suggest a structure like that outlined above, though parts of the rites are not mentioned.
266. Taken from Table 8 above.
267. Canon 101 mirrors ApTrad Ch. 20 and CH 19.
268. The catechumenal rites have collapsed into the prebaptismal rites.
269. Ch. 15.
270. One prayer is in BR-AC, the other, which is an intercession for those who have enrolled, is in the Euch-AC Σ50$^{va}$-51$^{ra}$ (H 30.5-21; D 82.6–84.2).
271. Ch. 17.
272. Ch. 17.
273. Chs. 15, 17, and 18. This likely occurred at the same service as that described in Chs. 35, 39, and 41.1-4; see Ch. 4 of our commentary.

| | | | | | | |
|---|---|---|---|---|---|---|
| -Scripture readings[274]<br>-Regular prayer with instruction[275] | -Scripture readings<br>-Regular prayer with instruction | | | | | |
| | | -Prayer for the Catechumens (P. 21) | | | -Prayer over catechumens | -Prayers over catechumens |
| -Hands laid on them[276] | -Hands laid on them | -Laying on of Hands of Catechumens (P. 28)[277] | -Prayer for handlaying on catechumens[278] | | | |
| -Expected to visit the widows and sick[279] | -Expected to visit the widows?? and sick | | | | | |

274. Chs. 15, 17, and 18. This likely occurred at the same service as that described in Chs. 35, 39, and 41.1-4; see Ch. 4 of our commentary.
275. Ch. 18. This likely occurred at the same service as that described in Chs. 35, 39, and 41.1-4; see Ch. 4 of our commentary.
276. Ch. 19.
277. Possibly here, and/or below; see n. 283.
278. Possibly here, and/or below; see n. 284. Taken from Euch-AC Σ49[ra] (H 36.13-23; D 102.14–104.6).
279. Ch. 20.1.

**Table 9: Structural Comparison of ApTrad's Rites of Initiation to the Egyptian Sources** (cont.)

| **ApTrad** | **CH** | **Sacramentary of Sarapion** | **Combined rites from BR- and Euch-AC** | **CB** | **Arb-TD.B** | **CR** |
|---|---|---|---|---|---|---|
| -Communal meals[281] | -Communal meals | | -Prayer of exorcism of those who bring bread, water, and oil[280]<br>-Blessed bread and water<br>-Anointing with oil (daily)[282] | | | |
| *Period Before Baptism (Ch. 20)*<br>-Enrollment with examination<br>-Daily exorcisms with handlaying | *Period Before Baptism*<br>-Enrollment with examination | | | | | |

280. The prayer in BR-AC may be a remnant of prayer for the catechumens; however, there is a prayer for catechumens in the Euch-AC $\Sigma 48^{vb}$-$49^{ra}$ (H 83.25–84.11). A similar set of prayers to the one in BR-AC occurs in Sarapion (Prayers 5 and 6, as well as 17). See Mihálykó, "Healing in Christian Liturgy," 176–79.

281. See Ch. 6 of our commentary.

282. Possibly here, and/or below; see n. 285.

| | | | | | | |
|---|---|---|---|---|---|---|
| -Washing<br>**Friday:**<br>-Fast<br>**Saturday**<br>-Prayer | -Washing<br>**Friday:**<br>-Fast<br>**Saturday** | | | | | |
| -Exorcism | -Handlaying with prayer of exorcism | -Laying on of hands of catechu-mens (P. 28)[283] | -[Prayer for handlaying on catechumens][284] | | | |
| -Breathing on them | -Breathing on face | | | | | |
| | | | | | | -Prayer over oil of catechumens |
| -Signs forehead, ears, nostrils | -Signs their breast, forehead, ears and nose | | -[Anointing with oil (daily)][285] | | | -Anointing of forehead<br>-Anointing of breast, hands, and back |
| -Vigil with readings and instruction | -Vigil with readings and instruction | | | | | |

283. Possibly here, and/or above; see n. 277.

284. Possibly here, and/or above; see n. 278. Taken from Euch-AC $\Sigma 49^{ra}$ (H 36.13-23; D 102.14–104.6).

285. Possibly here, and/or above; see n. 282.

**Table 9: Structural Comparison of ApTrad's Rites of Initiation to the Egyptian Sources** (cont.)

| ApTrad | CH | Sacramentary of Sarapion | Combined rites from BR- and Euch-AC | CB | Arb-TD.B | CR |
|---|---|---|---|---|---|---|
| | | | | | | -Prayers over catechumens<br>-Enrollment of names<br>-Handlaying |
| *Prebaptismal* | *Prebaptismal* | *Prebaptismal* | *Prebaptismal* | *Prebaptismal* | *Prebaptismal* | |
| -Prayer over water | -Preparation and sanctification of water | -Sanctification of Waters[286]<br><br>-[Prayer][287]<br>-Apotaxis and<br>-Syntaxis[288]<br>Handlaying(?)[291] | -Apotaxis[289]<br>-Syntaxis[290]<br>-Handlaying (exorcistic)[292] | -Prayer over water (oil poured in) | | |

286. Sanctification of Waters (Prayer 7).

287. Prayer for those being Baptized (Prayer 8).

288. Prayer after the Renunciation (Prayer 9) and perhaps Prayer after the Reception (Prayer 10).

289. Same as in Euch-AC $\Sigma 52^{ra}$-$52^{rb}$ (H 37.27–38.11; D 108.15–110.9).

290. See note above.

291. Prayer after the Reception (Prayer 10).

292. A slightly different prayer than the one in BR-AC appears in Euch-AC $\Sigma 52^{rb}$-$52^{va}$. The prayer in Euch-AC $\Sigma 52^{rb}$-$52^{va}$ is different from H 36.13-23, which is the prayer used in this location in H. H 36.13-23 is actually used earlier in Euch-AC for the Handlaying upon the catechumens

| | | | | | | |
|---|---|---|---|---|---|---|
| -De-robing<br>-Blessing of oil of thanksgiving<br>-Blessing of oil of exorcism<br>-Apotaxis | -De-robing<br>-Blessing of oil of exorcism<br>-Blessing of the oil of anoint-ing (= oil of thanksgiving)<br>-Apotaxis | | -Oil prayer (exorcistic)[293] | -Prayer over oil<br>-Prayer over chrism | -Prayer over oil | De-robing<br>-Apotaxis |
| -Anointing with oil of exorcism | -Anointing with oil of exorcism | -Anointing[294] | -Anointing (full-body) with prayer[295] | | -Exorcistic anointing (full-body) | |

(see n. 284). This prayer in Euch-AC Σ52$^{rb}$-52$^{va}$ is, however, very similar to the second half of the prayer in H 38.25–39.6 and D 112.10–114.2—the same prayer in the Baptismal Ritual 68.6-16. The prayer in H 38.25–39.6 and D 112.10–114.2 shares similarities in the first part of its prayer to H 36.13-23 and in the second part of its prayer to the prayer for the imposition of hands in Euch-AC Σ52$^{rb}$-52$^{va}$. All of this points to the complex reception of these prayers. As Bausi has noted to me, this prayer—as well as the prayers at nn. 295 and 300—are attributed to the Baptismal Ritual as split in the Sinodos, not the Euchologion.

293. A different prayer appears in the Euch-AC Σ52$^{ra}$ (H 34.10-19; D 96.8-15).

294. Prayer for the Oil of those being Baptized (Prayer 15).

295. Same as in Euch-AC: Anointing – Σ52$^{va}$-52$^{vb}$ (H 39.7-12; D 114.2-8); Prayer – Σ52$^{vb}$ (H 39.12-21; D 114.9-17). See also the note in n. 292. The anointing formula also appears in P. Ryl. III.471; see De Bruyn, "P. Ryl. III.471."

**Table 9: Structural Comparison of ApTrad's Rites of Initiation to the Egyptian Sources** (cont.)

| **ApTrad** | **CH** | **Sacramentary of Sarapion** | **Combined rites from BR- and Euch-AC** | **CB** | **Arb-TD.B** | **CR** |
|---|---|---|---|---|---|---|
| | | | -Blessing of water[296] | | | |
| | | | | | | -Breathing on the catechumens |
| | | | | -Exorcism prayer | | |
| | | | | | -Prayer after anointing | |
| | | | | -Apotaxis | -Apotaxis | |
| | | | | -Anointing with oil of incantation | | |
| | | | | -Pour oil into font | | |
| -Syntaxis (in Sahidic, Arabic II, and Ethiopic II, but not in Latin, Ethiopic I, or Arabic I) | -Syntaxis | | | -Syntaxis | -Syntaxis | -Syntaxis |

296. A different prayer occurs in the Euch-AC Σ51$^{vb}$-52$^{ra}$ (H 31.19–32.3; D 88.5-16), which appears at the start of the rite.

| | | | | | | |
|---|---|---|---|---|---|---|
| | | | | | | -Prayers over the catechumens<br>-Anointing with the oil of exor-cism on breast, arms, back, hands<br>-Handlaying and prayers<br>-Procession to font<br>-Pouring oil in the font<br>-Liturgy of the Word<br>-Prayer intercessions<br>-Prayer over font<br>-Three great petitions<br>-Creed |
| | | | | | -Oil in font with prayer | -Pouring of oil in the font with insufflations and consignations<br>-Pouring chrism in font with alleluia |

**Table 9: Structural Comparison of ApTrad's Rites of Initiation to the Egyptian Sources** (cont.)

| **ApTrad** | **CH** | **Sacramentary of Sarapion** | **Combined rites from BR- and Euch-AC** | **CB** | **Arb-TD.B** | **CR** |
|---|---|---|---|---|---|---|
| | | | | | -Font blessing | -Prayer of sancti-fication (dialogue, preface, *Sanctus*, etc.) |
| Interrogative form for baptism | Interrogative form for baptism with indicative formula | [Baptism] | Indicative form for Baptism[297] | Baptism in trini-tarian formula | Indicative form for Baptism | Indicative form for Baptism |
| *Postbaptismal* | *Postbaptismal* | *Postbaptismal* | *Postbaptismal* | *Postbaptismal* | *Postbaptismal* | *Postbaptismal* |
| | | -[Prayer][298] | -Clothing[299] | | -Clothing<br>-Prayer after clothing (pneumatic) | -De-consecration of the font |

297. Same as in Euch-AC Σ52$^{vb}$-53$^{ra}$ (H 39.20–40.2; D 114.17–116.9).
298. Prayer after being Baptized and Coming Up (Prayer 11).
299. The postbaptismal rites in BR- and Euch-AC show some rearrangement; see Chase, "Further Reflections."

| | | | | | | |
|---|---|---|---|---|---|---|
| -Anointing with oil of thanksgiving | -Anointing with oil of thanks-giving (= oil of anointing) on forehead, mouth, breast, body, head and face by presbyter | -Anointing with chrism[302] | -Handlaying[300]<br>-Prayer over oil[301]<br><br>-Breathing<br>-Anointing of fore-head and chest<br><br>-Anointing for those who are sick[303] | -Anointing of forehead, hips, hands, shoulders, two elbows, all the joints of the body, two ears, two eyes, nose, tongue, full-body | -Prayer over oil<br><br>-Anointing of various parts of the body | -Prayer over chrism<br><br>-Anointings over 30 parts of the body |
| | | | | -The bishop also prays a prayer over them labeled as the "Prayer after baptism" | -Prayer over the baptized | |

300. Same prayer in Euch-AC $\Sigma 53^{vb}$ (H 40.2-13; D 116.10–118.3), except the phrase "wie durch dich, dein einzelner Sohn Jesus Christus versprach, indem sie neu geboren aus Wasser und aus Geist waren," which appears in the prayer in the BR-AC. See also n. 292.

301. Different prayer in Euch-AC $\Sigma 53^{ra}$-$53^{va}$ (H 34.19–35.18; D 96.16–100.6).

302. Prayer for the Chrism with which the Baptized are Anointed (Prayer 16).

303. Very similar to the prayer in Euch-AC $\Sigma 53^{vb}$-$54^{ra}$ (H 33.25–34.10; D 94.15–96.7).

**Table 9: Structural Comparison of ApTrad's Rites of Initiation to the Egyptian Sources** (cont.)

| **ApTrad** | **CH** | **Sacramentary of Sarapion** | **Combined rites from BR- and Euch-AC** | **CB** | **Arb-TD.B** | **CR** |
|---|---|---|---|---|---|---|
| -Clothed<br>-Taken to church<br>-Bishop lays hands with prayer<br><br><br><br><br>-Bishop signs forehead with oil of anointing<br>-Communion<br>-Milk and honey | -Clothed<br>-Taken to church<br>-Bishop handlaying with prayer<br><br><br><br><br>-Bishop signs forehead with oil of anointing<br>-Communion<br>-Milk and honey | | -Communion<br>-Milk and honey<br>-Handlaying with concluding prayer for baptized | -Communion | | -Handlaying<br><br>-Insufflation with formula<br>-Dressing and crowning<br><br><br>-Communion<br><br>-Handlaying |

Comparisons between ApTrad and CH have been highlighted throughout the commentary above. As we have argued elsewhere, CH reflects a local derivation of ApTrad. Its central differences from its source document with regard to the rites of initiation include:

- A forty-day catechumenate instead of a three-year one;
- The lack of daily exorcisms;
- The reversal of the order of the blessings of the oil. In this way, CH is consistent with Ethiopic I;
- The addition of the indicative formulae for baptism;
- Possibly attesting to the older use of a single postbaptismal anointing.

On the whole, it is quite similar to ApTrad, except in possibly giving an earlier form of the postbaptismal rites, including the apparent Egyptian practice of anointing the full body. At the same time, the document does not represent Alexandrian practice. Thus, the full-body anointing and the form of the postbaptismal rites may be the result of earlier forms but also some degree of geographical/ecclesial differences. At the same time, CH indicates that the initiatory materials in ApTrad were thoroughly received in the Egyptian milieu in which CH was used.

Sarapion unfortunately does not provide an ordo of initiation that we can compare to ApTrad and CH. Moreover, its prayer texts appear to betray a local flavor. However, there is much that is consistent, or potentially consistent, with what can be seen in ApTrad and CH. The only difference is that only one postbaptismal anointing prayer is given, suggesting that we are again not looking at a double postbaptismal anointing in Sarapion. This, however, may have been the older form of both ApTrad and CH, and as such does not say much for or against Egyptian connections to ApTrad.

Comparing the combined rite in BR- and Euch-AC (BR-/Euch-AC) to ApTrad and CH also reveals some interesting similarities, but also some differences. While much of the catechumenate is not described, BR-/Euch-AC appear to point to extensive examination of the catechumens, as well as frequent laying on of hands and anointings of the catechumens. These are, of course, features prominent in ApTrad. Moreover, much of what is implied in BR-/Euch-AC seems filled out in Ethio-MC, which is roughly contemporaneous with them and also from Alexandria/Egypt.

Ethio-MC begins with a theological treatise on baptism (§1-6) followed by the moral demands of baptism and the need to avoid many of the types of people and practices described in ApTrad Ch. 16 (§7-8). There is also a strong exhortation to catechists (§9-11), all consistent with what is seen and implied in BR-/Euch-AC. Here again it is also consistent with ApTrad.

Additionally, as in ApTrad, CH, and perhaps Sarapion, bread but also water and oil are frequently brought during the catechumenate in BR-/Euch-AC.

Another significant similarity is the reference in BR-AC to a special "Confession for adults, children, and those who are unwell and mute," which in many ways replicates what is seen in ApTrad 21.4. In ways similar to ApTrad, BR-/Euch-AC also places the prebaptismal anointing after the *apotaxis*, but unlike ApTrad also after the *syntaxis*, though here the versions of ApTrad show some difference. A *syntaxis* only appears in Sahidic, Arabic II, and Ethiopic II, but not in the Latin, Ethiopic I, or Arabic I versions. Thus, not too much should be made of this difference between ApTrad and BR-/Euch-AC since there are signs of development here in both ApTrad and BR-/Euch-AC.

The first major difference with ApTrad comes with the location of the blessing of the waters, but here Euch-AC is in agreement in its placement with ApTrad and CH, perhaps suggesting some development in BR-AC. BR-/Euch-AC also includes a prebaptismal handlaying not contained in ApTrad and CH's prebaptismal rituals, but which does feature extensively in the catechumenates in both ApTrad and CH.

Another key development in BR-/Euch-AC is in the location of the blessing of the postbaptismal oil of anointing, though there are reasons to believe this was originally in the same location as ApTrad and CH, i.e. at the start of the rites of initiation.[322] The postbaptismal rites in BR- and Euch-AC show some rearrangement. BR-AC has the rubric: "And after he has been clothed again, the high priest or the priest shall say a prayer before anointing him with balsam (oil), which is thus consecrated."[305] This is then followed by the prayer for the handlaying, which notes that it is performed "after baptism,"[306] and then the prayer for the blessing of

322. Chase, "Further Reflections."

305. "Und nachdem er nun wieder bekleidet ist, soll der Oberpriester oder auch der Priester ein Gebet tun vor der Salbung mit Balsam(öl), das also geweiht ist." Bausi, "The *Baptismal Ritual*," 75.27-29. Translation ours.

306. "Nach der Taufe." Bausi, 75.22.

chrism. However, Euch-AC has the prayer for the consecration of the chrism directly after baptism. Following this is the prayer for the handlaying, but a rubric attached to that prayer notes that the handlaying precedes the sanctification of chrism. Euch-AC also does not mention when the chrismation itself occurs, but it is clear from both BR- and Euch-AC that the anointing with chrism occurred after the handlaying. Despite slight differences in each text, the blessing of chrism in both texts disrupts the flow of the rite. The fact that the CH and even CB (as can be seen in Table 8 above) have the prayer for the blessing of the postbaptismal anointing oil—"oil of anointing" in CH, "chrism" in CB—and the blessing of oil of exorcism together in the prebaptismal rites suggests that the prayer over the chrism in BR- and Euch-AC has recently been moved to the postbaptismal rites. This has caused some disruption and rearrangement in BR- and Euch-AC's postbaptismal rites. All of this hints that BR-/Euch-AC originally also followed the form given in ApTrad and CH of consecrating the oils at the start of the rites of initiation.

The rest of the prebaptismal rituals bear some close correspondences to ApTrad. Like ApTrad, BR-/Euch-AC point to directional change toward the West for the *apotaxis* and the East for the *syntaxis*. The form of the renunciation is also similar to ApTrad, particularly to Ethiopic II. BR-/Euch-AC also has a similar creedal *syntaxis* as that of ApTrad.

Perhaps the largest difference is that BR-/Euch-AC also now fully shifts to the indicative form of baptism.

Finally, there is the loss of the double postbaptismal anointing in between ApTrad and CH and BR-/Euch-AC. Though here it must be recalled that CH may be preserving an older witness here to ApTrad itself, and that ApTrad might be showing signs of innovations. Furthermore, CH is not from Alexandria, whereas BR-/Euch-AC may attest to Alexandrian use, though this is not entirely certain. So while an anointing of the forehead and chest in BR-/Euch-AC's postbaptismal anointing is somewhat consistent with CH's full-body presbyteral anointing and an episcopal anointing on forehead, here BR-/Euch-AC actually bears some closer resemblances to ApTrad. It is worth recalling that the manner of ApTrad's postbaptismal anointings is only described with regard to the anointing performed by the bishop. There it is done on the forehead. The presbyteral anointing is not described. BR-/Euch-AC's central postbaptismal anointing is, thus, not that different here from ApTrad's in displaying a focus on the forehead and chest, rather than the full-body anointing, as would be common in all the other Egyptian sources. It does have a slightly different formula, one that shows signs of development: "Anointing of sanctification and seal of the grace of the Holy Spirit."[307] But even this is in keeping with ApTrad's episcopal handlaying prayer, which focuses on grace.

Much like with CH, there are tantalizing connections here to the material in ApTrad and possible vestiges of an earlier shared tradition behind these texts. If CH is a testament to an earlier form of ApTrad that once contained a single postbaptismal anointing, then this fits in neatly with the evidence of BR-/Euch-AC and even Sarapion. The similarities between BR-/Euch-AC's and ApTrad's manner of anointing set them apart from the rest of the Egyptian tradition, but they are much in keeping with each other.

What also sets BR-AC apart, especially, is its possible double postbaptismal anointing for the sick. This is quite an odd practice. While it may attest to a unique context as the place of BR-AC's use, like a healing center, it may also in some way be a relic of a two-fold anointing in Alexandria that was by the time of BR-/Euch-AC's use no longer relevant. In fact, there is evidence to suggest that this is in fact what has occurred, namely that BR-/Euch-AC are preserving vestiges of a double anointing. The rubric in BR-AC 79.23-27, for instance, says:

> If it is a presbyter who baptizes, he shall take the balm from the bishop and shall anoint them after they have put on (the garments). And then the sequence of prosphora. Anointing oil, which the high priest prepares for those who receive the bath and for sick believers.[308]

This is followed by a prayer that could have been used for both initiation or the anointing of the sick, or even may indicate that there was a secondary anointing for the sick in the rite. This is paralleled in Euch-AC, which contains a similar "Prayer of oil for the new ones. Entrance of the

307. "Salbung der Heiligung und Siegel der Gnade des heiligen Geistes." Bausi, 79.20-21. Translation ours.

308. "Wenn es ein Presbyter ist, der tauft, soll er den Balsam vom Bischof nehmen und soll sie salben, nachdem sie (die Gewänder) angelegt haben. Und darauf die Folge der Prosphora. Salböl, das herstellt der Hohepriester für die, welche das Bad empfangen, und für kranke Gläubige." Bausi, 79.23-27. Translation ours.

catechumens to the sick" ($\Sigma 53^{vb}$-$54^{ra}$) after its baptismal rites.[309] Whether this is an indication that these prayers were multi-use or were used for the sick undergoing going initiation is not clear. Elsewhere in BR-AC there is a special form of the water bath for those who are sick, which may suggest that this anointing of the sick was an additional anointing during initiation for those who were sick. At the same time, the same rubric in BR-AC may provide a reason for why an original double anointing may have dropped out of the rites: "If it is a presbyter who baptizes, he shall take the balm from the bishop and shall anoint them after they have put on (the garments)." A similar rubric appears in Euch-AC attached to the prayer for the laying on of hands ($\Sigma 53^{vb}$) in the postbaptismal rites: "Thus the bishop or the presbyter who has baptised shall say." This seems to indicate that BR-/Euch-AC are starting to conform to a practice where the bishop was not always present at the rites of initiation. This may also point away from an Alexandrian context, and it may also explain why there is no double-anointing as in ApTrad. The bishop may simply no longer have been present enough in the rites of initiation to presuppose the possibility of a presbyteral and episcopal anointing. If this is the case, it may point away from BR-/Euch-AC's use by the patriarch in Alexandria. That the shift to presbyteral anointing alone in BR-/Euch-AC was a recent change is indicated by the inclusion still of the prayer for the consecration of chrism, which is only performed by the bishop.

The rites conclude, of course, with the giving of the milk and honey, as well as a handlaying. The latter is also a feature of Ethio-MC (§56). While not a uniquely Egyptian feature, this still bears a close resemblance to ApTrad and CH.

In any event, CH, Sarapion, and BR-/Euch-AC provide us with windows into Egyptian initiatory practice from slightly different times and slightly different places. CH and Sarapion certainly are indicative of a non-Alexandrian Egyptian context. BR-/Euch-AC at first glance appears to represent an Alexandrian rite of initiation, but there is clearly some accommodation, as well, to a context where the bishop is not always present. This may, in fact, also point to a non-Alexandrian Egyptian context.

So where does this leave us with regard to ApTrad and these earliest Egyptian sources? First, each of these sources shows some strong

309. See n. 261.

connections to ApTrad, at the very least indicating the early reception of ApTrad's rites of initiation within various Egyptian contexts. None of them, however, are an exact repetition of the rites in ApTrad, which is likely an indication of the tailoring of ApTrad's rites to various Egyptian times and places. It also leaves us with a bit of a void in the actual liturgy in Alexandria (at least the patriarchal liturgy) in the fourth century. It is not inconceivable that ApTrad's received text represented the fourth-century form of Alexandria's rites of initiation, of which these other forms—CH, Sarapion, and BR-/Euch-AC—attest to slightly different temporal and/or geographical adaptations.

Attention to the slightly later Egyptian rites of initiation may also reveal vestiges of ApTrad in Egypt. However, the later sources are challenging since CB is thought to represent a Syrian initiatory rite introduced into sixth-century Egypt, and both CB and Arb-TD.B show significant developments.[310] For instance, they each point to the truncation of the catechumenal rites into the baptism proper. However, with regard to the oil prayers, it should also be noted that CB follows the pattern seen in CH of praying over both baptismal oils together in the prebaptismal rites as in ApTrad and CH, again pointing to this likely being a novel development in BR-/Euch-AC, and the preservation of the original form of blessing of the oils in ApTrad. The same is the case with the blessing of the waters. CB and Arb-TD.B. lack the pre- and post-handlayings central to BR-/Euch-AC, though it is clear that they have here reworked the received tradition and likely also knew of an anointing–handlaying pattern.[311] Thus, even in these later initiatory rites there are still vestiges of ApTrad's influence, particularly in CB, which has the prebaptismal anointing after the *apotaxis*.

Finally, looking at the structure of CR, it is clear that it has undergone extensive development and elaboration from the earlier sources.[312] The rites of the catechumenate have become fused with the baptism proper and then compacted,[313] something that occurs across the various Christian

310. Chase, "Further Reflections."

311. Chase.

312. CR has also been adjusted to make it more eucharistic in structure and form; see DBL, 137.

313. Brakmann, "ⲃⲁⲡⲧⲓⲥⲙⲁ ⲁⲓⲛⲉⲥⲉⲱⲥ," 155 and 194.

liturgical traditions in the medieval period.[314] The postbaptismal rites in CR have undergone some rearrangement.[315] However, at the same time, it often preserves older forms, particularly in its prayers.[316] The chrismation formula is a case in point. The text in CR is as follows:

> [*In the Name of the Father and of the Son and of the Holy Ghost.*][317]
> An unction of the grace of the Holy Ghost.
> An unction of the pledge of the kingdom of heaven.
> An unction of participation in eternal and immortal life.
> A holy unction of Christ our God, and a seal that shall not be loosed.
> The perfection of the grace of the Holy Spirit, and the breastplate of the faith and the truth.
> *Thou art* anointed, son of N. with holy oil, *in the Name of the Father and of the Son and of the Holy Ghost. Amen.*

This prayer begins and ends with the trinitarian formula for the presbyteral anointing in CH, which is of course related to the episcopal anointing in ApTrad, but also includes pieces from BR-AC, CB, and even Arb-TD.B.[318] What this indicates is that CR at times can preserve ancient features while also showing interaction with other strands of the Egyptian tradition. But here we clearly see the CR preserving vestiages of ApTrad, though likely through the mediation of CH.

Given the diversity we see in the Egyptian sources above, but also the fact that later rites at times display signs of antiquity, it is not at all inconceivable that CR is at times preserving older forms. This includes the baptismal interrogations (see above); the use of the name "oil of gladness of the oil of exorcism" as in Ethiopic I; the postbaptismal full-body anointing with its formula; the lack of a signing or anointing or even kiss after the handlaying prayer; and a post-communion handlaying (though this does not appear in ApTrad or CH). In a more convoluted

314. Johnson, *The Rites of Christian Initiation*, 257–61 and 276.

315. Brakmann, "ⲂⲀⲠⲦⲒⲤⲘⲀ ⲀⲒⲚⲈⲤⲈⲰⲤ," 186–92.

316. Brakmann, esp. 155.

317. This appears to be absent in Codex Borg. copt. 112 and Codex Vat. Aeth. 4. It appears in CR 1 and CR 2, and at least by Pope Gabriel V (1411 CE); see 'Abdallah, *L'ordinamento liturgico di Gabriele V*, fol. 9v-10r. For more on the sources of the CR, see n. 116 of our Introduction.

318. Chase, "Further Reflections."

way, the reworking and retension of the traditional Egyptian postbaptismal handlaying prayer in CR, though now as a prayer after clothing, also shows the CR's preservation of liturgical formula from at least the fifth/sixth-century BR-/Euch-AC.[319] Thus, CR may also attest to an original anointing–handlaying postbaptismal sequence in the Egyptian tradition.

Before concluding the Egyptian parallels, it is also worth noting the timing of baptism in Egypt. As discussed above with regard to the timing of baptism in ApTrad (see pp. 197–200), namely that the document does not show a preference for Paschal baptism, further evidence can be presented that indicates Paschal baptism was not the norm in most places in Egypt. While the Pachomians celebrated Paschal baptism in their monasteries,[320] this was not the case for most of Egypt in this period as Bradshaw has shown.[321] Later evidence from the late-sixth and early-seventh centuries also indicates that the bishop would travel around throughout the year to celebrate baptism in parish churches.[322] All of this would fit comfortably with the lack of Paschal baptism in ApTrad, perhaps providing further Egyptian connections with the practices in this text.

## 9. Conclusion

As with all other sections of ApTrad the materials on Christian initiation also display various layers or strata of development, at the very least an earlier level with no explicit reference to the identity of ministers, followed next by rites pertaining to the bishop, and last by those rites pertaining to presbyters and deacons. Thanks to the work of Jean-Paul Bouhot in 1968, who claimed, as noted above, that the initiation rites reflect both Roman and African traditions,[323] it has been customary to view North

319. Chase.

320. Hugo Lundhaug, "Baptism in the Monasteries of Upper Egypt: The Pachomian Corpus and the Writings of Shenoute," in *Ablution, Initiation, and Baptism in Early Judaism, Graeco-Roman Religion, and Early Christianity*, ed. David Hellholm et al. (Berlin: Walter de Gruyter, 2011), 1350–51. An earlier study of baptism in the Pachomian Federation appears in Armand Veilleux, *La liturgie dans le cénobitisme pachômien au quatrième siècle* (Rome: "I. B. C." Libreria Herder, 1968), part 2, chap. 2.

321. Bradshaw, "Diem Baptismo Sollemniorem."

322. Wipszycka, *Alexandrian Church*, 109–10 and 327–28.

323. Bouhot, *La confirmation*, 38–45.

Africa as the locale where the final redaction of ApTrad took place. In this chapter, while we accept Bouhot's general approach to the distinctions of ministers as indicating strata, we have not accepted this view of North African redaction in favor of positing a final redaction in Egypt, and we have done so for the following reasons.

First, while there are several parallels in Chs. 15–19 with North African practice, especially as articulated by Tertullian and Cyprian, detailed evidence for the catechumenate is lacking elsewhere in early Christian sources. Nevertheless, as we have seen, even the ancient *Didache* refers to some of the same prohibited occupations noted in Tertullian. And, in a short passage in *Contra Celsum* Origen describes a similar catechumenal process, noting even the two-fold division of catechumens into beginners and advanced, much as ApTrad Ch. 20 makes a distinction between catehcumens and those elected to baptism.

Second, even the length of the catechumenate, whether three years as in ApTrad or forty days as in the earliest derivative document, CH, both speak to an Egyptian context. The forty days referred to in CH appear to be part of a long-standing practice within diverse contexts in Egypt, as do references to a three-year period for penitential and preparation periods, which have no parallels outside of Egypt in the early period.

Third, as we have seen above, contrary to Stewart, who claims a declaratory creed as an early Egyptian characteristic, we have argued that an interrogatory form of baptism is also a characteristic of early Egyptian baptismal liturgy as well and may be reflected in Origen's *Homilies on Numbers*, a letter from Dionysius of Alexandria, Athanasius, the *De trinitate* of Didymus the Blind, in Cyril of Alexandria, and in Mystagogical Catechesis II.4, attributed to Cyril of Jerusalem.[324] Further, based on our work on the Egyptian origins of CH,[325] we have followed Bradshaw here in affirming "the possibility that the original core of the baptismal rite in the *Apostolic Tradition* came from Egypt rather than North Africa."[326]

Fourth, we have argued against most of contemporary scholarship that the bishop's handlying prayer in the postbaptismal rites contains no explicit *epiclesis* of the Holy Spirit in *any* of the versions of ApTrad. The

324. See n. 187.

325. Chase and Johnson, *The Origins of the Canons of Hippolytus*.

326. Bradshaw, "Fourth-Century Egyptian Baptismal Practice."

only epiclesis there is for grace! Even where the Holy Spirit is expressly mentioned, the handlaying prayer asks for grace and not the Holy Spirit. Ethiopic I may provide an exception in asking that the neophytes "may be filled with the Holy Spirit," but the very means by which this happens is by "sending upon them your grace," and so even here there is no Spirit-epiclesis. Further, what appears to be the driving force for this handlaying prayer in all the versions (not just Latin) is Titus 3:5 ("he saved us . . . according to his mercy, through the water of rebirth and renewal by the Holy Spirit") and John 3:5 ("Very truly, I tell you, no one can enter the kingdom of God without being born of water and Spirit"). The handlaying prayer thus reflects this theology, though in all places this handlaying prayer will eventually become pneumaticized. Further, on the structural level, we have argued that CH likely reflects an earlier shape of the initiation rites in ApTrad, where a single postbaptismal anointing is closely associated with the handlaying prayer (again for grace specifically) and a signing or a kiss by the bishop. Such, as we have seen, is precisely what we see in the later Egyptian baptismal rites, including CH, Sarapion, BR- and Euch-AC, and even the current CR, and possibly CB and Arb-TD.B.

We might say, then, that while none of the initiatory rites in Egypt (not even CH) bear an exact relationship to ApTrad's rites of initiation, far from disproving a connection, the connections that do exist suggest that there is a good deal of continuity with ApTrad. There is no reason ApTrad may not represent the fourth-century practice of Alexandria, while the other early sources (CH, Sarapion, and BR-/Euch-AC) represent slightly different periods or places within Egypt, dependent, to various degrees, on the form of initiation described in ApTrad Chs. 20–21.

*Chapter 6*

# Eucharist, Foodstuffs, Firstfruits, and Meal Practices

## 1. Introduction

A number of chapters in ApTrad deal with the Eucharist and communion (Chs. 4; 9; 21.25-29 and 31-37; 22; 33; 36–38A), the blessing of foodstuffs connected to the Eucharist (Chs. 5–6; 21.27-29), firstfruits that are given to the church (Chs. 31–32), and, finally, communal meal practices (Chs. 23–33). The Eucharist is also dealt with in Euch-AC, which accompanies Ethiopic I. The presence of Euch-AC in the collection appears to have led to some changes to ApTrad, which will be dealt with below. Foodstuffs and meal practices have been included here alongside the Eucharist since, as we will see, these may be remnants of a time when the Eucharist was still being celebrated as a meal. In fact, ApTrad preserves a number of ancient practices that may have originally been associated with the Eucharist itself before gradually becoming more and more peripheral to the eucharistic celebration. As a result, it is worth beginning by contextualizing the shift from a meal to token distribution of bread and wine in the early church in order to understand how the chapters in ApTrad on the blessing of foodstuffs, firstfruits, and meal practices may be remnants of older eucharistic practices (section 2). This is especially necessary given shifting scholarly perspectives on eucharistic and non-eucharistic meal practices in the early church. The second part of the chapter (section 3) will then look directly at the structure of the eucharistic service as put together across ApTrad's chapters. Then we will turn to the blessing of foodstuffs and fruits (section 4), before concluding with the meal practices that are outlined in the text (section 5).

## 2. Early Christian Eucharistic and Non-Eucharistic Meal Practices and ApTrad[1]

Beginning with the New Testament accounts of the Last Supper and carrying into early eucharistic texts like *Didache* Chs. 9–10, it is clear that the eucharistic celebration began as a meal that included not only bread and wine but also other foodstuffs like cheese, olives, fish, milk, and honey.[2] These eucharistic meals were not just for ritual purposes but also for provisioning, and they were linked to food doles/benefits given to Christians by the church.[3] They were also rooted in older Greco-Roman and Jewish meal practices, the latter of which were largely based on broader Greco-Roman models.[4] The Greco-Roman world had rich

1. For the state of the question, see Nathan Chase, *Eucharistic Praying in Ritual Context: From the New Testament to the Classical Anaphoras*, Alcuin/GROW Joint Liturgical Studies (Norwich: Hymns Ancient and Modern, 2024), Ch. 2.

2. For a helpful summary, see Andrew McGowan, *Ascetic Eucharists: Food and Drink in Early Christian Ritual Meals* (Oxford: Clarendon Press, 1999), 39–45 and Ch. 3; Andrew McGowan, "'The Firstfruits of God's Creatures': Bread, Eucharist and the Ancient Economy," in *Full of Your Glory: Liturgy, Cosmos, Creation*, ed. Teresa Berger (Collegeville, MN: Liturgical Press, 2019), 69–86. For more on cheese, in particular, see more recently Elizabeth Klein, "Perpetua, Cheese, and Martyrdom as Public Liturgy in the *Passion of Perpetua and Felicity*," *Journal of Early Christian Studies* 28 (2020): 175–202.

3. McGowan, *Ascetic Eucharists*, 38–45; Clemens Leonhard, "Morning *Salutationes* and the Decline of Sympotic Eucharists in the Third Century," *Zeitschrift Für Antikes Christentum/Journal of Ancient Christianity* 18 (2014): 420–42; McGowan, "Firstfruits."

4. For a few studies, see Frank R. Trombley, *Hellenic Religion and Christianization c. 370–529*, vol. 2 (Boston: Brill, 2001); Frank R. Trombley, "Christian Demography in the *Territorium* of Antioch (4th–5th c.): Observations on the Epigraphy," in *Culture and Society in Later Roman Antioch*, ed. Isabella Sandwell and Janet Huskinson (Oxford: Oxbow Books, 2004), 59–85; Stephen Mitchell and Peter van Nuffelen, eds., *One God: Pagan Monotheism in the Roman Empire* (Cambridge: Cambridge University Press, 2010); Dennis Smith, *From Symposium to Eucharist: The Banquet in the Early Christian World* (Minneapolis: Fortress Press, 2003); Andrew McGowan, "Rethinking Agape and Eucharist in Early North African Christianity," *Studia Liturgica* 34 (2004): 165–76;

and codified practices for dining. Of those practices, the most influential on early Christian eucharistic celebrations appear to have been *symposia*, *collegia* (meals of associations), and morning *salutationes* (a daily meeting in the morning between a patron and their clients where food or money were distributed). Funerary meal customs known broadly as *refrigeria* also shaped early Christian eucharistic practice; however, the influence of this type of meal is not directly apparent in ApTrad except in one case, ApTrad 40.2 (see Ch. 7 of our commentary). Recent work has also noted the need to account, especially in the shift to a token bit of bread and wine, for Greco-Roman "breakfast" (*ientaculum*/*prandium*/ ἄριστον) practices.[5] Nevertheless, the afternoon/evening meal appears to have been the central model for the Christian Eucharist.

A *symposium* was an afternoon or evening meal. It consisted of "[1] a blessing of bread including wine in some cases [2] followed by its distribution and [3] which ends with a blessing over wine [4] also followed by its distribution."[6] While the *symposium*-style meal has long been seen by scholars as a possible forerunner to the Christian Eucharist, Clemens Leonhard notes issues with an uncritical acceptance of the *symposium*-style of meal as the predecessor to the eucharistic liturgies of the fourth

---

McGowan, "Firstfruits"; Valeriy Alikin, "Eating the Bread and Drinking the Cup in Corinth: Defining and Expressing the Identity of the Earliest Christians," in *Mahl und Religiöse Identität im Frühen Christentum/Meals and Religious Identity in Early Christianity*, ed. Matthias Klinghardt and Hal Taussig (Tübingen: Francke, 2012), 119–30; Hal Taussig, *In the Beginning Was the Meal: Social Experimentation and Early Christian Identity* (Minneapolis: Fortress Press, 2009); Hal Taussig, "Introduction: The Study of Identity and Religion in Relationship to Early Christian Meals," in *Mahl und Religiöse Identität*, ed. Klinghardt and Taussig, 15–23; Paul Bradshaw, "Jewish Influence on Early Christian Liturgy: A Reappraisal," in *Liturgies in East and West: Ecumenical Relevance of Early Liturgical Development; Acts of the International Symposium Vindobonense I, Vienna, November 17–20, 2007*, ed. Hans-Jürgen Feulner (Zürich: Lit Verlag, 2013), 47–59; David Grumett, *Material Eucharist* (Oxford: Oxford University Press, 2016). See also the essays in David Hellholm and Dieter Sänger, eds., *The Eucharist, Its Origins and Contexts: Sacred Meal, Communal Meal, Table Fellowship in Late Antiquity, Early Judaism, and Early Christianity*, 3 vols., Wissenschaftliche Untersuchungen zum Neuen Testament 376 (Tübingen: Mohr Siebeck, 2017).

5. Alistair Stewart, "Ἄριστον Μὲν Ὕδωρ: Ancient Breakfasts and the Development of Eucharistic Foods," *The Journal of Theological Studies* 71 (2020): 707–17.

6. Leonhard, "Morning *Salutationes*," 423.

century: "In sympotic celebrations, one would debate philosophical questions or affairs of one's group during the drinking party after the meal. A reconstruction of the early history of the Eucharist must account for what resembles a complete inversion of the sequence of the customary elements of *symposia*."[7]

Other early Christian eucharistic practices appear to bear a close relationship to the meal practices—known generally as *collegia*—of the Greco-Roman associations. These associations, which were established for a variety of reasons—religious, political, as funerary associations, or as guild's based on one's craft—periodically celebrated a common meal together.[8] The structure of these meals was usually a *symposium*, though at times particular adaptations were made to the *symposium* for each association. These associations also provided material aid to their members. The distribution of food to poor members of the church could be explained by the church functioning as an association.[9]

Finally, the morning *salutatio* was a Greco-Roman practice that occurred at the house of a wealthy patron, where "clients of wealthy and influential people used to assemble in the early morning. They were waiting there to be admitted into certain parts of their patron's house."[10] At the morning *salutatio*, clients would receive gifts (*sportulae*) that usually included food, often from a *symposium* the night before, but could also include money.[11] Rather than in a patron's home, Christians began to assemble at the church and waited on the bishop as chief Christian patron. In fact, some scholars have argued that the change in these practices might be the result of tensions

7. Leonhard, 423.

8. Smith, *From Symposium to Eucharist*, Ch. 5; John S. Kloppenborg and Richard S. Ascough, eds., *Greco-Roman Associations: Texts, Translations, and Commentary*, Beihefte Zur Zeitschrift Für Die Neutestamentliche Wissenschaft (Berlin: De Gruyter, 2011); Markus Öhler, "Mähler und Opferhandlungen in griechischrömischen Vereinigungen: Das frühchristliche Herrenmahl im Kontext," in *The Eucharist, Its Origins and Contexts: Sacred Meal, Communal Meal, Table Fellowship in Late Antiquity, Early Judaism, and Early Christianity*, ed. David Hellholm and Dieter Sänger, vol. 3, Wissenschaftliche Untersuchungen zum Neuen Testament 376 (Tübingen: Mohr Siebeck, 2017), 1413–439.

9. Smith, *From Symposium to Eucharist*, 106.

10. Leonhard, "Morning *Salutationes*," 425–30, here 425.

11. McGowan, *Ascetic Eucharists*, 38–45; McGowan, "Firstfruits," 80–81.

between older patronage practices and the emerging episcopate.[12] Parts of ApTrad likely reflect this tension, especially the directions surrounding the primacy of the bishop in the distribution of communion and food at the communal meals. It appears that Greco-Roman *ientaculum/prandium/* ἄριστον could easily coincide with or be related to the morning *salutatio*.

The influence of each of these Greco-Roman meal practices—*symposia*, *collegia*, and morning *salutationes*—on the early Christian community was not mutually exclusive. Christian eucharistic practices were undoubtedly influenced by all of these different meal practices. In fact, the coexistence and even synthesis of these various practices likely explains the different meal practices—eucharistic and non-eucharistic—described throughout ApTrad.

### *2.1. Early Meal Practices Behind ApTrad*

In its final form, ApTrad contains a curious mixture of early Christian meal practices that were likely the result of a combination of a variety of Greco-Roman practices. As we will see, ApTrad's final redaction seeks to distinguish clearly between eucharistic and non-eucharistic practices. Each of these meal practices in ApTrad's final redaction will be taken up in section 5 below. However, the fact that each of the meal practices described influenced early Christian eucharistic practices suggests that in earlier iterations of ApTrad meal practices now described in the text as non-eucharistic once likely were eucharistic. In fact, we can point to which parts of ApTrad

12. Tensions in patronage between bishops and laity may be seen in early sources like Ignatius of Antioch (Alistair C. Stewart, *Breaking Bread: The Emergence of Eucharist and Agape in Early Christian Communities* [Grand Rapids, MI: William B. Eerdmans, 2023], 68–72) and the *Didascalia* (Stewart, 104–5). It may explain later church orders, too, like ApTrad; see Charles Bobertz, "The Role of Patron in the *Cena Dominica* of Hippolytus' *Apostolic Tradition*," *Journal of Theological Studies* 44 (1993): 170–84; Stewart, *On the Apostolic Tradition*, for instance 179–80. His study dates this to second-century Rome. However, both the dating and provenance have been disputed by *Herm.Com.* 2002. It may also be behind the banning of meals in churches (cf. Stewart, *Breaking Bread*, 79) and was part of disputes between bishops and elites who had the Eucharist celebrated in their domestic spaces; see Kimberly Diane Bowes, *Private Worship, Public Values, and Religious Change in Late Antiquity* (Cambridge: Cambridge University Press, 2011), 62–63, 78–83, 101–2, 116–20, 161–87, and 218–20.

appear to have been influenced by which of these earlier eucharistic meal practices, some of which betray signs of multiple influences:

- *Symposia* or a *symposium*-style *collegia* meal practices—each of these chapters points to a meal context and the use of more than just token bits of bread and wine within a communal meal.
  - **Chs. 5–6** – *Concerning the offering of oil; Concerning the Offering of Cheese and Olives*
  - **Ch. 20.10** – the reference to the catechumens bringing at least bread, and perhaps other offerings, for the initiatory eucharistic celebration
  - **Ch. 21.28 and 33** – the reference to milk, honey, and water as part of the initiatory eucharistic celebration
  - **Ch. 23** – *Concerning Fasting.* The text indicates that members may share a meal after bringing offerings.
  - **Ch. 28 (and its doublet 29D)** – *That It Is Proper to Eat Judiciously and Moderately.*
  - **Ch. 29A** – *That It Is Proper to Eat with Thanksgiving*
  - **Ch. 29C (= Ch. 25)** – *Concerning the Bringing in of the Lamps at the Supper of the Congregation*
  - **Ch. 30A** – *Concerning the Supper of the Widows*
  - **Chs. 31–32** – *Concerning the Fruit That It Is Proper to Bring to the Bishop; The Blessing of Fruits*

  Strong patronage practices typical of *symposia* and/or *collegia* meals also feature strongly in Ch. 28 (and its doublet 29D) and Ch. 30A.

- *Collegia* membership and patronage practices—in addition to the celebration of *symposium*-style *collegia* meals, we can also see the way that *collegia* membership and patronage practices specifically shaped early Christian meal practices and provided support to its members beyond the meal itself.
  - **Chs. 26–28** – *Concerning the Hour of Eating; That It Is Not Proper for Catechumens to Eat with the Faithful; That It Is Proper to Eat Judiciously and Moderately.* These chapters make it clear that while the catechumens may participate in the communal meals, they are

still not full members and thus are excluded from the offering. This is reminiscent of the strict hierarchies surrounding *collegia* meal celebrations.

  - **Ch. 29B (= Ch. 24)** – *Concerning Gifts for the Sick.* This chapter implies the giving of the leftovers from the communal meal to those who are sick and were not able to attend. The support of its members was a key function of *collegia.*
  - **Ch. 30A** – *Concerning the Supper of the Widows.* The same concern for the support of the most vulnerable in the community appears with the meals of widows.
  - **Ch. 36-38** – *That It Is Proper to Receive the Eucharist Early at the Time It Will Be Offered, before They Taste Anything; That It Is Proper to Watch over the Eucharist Diligently; That It Is Not Proper to Spill Anything from the Cup.* These chapters indicate that only those who are Christian members (like *collegia* members) can partake of the eucharistic food.

- *Salutationes*—the practice of distributing foodstuffs or other aid from the patron, often, but not always, after a communal meal, to those not in attendance or not expected to attend, can be seen in several places throughout ApTrad:
  - **Chs. 5–6** – *Concerning the offering of oil; Concerning the Offering of Cheese and Olives.* These goods may have been blessed and distributed from the meal, to be taken home by the recipients.
  - **Ch. 22** – *Concerning Communion.* Here the text clearly implies a Sabbath distribution of communion. However, this need not mean that a meal or liturgy was celebrated. Rather, it may have begun as a simple distribution of foodstuffs (in particular the eucharistic bread and wine) by the bishop as the patron of the community.
  - **Ch. 29B (= Ch. 24)** – *Concerning Gifts for the Sick.* Here it is quite clear that this is a distribution of gifts to the sick for those who are not able to attend the Christian (eucharistic) meal.
  - **Ch. 30A** – *Concerning the Supper of the Widows.* Verse 2, in particular, seems to imply that the widows take with them leftovers from the communal meal, much like *sportulae.*

- **Chs. 31–32** – *Concerning the Fruit That It Is Proper to Bring to the Bishop; The Blessing of Fruits.* The firstfruits would, as we will see, often be distributed back to needier members of the Church, again much like *sportulae*.
- **Ch. 36–38** – *That It Is Proper to Receive the Eucharist Early at the Time It Will Be Offered, before They Taste Anything; That It Is Proper to Watch over the Eucharist Diligently; That It Is Not Proper to Spill Anything from the Cup*. These chapters, as we will see, seem to originally point to a home communion service, though Chs. 37 and 38 appear to have been reframed to now imply a eucharistic celebration. This seems to suggest the reception of the eucharistic gifts, like *sportulae*, that could be taken home for communion.

Thus, what we see at the core of ApTrad's meal practices is a diversity of influences, all rooted in early ways that Christians in the first three centuries, especially, came to celebrate the Eucharist. This diversity of forms and influences suggests that the practices outlined above in ApTrad may have their roots in second-century forms. However, by the third century things would begin to shift in eucharistic practice among Christians, and this would come to reshape this early material in ApTrad. No longer would all of these practices be seen as eucharistic, and the fact that ApTrad goes to pains to make this clear indicates that many of the meal practices outlined above predated this shift.

While already by the second and third century early Christians began to focus on the bread and wine in particular, the meal itself, and specifically the gathering of the whole assembly, was still a key part of early Christians' understanding of the presence of Christ among them.[13] The increased focus on the food was becoming particularly strong by the time of Cyprian. As Andrew McGowan has noted, by the time Cyprian was writing, "the understanding of the sacrality of the eucharistic food had developed to the point that it was the food itself more than the banquet that was the attraction."[14] Even then, however, Cyprian stresses the importance of both the eucharistic food and the gathering of the whole assembly.

13. For a longer treatment, see Chase, *Eucharistic Praying in Ritual Context*, Ch. 4.
14. McGowan, "Rethinking Agape," 176.

In the course of the third century, the increased sacrality of the eucharistic food, greater food security, and the increasing sizing of many assemblies, made the shift from a meal to a token distribution of bread and wine possible.[15] While some scholars again have tried to place this shift as early as the New Testament, it has been noted that "the transition from full meal to symbolic rite appears to have been gradual, taking place before the middle of the second century in some places, after the middle of the third century in others."[16] The heightened sacrality of the food itself continued in the fourth century,[17] where we also start to see the increasing use of transformation language—"may the bread and wine *become* (or "make" it—ποιέω) the body and blood of Christ"[18]—in the classical anaphoras. A shift in this direction, as we will see, was already underway in ApTrad Ch. 4. It would also be in this period that we would see the emergence of the *agape*.[19]

### *2.2. The Narrowing of the Eucharistic Meals and Practices in ApTrad*

Despite the meal practices in ApTrad displaying a strong continuity with eucharistic practices of the first three centuries, ApTrad also betrays signs of further development. In fact, those signs seem to suggest that the meal practices described above, while once eucharistic, were by the time of ApTrad's final redaction often no longer considered eucharistic, or were only tangentially tied to the eucharistic celebration. In fact, the received text of ApTrad makes it clear that there are only a few of these practices that were still clearly and unambiguously eucharistic:

15. McGowan, "Rethinking Agape," 176. For more, see Chase, *Eucharistic Praying in Ritual Context*.

16. Paul Bradshaw and Maxwell Johnson, *Eucharistic Liturgies: Their Evolution and Interpretation* (Collegeville, MN: Liturgical Press, 2012), 58; see also Chs. 1 and 2. For an earlier study of this shift, see Nathan Mitchell, *Cult and Controversy: The Worship of the Eucharist Outside Mass* (New York: Pueblo, 1982), Ch. 1. For the former position, see the dated, but still thought-provoking, work of Willi Marxsen, *The Lord's Supper as a Christological Problem* (Philadelphia: Fortress Press, 1970).

17. Bradshaw and Johnson, *Eucharistic Liturgies*, 132–35.

18. Nathan Chase, "From *Logos* to Spirit Revisited: The Development of the Epiclesis in Syria and Egypt," *Ecclesia Orans* 39 (2022): 29–64.

19. Nathan Chase, "Kitchens and Communion: The Eucharist and Communal Meals in the Fourth and Fifth Centuries," *Ex Fonte - Journal of Ecumenical Studies in Liturgy* 3 (2024): 217–95.

- **Ch. 4** – *Eucharistic Prayer*
- **Ch. 9.3-5** – eucharistic prayer could still be improvised
- **Ch. 21.25-29 and 31-37** – the initiatory Eucharist
- **Ch. 22** – *Concerning Communion*
- **Ch. 33** – *That It Is Not Proper for Anyone to Taste Anything in the Pascha before the Hour When It Is Proper to Eat*
- **Ch. 36-38** – *That It Is Proper to Receive the Eucharist Early at the Time It Will Be Offered, before They Taste Anything; That It Is Proper to Watch over the Eucharist Diligently; That It Is Not Proper to Spill Anything from the Cup.*

While the practices above were clearly understood to be eucharistic in the final redaction of ApTrad, there are indications that some of the older meal practices described above may still have been considered by some as eucharistic, prompting the need for some clarification, or in some cases were in the process of being de-eucharistized.[20] Perhaps the two best examples of this de-eucharistizing development in ApTrad can be seen in Chs. 23.4 and 29C (= Ch. 25). In both of these chapters, the communal meals, or parts of the communal meals, are described in some way as *not* being a Eucharist.

Ch. 23 appears at first to be about fasting, but the final verses 2-4 indicate that the faithful may sometimes wish to have an offering made. Ethiopic I and Arabic I both lack verse 4 in this chapter. Ethiopic I reads:

> The bishop may not fast except when all the people have fasted, because it happens that someone has brought something to offer it, and he may not refuse, because after he has broken the bread he will taste it.

This is strongly suggestive of a eucharistic celebration, since it breaks the fast. This apparently, however, was not how the Sahidic, Arabic II, and Ethiopic II versions wished the text to be interpreted, since they add verse 4:

20. Chase, "Kitchens and Communion."

> let them receive from the bishop's hand a single piece of bread before each one breaks his own bread. For it is a blessing and not a thanksgiving as in the body of the Lord (Sahidic).

This is, interestingly, precisely the same rubric that will come to be included in every version of ApTrad Ch. 29C.16.

Ch. 29C gives a long description of the evening lamp-lighting service and a communal supper. In this chapter, the communal meal seems to be described as *not* being a Eucharist. This is put forward in two places. Verse 6 otherwise follows the traditional pre-anaphoral dialogue, but notes that: "and 'Lift up your hearts' he will not say this, because it is said in the offering" (Ethiopic I). The need to clarify this seems to point to this once being a eucharistic celebration, since this expression was confined to the eucharistic celebration.[21] But the crux in interpreting this chapter is verse 16, which says: "And as those believers who are there are eating the supper, they are to take a little bread from the bishop's hand before they break their own bread, *because it is a blessing and not the Eucharist* like the body of our Lord." This verse is included in Ethiopic I ("Let the faithful who are present at the supper receive from the hand of the bishop a little bread, before they divide their own bread, for this is eulogy [e.g., blessed bread], not rendering of grace [e.g., thanksgiving] like the body"[22]) and Arabic I ("And at the supper together the present believers shall take from the hand of the bishop a little portion of bread, before they break their own bread, for this is partaking and it is not thanksgiving like the body").

There are two scholarly interpretations of this passage. The first views this meal as once being eucharistic, but no longer viewed as eucharistic by the community.[23] Stewart, however, suggests another interpretation of the italicized phrase. Rather than referring to the whole meal as non-eucharistic, he argues that this clause refers just to the bread brought and

21. For more on the pre-anaphoral dialogue and its history, see Nathan Chase, *The Anaphoral Tradition in the "Barcelona Papyrus,"* Studia Traditionis Theologiae 53 (Turnhout: Brepols, 2023), Ch. 5.

22. The Ethiopic terms are *ʾawlogiyā*, loanword from the Greek, "eulogy," and *ʾakkʷatet*, "thanksgiving, rendering of grace."

23. *Herm.Com.* 2002, 158–60; Nathan Chase, "Another Look at the 'Daily Office' in the Apostolic Tradition," *Studia Liturgica* 49 (2019): 5–25, here 12–13.

broken by the believers, namely "their own bread." In other words, there is a distinction between the eucharistic bread shared before the meal by the faithful and the non-eucharistic bread ("their own bread") brought by the faithful.[24] In either interpretation, this meal (and that given in Ch. 23) was once eucharistic in whole, but has now been totally de-eucharistized or, more likely, there is now a distinction between the eucharistic and non-eucharistic part of the meal.

Further support for a distinction between the eucharistic and non-eucharistic parts of the meal in ApTrad Chs. 23 and 29C can be seen in CH 32, which is derived from ApTrad 29C and which calls this "[a supper] of the Lord."[25] The text (translation taken from Stewart's edition) reads:

> If there is a meal [*walima*] or a supper [*'ašia*] that somebody gives for the poor, it is *kyriakon* [in a church] {or: "it is [a supper] of the Lord}. The bishop should be present when a lamp is lit. The deacon lights it and the bishop prays over them and over those who invited them. It is right that he make the thanksgiving [*alāwkhrisdya*, a transliteration of *eucharistia*] at the beginning of the liturgy [*quddās*] so that they can be dismissed before it is dark, and recite psalms before their departure.[26]

Stewart notes that this passage can also be interpreted in two different ways, depending on how the reference to the thanksgiving being offered first is interpreted:

> There have been attempts to understand this as a statement that the meal is to begin with a eucharist since the word translated 'liturgy' above (*quddās*) is that generally employed in the Canons of Hippolytus for the eucharistic liturgy. Thus the phrase could mean either that he is to conduct the eucha-

24. Alistair C. Stewart, *Breaking Bread: The Emergence of Eucharist and Agape in Early Christian Communities* (Grand Rapids, MI: William B. Eerdmans, 2023), 190.

25. For the various ways of interpreting this passage, see Stewart, *Breaking Bread*, 100–102.

26. Stewart, *Breaking Bread*, 101. Square brackets in Stewart. Curly brackets taken from Bradshaw, *The Canons of Hippolytus*, 32. For the difficulties of translating this section of the canon, see Alistair Stewart, *The Canons of Hippolytus: An English Version, with Introduction and Annotation and an Accompanying Arabic Text* (Macquarie Centre: SCD Press, 2021), 139n151. For a longer treatment of the issues with this text, see Chase, "Kitchens and Communion," 246–48.

> ristic liturgy at the beginning of the meal, or that he is to say certain words as a grace, which may possibly be the same words found at the opening of the eucharistic liturgy.[27]

Ultimately, Stewart concludes that "in this context it more probably refers to a grace before the meal; the canon is stating that the grace should use the same words as those used at the opening of the eucharistic liturgy."[28] However, the fact that a Eucharist may have been conducted at the beginning of the meal is actually more consistent with the above interpretation of both ApTrad Chs. 23 and 29C, where Stewart—at least in the case of Ch. 29C—has also argued that there was a distinction between the eucharistic bread shared before the meal by the faithful and the non-eucharistic bread at the meal.[29]

Here it also seems significant that the redactor of CH 32 does not include the note that "this is not the Eucharist," something also lacking in ApTrad Ch. 23.4 in Ethiopic I and Arabic I. In the case of CH 32, this is either because it was clear to those who were using that text that it was not the Eucharist, or in fact it was still understood as eucharistic. The latter case actually seems most reasonable, since CH tends to preserve the phraseology of ApTrad. Furthermore, according to Reinhard Meßner, the use of simply "supper" in ApTrad (Ethiopic I and II), versus the use of "Lord's Supper" as in CH, is possibly the result of an error in Ethiopic I, which also likely read "supper of the Lord," but possibly a deliberate change in Ethiopic II to move away from this meal being viewed as a eucharistic celebration.[30] This would seem to suggest that the reference to the meal in ApTrad Ch. 29C as "not [being] the Eucharist" is a recent addition and that here CH 32 is preserving an earlier form of these chapters.

While these are the clearest examples that the final redaction of ApTrad has reshaped its meal practices to distinguish more clearly between what was eucharistic and what was no longer a eucharistic celebration, ApTrad leaves other practices and whether they were eucharistic somewhat ambiguous. This also includes the material in ApTrad Chs.

27. Stewart, *Breaking Bread*, 102.

28. Stewart, 102. See also Stewart, *The Canons of Hippolytus*, 139n151.

29. Stewart, *Breaking Bread*, 190.

30. Reinhard Messner, "Die Angebliche *Traditio Apostolica*," *Archiv für Liturgiewissenschaft* 58/59 (2016): 1–58, here 40n153, which directs to a similar observation on 34n119.

26–30A.[31] This likely points to the continuation of older eucharistic meal practices—now no longer seen as eucharistic—alongside the more ritualized morning eucharistic celebrations that were becoming typical from the late third century onward.

At the same time, there are hints beyond ApTrad that a more substantial meal continued in some places.[32] The evidence for the continuation of house-churches into the fourth century may indicate the endurance of a more substantial eucharistic meal. Paul Bradshaw, for instance, notes that the *Passio SS. Dativi, Saturnini presb. et aliorum* "lists the names of the members of an African house-church arrested during the Diocletian persecution in February 304, totalling [sic] less than fifty persons."[33] Other evidence points to the continuation of house-churches in Rome, Constantinople, and other locations into the fourth and fifth centuries.[34] Legislation in East Syria also suggests the continuation of a meal there into the fifth century.[35] There are also several archaeological examples of domestic structures that were converted into churches in the fourth century. The best examples come from Lullingston (England)[36] and Egypt.[37]

31. Stewart has made a similar argument for ApTrad Chs. 26–30; see Stewart, *Breaking Bread*, 94–99. See also Stewart, *On the Apostolic Tradition*, 168; Bradshaw, *Apostolic Tradition*, 24, 88–89, and 90–91.

32. Chase, "Kitchens and Communion."

33. Paul Bradshaw, "The Fourth Century: A Golden Age for Liturgy?" in *Liturgie und Ritual in der alten Kirche: patristische Beiträge zum Studium der gottesdienstlichen Quellen der alten Kirche*, ed. Wolfram Kinzig, Ulrich Volp, and Jochen Schmidt, Studien der Patristischen Arbeitsgemeinschaft 11 (Leuven: Peeters, 2011), 104n17.

34. Harry Maier, "Heresy, Households, and the Disciplining of Diversity," in *Late Ancient Christianity*, ed. Virginia Burrus, A People's History of Christianity 2 (Minneapolis: Fortress Press, 2005), 213–33; Reinhard Meßner, "Die Synode von Seleukeia-Ktesiphon 410 und die Geschichte der ostsyrischen Messe," in *"Haec sacrosancta synodus:" Konzils- und kirchengeschichtliche Beiträge*, ed. Reinhard Meßner and Rudolf Pranzl (Regensburg, Germany: Friedrich Pustet, 2006), 59–85; Bowes, *Private Worship*.

35. Meßner, "Die Synode von Seleukeia-Ktesiphon 410."

36. See Edward Adams, *The Earliest Christian Meeting Places: Almost Exclusively Houses?* Library of New Testament Studies 450 (London: Bloomsbury T&T Clark, 2016), 110–11; Jenn Cianca, *Sacred Ritual, Profane Space: The Roman House as Early Christian Meeting Place*, Studies in Christianity and Judaism Series 1 (Montreal: McGill-Queen's University Press, 2018), 104–10. For other examples of villa churches, see Bowes, *Private Worship*, Ch. 3.

37. Possible examples from Egypt include the small East church at Kellis and the small church at Munisis, as well as the church at Kysis and maybe the church at 'Ain el-Gedida. Michel Reddé et al., eds., *Kysis: Fouilles de l'Ifao à Douch, Oasis de Kharga, 1985–1990*,

The archaeological evidence, especially in Egypt, provides stronger indications that in some places a substantial eucharistic meal continued in the fourth century.[38] In the fourth-century church complex at ʿAin el-Gedida in the Dakhla Oasis in Egypt (Figure 1), there are cooking spaces within the church complex (B6)[39] and next to it (B10).[40] Across the passageway (street B12) from the church complex there are also a series of ovens (B14–15).[41] It has even been suggested that the assembly room (A46) may have served as a refectory.[42] It is difficult to determine what type of community used this church complex. It may have been a monastic settlement, or more likely an *epoikion*, a small-scale agricultural settlement often housing temporary workers.[43]

But ʿAin el-Gedida is not the only extant fourth-century church complex in Egypt to contain food preparation spaces. Another example comes from the East churches at Kellis.[44] While some scholars have suggested that these food preparation spaces and their ovens were linked to the production of eucharistic bread, it is also possible that these were for the production and distribution of bread in the context of a eucharistic meal and/or outside of a ritual context. In fact, a few explanations can be advanced for the presence of these cooking spaces, namely, as places for (1) the production and distribution of food doles, (2) for the preparation of non-eucharistic clergy and community meals, and (3) even for

---

Douch 3 (Le Caire: Institut français d'archéologie orientale, 2004), 75–86; Nicola Aravecchia, *'Ain El-Gedida: 2006–2008 Excavations of a Late Antique Site in Egypt's Western Desert*, Amheida IV (New York: Institute for the Study of the Ancient World, New York University Press, 2018), 9–11 and 200–208, and Chs. 3 and 5. The West I house at Narmuthis may also be a *domus ecclesiae*; see Edda Bresciani, *Rapporto preliminare delle campagne di Scavo 1968 e 1969* (Milano: Istituto Editoriale Cisalpino, 1976), 25.

38. For a more detailed account, see Chase, "Kitchens and Communion."

39. Aravecchia, *'Ain El-Gedida*, 116–31.

40. Aravecchia, 143–51.

41. Aravecchia, 174–86.

42. Nicola Aravecchia, "Catechumens, Women, and Agricultural Laborers: Who Used the Fourth-Century Hall at the Church of ʿAin El-Gedida, Egypt?," *Journal of Late Antiquity* 15 (2022): 193–230.

43. Aravecchia, 220–24.

44. Gillian Bowen, "The Fourth-Century Churches at Ismant El-Kharab," in *Dakhleh Oasis Project: Preliminary Reports on the 1994–1995 to 1998–1999 Field Seasons*, ed. Colin A. Hope and Gillian E. Bowen, Dakhleh Oasis Project 11 (Oxford: Oxbow Books, 2002), 71.

the celebration of the Eucharist within a meal context.[45] None of these are mutually exclusive. Coupled with the evidence from East Syria and elsewhere, this may suggest a more gradual loss of the meal.[46]

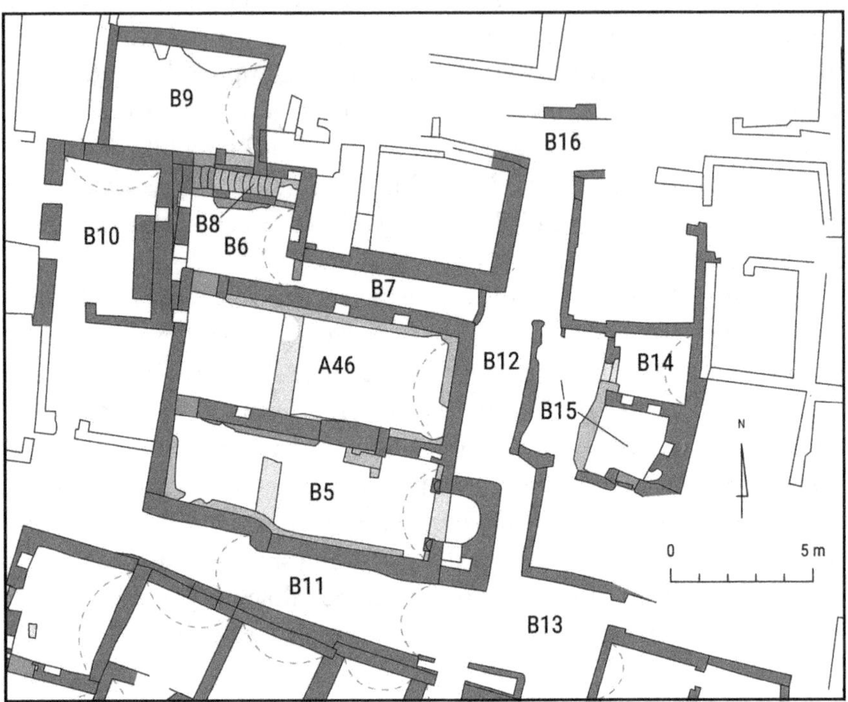


Figure 1. Plan of the church complex at ʿAin el-Gedida (© ʿAin el-Gedida Project; tracing by K. DeMondo). Used by permission.

## 3. The Eucharistic Celebration According to ApTrad

Having given an overview of the origins of the meal practices in ApTrad and the emergence of the clearly eucharistic celebrations of the document, we now turn to the practices that are clearly described as eucharistic in the document, before looking in more detail at the final shape of ApTrad's non-eucharistic meal practices.[47] ApTrad provides a pretty

45. Chase, "Kitchens and Communion."

46. See nn. 32–38.

47. *Herm.Com.* 2002; Messner, "Die Angebliche *Traditio Apostolica*"; Anders Ekenberg, "The Eucharist in Early Church Orders," in *The Eucharist, Its Origins and Contexts: Sacred*

full description of the eucharistic celebration. This includes discussions of the worship space, the preparation of the gifts, the eucharistic prayer, and the reception of the Eucharist, all of which are dealt with primarily, though not exclusively, in Chs. 4, 21.27, 22, and 36–38A. It should be noted that Ch. 22 is present only in Ethiopic I and II and Arabic I, as well as CH 30 and 31 and TD II.10. The presence of this chapter in Ethiopic I and II, Arabic I, CH 30 and 31, and TD II.10 suggests that it likely was original to the text of ApTrad or at least an early addition.[48] It must be noted, however, that the form of the Eucharist described in these chapters is for very specific celebrations: the ordination of a bishop (Ch. 4) and rites of initiation (Chs. 21 and 22).[49]

### *3.1. The Organization of the Worship Space*

Beginning already in the third century, early Christian sources mandate distinct areas in their worship spaces for clergy, widows, catechumens, and penitents. There was also a division in the worship space between the sexes. Sources that mention the arrangement of the worship space include the *Didascalia* Ch. 12, CH 18, and TD II.4, as well as a number of other Egyptian[50] and North African witnesses.[51] ApTrad also has some directives about the organization of the worship space, namely in ApTrad Ch. 18, but *Didascalia* 12 is also included as an expansion to ApTrad in Ethiopic I (see Ch. 8 of our commentary). *Didascalia* 12 provides much more information about the way the worship space should be organized

*Meal, Communal Meal, Table Fellowship in Late Antiquity, Early Judaism, and Early Christianity*, ed. David Hellholm and Dieter Sänger, vol. 2, Wissenschaftliche Untersuchungen zum Neuen Testament 376 (Tübingen: Mohr Siebeck, 2017), 957–92.

48. Scholars have long debated if it was original, see *Herm.Com.* 2002, 136.

49. This serves as a reminder of the different types of eucharistic celebrations in the early church. See Harald Buchinger, "Strukturwandel eucharistischen Betens: Zu Ursprung und Funktion der Postcommunio," in *Ecclesia de Liturgia: zur Bedeutung des Gottesdienstes für Kirche und Gesellschaft; Festschrift für Winfried Haunerland*, ed. Jürgen Bärsch, Stefan Kopp, and Christian Rentsch (Regensburg, Germany: Friedrich Pustet, 2021), 169–81.

50. The separation of the catechumens is clear in CA 25 (Arabic); Prayers 21 and 28 in the sacramentary of Sarapion of Thmuis; Ethio-MC §22. The separation of men and women in the worship space is also clear in CA 96 (Arabic) and possibly GCN 4.1.

51. J. Patout Burns and Robin Margaret Jensen, eds., *Christianity in Roman Africa: The Development of Its Practices and Beliefs* (Grand Rapids, MI: William B. Eerdmans, 2014), 158 and 354–55.

and how people in the space should conduct themselves, especially on how the youth, the infirm, the elderly, the clergy, men, and women should be arranged in the worship space.[52] Its inclusion in Ethiopic I embedded within ApTrad itself likely was an attempt to give that material the same authority as the rest of the document. It also points to the way the document evolved within the Egyptian milieu as a clear "living" document.

Within ApTrad itself, Ch. 18 implies that the catechumens prayed in a distinct room apart from the faithful: "After the teacher has finished instructing each day, they are to pray separated from the Christians." This separation was also maintained in meal practices—Chs. 26 and 27 note that the catechumens are to be segregated in some way from the believers during the meal and that that they are to be given exorcised bread, indicating originally that this was likely a eucharistic celebration.[53] ApTrad Ch. 18 also notes that men and women were separated in the worship space.[54] While there is no discussion about separate seating of clergy in ApTrad, this was a common feature in Christian worship spaces already by the third century. As Patout Burns and Robin Jensen note, "Cyprian identified [the] bishop's *cathedra* as one of the signs of the unity of the local church. It was a symbol of the teaching and governing authority of the bishop in Cyprian's attacks on the schismatics."[55] Archaeological evidence, especially in Egypt, provides further helpful support for this.[56] This is also addressed in *Didascalia* 12.

52. Alistair Stewart-Sykes, ed., *The Didascalia Apostolorum: An English Version*, Studia Traditionis Theologiae 1 (Turnhout: Brepols, 2009), 174–77.

53. *Herm.Com.* 2002, 142–45; Stewart, *On the Apostolic Tradition*, 175–76.

54. Bradshaw, *Apostolic Tradition*, 58–60.

55. Burns and Jensen, *Christianity in Roman Africa*, 288 and 432.

56. See, for instance, Peter Grossmann, *Christliche Architektur in Ägypten* (Leiden: Brill, 2002), 121–23 and 189–91. The apse contained seating for the clergy even in non-episcopal churches, since the bishop would often visit churches outside his cathedral to perform baptisms and other rituals. In churches lacking a bench, Grossmann notes that a wooden *cathedra* could be placed in the apse. Other clergy may have also used wooden chairs in some cases. In smaller churches, like those in Kellia, Grossmann believes the clergy sat in adjoining rooms, though it is equally possible, it seems, that they sat in portable chairs against one of the side walls/columns around the altar. Béatrice Caseau cites an inventory from the village church of Ibion in the Fayyum, which lists wooden seats; see Béatrice Caseau, "Objects in Churches: The Testimony of Inventories," in *Objects in Context, Objects in Use: Material Spatiality in Late Antiquity*, ed. Luke Lavan, Ellen Swift,

The posture of the assembly is not well known in this period and it is not described in ApTrad. Moreover, seating and standing patterns differed between regions in the ancient Christian world. There are some indications that the clergy and at times also the laity—specifically the infirm[57]—sat on benches or on the floor. Among the relevant sources are: *Didascalia* Ch. 12; Synod of Laodicea (fourth-century Asia Minor) canons 28 and 56;[58] and CB canon 97.[59] These, however, are all Eastern sources. In other places, like North Africa, it appears that sitting was less common, since Augustine of Hippo and Optatus of Milevis (in modern Algeria) indicate that only the clergy could/would sit.[60] There is also little to no evidence of seating in North African churches, except for the clergy and possibly the infirm.[61] In Egypt, outside of the citation to the *Didascalia* Ch. 12 included in Ethiopic I, there are no indications of whether the laity sat or stood during the liturgy, except in passing references in diaconal admonitions like the ones in Euch-AC and Ethio-MC—"You who are seated, stand up!"—as well as in Sarapion's Prayer 20: "Prayer After the Standing Up after the Homily." Additionally, Ethio-MC notes that at the start of the preface of the eucharistic prayer no one who is sitting, even the bishop, may continue to sit.[62] This, perhaps, indicates a mixture of sitting and standing practices in the Egyptian context. Thus, universal

---

and Toon Putzeys, Late Antique Archaeology 5 (Leiden: Brill, 2007), 560. However, it is unknown where exactly they would have been placed within the church and for whom.

57. Liturgical evidence for the elderly (and presumably the infirm) can be seen as early as the *Didascalia* Ch. 12.

58. Henry Percival, ed., *Nicene and Post-Nicene Fathers. Second Series*, vol. 14, Second Series (New York: Christian Literature, 1900), 157–58.

59. For the text, see Wilhelm Riedel, *Die Kirchenrechtsquellen des Patriarchats Alexandrien* (Leipzig: A. Deichert, 1900), 274. For discussions on the dating and provenance, see Alberto Camplani and Federico Contardi, "Remarks on the Textual Contribution of the Coptic Codices Preserving the Canons of Saint Basil, with Edition of the Ordination Rite for the Bishop (Canon 46)," in *Philologie, herméneutique et histoire des textes entre Orient et Occident: Mélanges en hommage à Sever J. Voicu*, ed. Francesca Prometea Barone, Caroline Macé, and Pablo Alejandro Ubierna (Turnhout: Brepols, 2017), 139–59. While it is thought that this text came from Syria, it circulated in Egypt at an early date.

60. Burns and Jensen, *Christianity in Roman Africa*, 158n300.

61. Burns and Jensen, 102–3 and 288.

62. For more on this, see Emmanuel Fritsch, "Two Ancient Ge'ez Witnesses of the Anaphora of Saint Mark," in *Explorations in Eastern Christian Liturgy: Selected Papers of the Sixth International Congress of the Society of Oriental Liturgy, Etchmiadzin, Armenia,*

norms cannot be established for the way that space was used in the early Church, and little further information can be gleaned from ApTrad.

### *3.2. The Preparation for the Eucharist*

The preparation for the Eucharist in ApTrad begins outside of the liturgical context and focuses primarily on the disposition of the faithful. For instance, a number of passages in ApTrad talk about the period of fasting prior to the eucharistic celebration (see also Ch. 8 in our commentary). Ch. 23 talks about general fasting practices for widows, presbyters, and laity but does not mention if this is explicitly a eucharistic fast. Ch. 23.2-4 references the fasting of the bishop, who can only fast when everyone fasts. While Ch. 23.2-4 does not seem to be related to the Eucharist, as noted above, Ch. 23.4 discusses the distribution of bread at the hands of the bishop in the church and makes it clear that this is *not* a Eucharist. While this passage now is a reference to a simple meal, it seems tantalizingly close to a eucharistic celebration. Interestingly, Ch. 23.4 is also missing from Ethiopic I and Arabic I, and the Latin has a lacuna here. References in ApTrad to something *not* being a Eucharist seem to imply at one point that it was. As a result, it could be that the reason why the bishop can only fast when everyone fasts is because otherwise someone will want the Eucharist offered and the bishop will have to receive the Eucharist at that celebration. This seems especially likely given that Ch. 23 continues after Ch. 22, which treats the distribution of communion.

Ch. 33 is connected to the eucharistic celebration, but specifically the two-day fast before the reception of the Eucharist at Pascha.[63] As a result, it is not really indicative of the normal eucharistic celebration. Nevertheless, it is worth noting that some people are given an abbreviated and/or modified fast, especially the sick and pregnant. Some may also observe the fast at another time, especially those who are traveling. Ch. 36 also mentions a fast before receiving the Eucharist, and this chapter is likely

---

*11–16 September 2016*, ed. Nina Glibetic and Gabriel Radle, Studies in Eastern Christian Liturgies 4 (Münster: Aschendorff Verlag, 2022), 300–301, 303–4, 313–14, and 317.

63. For more on the breaking of the pre-paschal fast, see Harald Buchinger, "Breaking the Fast: The Central Moment of the Paschal Celebration in Historical Context and Diachronic Perspective," in *Sanctifying Texts, Transforming Rituals: Encounters in Liturgical Studies; Essays in Honour of Gerard A.M. Rouwhorst*, ed. Paul van Geest, Marcel Poorthuis, and Els Rose, Brill's Studies in Catholic Theology 5 (Leiden: Brill, 2017), 191–205.

addressing daily or frequent reception of the Eucharist outside of the full eucharistic celebration, though the title in the Sahidic, Arabic II, and Ethiopic II will change this to refer not to private communion but the communal eucharistic celebration.[64] As a result, its provisions would still likely apply to the full eucharistic celebration. The additional material on fasting in Ethiopic I will be addressed in Ch. 8 of our commentary.

Besides fasting requirements, ApTrad also addresses the preparation of the gifts before the anaphora. This can be seen in Chs. 4.2, 21.27, and 23.3. It is possible that Chs. 31 and 32 (the blessing of the firstfruits) are also linked to the preparation of the gifts—directly or indirectly, especially since some of the eucharistic gifts may have been taken from the firstfruits discussed in Chs. 31 and 32 (see section 4 below for more). The preparation rite for the gifts is not thoroughly detailed in ApTrad, but it is clear in Chs. 4.2 and 21.27 that the deacon already played a key role in the preparation of the eucharistic offerings by presenting them to the bishop. At least in the case of the celebration of the Eucharist after baptism, it appears that it was the catechumens (Ch. 20.10) who brought the gifts.[65] This is not unlike what is seen in BR-AC, which contains a prayer for those who bring bread, water, or oil in Lent.[66] This prayer in BR-AC is specifically linked to the catechumens.

### *3.3. The Eucharistic Prayer in ApTrad Ch. 4*

While little of the eucharistic liturgy before the anaphora is described in ApTrad, there is a good deal of material on the anaphora and the distribution of communion. The central treatment of the anaphora in ApTrad is in Ch. 4 (Latin and Ethiopic II versions). The Sahidic and Arabic II versions of this chapter in ApTrad only give the pre-anaphoral dialogue. Ch. 4 is totally absent in Ethiopic I and Arabic I. Its absence in Ethiopic I is likely because of the presence of two anaphoras later in the Aksumite Collection

64. *Herm.Com.* 2002, 181; Stewart, *On the Apostolic Tradition*, 191–92. The issue of whether one could commune after eating was a debated topic in Egypt at this time; see Heinzgerd Brakmann, "Zur Geschichte der eucharistischen Nücternheit in Ägypten," *Le Muséon* 84 (1971): 197–211.

65. *Herm.Com.* 2002, 111.

66. Alessandro Bausi, "The *Baptismal Ritual* in the Earliest Ethiopic Canonical Liturgical Collection," in *»Neugeboren aus Wasser und Heiligem Geist« Kölner Kolloquium zur Initiatio Christiana*, ed. Heinzgerd Brakmann, Tinatin Chronz, and Claudia Sode (Münster: Aschendorff Verlag, 2020), 64/65.

in Euch-AC.[67] Euch-AC does not contain the version of the anaphora given in ApTrad Ch. 4 but instead gives the earliest fully extant form of MARK (Ethio-MARK I) and the earliest extant form of the Ethiopian Anaphora of the Apostles (Ethio-AA I).[68] This latter anaphora, as we will see, is a conflation of the anaphora in ApTrad Ch. 4 with Ethio-MARK I.

Despite the absence of the anaphora in the Sahidic and Arabic I and II, both texts include the pre-anaphoral dialogue and also mention that the eucharistic prayer is offered according to liturgical custom (Ch. 4.3). This still presupposes a model eucharistic prayer. This is also clear elsewhere

67. Predrag Bukovec, "Der Einsetzungsbericht: Die Genese des Eucharistischen Hochgebets" (PhD diss., Vienna, Universität Wien, 2016), 30; Bradshaw, *Apostolic Tradition*, 22.

68. No critical edition of Ethio-AA exists, though one is being prepared by Reinhard Meßner and Martin Lang; see Reinhard Meßner and Martin Lang, "Ethiopian Anaphoras: Status and Tasks in Current Research via an Edition of the Ethiopian Anaphora of the Apostles," in *Jewish and Christian Liturgy and Worship: New Insights into Its History and Interaction*, ed. Albert Gerhards and Clemens Leonhard (Leiden: Brill, 2007), 185–206. The earlier version of this prayer (Ethio-AA I) was recently discovered by Alessandro Bausi in the Aksumite Collection, but it has not yet been published. Emmanuael Fritsch has provided an English translation of the text; see Emmanuel Fritsch, "New Reflections on the Image of Late Antique and Medieval Ethiopian Liturgy," in *Liturgy's Imagined Past/s: Methodologies and Materials in the Writing of Liturgical History Today*, ed. Teresa Berger (Collegeville, MN: Liturgical Press, 2016), 47–54. For more information, see Emmanuel Fritsch, "The Anaphoras of the Ge'ez Churches: A Challenging Orthodoxy," in *The Anaphoral Genesis of the Institution Narrative in Light of the Anaphora of Addai and Mari*, ed. Cesare Giraudo, OCA 295 (Rome: Valore Italiano Lilamé, 2013), 275–82; Fritsch, "New Reflections"; Bukovec, "Der Einsetzungsbericht," 30–38, 571–72, and 607; Ágnes T. Mihálykó, *The Christian Liturgical Papyri: An Introduction*, Studien und Texte zu Antike und Christentum 114 (Tübingen: Mohr Siebeck, 2019), 43–44. For the received text of Ethio-AA (Ethio-AA II), one should consult the *textus receptus*; see Mäṣḥafä Qəddase, *መጽሐፈ፡ ቅዳሴ። በግዕዝና፡ በአማርኛ። አዲስ፡ አበባ፡ ፲፱፻፶፩፡ ዓመት፡ ምሕረት። Mäṣḥafä Qəddase. bä-Gəʿəz-ənna bä-Amarəñña [Book of the Liturgy. In Gəʿəz and Amharic]* (Addis Ababa: Täsfa Press, 1958). The date of Ethio-AA II has been a matter of debate; see Gabriele Winkler, *Das Sanctus: über den Ursprung und die Anfänge des Sanctus und sein Fortwirken*, Orientalia Christiana analecta 267 (Rome: Pontificio Istituto Orientale, 2002); Gabriele Winkler, "A New Witness to the Missing Institution Narrative," in *Studia Liturgica Diversa: Essays in Honor of Paul F. Bradshaw*, ed. Maxwell Johnson and L. Edward Phillips (Portland: Pastoral Press, 2004), 117–28; Heinzgerd Brakmann, "Schwarze Perlen aus Henochs Erbe? Zu <<Sanctus>> und <<Benedictus>> der äthiopischen Apostel-Anaphora," *Oriens Christianus* 91 (2007): 56–86.

in ApTrad Ch. 9.3-5, which indicates that the bishop still had the ability to improvise liturgical prayers. The eucharistic prayer is implied in the text. The following is the Sahidic:

> And (δέ) the bishop (ἐπίσκοπος) shall give thanks (εὐχαριστεῖν) according (κατά) to what we said before. It is not at all (οὐ πάντος) necessary (ἀναγκή) for him to repeat these same words that we said before as if (ὡς) recited (μελετᾶν) by rote (ἀναγκή) giving thanks (εὐχαριστεῖν) to God, but (ἀλλά) according to (κατά) each one's ability he shall pray. If on the one hand (μέν), he has ability to pray sufficiently (ἱκανός) with a prayer (προσευχή) that is honorable, then it is good (ἀγαθόν). But (δέ) if, on the other hand, he prays and recites a prayer (προσευχή) briefly, no one hinder (κωλύειν) him, only (μόνον) let him pray being sound in orthodoxy (ὀρθόδοξος).[69]

In fact, eucharistic prayers were shifting from improvised prayers to written texts in most regions in the third century, and this shift was nearly complete by the middle of the sixth.[70] The ability of the bishop to improvise eucharistic praying into the fourth century may provide a further reason for why the prayer is omitted in Ethiopic I, the Sahidic and Arabic (I and II) versions of ApTrad, and in CH 6.

Despite the absence of the eucharistic prayer in Ethiopic I, as well as the Sahidic and Arabic I and II versions of ApTrad, it is clear that it functioned as a model anaphoral text. The anaphora in ApTrad Ch. 4 served as the basis for at least two other anaphoras that will be taken up below: Ethio-AA I and TD. This confirms the fluidity of eucharistic praying in the places where ApTrad circulated, but also the early reception of ApTrad in two specific regions: Egypt and Syria. The anaphora also has, as we will see, been expanded over time. *Herm.Com.* 2002 notes that parts of the anaphora, in particular the institution narrative and anamnesis, are later additions.[71] Stewart also agrees that the text of the anaphora has been

69. *Herm.Com.* 2002, 68.

70. Allan Bouley, *From Freedom to Formula: The Evolution of the Eucharistic Prayer from Oral Improvisation to Written Texts*, Studies in Christian Antiquity 21 (Washington, DC: The Catholic University of America Press, 1981). See also Chase, *The Anaphoral Tradition in the "Barcelona Papyrus,"* 37–53.

71. *Herm.Com.* 2002, 44–48.

edited, though in ways different from *Herm.Com.* 2002. In particular, he says the prayer is the result of both the hands of $^{R}$El and $^{R}$CN.[72]

*Herm.Com.* 2002 tends to place the anaphora within a West Syrian context, while Stewart has placed it within the context of an Asian community in Rome. It is worth noting that Hanssens had argued that the anaphora in its preface, epiclesis, and doxology, as well as some of its phraseology and reception history, appears closer to the Alexandrian than Roman tradition.[73] The question of provenance will be dealt with as we discuss the text.

Turning specifically to the anaphora in ApTrad Ch. 4, the structure of the anaphora betrays an early date for its composition.[74] The anaphora lacks the *Sanctus* and expanded anaphoral intercessions, which, alongside the institution narrative and pneumatic epiclesis, were introduced into most anaphoral traditions in the fourth century. It is the absence of these units in some anaphoral texts into the fourth century that has led most scholars to argue that these units were added to earlier anaphoral forms in the course of the fourth century.[75] It is precisely in these units that Ethio-AA I and TD will diverge most from ApTrad Ch. 4, their source text.

The structure of the anaphora in ApTrad Ch. 4 may also help in determining its provenance, though in many ways it betrays a unique form not seen among any of the other classical anaphoras. The following is the structure of the anaphora in ApTrad Ch. 4:

- Pre-anaphoral dialogue
- Preface[76]

72. Stewart, *On the Apostolic Tradition*, 81–90.

73. Jean Michel Hanssens, *La liturgie d'Hippolyte: Ses documents, son titulaire, ses origines et son charactère*, Orientalia Christiana Analecta 155 (Rome: Pontificium Institutum Orientalium Studiorum, 1959), 352–70 and 426–41.

74. For a helpful summary of scholarship, see Bradshaw, *Apostolic Tradition*, 23–33.

75. For a summary of anaphoras lacking these units, see Chase, *Eucharistic Praying in Ritual Context*, 7.

76. Given the absence of a *Sanctus* in this text, there is no real preface in the traditional sense, but rather an extended Thanksgiving that will flow into the institution narrative. However, in order to facilitate a comparison to other texts with a proper preface, the language of *preface* will be used here to denote all the material in ApTrad Ch. 4 up to the introduction to the institution narrative.

- Institution Narrative
- Anamnesis
- Offering
- Epiclesis
- Fruits of Communion
- Doxology

Missing is the *Sanctus* and anaphoral intercessions.

The earliest classical anaphoras can be divided into different anaphoral patterns. These anaphoral patterns largely (though not exclusively) broke along regional lines before the widespread adoption of certain anaphoral texts and patterns like the anaphora of St. Basil (BAS) and the West Syrian form. However, some regions knew of more than one way to construct an anaphora even after this period of homogenization (see Table 1 below). In general, the anaphora in ApTrad Ch. 4 mirrors most closely the West Syrian anaphoral pattern in placing a single epiclesis after the institution narrative.[77] However, the absence of the *Sanctus* in the text, as well as the lack of intercessions, means that it cannot be identified with any of the patterns from the fourth century onward. For this reason, the anaphora in ApTrad Ch. 4 should really not be classified among the West Syrian anaphoral pattern. This is especially the case since the pattern seems to imply a Syrian provenance for the text, something that is by no means certain. The absence of a *Sanctus* and anaphoral intercessions also does not help with the provenance of the text, since the lack of both of these units can be seen across different geographical regions from Rome to Syria to Egypt.[78]

77. Matthieu Smyth, "The Anaphora of the So-Called 'Apostolic Tradition' and the Roman Eucharistic Prayer," in *Issues in Eucharistic Praying in East and West*, ed. Maxwell Johnson (Collegeville, MN: Liturgical Press, 2011), 71–97.

78. See n. 75.

**Table 1: Anaphoral Patterns**[79]

| **West Syrian** | **East Syrian** | **Egyptian** | | **Gallican/Hispano-Mozarabic** | **Roman** |
|---|---|---|---|---|---|
| | | **MARKan** | **BARCelonan** | | |
| Preface | Preface | Preface | Preface | Preface | Preface |
| | | [Intercessions] | | | |
| *Sanctus* | *Sanctus* | *Sanctus* | *Sanctus* | *Sanctus* | *Sanctus* |
| Post-*Sanctus* | Post-*Sanctus* | [Post-*Sanctus*] | Post-*Sanctus* | Post-*Sanctus* | |
| | | | | | Intercessions |
| | | Epiclesis 1 | Epiclesis | | Offering Language/Epiclesis 1 |
| Institution Narr. | [Institution Narr.] | Institution Narr. | Institution Narr. | Institution Narr. | Institution Narr. |
| Anamnesis | Anamnesis | Anamnesis | Anamnesis | Anamnesis | Anamnesis |
| Epiclesis | | Epiclesis 2 | | | Offering Language/Epiclesis 2 |
| Intercessions | Intercessions | [Intercessions] | Fruits of comm. | Fruits of comm. | Intercessions |
| | Epiclesis | | | | |
| Doxology | Doxology | Doxology | Doxology | Doxology | Doxology |

79. Adapted and expanded from Bradshaw and Johnson, *Eucharistic Liturgies*, 77.

| **Examples of each pattern (anaphoras)**[80] | | | | | |
|---|---|---|---|---|---|
| • Basil<br>• JAS<br>• ApCons 8<br>• Twelve Apostles<br>• Chrysostom<br>• Gregory[81]<br>• Many others | • Addai and Mari<br>• Sharar<br>• Mar Theodore<br>• Mar Nestorius[82]<br>• The "Persian Anaphora"[83]<br>• Others | • MARK<br>• SAR<br>• Fragments | • BARC<br>• The anaphora in the Deir Balyzeh Papyrus<br>• The anaphora in the Sunnarti fragments[84]<br>• Fragments | • All Gallican and Hispano-Mozarabic prayers | • Roman Canon |

80. Almost all of the anaphoras in this table can be found in PEER4e. Those that are not in PEER4e will be noted with a footnote.

81. The Egyptian anaphora of St. Gregory; see Ernst Hammerschmidt, *Die Koptische Gregoriosanaphora* (Berlin: Akademie-Verlag, 1957); Albert Gerhards, *Die griechische Gregoriosanaphora. Ein beitrag* zur Geschichte des eucharistischen Hoc*hgebets* (Münster Westfalen: Aschendorff, 1984).

82. Bryan Spinks, *Mar Nestorius and Mar Theodore, the Interpreter: The Forgotten Eucharistic Prayers of East Syria* (Cambridge: Grove Books, 1999).

83. R. H. Connolly, "Sixth-Century Fragments of an East-Syrian Anaphora," Oriens Christianus 12–14 (1925): 99–128.

84. Alistair Stewart, *Two Early Egyptian Liturgical Papyri: The Deir Balyzeh Papyrus and the Barcelona Papyrus with Appendices Containing Comparative Material*, Joint Liturgical Studies 70 (Norwich: Hymns Ancient and Modern, 2010), 45–47.

Turning now from the structure of the anaphora in ApTrad Ch. 4 to the content of the prayer itself, the text of the anaphora shows signs of antiquity.[85] Matthieu Smyth has summarized these points of antiquity as follows:

- a direct address to the Father ("We thank you, O God, through your beloved servant, Jesus Christ") comparable to that of *Didache* 9, and anterior to the diffusion of the rhetorical catchphrase ("it is right and just to give you thanks," *Axion kai dikaion* . . . ) of narrative style
- mention of the especially archaic christological title of "servant" (*pais*) taken from *Didache* 9, a title already outdated by the time of the redaction of the New Testament, where it is only witnessed in the early records of Acts 3:13-26 and 4:27-30
- the vestige from *Didache* 9–10 ("gathering them in unity") at the heart of the intercessions
- the presence in the oration of *carmen Christo quasi deo* woven from characteristic conceptions notably to be found in pre-Nicene paschal homilies, illustrated from *On the Pascha* of Pseudo-Hippolytus and of Melito of Sardis, and marked by the New Testament christological rhetoric of the antithetical parallels of humbling/exaltation ("while suffering to deliver from suffering")
- the absence of the *Sanctus* and the epiclesis for the transformation of the gifts
- the soberness of the anamnesis in relation to other later anaphoras.[86]

To this should also be added a few additional signs of antiquity.

First, the transition from the pre-anaphoral dialogue to the "preface"[87] is not the transition typically seen in the classical anaphoras. The anaphora simply has "We render thanks to you," but most of the classical anaphoras pick up on "It is right and just" in the pre-anaphoral dialogue and begin their preface with "It is truly right and just."[88] The anaphora also lacks the expansion of the praise verbs introducing the preface, something seen in

85. For a helpful summary of scholarship, see Bradshaw, *Apostolic Tradition*, 23–33.

86. Smyth, "Anaphora of the So-Called 'Apostolic Tradition,'" 79–80. For further reflection, see Enrico Mazza, *The Origins of the Eucharistic Prayer* (Collegeville, MN: Liturgical Press, 1995), Ch. 4.

87. See n. 76.

88. Chase, *The Anaphoral Tradition in the "Barcelona Papyrus,"* 156–57.

many of the classical anaphoras from the mid-fourth century onward.[89] This suggests an early dating for the introduction to ApTrad Ch. 4's preface. In fact, there is nothing about this that would preclude a second-century date. While likely a later addition, the institution narrative in ApTrad is one of the earliest examples of the introduction of the institution narrative in anaphoral praying. This can be seen in comparing the form of the institution narrative against other examples from the mid-fourth century, like BARC and SAR.[90] The fruits of communion unit in ApTrad Ch. 4 is also underdeveloped in comparison to other classical anaphoras. This again points to an early date for this part of the prayer, possibly as early as the second century.[91] These features in the anaphora in ApTrad Ch. 4 may point to a second- or third-century origin for parts of the prayer.

While it is clear that the anaphora in ApTrad Ch. 4 shows signs of antiquity, in other ways the anaphora shows signs of development. ApTrad Ch. 4's use of some of the archaic phrases above actually suggests some further development in the text.[92] While the preface of the prayer bears some resemblance to earlier paschal homilies,[93] there are also signs of later reworkings, like the addition of some creedal language. An example of this is the reference to Christ being "born from the Holy Spirit and the Virgin."[94] The way the institution narrative has been blended into the text also shows signs of later editing.[95] But perhaps the most significant sign of development in the text is the pneumatology in the epiclesis.[96]

Based on comparative evidence and the derivates of the text (which will be discussed below) the *terminus ante quem* of the anaphora cannot be later than the mid-fourth century, but the *terminus post quem* is much more difficult to determine. It is possible, as Enrico Mazza has suggested,

89. Chase, 156–57.

90. Bukovec, "Der Einsetzungsbericht," 16–72, 90–102, and 222–38; Chase, *The Anaphoral Tradition in the "Barcelona Papyrus,"* Ch. 10.

91. Nathan Chase, "The Fruits of Communion in the Classical Anaphoras," *Orientalia Christiana Periodica* 87 (2021): 14–15; Chase, *The Anaphoral Tradition in the "Barcelona Papyrus,"* Ch. 12. See also the recent work on the anaphora in the Milan Euchologion: Ágnes T. Mihálykó and Nathan Chase, "The 'Milan Euchologion': Reconstructing an Unknown Fourth-Century Anaphora and Its Post-Anaphoral Prayers," *Vigiliae Christianae*, forthcoming.

92. Smyth, "Anaphora of the So-Called 'Apostolic Tradition,'" 80.

93. *Herm.Com.* 2002, 44–45.

94. *Herm.Com.* 2002, 46–47.

95. Smyth, "Anaphora of the So-Called 'Apostolic Tradition,'" 82–83.

96. Smyth, 84.

that the preface in particular might be rooted in an early form;[97] however, Smyth has rightly noted that this could be an intentional archaism. Bradshaw has also argued recently for a second-century date for the core of the prayer.[98] Thus, it is not unreasonable that some parts of ApTrad Ch. 4 might very well have their origins in the second or third century; however, the addition of the institution narrative, which otherwise does not appear in eucharistic praying before the fourth century,[99] and the presence of a well-developed pneumatic epiclesis requesting the change of the bread and wine into the body and blood of Christ, points to the fourth century as the final period for the redaction of the anaphora in ApTrad Ch. 4.[100]

The provenance and original core of the prayer will be taken up after looking at its early derivatives: Ethio-AA I and TD. What is important to again bear in mind is that the only two witnesses to ApTrad Ch. 4 are the Latin and Ethiopic II versions of ApTrad. This anaphora is conspicuously absent in every version of ApTrad within the Egyptian orbit (Ethiopic I, Sahidic, and Arabic I and II, including CH 3b), except Ethiopic II and TD. In all of the Egyptian-orbit versions of the text, except Ethiopic II and TD, only the dialogue is given. Perhaps even more significantly, ApTrad Ch. 4 had absolutely no impact on Western liturgical sources until the Second Vatican Council, indicating that the text was not received in the West, particularly the Roman West.[101] A turn to these derivatives, which are very close in date to ApTrad's anaphora, then, can provide key insights into the reception of ApTrad's anaphora that may also shed light on its origins.

### *3.4. Derivatives of the Eucharistic Prayer in ApTrad Ch. 4*

Part of the key to interpreting the anaphora in ApTrad Ch. 4 is its derivatives, namely Ethio-AA I and TD (I.23). It was not until recently that Ethio-AA (I and II) were seen as derived in some way from a conflation of ApTrad Ch. 4 with MARK. The first to suggest this interpretation was Reinhard Meßner and Martin Lang based on a comparison to Ethio-AA

97. Mazza, *The Origins*, 102–29.

98. Paul Bradshaw, "The Formation of the Eucharistic Prayer in the *Apostolic Tradition*," *Theology* 125 (2022): 101–8.

99. Robert Taft, "Mass without the Consecration?: The Historic Agreement on the Eucharist between the Catholic Church and the Assyrian Church of the East Promulgated 26 October 2001," *Worship* 77 (2003): 482–509.

100. Chase, "From *Logos* to Spirit Revisited."

101. Maxwell Johnson, "Imagining Early Christian Liturgy: The *Traditio Apostolica*—A Case Study," in *Liturgy's Imagined Past/s*, ed. Berger, 93–120.

II,[102] and their study was followed shortly by another.[103] However, as we will see, the recent discovery and work done on Ethio-AA I contained in Euch-AC, indicates that ApTrad Ch. 4 was conflated with MARK, particularly Ethio-MARK I, to form Ethio-AA I. Thus, ApTrad Ch. 4 was repurposed at an early date within the Egyptian orbit.

Prior to the recent work on Ethio-AA I, scholars have tended to focus on parallels between ApTrad Ch. 4 and other Syrian anaphoras. This led them to strongly suggest that at the very least ApTrad Ch. 4 circulated primarily in a Syrian context and that its origins likely lay in Syria.[104] One of the texts used to point to a Syrian context had parallels to ApCons 8; however, the parallels are minimal in light of heavy expansions and edits made by the redactor of the text.[105] If ApCons 8 was indeed derived from the hypothetically postulated Anaphora of the Apostles,[106] this could indicate some sort of conflations between the Anaphora of the Apostles and the anaphora in ApTrad Ch. 4 to form ApCons 8. In any event, ApCons 8 will not be taken up here since the additions from ApTrad Ch. 4 are minimal, though it clearly shows the circulation of the anaphora in the Antiochene context. The other source of evidence seemingly pointing to a Syrian context for ApTrad Ch. 4 was the presence of an expanded form of the anaphora in TD. However, as we will see, there are issues with the provenance of this document, and it is known to have circulated in Egypt at an early date as well.

In looking at ApTrad Ch. 4's main derivatives, it is perhaps best to begin with Ethio-AA I, because Ethio-AA I has been expanded more from the anaphora in ApTrad Ch. 4 than TD. Table 2 below gives the texts of ApTrad Ch. 4, Ethio-AA I, and Ethio-MARK I, as well as Syr-TD, which will be used as the base text of TD. Differences between Syr-TD, Ethio-TD, and Arb-TD.M will be marked in the footnotes in the table.

102. Meßner and Lang, "Ethiopian Anaphoras."

103. Maxwell Johnson, "Recent Research on the Anaphoral *Sanctus*: An Update and Hypothesis," in *Issues in Eucharistic Praying in East and West*, ed. Johnson, 161–88.

104. Cf. Paul Bradshaw, "The Formation of the Eucharistic Prayer in the *Apostolic Tradition*," *Theology* 125 (2022): 101–8.

105. Raphael Graves, "The Anaphora of the Eighth Book of the Apostolic Constitutions," in *Essays on Early Eastern Eucharistic Prayers*, ed. Paul Bradshaw (Collegeville, MN: Liturgical Press, 1997), 178–79; Smyth, "Anaphora of the So-Called 'Apostolic Tradition,'" 87–88.

106. See especially John R. K. Fenwick, *"The Missing Oblation": The Contents of the Early Antiochene Anaphora*, Joint Liturgical Studies (Bramcote: Grove Books, 1989). For a summary, see Chase, *The Anaphoral Tradition in the "Barcelona Papyrus,"* 330–31.

**Table 2: ApTrad Ch. 4 and Its Derivatives**

| | **ApTrad Ch. 4 (Latin)** | **Formation of Ethio-AA I** | | **Syr-TD**[107] |
|---|---|---|---|---|
| | | **Ethio-AA I**[108] | **Ethio-MARK I**[109] | |
| *Dialogue* | The Lord [be] with you.<br>And with your spirit.<br>Up [with your] hearts.<br>We have [them] to the Lord.<br>Let us give thanks to the Lord.<br>It is worthy and just. | The Lord [be] with you all.<br>With your spirit.<br>Lift up your hearts!<br>We pray to the Lord.<br>Let us give thanks to the Lord!<br>It is right and just, he is worthy. | The Lord [be] with you all.<br>And with your Spirit.<br>Lift up your hearts!<br>We have them with the Lord.<br>Let us give thanks to the Lord!<br>It is right and just. | Our Lord be with you.<br>And with your spirit.<br>Up with your hearts.<br>We have them with the Lord.<br>Let us give thanks to the Lord.<br>It is fitting and right. [*Sanctus*][110]<br>The holy things for the holy people.<br>In heaven and on earth<br>unceasingly. |
| *Preface* | We render thanks to you, God, | We give you thanks, O Lord, | It is right and just that we praise you, glorify you, bless you.<br><br>We confess you by night and by day. To you who made heaven and all that is in it, the earth and | We render thanks to you, Holy God, strengthener of your souls, giver of our life, treasure of incorruptibility, |

107. Text adapted from PEER3e, 138–141. Significant departures from Ethio-TD and Arb-TD.M will be noted in the text.

108. Text adapted from Fritsch, "New Reflections," in Liturgy's Imagined Past/s, ed. Berger, 47–54.

109. Text adapted from Fritsch, 47–54.

110. The Sanctus is inserted here instead of "The holy things for the holy people" in Arb-TD.M, see Martin Lüstraeten, "The Eucharistic Prayer in the Arabic Tradition of the *Testamentum Domini*," forthcoming in the proceedings from The Eighth International Congress of the Society of Oriental Liturgy; 13–18 June 2022, Thessaloniki, Greece.

| | | | | |
|---|---|---|---|---|
| | | | all that is on the earth, the sea and all that is in it; to you who created man in your own image and likeness, you created all by this your wisdom, the true light, | |
| | through your beloved servant Jesus Christ, | through your beloved Son our Saviour Jesus Christ | the Lord our Saviour Jesus Christ, through whom to you, with him and through the Holy Spirit, as we give thanks | Father of your only-begotten, our Savior, |
| | | | we offer the reasonable sacrifice, this bloodless worship of yours, which all the peoples offer to you from the rising of the sun to the west, from south to north, for your name is great among all nations and in every place incense is offered to your holy name and a pure sacrifice. | |
| | whom in the last times you sent to us as savior and redeemer and angel of your will, | whom in the last days you sent to us as saviour and redeemer and the angel of your council. | | whom in the last times you sent to us as Savior and proclaimer of your will.<br>For it is your purpose that we should be saved through you. Our heart, mind, and soul, with all |

**Table 2: ApTrad Ch. 4 and Its Derivatives** (cont.)

| | ApTrad Ch. 4 (Latin) | Formation of Ethio-AA I | | Syr-TD |
|---|---|---|---|---|
| | | Ethio-AA I | Ethio-MARK I | |
| *Preface* (cont.) | | | | its thinking, gives thanks to you, [Lord, that your grace may come upon us; Lord, that we may continually praise you and your only-begotten Son and your Holy Spirit, now and always and to the ages of ages.][111] O power of the Father, grace of the nations, knowledge, true wisdom, the exaltation of the meek, the medicine of souls, the confidence of us who believe, you are the strength of the righteous, the hope of the persecuted, the haven of the buffeted, the illuminator of the perfect, the Son of the living God. Make to arise on us, out of your unsearchable gift, courage, might, reliance, wisdom, strength, unlapsing faith, unshaken hope, the knowledge of your Spirit, meekness, uprightness, so what we your servants and all your people may always praise you purely, bless |

111. Not in Ethio-TD and a different line in Arb-TD.M: "so that your salvation may come upon us! O Christ . . ."

| | | | | |
|---|---|---|---|---|
| | | | | you, give thanks to you, Lord, and entreat you at all times. Lord, the founder of the heights, king of the treasuries of light, visitor of the heavenly Zion, [king of the orders of archangels, of dominions, praises, thrones, vestures, lights, joys, and delights, father of kings,][112] you hold all things in your hand and guide them by your counsel, through your only-begotten Son, who was crucified for our sins |
| | who is your inseparable word, through whom you made all things and it was well pleasing to you, [whom] you sent from heaven into the virgin's womb, | He is the Word while he is faithful, him through whom you made all things, you have decided, and you sent him from heaven into the womb of a virgin. | | You sent your Word, Lord, the sharer of your counsel and covenant, through whom you made all things, and in whom you were well-pleased into a virgin's womb. |
| | | | In this sacrifice and offering we pray and beseech you: remember the one, your holy Church which is spread everywhere | |

112. Slightly different in Ethio-TD: "Lord of the powers, of the archangels, the power of lordships and the glory of the thrones, garments of light, joy of delight, king of kings." Slightly different in Arb-TD.M: "O you, you are the overseer, the jubilation of the ranks of the arch(angel)s and the angels, glorified by the lords, the jubilation of the lights, the force of the kings."

**Table 2: ApTrad Ch. 4 and Its Derivatives** (cont.)

| | **ApTrad Ch. 4 (Latin)** | **Formation of Ethio-AA I** | | **Syr-TD** |
|---|---|---|---|---|
| | | **Ethio-AA I** | **Ethio-MARK I** | |
| *Preface* (cont.) | | <The diptychs are to be read here> | . . . [Intercessions] . . . | |
| | and who conceived in the womb was incarnate and manifested as your Son, | He became flesh and was carried in the womb and your Son was known from the Holy Spirit. | | When he was conceived and made flesh, he was manifested as your Son, being born of the Holy Spirit and the Virgin. Fulfilling your will and gaining a holy people, he stretched out his hands to suffering, that he might release from suffering and the corruption of death those who have hoped in you. |
| *Pre-Sanctus and Sanctus* | | To you, whom sanctify the thousands and countless thousands of holy angels and archangels and your glorious animals, | It is you who are above every rank and authority and power and dominations and every name which is named; before you stand millions of millions and myriads of holy angels and archangels; before you stand your glorious living creatures, | |
| | | the seraphim and cherubim who have six wings, with two wings they cover the face, and with two | the seraphs with six wings and the cherubs. With two wings they cover their face, with two their | |

| | | | | |
|---|---|---|---|---|
| | | they cover their feet, and with two of their wings they fly and all of them continuously sanctify you<br><br>together with all those who sanctify you, accept our own sanctification as we say to you: Holy! And the people say together with the one who offers:<br><br>Holy, Holy, Holy, Lord Sabaoth! Heaven and earth are filled with the holiness of your glory! | feet, with two they fly and all of them always sanctify you.<br><br>Accept our own sanctification as, together with all those who sanctify you, we say to you:<br><br>Holy, Holy, Holy Lord Sabaoth! | |
| *Post-Sanctus* | born from the Holy Spirit and the virgin; who fulfilling your will and gaining for you a holy people stretched out [his] hands when he was suffering, that he might release from suffering those who believed in you; | Truly the holiness of your glory fills heaven and earth through our Lord and our Saviour Jesus Christ.<br><br>Your holy Son having been born of a virgin in order to fulfill your will and to make a people for you, stretch his hand(s), suffering in order to set the sufferers free, those who rely on you, | Perfect therefore is all the heaven and the earth by the holiness of your glory through the Lord our Saviour Jesus Christ. | |

**Table 2: ApTrad Ch. 4 and Its Derivatives** (cont.)

| | ApTrad Ch. 4 (Latin) | Formation of Ethio-AA I | | Syr-TD |
|---|---|---|---|---|
| | | Ethio-AA I | Ethio-MARK I | |
| *Epiclesis (1)* | | | Perfect, O Lord, this sacrifice which is a blessing from you by the Holy Spirit because it is your only Son, the Lord and God and our King over all, Jesus Christ. | |
| *Institution Narrative* | who when he was being handed over to voluntary suffering, that he might destroy death and break the bonds of the devil, and tread down hell and illuminate the righteous, and fix a limit and manifest the resurrection, taking bread [and] giving thanks to you, he said: | he has given to suffering by his will in order to overcome death and break the bounds of [the devil/Satan] and tram[ple she]ol and lead the holy ones and establish a covenant, and make known the resurrection. | | When he was betrayed to voluntary suffering that he might set upright those who had stumbled, and find the lost, and give life to the dead, and destroy death, and break the bonds of the devil, and fulfill the counsel of the Father, and tread down hell, and open the way of life, and guide the righteous to light, and fix a limit, and lighten the darkness, and nurture babes, and manifest the Resurrection, |

| | | | | |
|---|---|---|---|---|
| | | In the night in which they betrayed him he took bread in his holy [hand] and looked up towards you, towards his Father, and blessed and broke and gave to them his own disciples and said to them: | In the night when they handed him over, he took bread with his holy and blessed hands and, having blessed and broken it, he gave it to his very disciples and to his apostles as he said: | he took bread [ ][113] and gave it to his disciples, saying, |
| | "Take, eat, this is my body that will be broken for you." | "Take, eat, all of you: This is my body. It is given to you, | "Take, eat from it all of you: this is my body which is given for you | "Take, eat; this is my body, |
| | | this by which sin is remitted." | unto the remission of sin." | which is broken for you for forgiveness of sins. |
| | | | | When you shall do this, you shall make my [resurrection]."[114] |
| | Likewise also the cup, saying, "This is my blood that is shed for you. | And likewise the chalice, having given thanks he said: "Take, drink all of you, this is my blood which will be poured for you, | Again, likewise for the chalice after they had supper, having taken it, he gave thanks and gave as he said: "Take, drink from it all of you: this is my blood | Also the cup of wine which he mixed, he gave for a type of the blood |
| | | | of the new covenant | |

113. Ethio-TD: "in his holy and blessed hands, which are spotless, he broke it."
114. Ethio-TD and Arb-TD.M: "commemoration."

**Table 2: ApTrad Ch. 4 and Its Derivatives** (cont.)

| | **ApTrad Ch. 4 (Latin)** | **Formation of Ethio-AA I** | | **Syr-TD** |
|---|---|---|---|---|
| | | **Ethio-AA I** | **Ethio-MARK I** | |
| *Institution Narrative* (cont.) | | by which sin is remitted." | which is poured for you unto the forgiveness of sins." | which was shed for us.[115] |
| | When you do this, you do my remembrance." | When you do this, you will do it for the commemoration of me. | As often as you | |
| | | | eat this bread and drink this cup then you announce this my death and you believe in my resurrection. | |
| *Anamnesis* | Remembering therefore his death and resurrection, | As we commemorate his death and resurrection, | As we announce the death of my Lord almighty, your Only Son, the Lord and God, the king over all and our Saviour Jesus Christ, as we believe in his resurrection, | Remembering therefore your death and resurrection, [ ][116] |
| | | | his ascension in the heavens, | |

115. Arb-TD.M: "And he mixed the cup of wine and blessed (it) and gave (it) to them, saying: 'Take (it), drink from this, all of you. This is my blood, which is poured out for you.'"

116. Ethio-TD: "we believe in you."

| | | | | |
|---|---|---|---|---|
| | we offer to you the bread and cup,<br><br>giving thanks to you because you have held us worthy to stand before you and minister to you. | we offer to you this bread and cup as we thank you.<br><br>Thereby you made . . . for us so that we may stand (before) you and serve you sacerdotally. | we have offered to you this your own gift from your own gift. | we offer you bread and the cup, giving thanks to you<br><br>who alone are God for ever and our Savior, because you have held us worthy to stand before you and serve you as priests.<br><br>Therefore, we your servants, Lord, render thanks to you. (*The people say likewise.*) We offer you this thanksgiving, eternal Trinity, Lord Jesus Christ, Lord the Father, before whom all creation and all nature trembles, fleeing into itself [ ][117]; |
| *Epiclesis (2)* | And we ask that you would send your Holy Spirit in the oblation of [your] holy church, | We pray and beseech you so that you may send the Holy Spirit and power to this bread and cup<br><br>and (that) you may make it the body and the blood of the Lord our Saviour Jesus Christ. Amen. | We pray and beseech you to send the Holy Spirit and power in this offering upon the bread and the cup<br><br>and to make the bread the body and the cup the blood of the new covenant of the Lord God, our King everywhere, Jesus Christ. | | Lord, send the Holy Spirit upon this drink and this your holy food; |

117. Arb-TD.M: "and the Holy Spirit."

**Table 2: ApTrad Ch. 4 and Its Derivatives** (cont.)

| | ApTrad Ch. 4 (Latin) | Formation of Ethio-AA I | | Syr-TD |
|---|---|---|---|---|
| | | Ethio-AA I | Ethio-MARK I | |
| *Fruits of Communion or Intercessions* | | | | cause them to be to us, not for condemnation \|[118] nor reproach nor destruction, but for the healing and strengthening of our Spirit.<br><br>(*Intercessions*)<br><br>Yea, O God, grant us that by your Name every thought of things displeasing to you may flee away. Grant, O God, that every proud conception may be driven away |

118. Syr-TD: It should be noted that Louis Bouyer has argued that the phrase "Lord, send the Holy Spirit upon this drink and this your holy food"—as Botte has it—is not how this text should be read, but rather: "Lord Holy Spirit, obtain for us this food of your holiness, so that it may not turn to our judgment." Louis Bouyer, Eucharist (Notre Dame: University of Notre Dame Press, 1989), 170–75, here 174. Ethio-TD appears to also be complicated here. Reinhard Meßner and Martin Lang note that "the text is hardly understandable." Meßner and Lang, "Ethiopian Anaphoras," 193n1. They have proposed the following for the epiclesis in Ethio-TD: "Furthermore we offer to you this thanksgiving, eternal trinity, O Lord, Father of Jesus Christ, before whom every creature and (every) soul is trembling; and be poured out in it [??] by you [??] this gift, not food and drink, that we have offered to you, make them for us your holy (things) [???]. Not be it for us in judgement." Meßner and Lang, 193. Arb-TD.M: "Make for us this sanctified food and the drink for your sanctification, (it should be) neither for the judgment."

| | | | | |
|---|---|---|---|---|
| | | | | from us by your Name, which is written within the veils of your sanctuaries, those high ones. When Sheol hears that Name, it is amazed, the depth is rent, [ ][119] the spirits are driven away, the dragon is [bruised],[120] [unbelief is cast out, disobedience is subdued, anger is appeased, envy works not, pride is reproved, avarice rooted out, boasting taken away, arrogance humbled, every root of bitterness destroyed.][121] Grant therefore, Lord, to our innermost eyes to see you, praising you and glorifying you, commemorating you, serving you, having a portion in you alone, Son and Word of God, to whom all things are subdued. Sustain to the end those who have gifts of |

119. Ethio-TD: "let the enemy be trampled."

120. Ethio-TD: "retreat." Arb-TD.M: "dies."

121. Ethio-TD is different here: "let envy always be useless, let it be punished, let those who love gold be eradicated, let affliction be removed, let the deceiver be humbled and let all that is a principle of bitterness be dispelled."

**Table 2: ApTrad Ch. 4 and Its Derivatives** (cont.)

| | **ApTrad Ch. 4 (Latin)** | **Formation of Ethio-AA I** | | **Syr-TD** |
|---|---|---|---|---|
| | | **Ethio-AA I** | **Ethio-MARK I** | |
| *Fruits of Communion or Intercessions* (cont.) | | | | revelations; confirm those who have a gift of healing; [make those who have the gift of tongues courageous. Keep those who have the word of doctrine upright;][122] care for those who do your will always. Visit the widows; help the orphans; remember those who have fallen asleep in the faith; and grant us an inheritance with your saints, and bestow the power to please you as they also pleased you. Feed the people in uprightness; sanctify us all, O God;<br><br>(*Fruits of communion resume*) |

122. Ethio-TD: "guard those who by the power of the tongue glorify the faith, direct those who are instructed by the word."

| | | | | |
|---|---|---|---|---|
| | [that] gathering [them] into one you will give to all who partake of the holy things [to partake] | Having united, may you give to all those who take (of it) that they will be for holiness | So that it may be for all who take from it | but grant that all who partake and receive of your holy things may be united to you so that they may be filled with the Holy Spirit for the strengthening of faith in truth; |
| | in the fullness of the Holy Spirit, | and the fullness of the Holy Spirit, | | |
| | for the strengthening of faith in truth, | [the strengthening] of the (true) faith | for faith, for understanding, | |
| | | | for healing, for a renewal of soul, body and spirit, | |
| *Doxology* | that we may praise and glorify you through your servant Jesus Christ, through whom [be] glory and honor to you, Father and Son with the Holy Spirit, | so that they may glorify and praise you and your Son our Saviour Jesus Christ with the Holy Spirit. | So that to you, in this as in all things, be glorified your holy and blessed name in everything, with Jesus Christ and the Holy Spirit. | that they may always lift up a doxology to you and your beloved Son Jesus Christ, through whom be glory and might to you with your holy Spirit |
| | in your holy church, | | | |
| | both now and to the ages of ages. Amen. | As it was, is, and shall be for ever and ever. Amen. | As it was, is and shall be, and become for generations of generations for ever and ever. Amen. | to the ages of ages. Amen. |

### *3.4.1. Ethio-AA I*

Ethio-AA I is clearly an Egyptian and/or Aksumite (Ethiopian) derivative of the anaphora in ApTrad Ch. 4 that was constructed through a conflation of the anaphora in ApTrad Ch. 4 with an early version of MARK, particularly Ethio-MARK I.[123] Ethio-MARK I circulated alongside Ethio-AA I in the Euch-AC, where both appear to have functioned as recent replacements for the anaphora in ApTrad Ch. 4. In the construction of Ethio-AA I, the anaphora in ApTrad Ch. 4 has been supplemented in the very places where it lacks units that had become commonplace in eucharistic praying in the fourth century. The materials added from MARK include:

- Nascent intercessions/diptychs
- All of the Pre-*Sanctus* and *Sanctus*
- Parts of the introduction to the institution narrative
- The transformation language in Ethio-AA's epiclesis [see Epiclesis (2) above]

What this suggests is that developments in eucharistic praying in the early church meant that the anaphora in ApTrad Ch. 4 was no longer seen as appropriate for the Egyptian and Aksumite context.

Given that Ethio-AA I is part of a collection dated to the end of the fifth or beginning of the sixth century, this provides a *terminus ante quem* for Ethio-AA I. But the *terminus post quem* is harder to determine; it must be sometime in the early fourth century when the earliest witnesses of MARK appear to have begun to be codified in written form.[124] Further

123. See nn. 68, 102, and 103, as well as Emmanuel Fritsch, "How the Antiochene Anaphora of the Apostolic Tradition Became the Ge'ez Anaphora of the Apostles," in *Holy Spirit University of Kaslik, Faculty of Religious and Oriental Sciences, Institute of Liturgy and Department of Syriac and Antiochian Sciences, International Conference "Anaphora in Syriac Rites" 26–28 April 2017* (Beirut: USEK, 2017), 115–58; Hlabse, "Shaping the Classical Anaphoras."

124. Heinzgerd Brakmann, "Die alexandrinische Markus-Liturgie und ihre arabische Version im Codex Sinaticus arabicus 237," in *La Liturgie de S. Marc dans le Sinaï arabe 237: Édition et traduction annotée*, ed. Ugo Zanetti (Münster: Aschendorff Verlag, 2021), 9–40. See also a recently joined and published version of MARK: Ágnes T. Mihálykó and Kon Panegyres, "Two Liturgical Papyri from the Bodleian Library," *Archiv Für Papyrusforschung* 70 (2024): 317–70.

study of a constellation of Egyptian and Hagiopolite anaphoras is needed to get a better understanding of the codification of MARK and thus Ethio-AA I, but this does not shed light on ApTrad Ch. 4.

How Ethio-AA I does shed light on ApTrad Ch. 4, however, is that it helps provide an explanation for the omission of ApTrad Ch. 4 from the Ethiopic I, Arabic I and II, and the Sahidic versions of ApTrad, as well as the omission of the anaphora from CH 3b. Clearly the anaphora in ApTrad Ch. 4 was no longer suitable as a model for eucharistic praying in Egypt and Ethiopia, which is why it was supplemented to create Ethio-AA I and why Ethio-MARK I was also included alongside it in Euch-AC. But this also indicates, alongside Ethiopic II—which for some reason is more conservative than the other Egyptian versions of ApTrad and its derivatives here—that ApTrad Ch. 4 was originally known within the Egyptian orbit, but that it dropped out at a very early date. In other words, even the sources within the Egyptian orbit knew of the text at one point, but opted to omit it from their versions of ApTrad. This is not unlike CH's preference in general to ignore prayers from ApTrad in favor of local tradition.[125] It also shows a willingness on the part of the Egyptian redactors of ApTrad, unlike the Latin, to continue to modify ApTrad to suit their purposes.

Furthermore, the omission of ApTrad Ch. 4 in these Egyptian versions also cannot be used to imply that ApTrad Ch. 4 was not originally an Egyptian text. Again, the liberty which the Egyptian witnesses were willing to use to throw out this supposed "model text" serves only to show that they did not feel the need to conserve a text that was no longer appropriate to their context and they felt comfortable modifying ApTrad Ch. 4 accordingly. This also suggests a certain familiarity and ownership of the text indicative of extensive use in the Egyptian context, a context that was also known for a variety of competing anaphoras and anaphoral forms. It is an indication that ApTrad Ch. 4 was "living" within the Egyptian milieu.

### *3.4.2. TD (I.23)*

The other key derivative of the anaphora in ApTrad Ch. 4 is TD (I.23). TD exists in a number of different forms and the various recensions of TD and their relationship is rather complex and in need of much further

125. Bradshaw, *The Canons of Hippolytus*, 12.

study.[126] There are three main witnesses to the anaphora in this church order: the Syriac (Syr-TD),[127] the Ethiopic (Ethio-TD),[128] and the Arabic (Arb-TD). The Arabic is itself divided into four separate recensions: B, L, M, and D. Of those recensions, only B (Arab-TD.B)[129] and M (Arb-TD.M)[130] preserve the anaphora; however, the anaphora in Arb-TD.B is a conflation of BAS with MARK dated to the eighth/ninth century.[131] As a

126. For an overview of the sources, see Lüstraeten, "The Eucharistic Prayer in the Arabic Tradition of the *Testamentum Domini*." An English translation of Syr-TD appears in PEER[3e], 138–41. For more, see our Introduction.

127. I. E. Rahmani, *Testamentum Domini nostri Iesu Christi* (Moguntiae: F. Kirchheim, 1899), 39–45; Bernard Botte, "L'Épiclèse de l'Anaphore d'Hippolyte," *Recherches de Théologie ancienne et médiévale* 14 (1947): 241–51; Anton Hänggi and Irmgard Pahl, eds., *Prex Eucharistica: Textus e Variis Liturgiis Antiquioribus Selecti*, 2nd ed., Spicilegium Friburgense 12 (Fribourg: Éditions Universitaires Fribourg Suisse, 1968), 219–22.

128. Robert Beylot, *Testamentum Domini éthiopien* (Louvain: Peeters, 1984), 167–71. See also Emmanuel Fritsch, "A Fresh Look at Certain Aspects of the Ge'ez Liturgical Edition of the Anaphora of the *Testamentum Domini* as the *Anaphora of Our Lord Jesus Christ*," in *Proceedings of the "First International Conference on Ethiopian Texts" May 27–30, 2013 St. Francis Friary, Asko* (Addis Ababa: CFRRC Press, 2016), 21–53.

129. Anton Baumstark, "Eine ägyptische Mess- und Taufliturgie vermutlich des 6. Jahrhunderts," *Oriens Christianus* 1 (1901): 1–45.

130. Gérard Troupeau, "Une version arabe de l'anaphore du Testamentum Domini," in *Christianisme oriental. Kérygme et histoire, mélanges offerts au père Michel Hayek*, ed. Šārl Šartūnī (Paris: Geuthner, 2007), 247–56; Lüstraeten, "The Eucharistic Prayer in the Arabic Tradition of the Testamentum Domini."

131. The Arabic, known colloquially as "the Baumstark liturgy," reflects an Egyptian redaction. For more on this redaction, see especially Heinzgerd Brakmann, "Le déroulement de la Messe copte. Structure et histoire," in *L'eucharistie: célébrations, rites, piétés*, ed. A.M. Triacca and A. Pistoia (Rome: C.L.V. - Edizione Liturgiche, 1995), 107–32; Achim Budde, *Die ägyptische Basilios-Anaphora: Text, Kommentar, Geschichte*, Jerusalemer theologisches Forum, Bd. 7 (Münster: Aschendorff, 2004), 583; Heinzgerd Brakmann, "ⲂⲀⲠⲦⲒⲤⲘⲀ ⲀⲒⲚⲈⲤⲈⲰⲤ: Ordines und Orationen kirchlicher Eingliederung in Alexandrien und Ägypten," in *»Neugeboren aus Wasser und Heiligem Geist«*, ed. Brakmann, Chronz, and Sode, 126–37; Mihálykó, *The Christian Liturgical Papyri*, 45–46; Heinzgerd Brakmann, "Die alexandrinische Markus-Liturgie und ihre arabische Version im Codex Sinaticus arabicus 237," in *La Liturgie de S. Marc dans le Sinaï arabe 237: Édition et traduction annotée*, ed. Ugo Zanetti (Münster: Aschendorff Verlag, 2021), 20. For more context, see also Andreas Johannes Ellwardt, "Die Kirchenordnung aus dem Testamentum Domini Nostri Jesu Christi nach den Redaktionen der Handschriften Borg. arab. 22 und Petersburg or. 3" (PhD diss., Kehl, Eberhard Karls Universität Tübingen, 2018).

result, Arb-TD.B represents a distinct anaphoral tradition that is beyond our scope. While TD is traditionally ascribed to a Syrian context, it also circulated in Egypt at an early date, and this must be considered when assessing ApTrad Ch. 4.[132]

There are a number of issues with the editions of Syr- and Ethio-TD. While Syr- and Ethio-TD have usually been considered the best representatives of TD, Martin Lüstraeten has recently noted issues with these witnesses and their editions and has instead suggested that scholars should rely more on Arb-TD.M.[133] While Syr- and Ethio-TD will still remain the central witnesses used here, key differences in Arb-TD.M are noted in the footnotes in Table 2 above.

In comparison to the anaphora in ApTrad Ch. 4, Syr- and Ethio-TD at times preserve an older reading.[134] This especially appears to be the case in the institution narrative and in the epiclesis. The lack of the words over the cup may be a remnant of an older form of the institution narrative than that seen in the anaphora in ApTrad Ch. 4.[135] However, the words over the cup are preserved in full in Arb-TD.M.[136] The epiclesis in TD is also odd and could represent an earlier stage in epicletic development.[137] But TD also shows signs of extensive elaboration, more so at times than even Ethio-AA I. This is especially clear in the so-called "preface"[138] of

132. Alessandro Bausi, "Testamentum Domini," in *Encyclopaedia Aethiopica*, ed. Siegbert Uhlig and Alessandro Bausi, vol. 4 (Wiesbaden: Harrassowitz, 2010), 928. For more on this, see also Fritsch, "A Fresh Look at Certain Aspects of the Ge'ez Liturgical Edition."

133. Lüstraeten, "The Eucharistic Prayer in the Arabic Tradition of the *Testamentum Domini*."

134. *Herm.Com.* 2002, 42.

135. Chase, *The Anaphoral Tradition in the "Barcelona Papyrus."*

136. Lüstraeten, "The Eucharistic Prayer in the Arabic Tradition of the *Testamentum Domini*."

137. See n. 118. See also Smyth, "Anaphora of the So-Called 'Apostolic Tradition,'" 88. The form in Bouyer's recommendation of Syr-TD does not quite correspond to our general theory of the development of the epiclesis; see Chase, "From *Logos* to Spirit Revisited."

138. Like with ApTrad Ch. 4 (see n. 87), given the absence of a *Sanctus* in this text, there is no real preface in the traditional sense, but rather an extended Thanksgiving that will flow into the institution narrative. However, in order to facilitate a comparison to other texts with a proper preface, the language of *preface* will be used here to denote all the material in TD up to the introduction to the institution narrative.

TD, the introduction to the institution narrative, and the anamnesis. The fruits of communion have also been bisected with the insertion of nascent anaphoral intercessions. These intercessions are likely recent additions to TD.[139] Conspicuously absent from TD is the *Sanctus*. Intriguingly, however, there is phraseology in the preface of TD that mirrors an anaphoral Pre-*Sanctus*: "king of the orders of archangels, of dominions, praises, thrones, vestures, lights, joys, and delights, father of kings." Perhaps this is an indication of the increased use of the *Sanctus* within the larger context in which TD is celebrated, even though TD has not incorporated the *Sanctus*. Arb-TD.M, however, does contain a recitation of the *Sanctus* before the anaphora proper.[140] This seems to support the increased use of the *Sanctus* around TD.

As with Ethio-AA I, TD can shed some light on ApTrad Ch. 4 and its provenance. This is especially true since at times the text may actually preserve earlier features than those seen in ApTrad Ch. 4 (institution narrative and in the epiclesis). However, the text also witnesses to some significant expansions (*Sanctus* [Arb-TD.M], preface, introduction to the institution narrative, anamnesis, and intercessions). As with Ethio-AA I, TD is an indication that ApTrad Ch. 4 was considered a model text, but one which was open to emendation. Unlike the Egyptian versions of ApTrad and CH, however, TD was more conservative in nature, both in the changes that it made to ApTrad Ch. 4 and in continuing to include it alongside the material it reworked from ApTrad. While TD clearly circulated in Egypt at an early date, its anaphora does not appear to have had a huge impact on Egyptian anaphoral praying, except in Arb-TD.M and in the Ethiopian Anaphora of Our Lord.[141] Here, again, like with Ethiopic II, we see the conservative nature of later Ethiopian sources.

139. Chase, "Fruits of Communion," 26–28.

140. Lüstraeten, "The Eucharistic Prayer in the Arabic Tradition of the *Testamentum Domini*."

141. For the Ge'ez and English translation, see Mäṣḥafä Qəddase, *The Liturgy of the Ethiopian Orthodox Church* (Addis Ababa: Tensae, 2010). For some scholarly discussions on this anaphora, see Meßner and Lang, "Ethiopian Anaphoras," in *Jewish and Christian Liturgy and Worship*, ed. Gerhards and Leonhard, 185–206; Emmanuel Fritsch, "The Anaphoras of the Ge'ez Churches: A Challenging Orthodoxy," in *The Anaphoral Genesis of the Institution Narrative in Light of the Anaphora of Addai and Mari*, ed. Cesare Giraudo,

The question, though, that swirls around TD is whether this document should be seen primarily as Syrian or Egyptian. At this time, little more can be said with regard to TD's larger provenance as a church order. With regard to the anaphora, however, there is nothing inherently Syrian about TD and its early circulation in Egypt allows for its prayer to be as at home there as in Syria, especially when one realizes that ApTrad Ch. 4 and TD do not follow a West Syrian anaphoral pattern. That TD shows some possibly older features than ApTrad Ch. 4, and that it circulated in Egypt for a time—undergoing some development as perhaps evidenced by Arb-TD.M but certainly by the Ethiopian Anaphora of Our Lord—indicate that it was known for a time in Egyptian circles. In any event, TD's circulation in Egypt, and its later use in Arb-TD.M and the Ethiopian Anaphora of Our Lord, provide further evidence that ApTrad Ch. 4 itself, from which it is clearly derived, must have also circulated within the Egyptian orbit as well. This further confirms what Ethio-AA I already indicated. However, it is also clear that TD underwent a different line of development than Ethio-AA I. Thus, like with Ethio-AA I, TD cannot be used to imply that ApTrad Ch. 4 was not known in Egypt or that it was not originally an Egyptian text. In fact, it suggests quite the opposite and again indicates that ApTrad Ch. 4 was at an early date "living" within the Egyptian milieu.

### *3.4.3. The Provenance of the Anaphora in ApTrad Ch. 4*

Having looked at the derivatives of ApTrad, it is worth returning to the provenance of the anaphora in ApTrad Ch. 4. The provenance of the prayer is difficult to determine since the prayer is likely the product of several stages of development. It is also possible that it originated in one region before being expanded and developed in another. Both derivatives of the anaphora in ApTrad Ch. 4 supplement the anaphora in ApTrad in order to fill in material that is missing. Ethio-AA I supplements ApTrad Ch. 4 primarily by bringing in MARK's *Sanctus*. Ethio-AA I lacks MARK's expanded intercessions, though it does include diptychs. TD contains a

OCA 295 (Rome: Valore Italiano Lilamé, 2013), 275–316; Fritsch, "A Fresh Look at Certain Aspects of the Ge'ez Liturgical Edition," 21–53.

number of expanded intercessions, but still lacks the *Sanctus*, at least in its typical location (see Arb-TD.M). That these derivatives supplement ApTrad Ch. 4 in different ways may indicate different settings for where these derivatives were formed. As the above analysis has demonstrated, however, Egypt remains a likely place for both derivatives.

It is worth considering a possible Western provenance for all or part of the prayer. The most probable regions in the West would be either North Africa or Rome. There are, however, no extant anaphoras from North Africa, and the Roman tradition—exemplified by the Roman Canon—knew of a different anaphoral structure (see above) that was highly variable, especially in its preface.[142] The only other possible Western traditions that could mirror the anaphora seen in ApTrad Ch. 4 are the Gallican and Hispano-Mozarabic traditions. These latter traditions are closely related and followed the same anaphoral structure.[143] The structure of their anaphoras consisted of a variable preface, followed by the *Sanctus*, a variable Post-*Sanctus*, institution narrative, fruits of communion, and sometimes epiclesis, concluded by a doxology.[144] Removing the *Sanctus* and Post-*Sanctus*—which is not unreasonable given the later addition of this unit in a number of Western sources[145]—would actually leave a structure not that unlike the anaphora in ApTrad Ch. 4. However, given the variable nature of many of these sections, even if there were textual parallels to ApTrad in the Gallican and Hispano-Mozarabic corpus, it would be too difficult to determine the direction of influence.

There are two reasons, however, why the eucharistic prayer in ApTrad likely did not originate in the West. The first is that ApTrad Ch. 4's developed epiclesis is rather unusual for the Western tradition, which otherwise does not usually contain a request for the descent of the Holy

142. Bouley, *From Freedom to Formula*, 200–215.

143. Nathan Chase, "Liturgical Preservation, Innovation, and Exchange at the Crossroads of the Visigothic and Merovingian Kingdoms," *Worship* 92 (2018): 415–35.

144. Bryan Spinks, *Do This in Remembrance of Me: The Eucharist from the Early Church to the Present Day*, SCM Studies in Worship and Liturgy (London: SCM Press, 2013), 190–200.

145. This includes the early form of the RC. For more, see Chase, *Eucharistic Praying in Ritual Context*, 7.

Spirit.[146] Furthermore, as already noted, until the modern period,[147] the anaphora in ApTrad Ch. 4 did not have a major circulation in the West. As a result, it is better to look for provenance in the East.

In the East, the two most likely traditions from which the prayer in ApTrad Ch. 4 could be derived are the Egyptian and Syrian traditions. In fact, it is in these traditions that the anaphora circulated, as indicated primarily by Ethio-AA I and TD, and secondarily by ApCons 8. Based on the witness of Ethio-AA I, ApTrad Ch. 4's circulation in Egypt must have been between the end of the fifth and the beginning of the sixth century *at the latest*, but an earlier date is also possible and even more likely. In fact, Emmanuel Fristch has suggested this prayer must have an earlier history than the version seen in Euch-AC and has pointed to a fourth-century context.[148]

In Syria, the circulation of the anaphora in ApTrad Ch. 4 could be no later than the first half of the fourth century, since the text appears to have influenced—or in some way been utilized in—ApCons 8,[149] but these connections are somewhat superficial. More useful is the connection to TD, which circulated in Syria by the fifth century. Unfortunately, this does not shed much light on the possible provenance of the anaphora in ApTrad Ch. 4 either, since the first evidence for TD circulation in Egypt and Syria is roughly contemporaneous. In fact, what is abundantly clear from the study of Ethio-AA I and TD above is that ApTrad Ch. 4 *must* have been known in Egypt at an early date and it *must* have been undergoing developments there. The same cannot be said of the Syrian tradition, which only knows of ApTrad Ch. 4 through its limited use in ApCons 8

146. John McKenna, *The Eucharistic Epiclesis: A Detailed History from the Patristic to the Modern Era*, 2nd ed. (Chicago: Hillenbrand Books, 2009), 33–39; Anne McGowan, *Eucharistic Epicleses, Ancient and Modern: Speaking of the Spirit in Eucharistic Prayer* (Collegeville, MN: Liturgical Press, 2014), 96–101.

147. Maxwell E. Johnson, "Imagining Early Christian Liturgy: The *Traditio Apostolica*—A Case Study," in *Liturgy's Imagined Past/s: Methodologies and Materials in the Writing of Liturgical History Today*, ed. Teresa Berger and Bryan D. Spinks (Collegeville, MN: Liturgical Press, 2016), 93–120.

148. Fritsch, "How the Antiochene Anaphora," esp. 128.

149. Raphael Graves, "The Anaphora of the Eighth Book of the Apostolic Constitutions," in *Essays on Early Eastern Eucharistic Prayers*, ed. Paul F. Bradshaw (Collegeville, MN: Liturgical Press, 1997), 173–94.

and in its circulation of TD, a clear derivative of ApTrad. In other words, only Egypt was willing to innovate with ApTrad Ch. 4 and only Egypt was also willing to omit the text from its earliest form of ApTrad (Ethiopic I and CH 3b). Its willingness to innovate but also to throw out the text suggests a strong sense of ownership over the anaphora.

Thus, it is worth looking at how ApTrad Ch. 4 may have fit within the Egyptian anaphoral milieu. One cannot begin by overstating the flexibility and adaptability of the Egyptian tradition, which unlike the East and West Syrian traditions, would allow for multiple models and textual forms to coexist (see Table 1 above). With regard to the Egyptian anaphoral tradition, scholars have increasingly come to realize that the Egyptian tradition knew several ways of constructing an anaphora.[150] The first, represented by MARK/CYRIL and related fragments, consists of the expected sequence: *Sanctus* → Epiclesis → Institution Narrative. The second, represented by BARC, related fragments, and the anaphora in the Sunnarti fragments, follows a *Sanctus* → Post-*Sanctus* → Epiclesis → Institution Narrative sequence. A third type, represented by the anaphora in the Deir Balyzeh Papyrus and SAR (and likely Ethio-MC) "witness[es] an interference between both types."[151] To these should likely be added a fourth type, represented by the Egyptian version of the anaphora of St. Basil (E-BAS), the Egyptian anaphora of Gregory, and other "Syrian" anaphoral patterns, that consists of a *Sanctus* → Post-*Sanctus* → Institution Narrative → Epiclesis sequence; and a fifth type, represented by the anaphora of St. Thomas, which presumably has a *Sanctus* → Epiclesis → Post-*Sanctus* → Institution Narrative sequence.[152]

Despite the variety in patterns, the prayer in ApTrad Ch. 4 does not follow the most prevalent Egyptian patterns, which include a single epiclesis before the institution narrative or an epiclesis before and after it. In fact, in Egypt the presence of a single consecratory epiclesis after the

150. See especially Sebastià Janeras, "Sanctus et Post-Sanctus dans L'Anaphore du P.Monts.Roca inv. n° 154b-155a," *Studi sull'Oriente Cristiano* 11 (2007): 9–13; Michael Zheltov, "The Sanctus and the First Epiclesis in the Anaphoras of the Egyptian Type," *Studia Patristica* 45 (2010): 105–13.

151. Michael Zheltov, "The Anaphora and the Thanksgiving Prayer from the Barcelona Papyrus: An Underestimated Testimony to the Anaphoral History in the Fourth Century," *Vigiliae Christianae* 62 (2008): 494n112.

152. Chase, *The Anaphoral Tradition in the "Barcelona Papyrus,"* 199.

institution narrative may be the result of Syrian influence.[153] Similarly, most of the native Egyptian anaphoras have a strong link between the *Sanctus* and epiclesis, which indicates that in the Egyptian tradition they may have been introduced together.[154] The *Sanctus* is totally absent in ApTrad Ch. 4; however, even in Ethio-AA I (which is most certainly Egyptian or Aksumite) the strong link between the *Sanctus* and epiclesis is absent. This is likely a result of a preference to maintain the structure of the anaphora in ApTrad Ch. 4.

But the lack of structural similarity between ApTrad Ch. 4 and the known Egyptian anaphoral patterns does not preclude ApTrad being native to Egypt either; it just indicates that ApTrad Ch. 4's pattern was no longer favored within the Egyptian milieu from the fourth century onward, something that we have already amply demonstrated. In fact, ApTrad Ch. 4 does bear some resemblance to a trajectory of development in Egypt that appears at the end of the third and the turn of the fourth century at the latest, one which is actually shared with Palestine, further muddying clear geographical distinctions (see below). If parts of ApTrad Ch. 4 are quite early, ApTrad Ch. 4 may be yet another witness along this trajectory, but one which would ultimately take a different form.

In looking at the relationship between BARC, MARK, MC 5, and JAS it becomes apparent that these are rooted in a common narrative tradition with shared structural and textual developments.[155] It is the shared textual developments that set these texts apart from ApTrad Ch. 4 (see below). In any event, the following stages can be outlined in their structural trajectory:

153. Maxwell Johnson, *Liturgy in Early Christian Egypt* (Cambridge: Grove Books, 1995), 25–27 and 30; Chase, *The Anaphoral Tradition in the "Barcelona Papyrus."*

154. Chase, *The Anaphoral Tradition in the "Barcelona Papyrus."*

155. Maxwell E. Johnson, "The Anaphora in *Mystagogical Catechesis V* attributed to St Cyril of Jerusalem and the Anaphora of St James," *Interdisciplinary Symposium: The Liturgy of St James, Origins, Contexts, and Receptions in East and West*, Regensburg, Germany: University of Regensburg, June 8, 2022, in Studies in Eastern Christian Liturgies series (Münster: Aschendorff, 2024); Nathan Chase, "The Anaphoras of the Barcelona Papyrus, St. Mark, and St. James: An Anaphoral Hydra?," in *Symposium on the Liturgy of Saint James, Regensburg, Germany, June 2022*, forthcoming; Nathan Chase, "Evaluating Eusebius' Anaphora in Light of Additional Evidence: More Egyptian-Palestinian Anaphoral Parallels," *Ecclesia Orans*, forthcoming.

| **Stage 1: Eusebius** | **Stage 2: Earlier form of BARC** | **Stage 3: MC 5** | **Stage 4: The received form of JAS, MARK, and BARC** |
|---|---|---|---|
| Prayers of the faithful | | | |
| Preface | Preface | Preface | |
| Pre-*Sanctus* | Pre-*Sanctus* | Pre-*Sanctus* | |
| [*Sanctus*] | *Sanctus* | *Sanctus* | |
| Offering | Offering | Offering | |
| | Epiclesis | Epiclesis | |
| | Fruits of communion | Intercessions | |
| [Doxology] | Doxology | Doxology | |

What would then lead to the differing structures in the received texts of the classical anaphoras in JAS, MARK, and BARC (Stage 4) is primarily the location in which the institution narrative was interpolated. BARC and MARK are products of a shared oral and emerging written tradition that primarily diverges with 1) the interpolation or addition of the intercessions into MARK, which disrupts the creation-*Sanctus* link that underlies this common tradition; and 2) the insertion of the institution narrative. This has resulted in the emergence of two distinct patterns from this earlier shared tradition: the BARCelonan and the MARKan (see Table 1 above).[156] Similarly, in the creation of JAS from MC 5, the institution narrative was interpolated into MC 5 between the *Sanctus* and/or nascent christological Post-*Sanctus* and the offering/epiclesis in MC 5. JAS would

156. Nathan Chase, "The Antiochenization of the Egyptian Tradition: An Alternate Approach to The Barcelona Papyrus and Anaphoral Development," *Ecclesia Orans* 34 (2017): 319–67; Chase, *The Anaphoral Tradition in the "Barcelona Papyrus,"* Ch. 4. For other differences, particularly in the preface and Pre-*Sanctus*, see Nathan Chase, "The Egyptian Sanctus and the Apse Iconography of the Red Monastery Church: The Early Use of the Sanctus in the Shenoutean Federation," *Le Muséon* 136 (2023): 339–403.

further develop way from MC 5 and the Egyptian tradition through the expansion of its christological Post-*Sanctus*.[157]

ApTrad Ch. 4 with the absence of a *Sanctus* and the incorporation of an institution narrative and anamnesis fits neatly into these early Egyptian and Hagiopolite forms:

| **ApTrad Ch. 4** | **Eusebius's anaphora** | **Earlier form of BARC** |
|---|---|---|
| Preface | Preface | Preface |
| | Pre-*Sanctus* | Pre-*Sanctus* |
| | [*Sanctus*] | *Sanctus* |
| Institution narrative | | |
| Anamnesis | | |
| Offering | Offering | Offering |
| Epiclesis | | Epiclesis |
| Fruits of communion | | Fruits of communion |
| Doxology | [Doxology] | Doxology |

In fact, removing the institution narrative and anamnesis from ApTrad Ch. 4 leaves a structure almost identical to Eusebius and an earlier form of BARC, a form also largely shared with MC 5 and MARK. The fruits of communion between ApTrad Ch. 4 and BARC also remain quite early in form, suggesting that ApTrad Ch. 4 is odd in lacking the *Sanctus*, but has also updated its fruits of communion along the lines of that seen in BARC. Thus, the only real oddity, especially from the Egyptian perspective, is the lack of the *Sanctus*. But this may speak more to the antiquity of ApTrad Ch. 4 than to anything else, and there is no reason to presume that the addition of anaphoral units within an anaphoral tradition always occurred in the same way. ApTrad Ch. 4 may very well represent an early Egyptian form and an early way of updating that form in light of changing eucharistic practices.

157. Chase, "The Antiochenization of the Egyptian Tradition," 353–57.

In fact, a number of scholars have argued that a pattern of Thanksgiving [- Offering]—Supplication seems to have been used as the basis for a number of anaphoras and have turned to the Strasbourg Papyrus (Strasbourg PGr 254) as a possible witness to a complete anaphora that followed this form.[158] However, beyond the arguments advanced by some against the idea that the text in the Strasbourg Papyrus is a complete anaphora, there are also papyrological and codicological indications that the text was part of a codex.[159] Ágnes Mihálykó notes, however, that "while this settles the question of format, it does not necessarily suggest that the text of the anaphora cannot end, as the surviving fragment

158. A number of scholars have suggested that the Strasbourg Papyrus is a complete anaphora: H. Wegman, "Généalogie hypothétique de la prière eucharistique," *Questions liturgiques* 61 (1980): 263–78; H. Wegman, "Une anaphore incomplete? Les Fragments sur Papyrus Strasbourgh Gr. 254," in *Studies in Gnosticism and Hellenistic Religions*, ed. R. van den Broek and M. J. Vermeseren (Leiden: Brill, 1981), 432–50; Enrico Mazza, "L'anafora di Serapione: Una ipotesi di interpretazione," *Ephemerides Liturgicae* 95 (1981): 510–28; Enrico Mazza, "Una anafora incompleta? Il papiro Strasbourg Gr. 254," *Ephemerides Liturgicae* 99 (1985): 425–36; Mazza, *The Origins*; Geoffrey Cuming, "The Anaphora of St. Mark: A Study in Development," *Le Muséon* 95 (1982): 115–29; Geoffrey Cuming, "The Shape of the Anaphora," *Studia Patristica* 20 (1989): 333–45; Walter Ray, "The Strasbourg Papyrus," in *Essays on Early Eastern Eucharistic Prayers* (Collegeville, MN: Liturgical Press, 1997), 39–56; Walter Ray, "Rome and Alexandria: Two Cities, One Anaphoral Tradition," in *Issues in Eucharistic Praying in East and West*, ed. Johnson, 99–128; Walter Ray, "The Strasbourg Papyrus and the Roman Canon: Thoughts on Chapter Seven of Enrico Mazza's *The Origins of the Eucharistic Prayer*," *Studia Liturgica* 39, no. 1 (2009): 40–62; Walter Ray, "The Priority of the Strasbourg Papyrus's Tripartite Structure in Some Early Egyptian Eucharistic Prayers," *Ecclesia Orans* 34 (2017): 47–94; Maxwell Johnson, *The Prayers of Sarapion of Thmuis: A Literary, Liturgical, and Theological Analysis*, Orientalia Christiana Analecta 249 (Rome: Pontifico Istituto Orientale, 1995), esp. 255–59. However, both Spinks and Zheltov have argued against seeing this text as a complete anaphora: Bryan Spinks, "A Complete Anaphora? A Note on Strasbourg Gr. 254," *Heythrop Journal* 25 (1984): 51–59; Michael Zheltov, "The Anaphora and the Thanksgiving Prayer from the Barcelona Papyrus: An Underestimated Testimony to the Anaphoral History in the Fourth Century," *Vigiliae Christianae* 62 (2008): 467–504. Chase has also resisted viewing this text as anything but a fragment of the start of the anaphora of MARK; see Chase, *The Anaphoral Tradition in the "Barcelona Papyrus,"* 137–41 and 286–89.

159. See Mihálykó, *The Christian Liturgical Papyri*, 156. For Hammerstaedt's observations, see Jürgen Hammerstaedt, *Griechische Anaphorenfragmente aus Ägypten und Nubien*, Abhandlungen der Nordrhein-Westfälischen Akademie der Wissenschaften (Opladen: VS Verlag für Sozialwissenschaften, 2013), 23.

does, before the *Sanctus*, since the anaphora could have been followed by other texts in a prayer book."[160] Thus, the question of the Strasbourg Papyrus's completeness or incompleteness still remains. What is key here, really, is not whether the Strasbourg Papyrus was a complete anaphora, but whether at one point a structure like what is seen in the text, the structure of Thanksgiving [– Offering]—Supplication, was at one point a complete anaphora.

For this there appears to be ample evidence; some of it is already noted above. Additionally, however, a Thanksgiving—Supplication structure, with perhaps an intervening offering not unlike what is seen in the Strasbourg Papyrus, lay at the origins of Christian worship practices, as can be seen already in Justin Martyr's *Dialogue with Trypho* (41.1-3; 70.4; 117.1-3).[161] There we see a structure of Thanksgiving—Offering (via Malachi)—Supplication that mirrors the Strasbourg Papyrus and *Didache* 9-10.[162] This structure would come to undergird the anaphora described by Eusebius, BARC, MARK, MC 5, and JAS,[163] as well as SAR[164] and even the other West and East Syrian anaphoras.[165]

In fact, our proposal that the original form of the anaphora in Ch. 4 followed a Thanksgiving—Offering—Supplication pattern does not differ greatly from Bradshaw's proposal for the earliest form of ApTrad Ch. 4, dated possibly as early as the second century (text in *italics* is judged by Bradshaw to be later additions):[166]

> We render thanks to you, God, through your beloved servant Jesus Christ, whom *in the last times* you sent to us as saviour and redeemer and messenger of your will, *who is your inseparable word, through whom you made all things and it was well pleasing to you,* (whom) you sent from heaven into the virgin's womb, *and who conceived in the womb was incarnate and manifested as your Son, born from the Holy Spirit and the virgin*; who fulfilling

160. Mihálykó, *The Christian Liturgical Papyri*, 156n13.

161. PEER[4e], 24–25.

162. Alistair Stewart-Sykes, "The Anaphora of *Catecheses Mystagogicae* 5 and the *Birkath Ha-Mazon*: A Study in Development," *Augustinianum* 45, no. 2 (2005): 309–47.

163. Chase, *The Anaphoral Tradition in the "Barcelona Papyrus,"* 137–41; Chase, "Evaluating Eusebius' Anaphora in Light of Additional Evidence."

164. Johnson, *The Prayers of Sarapion*, 256.

165. Chase, *The Anaphoral Tradition in the "Barcelona Papyrus,"* 299–304.

166. Bradshaw, "The Formation of the Eucharistic Prayer in the *Apostolic Tradition*."

> your will and gaining for you a holy people, stretched out (his) hands when he was suffering, that he might release from suffering those who believed in you; who *when he* was *being* handed over to voluntary suffering, that he might destroy death and break the bonds of the devil, and tread down hell and illuminate the righteous, and fix a limit and manifest the resurrection, *taking bread [and] giving thanks to you, he said: 'Take, eat, this is my body that will be broken for you.' Likewise also the cup, saying, 'This is my blood that is shed for you. When you do this, you do my remembrance.'*
>
> REMEMBERING THEREFORE HIS DEATH AND RESURRECTION, we offer to you the bread and cup, giving thanks to you because you have held us worthy to stand before you and minister to you. And we ask **that you *would send your Holy Spirit on the oblation of the Holy Church***, gathering (us) into one, you will give to all who partake of the holy things (to partake) in the fullness of the Holy Spirit, for the strengthening of faith in truth, that we may praise and glorify you through your servant Jesus Christ, *through whom (be) glory and honour to you, Father and Son with the Holy Spirit,* in your Holy Church, both now and to the ages of ages. Amen.

What remains fits comfortably within a second-century context. Our only revision to Bradshaw's proposal would be to see a more Christic invocation reminiscent of *Didache* 9 and 10, especially the "marana tha" petition, behind the **bolded text**, something like: "that you (Christ) would come upon the offering,"[167] and to perhaps omit the nascent anamnesis (in SMALL CAPS).

It is worth considering whether there are textual parallels that could be useful in determining provenance as well. The points of comparison—like the use of *pais*; the images of light, knowledge, and life; common fruits of communion—that might suggest a connection to the Egyptian tradition, especially to early Egyptian texts like BARC, do not seem strong enough to overcome the dissimilarities.[168] In fact, the real issue is that the prayer appears to have such ancient roots. Bradshaw's study of the text has shown textual parallels across the ancient Christian world (not

167. Chase, "From *Logos* to Spirit Revisited."

168. Paul Bradshaw, "The Barcelona Papyrus and the Development of Early Eucharistic Prayers," in *Issues in Eucharistic Praying in East and West*, ed. Johnson, 129–38; Chase, "Fruits of Communion," 15; Chase, *The Anaphoral Tradition in the "Barcelona Papyrus."*

a single area is privileged) and as far back as the second century. Thus, its reception, again, appears to indicate more about its final redaction than its origins. In this regard, it is interesting that the unique form of the doxology in the prayer "the Holy Spirit, in your Holy Church, both now and to the ages of ages" appears in the doxology of an unknown and unnamed anaphora in the *Great Euchologion* from the White Monastery, indicating the continued circulation of this style of doxology in Egypt.[169] This form is rare in the classical anaphoras, only appearing in the Egyptian anaphora of St. Matthew, ApTrad Ch. 4, the Egyptian Sahidic form of St. Basil, Addai and Mari, and Sharar.[170] Outside of the classical anaphoras, this form of the doxology appears in Euch-AC in the "Prayer for the Papas"[171] and the fraction prayer that accompanies Ethio-AA I.[172] This form also appears in ApTrad 6, 7, and 21.21. However, the lack of textual parallels again does not point away from an Egyptian context; it simply is further indication that Egypt knew of multiple anaphoras. In fact, that much of ApTrad Ch. 4 was taken over into Ethio-AA I is an indication that the Egyptian milieu was very comfortable with the text of the prayer, more so, as we will see, than Syria was.

Finally, it must be considered whether Syria could also be the place of ApTrad Ch. 4's origin. First, TD's institution narrative and epiclesis represent earlier forms of the institution narrative and epiclesis than even those seen in ApTrad Ch. 4, from which Syr- and Ethio-TD is derived; this suggests that an earlier form of ApTrad was circulating in Syria at a very early date. But again, it must be remembered that TD also circulated in Egypt at an early date, and so this does not tip the scales in Syria's favor.[173] Furthermore, there are issues with the editions of Syr- and Ethio-TD,

169. Alois Grillmeier, *Christ in Christian Tradition: Vol. 2, From the Council of Chalcedon (451) to Gregory the Great (590–604); Part 4, The Church of Alexandria with Nubia and Ethiopia after 451*, vol. 2.4 (London: Mowbrays, 1996), 250. For the text of the anaphora, see Emmanuel Lanne, "Le Grand Euchologe du Monastère Blanc," *Patrologia Orientalis* 28, no. 2 (1958): 269–406, §137.20-21.

170. For a summary and the editions of these sources, see Chase, *The Anaphoral Tradition in the "Barcelona Papyrus,"* 280 and 281.

171. Σ51$^{ra}$-51$^{va}$ (H 86.17-87.8).

172. Fritsch, "New Reflections," in *Liturgy's Imagined Past/s*, ed. Berger, 52. For a summary and analysis, see Alistair Stewart-Sykes, "The Integrity of the Hippolytean Ordination Rites," *Augustinianum* 39 (1999): 108ff.

173. See n. 132.

suggesting that much more work is necessary to determine exactly if TD is preserving an earlier form.

Second, unlike the reworked version of ApTrad seen in Egypt (Ethio-AA I), TD is still lacking the *Sanctus*. The lack of a *Sanctus* in Syria is still possible into the fifth century, as indicated by Theodore of Mopsuestia and a number of different sources.[174] There is evidence of the continued absence of the *Sanctus* in later sources within the Egyptian orbit, namely the Ethiopian Anaphora of Our Lord Jesus Christ.[175] However, this is very uncommon, especially given the important link between the *Sanctus* and epiclesis in Egypt. Again, however, this does not actually point to Syria as a location for ApTrad Ch. 4's creation; it can only suggest that Syria was willing to tolerate the absence of a *Sanctus* longer than Egypt.

Finally, the argument most favored for a Syrian origin for the text is that ApTrad supposedly shows strong parallels to the structure of later Syrian anaphoras. But this is simply not the case, since the only thing suggesting a Syrian structure is the location of the epiclesis after the institution narrative and anamnesis, something that is not a strong enough indicator of provenance, especially when considering the variety of Egyptian anaphoral patterns.

In fact, pointing against ApTrad Ch. 4 being a Syrian text is its utter lack of adoption in Syria except in very minimal form in ApCons 8, a church order that on the whole shows influence from and correspondences with ApTrad throughout; and in its circulation in TD, a text that circulated in Syria and Egypt, but which actually (from the perspective of the Eucharist) appears to have only had an influence in the Egyptian milieu! Since the provenance of the core of the prayer in ApTrad Ch. 4 cannot be definitively determined—especially given that it may have developed in stages in different places—it seems most likely that at least in its final redaction, the prayer comes from an Egyptian orbit.

### *3.5. Reception of the Eucharist*

Regarding the reception of communion, ApTrad addresses two different contexts in which the Eucharist is received. First is the regular reception of communion on a weekly basis as outlined in Chs. 22 and 36. The

174. For more on these sources, see Chase, *Eucharistic Praying in Ritual Context*, 7.

175. See Chase, 7.

description of this in these chapters is rather short. Ch. 22 indicates that the Eucharist was still celebrated primarily once a week on the Sabbath (Ethiopic I and II) or Sunday (Arabic I). The primary minister for the distribution of communion is the bishop; however, the presbyters and deacons may also break the bread. Contra Stewart's interpretation, this chapter is not dealing with the Roman practice of the *fermentum*.[176] This chapter is only preserved in Ethiopic I and II, Arabic I, CH 30 and 31, and TD II.10; and Ethiopic II adds the phrase "and on the first [day of] the week" after the reference to the celebration on the Sabbath. It is clear that this chapter was originally part of ApTrad, and its omission from the Sahidic and Arabic II is not clearly understood.

ApTrad is the first liturgical source to focus on the breaking of the bread and the fraction rites. The need for the physical breaking of bread during the eucharistic celebration, of course, originates already in the New Testament texts where it appears in the accounts of the Last Supper (Matthew 26:20-29; Mark 14:17-25; Luke 22:14-20; and 1 Corinthians 11:23-26) as well as in the feeding narratives (e.g., John 6) and Jesus' post-resurrection meals (e.g., Luke 24:13-35).[177] A reverse-fraction rite, if you will, appears also in the *Didache* (Ch. 9)—"As this broken bread (*klasma*) was scattered upon the mountains and having been gathered together became one, so may your church be gathered together from the ends of the earth into your kingdom"—as does a reference to the breaking of bread in Ch. 14. A number of early Christian writers also imply the fraction of the bread: Ignatius of Antioch's *Letter to the Ephesians* 20 and Justin Martyr's *First Apology* 65 and 67. All of these sources indicate that there was a fraction rite, but do not indicate if it was formalized, i.e., that there were not yet prayers or ritual actions that had accrued to this rite other than the physical act of breaking the bread.

Moreover, as Andrew McGowan has recently shown, the need to physically break the bread was a result of the physical characteristics of the

176. Stewart, *On the Apostolic Tradition*, 160. For more on this and related practices, see Robert Taft, "One Bread, One Body: Ritual Symbols of Ecclesial Communion in the Patristic Period," in *Nova Doctrina Vetusque: Essays on Early Christianity in Honor of Fredric W. Schlatter, S.J.*, ed. Douglas Kries and Catherine Brown Tkacz (New York: Peter Lang, 1999), 23–50.

177. For a summary of scholarship on the history of the fraction rite, see Robert Taft, *The Precommunion Rites*, OCA 261 (Rome: Pontificio Istituto Orientale, 2000), Ch. 7.

bread used in antiquity. The bread produced was often made commercially (at least in urban centers) and in the shape of a round loaf that was "divided into sections (*quadrae*)."[178] This allowed for the easy breaking and distribution of bread, both in secular and religious meal settings. Reflecting on the eucharistic texts in the *Didache*, McGowan notes that the reference to "broken bread (*klasma*)" should be understood as the single diner's piece, a *quadra* in Latin, produced when the *panis quadratus* was "broken according to its pre-shaped form."[179] Thus, even the physical bread itself assisted and implied its fraction.

Undoubtedly, the earliest eucharistic celebrations did not include a prayer or any other liturgical actions to accompany this ritual action of breaking the bread, even though this action likely had a strong ecclesiological meaning. This seems to be evidenced by the *Didache*, which simply mentions the breaking of the bread, as well as the cursory references in Ignatius of Antioch and Justin Martyr. The fraction rite was primarily a utilitarian action, which, as McGowan notes, was even embedded in the form of the bread itself. However, as Robert Taft and others have repeatedly shown, it is not uncommon for a utilitarian action to accrue symbolic meaning and to be a soft point in the liturgy to which other prayers and actions would gravitate.[180] We can trace this latter development in the liturgical sources.

One of the first liturgical witnesses to describe the fraction rite is ApTrad Chs. 21.31-40 and 22, and to a lesser extent 29C. While this latter chapter is described as a communal meal, it is clear that they once referred to a Eucharist, though the dating of the layers in ApTrad is difficult.[181] Chs. 21.31 and 29C16 simply mention that the bread is broken and distributed, while Ch. 21 also gives distribution formulas. Ch. 22 seems to

178. Andrew McGowan, "'The Firstfruits of God's Creatures': Bread, Eucharist and the Ancient Economy," in *Full of Your Glory: Liturgy, Cosmos, Creation*, ed. Teresa Berger (Collegeville, MN: Liturgical Press, 2019), 72.

179. McGowan, "'The Firstfruits of God's Creatures,'" 81.

180. Two of the principles of comparative liturgy are at play here, mainly: law 10, "the law of the later symbolization of originally utilitarian liturgical actions"; and law 16, "liturgies evolve at their 'soft points'"; see Robert Taft, "Anton Baumstark's Comparative Liturgy Revisited," in *Comparative Liturgy Fifty Years after Anton Baumstark (1872–1948)*, ed. Robert Taft and Gabriele Winkler (Rome: Pontificio Istituto Orientale, 2001), 209–10 and 213–14 respectively.

181. *Herm.Com.* 2002.

begin to articulate a theology/ecclesiology behind the fraction rite, but on the whole ApTrad does not yet seem to know of an elaborate rite with an accompanying prayer. The layering of prayers within the fraction rite begins to appear in the sacramentary of Sarapion of Thmuis, Prayer 2, entitled "the fraction after the prayer and the prayer during the fraction." However, as Taft observed, "though recited during the faction, it is a prayer of preparation for communion, not a 'Prayer of the Fraction,' as it is sometimes called."[182] It is with Theodore of Mopsuestia "where we see for the first time a fully ritualized fraction."[183] But perhaps the earliest testament to the emerging fraction rites comes from the fourth-century "Milan Euchologion" from Egypt, where we see, following the anaphora, "a prayer of fraction with a reference to communion, formulas referring to the Last Supper, and a request for the sending of the Holy Spirit on the congregation (fr. 3–fr. 4, 5)," followed by "a prayer of thanksgiving after communion (fr. 4, 6-12)."[184]

The exact time implied for the distribution of communion in ApTrad is an open question. In most places in the course of the third century it appears that there was a shift from an evening to a morning eucharistic celebration.[185] At the same time, it is clear that in certain places, like Egypt, the evening eucharistic meal endured for a longer time, especially outside of Alexandria. In support of this, Bradshaw quotes the church historian Socrates (*Historia ecclesiastica* 5.22):

> The Egyptians in the neighbourhood of Alexandria, and the inhabitants of Thebaïs, hold their religious assemblies on the sabbath, but do not participate of the mysteries in the manner usual among Christians in general: for after having eaten and satisfied themselves with food of all kinds, in the evening making their offerings, they partake of the mysteries.[186]

182. Taft, *The Precommunion Rites*, 325.

183. Taft, 325.

184. Mihálykó and Chase, "The 'Milan Euchologion.' "

185. McGowan, "Rethinking Agape"; Leonhard, "Morning *Salutationes*"; Paul Bradshaw, "The Earliest Eucharist: Saturday or Sunday?," *Ecclesia Orans* 36 (2019): 225–40; Stewart, *Breaking Bread*, esp. Ch. 1.

186. Bradshaw, "The Earliest Eucharist," 236. Translation taken from *Nicene and Post-Nicene Fathers. Second Series*, vol. 2 (New York: Christian Literature, 1890), 132. Stewart cites this to suggest that Alexandrian Christians did not celebrate the Eucharist on the

Other evidence indicates that eucharistic celebrations that were meals in the evening occurred in other regions, such as East Syria, and a result of the continuation of some house-churches into the fifth century.[187]

The factors that led to this shift from an evening to morning eucharistic celebration are not entirely clear. The shift may have been the result of the adoption of Roman food distribution practices like the morning *salutationes*, and/or the morning distribution of goods to the needy. Imperial legislation likely also motivated this shift. Pliny the Younger's letter to Emperor Trajan in 112 CE notes that new imperial legislation prohibited evening gatherings of associations. The desire to not cause scandal may have also been a reason.[188] Nevertheless, the first explicitly documented reference to a morning Eucharist is in Tertullian. Whether these morning Eucharists at first were full eucharistic celebrations, or simply times for the reception of communion, is not clear. However, it seems that they were initially simply a chance for the reception/distribution of communion and possibly other foodstuffs. Furthermore, these morning (Sunday?) Eucharists may have specifically been times for the distributions of leftovers from the communal meal the night before (Saturday?).[189] It is possible that these shifts may be behind the differences between Ethiopic I and II, and the discussion behind Christian meal practices elsewhere in ApTrad (see section 5 below).

While Ch. 22 seems to imply one weekly celebration of the Eucharist by the assembly, there are indications that Christians were frequently or

sabbath, but the opposite is supported by Socrates; see Stewart, *On the Apostolic Tradition*, 159.

187. Harry Maier, "Heresy, Households, and the Disciplining of Diversity," in *Late Ancient Christianity*, ed. Virginia Burrus, A People's History of Christianity 2 (Minneapolis: Fortress Press, 2005), 213–33; Meßner, "Die Synode von Seleukeia-Ktesiphon 410"; Bowes, *Private Worship*; Bradshaw, "The Fourth Century." See also Chase, "Kitchens and Communion."

188. See Nicholas Russo, "Certe occultis ac nocturnis sacris adposita suspicion, Certainly suspicion is applicable to secret and nocturnal rites: Part 1: Rumors of Christian Nocturnal Debauchery and Other Factors Prompting the Shift to a Morning Eucharist," presented to the Problems in the Early History of Liturgy Seminary, North American Academy of Liturgy (January 2022), unpublished. Used by permission of the author.

189. Leonhard appears to dispute this idea; see Leonhard, "Morning *Salutationes*," 427; Clemens Leonhard, "Establishing Short-Term Communities in Eucharistic Celebrations of Antiquity," *Religion in the Roman Empire* 3 (2017): 79.

daily receiving the Eucharist in a domestic context.[190] This is implied by Ch. 36, which enjoins "every faithful [person to] take care to receive the Eucharist before he tastes anything else."[191] It is possible that a similar practice undergirds Ch. 37 as well, which is clearly concerned about unbelievers and mice(!) receiving the Eucharist. At the same time, Stewart suggests that Chs. 36–38 originally referred to one's conduct at a meal where the Eucharist is celebrated, likely explaining the mention of unbelievers, before becoming rules for private reception at home.[192] In any event, these chapters give tantalizing clues about the distribution and reception of communion in a domestic setting, something that continued beyond the fourth century in some locations.[193]

The longer and more detailed treatment of the reception of communion in ApTrad occurs in the discussion of the administration of communion in the full eucharistic celebration after the rites of initiation. This is outlined in Ch. 21.25-29, 31-37. It should first be noted that the administration of communion in Ch. 21 has clearly undergone some development. In vv. 27-29, the Latin, Ethiopic I, and Arabic I versions of ApTrad note a prayer of thanksgiving over a number of items: the bread, a mixed cup of water and wine, a mixed cup of milk and honey, and a cup of water. The other versions of ApTrad exclude the final cup of water. The corresponding administration of the bread and cups is given in vv. 31-37. Perhaps the foodstuffs most closely related to the Eucharist in ApTrad

190. For a larger discussion of the domestic reservation and reception of communion, see Robert Taft, "The Frequency of the Celebration of the Eucharist Throughout History," in *Between Memory and Hope: Readings on the Liturgical Year*, ed. Maxwell Johnson (Collegeville, MN: Liturgical Press, 2000), 77–96. See also Nathan Chase, "Reprising the Evidence for the Origins of Daily Eucharistic Celebrations," to be published in the proceedings of "Fractio panis" symposium at Pusey House Oxford, England, August 2024. Published in the series "Studia Traditionis Theologiae" by Brepols.

191. Nathan Chase, "Another Look at the 'Daily Office' in the Apostolic Tradition," *Studia Liturgica* 49 (2019): 14, 17, and 18.

192. Stewart, *On the Apostolic Tradition*, 193–95.

193. A perfect example is the eucharistic ritual of a female ascetic described in Pseudo-Athanasius in the fourth/fifth century; see Teresa Berger, *Gender Differences and the Making of Liturgical History: Lifting a Veil on Liturgy's Past* (Burlington, VT: Ashgate, 2011), 88–93. There are also references to eucharistic meals in houses in the fourth and fifth centuries; see Bowes, *Private Worship*. It is not inconceivable that this practice is partly rooted in pagan rituals, where portions from the temple sacrifice "were often taken home by participants." McGowan, *Ascetic Eucharists*, 62.

are the cup(s) of milk and honey that appear to have been blessed in conjunction with the bread and wine (Ch. 21.27-29).[194]

There is no dispute about how the bread is administered. This appears to have normally been done by the bishop and presbyters, something confirmed by Chs. 22 and 25, though there appears to be some tension with respect to who can perform these functions.[195] The need to reference the bishop and presbyters as the ordinary distributors is likely the result of shifting patronage practices.[196] Despite the clarity in who is to distribute communion, the formula for the administration of the bread is different in the Latin and Ethiopic I than in the other versions of ApTrad. The Latin, Ethiopic I, and Arabic I have: "Heavenly bread in Christ Jesus," while the other versions of ApTrad explicitly reference the bread as the body of Christ: "This is the bread of heaven, the body of Christ Jesus." This could denote a development in the theology of the Eucharist.[197] In all cases the faithful say "Amen."

The next section in Ch. 21 about the administration of the cups (vv. 33-36) is very muddled in the various versions of ApTrad.[198] What is clear is that the deacon is the minister of the cup if there are not a sufficient number of presbyters to assist with communion. The Latin contains the practice of three cups (mixed water/wine, mixed milk/honey, and water), while the other versions of ApTrad include only two cups (mixed water/wine and mixed milk/honey). However, Ethiopic I (which earlier had three cups like the Latin) and Ethiopic II (which earlier only had two cups) now both reference three different cups: honey, milk, and mixed water/wine. Again, Arabic I is also slightly different: cup of water, cup of milk, cup of wine. Stewart argues that there are likely some changes

194. *Herm.Com.* 2002, 134–35.

195. Bradshaw, *Apostolic Tradition*, 83 and 90.

196. See n. 12.

197. Bradshaw has shown the tension in the early sources between the feeding narratives, Jesus Christ as bread, and the "body and blood sayings"; see Paul Bradshaw, "Did Jesus Institute the Eucharist at the Last Supper?," in *Issues in Eucharistic Praying in East and West*, ed. Johnson, 1–20. While it would be late between the Latin and Ethiopic I versions of ApTrad and the Sahidic, Arabic I and II, and Ethiopic II versions of ApTrad for this change, it is possible that there is a desire to modify the older language to conform it to the cup words and to make it theologically more refined.

198. *Herm.Com.* 2002, 129 and 134–35; Bradshaw, *Apostolic Tradition*, 79–82.

being made in these texts to conform them to local customs.[199] Alongside a reduction in the number of cups, the Sahidic and Arabic II versions of ApTrad—as well as CH 19c—have also re-ordered the cups. The Latin has the following order: water, milk, wine. Ethiopic I and II have honey, milk, and wine. The Sahidic, Arabic II, and CH 19c have wine then milk/honey. The Latin is clearly preserving the earlier practice here, which has become muddled in the various versions of ApTrad, including Ethiopic I. That a change has occurred in Ethiopic I is clear from the fact that the number of cups has remained the same, but not what is in the cups.

The corresponding formulas accompanying the administration of the cups in the various versions of ApTrad have also undergone some revisions which has made the administration difficult to understand (see Table 3 below). The Latin version has a trinitarian formula that goes along with the administration of the cups: "'In God the Father Almighty.' And let him who receives say, 'Amen.' 'And in the Lord Jesus Christ.' 'And in the Holy Spirit and the holy church.' And let him say, 'Amen.'" Arabic I follows this closely: "In God, the Father, the almighty, and Christ Jesus and the Holy Spirit and the sanctified church." However, Ethiopic I shows a shift here, noting that the one giving the cups says three times: "In the Lord Father Almighty," to which the faithful reply "Amen. Amen." But then there appears to be a reference to the prior administration of the bread, now with the wine/water cup: "And in the body. Amen" and "'And in the blood. Amen.' in the image of the Trinity." This might be what we see in Ethiopic II, which circles back to the bread and cup as well. The reference to the image of the Trinity in Ethiopic I is muddled as a result. This is likely why Ethiopic II attaches this trinitarian reference to the following verse. It should be noted that here Ethio-MC (§55) follows the distribution formulas for the bread and wine given in ApTrad, with the exception of the reference to "This heavenly bread" in ApTrad. What is interesting is that while most of the sources indicate one amen after the bread and cup, Ethiopic I and II and Ethio-MC note a double amen ("amen and amen") after the cup. This points to the early reception of this practice in Egypt, and possibly an Egyptian formulation.[200]

199. Stewart, *On the Apostolic Tradition*, 142.

200. Hanssens at least believed the practice outlined here could not be a Roman practice; see Hanssens, *La liturgie d'Hippolyte*, 481–88.

**Table 3: Comparison of Cup Formulas**

| | Latin | Sahidic | Arabic II | Ethiopic II | Ethiopic I | Arabic I |
|---|---|---|---|---|---|---|
| v. 33 | And if the presbyters are not sufficient, let the deacons also hold the cups, and let them stand with appropriateness and with restraint: first he who holds the water, second he who [holds] the milk, third he who [holds] the wine. | And if there are not sufficient presbyters there, let the deacons take possession of the cup and stand in proper order and give them the blood of Christ Jesus our Lord, and the one with the milk and honey. | If there are not enough presbyters, let the deacons hold the cup. And they stand in order and distribute the body of our Master Jesus Christ, and this is the milk and honey. | And if there are not enough presbyters, the deacons are to take the cups and stand in order—the first with the honey and the second with the milk. | The presbyters then, if there is not enough, let the deacons take the chalices and stand in good order, the chalice of honey first, the chalice of milk second, and the chalice of wine third; | And if the present presbyters are not sufficient for holding the cups, the deacons shall stand in the [following] order: first the water, second the milk, third the wine. |

| | | | | | | |
|---|---|---|---|---|---|---|
| v. 34 | And let those who receive taste of each, he who gives saying three times, "In God the Father Almighty." And let him who receives say, "Amen." | Let the one who gives the cup say, "This is the blood of Jesus Christ our Lord." And let the one who receives it answer, "Amen." | And the one who gives the cup says, "This is the blood of our Master Jesus Christ." And the one who partakes says, "Amen." | And the one who hands [it] over is to say: "In God the Father, Lord of all." And the third [is the] one with the wine. And the one who hands over the cup is to say: "This is the blood of our Lord Jesus Christ." And the one who receives is to say, "Amen and amen." And when he receives the body, he is to say, "Amen." And with the blood | and those who have been initiated shall taste of it, saying [three times] he who [gives it]: "In the Lord the Father Al[mighty];" and he who receives it shall then say: "Amen. Amen. | And for the reception of the three, the one giving it to them says to them: "In God, the Father, the almighty, |
| v. 35 | "And in the Lord Jesus Christ." | | | | And in the body. Amen." "And in the blood. Amen," in the image of the Trinity. | and Christ Jesus |
| v. 36 | "And in the Holy Spirit and the holy church." And let him say, "Amen." | | | | | and the Holy Spirit and the sanctified church." And he shall say: "Amen." |

**Table 3: Comparison of Cup Formulas** (cont.)

| | Latin | Sahidic | Arabic II | Ethiopic II | Ethiopic I | Arabic I |
|---|---|---|---|---|---|---|
| v. 37 [and v. 38 in Ethiopic II] | So let it be done with each one. | | | is to say, "Amen and amen." [v. 38 only in Ethiopic II begins] As therefore this Trinity takes place. | | Thus with everyone. |

The shift from administering the bread separately from the three cups, to administering the bread alongside the wine—a bread-mixed wine couplet—followed by the administration of the milk and honey likely represents a theological shift, focusing now on the special nature of the bread and wine over and against other foodstuffs offered in/with the Eucharist (see more below). This shift has solidified by CH 19c, where the procedure for administering the bread, wine, and milk and honey is much clearer. This is almost certainly the result of a change in eucharistic theology. While scholars today would see the milk and honey as not being eucharistic in ApTrad, early sources suggest that originally they were. As Teresa Berger has noted, there was a strong legacy in early writers like Clement of Alexandria, the *Odes of Solomon*, Irenaeus of Lyons, and Augustine of Hippo of associating breast milk with blood and by extension the Eucharist.[201] The fact that a distinction in the blessing of the milk and honey from the bread and wine had to be insisted upon by the Third Council of Carthage (canon 24) in 397 suggests a very close association between them in the ancient world.[202] This also corresponds to a limiting of the firstfruits offered on the altar in African legislation (*Breviarium Hipponense* 23) and in ApCons VIII.47.3.[203] Thus, originally in ApTrad they were likely considered eucharistic as well.[204]

The chapters on the reception of the Eucharist also provide some theological reflection on the Eucharist beyond the anaphoral prayer in ApTrad Ch. 4. The first theological reference is in Ch. 21.25-28, which articulates a few key principles about the Eucharist: it is for the baptized only, uses the language of type and antitype,[205] uses terminology that is consistent with later understandings of real presence, and articulates the Eucharist as nourishment. These are reaffirmed in Chs. 36–38A. Ch. 36 also gives the Eucharist some apotropaic dimensions. Finally, Chs. 37 and 38A note that the Eucharist is only for believers and should be handled with care.

201. Berger, *Gender Differences and the Making of Liturgical History*, 72–88.

202. Stewart, *On the Apostolic Tradition*, 155.

203. For more, see Stewart, *Breaking Bread*, 240. For *Breviarium Hipponense* 23, see Charles Munier, *Concilia Africae A.345-A.525*, CCSL 149 (1974).

204. McGowan, *Ascetic Eucharists*, 110.

205. For more, see Edward Kilmartin, *The Eucharist in the West: History and Theology*, ed. R. J. Daly (Collegeville, MN: Liturgical Press, 2015), 41 and 49–51; Bradshaw and Johnson, *Eucharistic Liturgies*, 133; Kevin W. Irwin, *Models of the Eucharist*, 2nd ed. (New York: Paulist Press, 2020), 232–42.

With regard to provenance, there is nothing in the preparation or the reception of communion that points to a particular region except the unique form of the formulas for the distribution shared between ApTrad (21.31-32 and 34-36) and Ethio-MC and the practice of giving milk and honey to the initiates in the Eucharist after their baptism. The former practice is specifically Egyptian, while the latter practice appears to be confined primarily to Egypt, North Africa, or Rome.[206] The latter practice was also specifically carried over into CH 19c and later Egyptian and Ethiopian sources.[207] This may suggest that this treatment of the distribution of the Eucharist in ApTrad, at least in its final redaction, has occurred in Egypt, North Africa, or Rome, though Ethio-MC tips the scales in Egypt's favor.

## 4. The Blessing of Foodstuffs and Fruits

Throughout ApTrad, other foodstuffs also appear to have been blessed with or alongside the Eucharist. This includes the blessing of oil, cheese, and olives in ApTrad Chs. 5–6, which follow the eucharistic prayer in Ch. 4, except in Ethiopic I where they have been displaced and in Arabic I where they are entirely absent. Ethiopic I (and Arabic I) do not include Ch. 4, and this likely explains the displacement of Chs. 5 and 6 in Ethiopic I, at least, to after the treatment of confessors and before newcomers.[208]

The practice of blessing additional foodstuffs and oil after or within the Eucharist in this period can be seen in the sacramentary of Sarapion of Thmuis and in the Barcelona Papyrus, as well as in the Coptic form of *Didache* 10, where a prayer for the anointing of the sick or initiation was inserted at the end.[209] The sacramentary of Sarapion has two prayers for the blessing of oils and water that follow the eucharistic liturgy: "Those offering Oils and Water" (Prayer 5) and "Laying on of Hand after the Blessing of Water and Oil" (Prayer 6).[210] While not directly linked to the

206. *Herm.Com.* 2002, 134.

207. This includes BR-AC, Arb-TD I, and the Ethiopic Rite. There are also some other sources that indicate the continuation of the practice. For an overview, see Brakmann, "ⲃⲁⲡⲧⲓⲥⲙⲁ ⲁⲓⲛⲉⲥⲉⲱⲥ," 111, 124, 126, 134, 140, 144, and 193.

208. Bradshaw, *Apostolic Tradition*, 33–35.

209. Kurt Niederwimmer and Harold W. Attridge, *The Didache: A Commentary* (Minneapolis: Fortress Press, 1998), 165–67.

210. Johnson, *The Prayers of Sarapion*, 52–53.

Eucharist, these follow the prayer for the distribution of communion in the text. The euchologion in the Barcelona Papyrus contains an exorcism of oil that follows the anaphora BARC. However, it is not clear if the prayer for the exorcism of oil occurred in this place in the liturgical celebration or if it was even used in a eucharistic setting.[211] Nevertheless, the close proximity of these prayers to the eucharistic prayer in their collections supports a strong connection between these types of prayers. It provides some further possible support to the practice seen in Chs. 5 and 6 of ApTrad of blessing the foodstuffs in or alongside the eucharistic prayer.[212] It is peculiar, as Stewart notes, that in Ch. 5 "the preceding rubric is odd, in that whereas it directs that the prayer over the oil is to be a thanksgiving similar to that over the bread and wine, the prayer which follows bears no resemblance to the prayer of offering which preceded it."[213] He sees this prayer and that in Ch. 6 as perhaps originally connected to the eucharistic celebration, but which has now become freestanding. As he notes with regard to Ch. 6, this seems to suggest a de-eucharistizing of these foodstuffs, or at least increased distinctions between the eucharistic and non-eucharistic foods.[214] The fact that Ch. 6 mentions the *artotyrites* (eucharistic cheese-eaters) may point to an early date for this part of the text, since this becomes a controversy in the fifth century as the practice comes to be identified solely with Montanists.[215] While Hanssens thought that the blessing of oil and other foodstuffs in these chapters was certainly a sign of Egyptian influence,[216] in all likelihood this is really preserving an older practice common throughout the East and West of celebrating the Eucharist in the context of a meal. What we see, then, is that these

211. Ramón Roca-Puig, *Anàfora de Barcelona I alters pregàries: Missa del segle IV* (Barcelona: privately published, 1999); Cornelia Eva Römer, Robert Walter Daniel, and Klaas Anthony Worp, "Das Gebet zur Handauflegung bei Kranken in P. Barc. 155, 19-156, 5 und P. Kellis I 88," *Zeitschrift für Papyrologie und Epigraphik* 119 (1997): 128–31; Wolfgang Luppe, "Christliche Weihung von Öl: Zum Papyrus Barc. 156a/b," *Zeitschrift Für Papyrologie Und Epigraphik* 95 (1993): 70; ET: Stewart, *Two Early Egyptian Liturgical Papyri*, 22–38.

212. *Herm.Com.* 2002, 49. See also Stewart, *On the Apostolic Tradition*, 90–96.

213. Stewart, *On the Apostolic Tradition*, 91.

214. Stewart, 94–95.

215. Stewart, 93.

216. Hanssens, *La liturgie d'Hippolyte*, 411–24.

types of prayers were connected with the Eucharist and circulated with its prayer texts at an early date.

There are also some issues with the text of Chs. 5 and 6, and some have seen the prayers as later additions.[217] Some scholars have argued that the first use of "health" in Ch. 5.2 in the Latin text was the result of a translation error. However, "health" is used in Ethiopic I, thus likely confirming the original use of "health" in the Latin text as was previously argued by Eric Segelberg.[218] The use of the phrase "fruit of the olive" in close proximity to "tree in life" in Ch. 6.3 is also an important feature. This language mirrors the Pseudo-Clementine *Recognitions'* reference to the chrism oil coming from "the wood of the tree of life" (1.45).[219] This section of the *Recognitions* is dated to the mid-second century and is located in a community of rabbinic Jewish Christians.[220] But these are not the only early parallels. This phraseology is also mentioned in *The Life of Adam and Eve* 36.2 and the *Gospel of Nicodemus* B (fifth/sixth century), Ch. 19.[221] This imagery also circulated in Orthodox circles in the Egyptian tradition: (1) BR-AC (very similar to Euch-AC here): "Unction of holy anointing against every work that opposes, and for planting in the beautiful olive tree of your church: and create blessing. And he shall answer: Amen."[222] (2) Arb-TD.B, Prayer No. 3: "The oil for driving out all the operations of the adversary and for planting those who have been anointed in the

217. Bradshaw, *Apostolic Tradition*, 33–35.

218. *Herm.Com.* 2002, 49; Eric Segelberg, "The Benedictio Olei in the Apostolic Tradition of Hippolytus," *Oriens Christianus* 48 (1964): 268–79.

219. English translation in Alexander Roberts and James Donaldson, eds., *Ante-Nicene Christian Library, Vol. 3: Tatian, Theophilus, and the Clementine Recognitions* (Edinburgh: T&T Clark, 1867), here 173–75.

220. Jonathan Bourgel, "The Holders of the 'Word of Truth': The Pharisees in Pseudo-Clementine *Recognitions* 1.27-71," *Journal of Early Christian Studies* 25 (2017): 171–200.

221. See Bart D. Ehrman and Zlatko Pleše, eds., *The Apocryphal Gospels: Texts and Translations* (New York: Oxford University Press, 2011), 465–89. For a general overview and the first part of the gospel, see the *Gospel of Nicodemus* A, 419–63. Ch. 19 of the *Gospel of Nicodemus* B talks about the oil coming from the "tree of mercy" in Paradise that can cure the sickness and death of Adam. This oil is then described as the oil that will be used on him and his descendants before he is washed in water in the Holy Spirit.

222. "Salböl der heiliger Salbung, gegen alles Werk, das widerstrebt, und zur Einpflanzung in den schönen Ölbaum deiner Kirche: und schaffe Segen. Und er soll antworten: Amen." Bausi, "The *Baptismal Ritual*," 70/71. This is the same prayer in Euch-AC – Σ52[vb] (H 39.12-21; D 114.9-17). Translation ours.

sacred universal church."[223] (3) CR: "Thou art anointed, child of N., with the oil of gladness, availing against all the workings of the adversary, unto thy grafting into the sweet olive tree of the holy catholic Church of God. Amen."[224] (4) The same language also appears in P. Ryl. III.471.[225] Interestingly, this imagery is located within initiatory texts, while the prayer in ApTrad seems directed towards healing. However, anointing prayers for initiation and sickness were porous in this period (see Ch. 7 of our commentary). Additionally, the connections to the Egyptian orbit noted above are strongly suggestive of an Egyptian context for this prayer.

Turning to the prayer in Ch. 6, the doxology in Ch. 6.4 is likely a later addition given its form.[226] However, it also has parallels to initiatory prayers like those noted above. Furthermore, it parallels the conclusion of the prayer over the fraction in the Euch-AC that follows Ethio-AA I: "to those who serve you with mildness of heart and those who offer to you good perfume, that is for our Lord Jesus Christ, to you and to whom, glory and honour, to the Father, the Son, and the Holy Spirit, and the holy Church."[227] As noted above, a similar doxology also appears at the end of an unknown and unnamed anaphora in the *Great Euchologion* from the White Monastery, as well as some other anaphoras and prayers, indicating the continued circulation of this style of doxology in Egypt.[228] Here the use of "perfume" is fascinating given its initiatory undertones. Reference should also be made here again to the Coptic form of *Didache* 10, where a prayer for the anointing of the sick or initiation that was inserted at the end mentioned myron, a perfumed oil.[229] The use of this doxological form in Euch-AC may point to a common milieu with ApTrad Ch. 6 or it may simply indicate the borrowing of this form from Ethiopic I.

223. "Oleum effugans omnes operations adversarii et plantas illos, qui eo illinuntur, in sacra universali ecclesia." Baumstark, "Eine ägyptische Mess- und Taufliturgie," 34/35. Translation ours.

224. DBL, 136. For more on the development of this formula in the Coptic Rite, see Brakmann, "ⲂⲀⲠⲦⲒⲤⲘⲀ ⲀⲒⲚⲈⲤⲈⲰⲤ," 163–64.

225. Theodore De Bruyn, "P. Ryl. III.471: A Baptismal Anointing Formula Used as an Amulet," *The Journal of Theological Studies* 57 (2006): 94–109.

226. *Herm.Com.* 2002, 52–53.

227. Euch-AC $\Sigma 62^{vb}$. Cf. Fritsch, "How the Antiochene Anaphora," 142–43.

228. Grillmeier, *Christ in Christian Tradition. Pt. 4*, 2.4:250. For the text of the anaphora, see Lanne, "Le Grand Euchologe," §137.20-21. For a full list of parallels, see pp. 110–11.

229. Niederwimmer and Attridge, *The Didache: A Commentary*, 165–67.

Given the rarity of this phrase (it does not occur in either Ethio-AA I or the anaphora in TD despite this doxology appearing at the end of the anaphora in ApTrad Ch. 4!), alongside the other parallels to Egyptian initiatory texts, it seems very possible that this chapter in ApTrad was derived from an Egyptian context.

The blessings of oil, cheese, and other foods in ApTrad may be more than just the blessing of important foodstuffs. As noted in section 2 above, they may also be remnants of a eucharistic meal, rather than a token distribution of bread and wine. Early Christian Eucharists were a meal that consisted not only of the token bits of bread and wine that we normally associate with the Christian Eucharist, but also other foodstuffs like cheese, olives, fish, milk, and honey. The shift from a meal to a token distribution of bread and wine in most places in the third century could have resulted in the token mention of the blessing of other foods seen in Chs. 5–6 before this practice too fell away. Except for the blessing of oils used specifically in the rites of initiation and the anointing of the sick, the practice of the blessing other foodstuffs in Chs. 5–6 appears to have fallen away by the late fourth and early fifth century as indicated by ApCons (which lacks any comparable practice, though it mentions the firstfruits in 2.25 and 28 despite prohibiting the offering of other fruits[230]) and TD I.24 (which makes this the blessing for the oil of the sick).

Chs. 31 and 32 also deal with the blessings of the firstfruits of the faithful. The list of fruits that can be offered varied and appears to have been well known across the ancient world. All of them were prominent in ancient Egypt, though Hanssens is likely correct that the listing of the foodstuffs in these chapters does not help point to a particular place.[231] While in ApTrad these appear to not be associated directly with the eucharistic meal, they almost certainly were for most communities. Perhaps, however,

230. See n. 240.

231. Hanssens, *La liturgie d'Hippolyte*, 491–92. For a general list that treats many of the foodstuffs in Ch. 32, see Paul T. Nicholson and Ian Shaw, eds., *Ancient Egyptian Materials and Technology* (Cambridge: Cambridge University Press, 2000), Part III; Naomi Miller and Wilma Wetterstrom, "V.A. The Beginnings of Agriculture: The Ancient Near East and North Africa," in *Cambridge World History of Food*, ed. Kenneth Kiple and Kriemhild Conee Ornelas (Cambridge: Cambridge University Press, 2000), 1128–35; Magda Mehdawy and Amr Hussein, *The Pharaoh's Kitchen: Recipes from Ancient Egypt's Enduring Food Traditions* (Cairo: American University in Cairo Press, 2010).

these were offered before the meal. This would be in keeping with how the offerings were handled in much of the East—but not necessarily Egypt—in the early Church.[232] The reference to the bishop "nam[ing] the one who offered," as Taft also notes in the Byzantine sources, would be hard to do if the gifts were brought up in the context of the liturgy itself. Stewart interestingly observes that there is no naming of the individual in the prayer itself, despite this being what the rubric says is to be done.[233] This likely points to the prayer being a later addition.

In any event, Irenaeus in *Haer.* 4.17.5 and 4.18.1 correlates the bread and wine in the Eucharist with part of the firstfruits of creation. While the connection is not made to any other foodstuffs, there Irenaeus makes a direct connection between the Eucharist and the firstfruits that are offered. CH 3c, after the quotation of the pre-anaphoral dialogue, has a rubric that appears to conflate ApTrad 6 with 31 and 32: "If there is any oil, he prays over it in this manner, though not the same expressions, but the same meaning. If there are any first fruits, anything edible, which someone has brought, he prays over it, and blesses the fruit which is brought to him, in his prayer" (CH 3c). CA parallels these chapters from ApTrad.[234] CA canon 7 (Arabic) references "the first fruits of the altar."[235] But perhaps the strongest evidence that these would be used in the eucharistic celebration comes from canons 2-4 attached to the ApCons. These canons prohibit the practice of offering these firstfruits (except wheat and grapes and oil) during the Eucharist.[236] This all may point to the once meal-quality of

232. Robert Taft, "Toward the Origins of the Offertory Procession in the Syro-Byzantine East," *Orientalia Christiana Periodica* 36 (1970): 73–107. For a treatment of the Egyptian sources, see Ramez Mikhail, *The Presentation of the Lamb: The Prothesis and Preparatory Rites of the Coptic Liturgy*, Studies in Eastern Christian Liturgies, vol. 2 (Münster: Aschendorff Verlag, 2020), Chs. 1 and 2.

233. Stewart, *On the Apostolic Tradition*, 183.

234. CA 3 (Arabic); 61 (Arabic and Coptic); 63 (Arabic and Coptic); 69 (Arabic and Coptic); 82 (Arabic); and 86 (Arabic).

235. Wilhelm Riedel and W. E. Crum, *The Canons of Athanasius of Alexandria: The Arabic and Coptic Versions* (London: Williams and Norgate, 1904), 14.

236. M. Metzger, *Les Constitutions Apostoliques*, SC 320, 329, 336 (Paris: Editions du Cerf, 1985), III:274–77; Paul Bradshaw, "The Offering of the Firstfruits of Creation: An Historical Study," in *Creation and Liturgy: Studies in Honor of H. Boone Porter*, ed. Ralph McMichael Jr. (Washington, DC: Pastoral Press, 1993), 36.

the Eucharist like in a *symposium* or *collegia* meal. In fact, there are also connections here to the communal meals at Qumran.[237]

GCN 15.7 also links the giving of the firstfruits and offerings to the Eucharist, which in the larger context of Ch. 15 seems to suggest outreach to the poor and those in need.[238] In fact, the tithing of the firstfruits to the church was primarily connected to the eucharistic gathering, but also the support of the clergy, the poor, the sick, and widows within the community.[239] These, undoubtedly, were part of the communal meals and distributions of food. It was not until the fourth century that these would come to

237. 1QS VI, 2-6. See Stewart, *Breaking Bread*, 181–82.

238. Alistair Stewart, ed., *The Gnomai of the Council of Nicea (CC 0021): Critical Text with Translation, Introduction and Commentary*, Texts from Christian Late Antiquity 35 (Piscataway, NJ: Gorgias Press, 2015), 83.

239. Lukas Vischer, *Tithing in the Early Church* (Philadelphia: Fortress Press, 1966), 15–30; Bradshaw, "The Offering of the Firstfruits of Creation"; Chase, "Kitchens and Communion." The connection between the Eucharist and meal practices and distributions for the poor, sick, widows, and clergy can be seen in a number of other sources. We can see connections between the support of the poor and other groups and the eucharistic celebration in Ignatius of Antioch (even if this may be shifting toward charitable meals; see Stewart, *Breaking Bread*, 71) and Clement of Alexandria (81–83), as well as later sources. *Didascalia* 2.27.3-4, 2.28.1-2, 2.36.4, and 2.57.6, which link the Eucharist and meals to the support of the poor, widows, and clergy; Stewart, 103–5. ACO links the Eucharist and the poor, as well as clergy; see Stewart, 107–8. ApTrad Chs. 29B and 30A also address the material support of the widows, sick, and the poor, and were likely at one point Eucharist; see Stewart, 94–99. This also appears in CH 32, 34, and 35, which again may have also been, or at one point were, eucharistic; see Stewart, 100–102. In the CA, the firstfruits and offerings given to the clergy within the context of the Eucharist (Arabic and Coptic canon 63), are distributed to the clergy and for church use, as well as being distributed to the poor, widows, and sick by the bishop or his steward (Arabic canons: 3, 14-16, 61, 65, 69, and 82; Coptic canons: 47, 61, 62, 65, and 87); see Riedel and Crum, *The Canons of Athanasius of Alexandria: The Arabic and Coptic Versions*. ApCons II.25 and 28 also links the firstfruits to the Eucharist, as well as distributions to the poor and clergy; however, see also ApCons 8.31.1-3, which restricts leftovers from the offerings to the clergy. For more, see also Ewa Wipszycka, *Les ressources et les activités économiques des églises en Égypte du IVe au VIIIe siècle* (Brussels: Fondation Égyptologique Reine Élisabeth, 1972), 64–92; Daniel Caner, "Towards a Miraculous Economy: Christian Gifts and Material 'Blessings' in Late Antiquity," *Journal of Early Christian Studies* 14 (2006): 329–77; Ewa Wipszycka, *The Alexandrian Church: People and Institutions*, The Journal of Juristic Papyrology Supplement 25 (Warsaw: Faculty of Law and Administration of the University of Warsaw, 2015), 202.

be disconnected from the eucharistic celebration.[240] An interesting addition to ApTrad in Ethiopic I and II between Ch. 43.3 and 43.4 also discusses the firstfruits given to the prophets or to the poor (see Ch. 8 below).

While some of the fruits described in Ch. 32 are not directly connected to the eucharistic meal, like flowers, others many have been used in the eucharistic meal (grape, fig, pomegranate, olive, pear, apple, mulberry, peach, cherry, almond, and plum)[241] or may have been used to produce foodstuffs used in the liturgy (grapes for wine and olives for olive oil). It is well known that the church, and monasteries in particular, were centers for wine and oil production.[242] At the same time, the exclusion of vegetables and other foodstuffs regularly used in common meals and in the eucharistic meal in particular—namely, wheat, barley, honey, etc.—suggests that Ch. 32, at least, may not bear a direct relationship to the eucharistic meals. McGowan suggests, however, that this may be the result of "some fear of confusion of the first-fruits ceremony with the eucharistic meal; if bread or grain were to be offered, how would their blessing be understood?"[243] He suggests that these were, at their core, part of the eucharistic meal. Thus, like with the meal practices that will be taken up below, it is possible that this is the result of recent changes in practice.

## 5. Meal Practices

Just as the blessing of foodstuffs other than bread and wine in close proximity to the Eucharist and the eucharistic prayer in ApTrad has suggested an earlier eucharistic connection, the meal traditions in ApTrad have to be further investigated to determine whether they might actually be vestiges

240. For a summary, see McGowan, *Ascetic Eucharists*, 89 and 127. See also *Breviarium Hipponense* 23 and ApCons 8.47.3.

241. McGowan, *Ascetic Eucharists*, Ch. 3; Stewart, "Ἄριστον Μὲν Ὕδωρ: Ancient Breakfasts."

242. For general information on the church's role in olive oil production, see Tomasz Waliszewski, *Elaion: Olive Oil Production in Roman and Byzantine Syria-Palestine*, PAM Monograph Series 6 (Warsaw: Warsaw University Press [u.a.], 2014), esp. 245–51 and 275. For the church's involvement in wine production, see David Grumett, *Material Eucharist* (Oxford: Oxford University Press, 2016), 58–59. For examples about the monastic production of wine, see Ewa Wipszycka, "Resources and Economic Activities of the Egyptian Monastic Communities (4th–8th Century)," *The Journal of Juristic Papyrology* 41 (2011): 159–263.

243. McGowan, *Ascetic Eucharists*, 126–27, here 126.

of a eucharistic meal. This is especially true of a number of meal practices that explicitly note that they are *not*—in whole or in part—eucharistic celebrations. There is a whole section in ApTrad that is primarily directed toward the Eucharist and meal practices—Chs. 22–38A. The only chapters that do not deal with the Eucharist or a meal in this block in ApTrad are Chs. 34 and 35. Ch. 34 is about visits to the sick and Ch. 35 is about morning prayer. Ch. 35 is omitted in Ethiopic I, and Ethiopic I confirms the placement of 29B and 29C as Chs. 24 and 25 as proposed by *Herm.Com.* 2002.[244]

As noted above,[245] Ch. 23 mentions fasting practices and at first glance talks about a non-eucharistic meal with the bishop. However, as noted above, it contains a curious remark in v. 4 that "this is a blessing and not a thanksgiving as in the body of the Lord." Was this once also a Eucharist? This is not improbable, as we saw a similar phrase appear in Ch. 29C (= Ch. 25). Again, Ethiopic I and Arabic I do not contain Ch. 23.4, and thus the reference to this not being the Eucharist.

The next reference to a meal occurs in 29B (= 24). This is a discussion about taking food to the sick, poor, and widows. This chapter is divided into two chapters in Ethiopic I (§20 and §21). Here Ethiopic I appears to be preserving the original form since it makes the most sense of the material. Ch. 29B.1-2 appears to be dealing with the administration of the Eucharist to the sick, but v. 2 in particular "is so unintelligible in the Ethiopic [II] that it is impossible to know precisely what is meant, beyond that it has something to do with the distribution of food and its blessing."[246] Interestingly, Ethiopic I omits any reference to blessing and places this with the following material in vv. 3-4, partially as a title. It seems here we are dealing with the communion of the sick, though the term "eulogy [i.e., blessed bread]" is used.[247] Furthermore, Ethiopic I appears to preserve the original sense of vv. 3-4. It describes this as a service of blessing and charity that included bringing the Eucharist to widows, the

244. *Herm.Com.* 2002, 15, 141, 154, and 158. See also Bradshaw, *Apostolic Tradition*, 85 and 88.

245. See pp. 280–86, 290.

246. *Herm.Com.* 2002, 155. See also Messner, "Die Angebliche *Traditio Apostolica*," 30–31; Bradshaw, *Apostolic Tradition*, 85–86. Here it appears to be paralleling CA 15, 36, and 47.

247. For more context, see n. 22.

sick, and others. It appears that Ethiopic II did not understand what was happening here, and as a result conflated the title that properly belongs to the ritual in vv. 3-4 with the ending of the ritual in vv. 1-2.

The following chapter (29C = 25), as we have already seen above,[248] is a significant witness to the possibility that ApTrad once knew of a eucharistic meal. Ch. 29C (= 25) is only preserved in Ethiopic I and II, as well as in Arabic I. As it stands now, the chapter talks about an evening lamp-lighting ceremony that was accompanied by a meal. Furthermore, in the middle of the chapter, there is a long section (vv. 10-15) that talks about the "mixed cup of the oblation." This section contains many eucharistic hints but is missing in Ethiopic I and Arabic I (though Arabic I preserves v. 10); the whole chapter is extremely abbreviated in CH 32. This section is seen by *Herm.Com.* 2002 as a subsequent expansion.[249] Meßner has suggested that this section dropped out of the original, since CH 32 and TD II.11 make it clear that this passage did not originate in Ethiopia.[250] Ethiopic I and Arabic I still preserve the note in Ch. 29C.16 that "this is not the Eucharist." This seems to indicate that this supper once actually *was* a Eucharist, as discussed above. In fact, it seems in vv. 10-15 that Ethiopic II is preserving an earlier form of this chapter, even if this section was a later addition to ApTrad as *Herm.Com.* 2002 suggests.[251] Given the clear use of psalmody, a fourth-century context would not be unreasonable for this material,[252] though Stewart points to some evidence that this was known in the Hippolytean community.[253] Thus, it seems that Ethiopic I has omitted vv. 10-15 to prevent any confusion with the Eucharist, further affirming our earlier comments above that this meal was once a Eucharist.

Originally Chs. 26 and 27 followed Ch. 29C (= Ch. 25). Chs. 26 and 27 further describe the practices of a communal meal and, given their placement, they are likely talking about the same supper/Eucharist in Ch.

248. See pp. 280–82.

249. *Herm.Com.* 2002, 159. See also Bradshaw, *Apostolic Tradition*, 88–89.

250. Messner, "Die Angebliche *Traditio Apostolica*," 34.

251. *Herm.Com.* 2002, 159.

252. Everett Ferguson, *The Early Church at Work and Worship, Volume Three: Worship, Eucharist, Music, and Gregory of Nyssa* (Eugene, OR: Cascade Books, 2017), Ch. 6.

253. Stewart, *On the Apostolic Tradition*, 168.

29C.[254] These chapters further suggest—something 29C already does—that the faithful and catechumens are to be segregated in some way and that the catechumens are given exorcised bread.[255] Interestingly, Ethiopic I adds a reference to washing in Ch. 26.1: "Before everyone drinks, *once they have washed themselves* [emphasis added], you will give thanks to the chalice." Perhaps this harkens to some form of ritual washing (see Ch. 8 of our commentary). Ch. 27 lends itself even more to eucharistic connotations as all of the versions, except Ethiopic I and Arabic I, describe this as "the Lord's Supper." Here this likely further confirms the shift from "Lord's Supper" to "supper" in Ch. 29C of Ethiopic I and II. Here in Ch. 27 Ethiopic I and Arabic I have "at the supper" to which Ethiopic I adds "of the congregation." Again Meßner has noted that this is a change, and perhaps a deliberate one, in Ethiopic I, and to this we may add Arabic I.[256] It is very possible that Ch. 26 was added when 29C was shifted toward a non-eucharistic supper and that Ch. 27 originally followed 29C. This may be suggested by the lack of a title in the Latin. Ethiopic I and Arabic I do continue the language of "offer/offering," which is otherwise unique to the Latin and which has suggested to some a eucharistic context.[257] This may again further support the antiquity of Ch. 29C.10-15, which continues the offering language in Ch. 29C.

Throughout the discussion of these meal practices, Ethiopic I and Arabic I appear to eliminate eucharistic connotations. This seems the most probable explanation for the discrepancies between the different versions of ApTrad since it makes no sense for the other versions of ApTrad to make this meal *more* eucharistic by describing it as the Lord's Supper. It also likely indicates that CH 32 preserves an earlier form of ApTrad in this place.

Ch. 28 also continues to talk about eating. Again, the Latin does not contain a title. It could easily again be the same supper described in Ch. 29C (=25), 26, and 27, which may once have been a Eucharist. There are some parallels here with CA §66 and §67, especially in ApTrad Ch. 28.4. Similarly,

254. The ordering of the chapters here in ApTrad have been rearranged; see the Introduction of our commentary. See also Stewart, *On the Apostolic Tradition*, 171–76.

255. *Herm.Com.* 2002, 142–45.

256. Messner, "Die Angebliche *Traditio Apostolica*," 40n153, directs to a similar observation on 34n119.

257. *Herm.Com.* 2002, 144–45.

Ch. 29A follows closely on 28.4-6, again without a title in the Latin. Stewart suggests that the reference in Ch. 28.3 may be a reference to the giving of a *sportula*, and thus would be similar to the practice of the *salutatio*.[258]

The lack of titles is not the only oddity in Chs. 26-29A that requires further examination. Ch. 26 begins in the Latin in the second person plural, before switching to the third person. This only occurs in the Latin version, which is very fragmentary but which also seems to be speaking from a totally different context in Ch. 26.1 than the other versions of ApTrad.[259] Ch. 28.1-3 is also in the second person plural in all the versions of ApTrad except the very start of Arabic I, which is in the third person plural.[260] Vv. 1-3 are, like part of Ch. 26, in the second-person plural, while vv. 4-6 are in the third person.[261] Meßner has also noted that the latter half of Ch. 27.2 in Ethiopic I uses the second person plural, unlike in Ch. 27.1.[262] All of this suggests that two sources of material have been brought together here in Chs. 26–28 and made to look like they all refer to the same communal (now de-eucharistized!) meal. Creating a composite of the versions of ApTrad, two sources of material can likely be seen behind these chapters:

| | **Second Person Material** | **Third Person Material** |
|---|---|---|
| *Ch. 26* | . . . you who are present, and so feast. | It is proper before all drink, after they have washed, to give thanks over the cup, and for those present to taste it and then eat. But to the catechumens let exorcised bread be given and let them each offer a cup. |
| *Ch. 27* | For that is why he asked you to come under the roof of his house. | Let a catechumen not sit at the Lord's Supper. But through the whole offering let him who offers be mindful of him who invited him. |

258. Stewart, *On the Apostolic Tradition*, 178–79.

259. *Herm.Com.* 2002, 142; Messner, "Die Angebliche *Traditio Apostolica*," 39n144.

260. *Herm.Com.* 2002, 150; Messner, "Die Angebliche *Traditio Apostolica*," 41–46.

261. *Herm.Com.* 2002, 150.

262. Messner, "Die Angebliche *Traditio Apostolica*," 41n163.

| | **Second Person Material** (cont.) | **Third Person Material** (cont.) |
|---|---|---|
| *Ch. 28* | When eating and drinking, do it with appropriateness and not to the point of drunkenness, and not so that anyone may ridicule [you] or he that invites you may be grieved by your disorderly behavior, but that he may pray that he may be made worthy that the saints may enter in to him, for "you," he said, "are the salt of the earth." But if an offering is made in common to all, which is called in Greek *apophoreton*, take of it. But if [it is] so that all may eat enough, eat so that both some may remain and he who invited you may send [it] to whomever he wishes, as through from the leftovers of the saints, and he may rejoice in confidence. | And let those who are invited, when eating, receive in silence, not contending with words but what the bishop has exhorted, and if he has asked anything, reply shall be given to him. And when the bishop says a word, let everyone keep silent, praising him with modesty, until he again asks. Even if without the bishop the faithful are at the supper, with a presbyter or deacon present, let them similarly eat appropriately. And let everyone hasten to receive the blessing from the hand, whether from a presbyter or from a deacon. Similarly a catechumen also shall receive it exorcised. If the laity are together, let them act with moderation, for a layman cannot make the blessing. |
| *Ch. 29A* | | Let everyone eat in the name of the Lord. For this is pleasing to God, that we should be competitors also among the nations, all alike and sober. |

Each of these is fairly self-contained, suggesting two sets of material have been merged together.

Ch. 30A deals with the supper of the widows. Given what is said in Chs. 28 and 29B about leftovers and distribution, this could be either food and/or the Eucharist.[263]

263. *Herm.Com.* 2002, 162.

Finally, Chs. 31–32 may point to the common supper or, at one point, a eucharistic meal. The titles in Chs. 31 and 32 appear to be flipped,[264] and so it is actually better to first deal with Ch. 32, which talks about the fruits themselves, before going to Ch. 31, which contains the rubrics and prayer for the blessing of the fruits. The fruits that are to be brought to the bishop vary between the different versions of ApTrad; however, the following fruits are mentioned in the different versions: grape, fig, pomegranate, olive, pear, apple, mulberry, peach, cherry, almond, plum, prunes, quinces, and *kastamēn*. Arabic I adds a host of other fruits before these: barley, fava beans, lentil, peavine, bean, chickpea, cauliflower, and rice, as well as pignolia and citron. The following fruits are not blessed: pumpkin, melon, cucumber, onion, garlic, pulses, gourd, nor any other fruits or vegetables (ApTrad does not specify what these other possible fruits and vegetables are). Interestingly, sycamore figs are allowed to be blessed in Ethiopic I but are not in the Sahidic or Arabic I. Sometimes flowers are allowed, but those are restricted to roses and, in the Latin and Sahidic, lilies. Ch. 31 contains the blessing of the firstfruits which are brought to the bishop.

While the current text of ApTrad associates this blessing of firstfruits with the common supper, there is an intriguing hint in CH 3 that perhaps this was not always the case. In CH 3c, which includes the dialogue introducing the eucharistic prayer, CH has two notes that parallel ApTrad Chs. 5–6:

> After [the dialogue], [the bishop] says the prayer and completes the liturgy. If there is any oil, he prays over it in this manner, though not the same expression, but the same meaning. If there are any firstfruits, anything edible, which someone has brought, he prays over it, and blesses the fruit which is brought to him, in his prayer.[265]

In ApTrad Chs. 5–6 these prayers directly followed the eucharistic prayer in the liturgy. CH 3c witnesses to a later shift here where these blessings now occur, it seems, after the liturgy. At the same time, CH 3c appears to preserve an earlier practice of blessing all the firstfruits, presumably after

264. Bradshaw, *Apostolic Tradition*, 96–97.

265. Paul F. Bradshaw, ed., *The Canons of Hippolytus*, Alcuin/Grow Liturgical Study 2 (Bramcote: Grove Books, 1987), 13.

the eucharistic prayer as was likely their original location and as was done in ApTrad Chs. 5–6. It may, then, be that at some point Chs. 31–32 were associated with an earlier eucharistic meal, before later being blessed after the eucharistic prayer, and finally removed from the eucharistic liturgy entirely as seems to be the case in the final redaction of ApTrad.

What all of this evidence seems to suggest is that Chs. 22–25(=29C) and 27.4-28 and perhaps 30A–32 may all, at one time, have been references to a eucharistic meal(s). As Christians moved from a eucharistic meal to a token distribution of bread and wine, these chapters were then gradually edited with various degrees of success to reflect non-eucharistic meal practices. This appears to also correspond to the shift in the time of the meal (see section 2 above). While this helps in dating these sections and their redaction, there is little in these passages that points to one region over another. At the same time, it is clear that the shift from an evening eucharistic meal to a morning distribution of token bits of bread and wine occurred in various places from the third to fifth centuries. The last places to adopt this shift appear to have been East Syria and some places in Egypt.[266] The endurance of these meals and their recent non-eucharistic interpretation may point to one of these centers for the final compilation of the document. Given the wide circulation of the document, somewhere in the empire seems most likely. While its elite character in places (see Ch. 4 in our commentary) may suggest an elite household, the clear preference for episcopal patronage in the document points to a traditional ecclesial setting. Egypt, especially, lends itself to each of these conditions.

## 6. Conclusion

It is clear that the discussion of meal and eucharistic practices in ApTrad is the result of several layers of development. With regard to the chronological developments in the text, it is easiest to start with the end result, which dates to the mid-fourth century. The final form of ApTrad outlines five different ritual practices: 1) the Eucharist proper (Chs. 4; 21.25-29 and 31-37; 22; 33; 36–38A); 2) the blessing of foodstuffs in conjunction with the Eucharist (Chs. 5; 6; and 21.27-29); 3) the blessing of firstfruits

266. See pp. 284–86.

(Chs. 31–32); and 4) rules surrounding communal meals (Chs. 23–32), in particular 5) the communal meal in the evening (Ch. 29C). These are likely based on a variety of older Greco-Roman meal practices, like *symposia, collegia*, and the morning *salutationes*.

The discussion of the Eucharist proper points to several levels of development. Within the anaphora in ApTrad Ch. 4, it is clear that there have been several fourth-century developments, mainly the addition of the institution narrative, a pneumatological epiclesis, and some creedal language. These need not have all been interpolations, but also the result of other anaphoral construction techniques and editorial processes like agglomeration, conflation, and the expansion and codification of older phrases.[267] It is possible, however, that the core of the anaphora dates to the second or third century. Within Chs. 21.25-29 and 31–37 there is some development in the administration of the cup. This appears to be the result of third- to fourth-century developments in the understanding and theology of the Eucharist, which led to changes in how the bread and cups are administered. Other later additions include the ministerial directions in Ch. 21.25-29 and 31–37, and, for a similar reason, most of Ch. 22, though this was likely rooted in an older practice of distributing communion. Chs. 36–38A may preserve remnants of older traditions, but they have also been developed in the fourth century as a result of changes in eucharistic theology. Changes in patronage practices and the desire to see the bishop as the central patron of the Christian community may have also motivated the explicit references to the role of the bishop in the distribution of the Eucharist and other foods in ApTrad. The rest of the material could easily date to the second or third centuries.

The separation of the blessing of fruits from the blessing of foodstuffs likely represents a later development, perhaps of the late third or early fourth century. At an earlier point, these were likely all blessed together in the context of the eucharistic liturgy just as the foodstuffs in ApTrad Chs. 5–6 were described. Moreover, these likely were also all vestiges of an even earlier practice of celebrating the Eucharist as a meal. This practice ceased in most places at the end of the third century.

267. For a summary of these approaches, see Chase, *The Anaphoral Tradition in the "Barcelona Papyrus,"* 60–61.

Finally, the rules surrounding communal meals, in particular the evening supper, are clearly fourth-century developments, though likely rooted in earlier forms. In fact, these rules likely are vestiges of earlier second- or third-century rules surrounding a eucharistic meal. They have been reformulated as general meal rules as a result of the shift from a eucharistic meal to a token distribution of bread and wine in the course of the third century and possibly into the early fourth.

What we see, then, is that there are several layers of development in ApTrad that extend from the second to fourth centuries. This was the result of shifting understandings of the Eucharist and ministry in this period.

Concerning the provenance of these sections in ApTrad, each section and the editing of the different layers did not have to happen in the same place. There is nothing unique enough in the sections on the fruits and the meal practices to indicate where these may have come from. However, it should be noted that the firstfruits are extensively described in the CA[268] along with a meal that parallels ApTrad Ch. 28.4.[269] The section on the blessing of foodstuffs, however, may provide a few indications. As noted above, the Egyptian tradition maintained a strong connection between the blessing of foodstuffs apart from oil—which continued to be blessed close to the Eucharist in most places[270]—and the Eucharist into the fourth century. This can especially be seen in the sacramentary of Sarapion of Thmuis. Additionally, the practice of giving milk and honey with the baptismal Eucharist occurs in a few specific locations, namely North Africa, Egypt, and Rome.

Turning now to the anaphora, the anaphora in ApTrad Ch. 4 appears to have received its final redaction in an Egyptian context. However, it clearly circulated in both Egypt and Syria by the fourth/fifth century as indicated by ApCons 8, Ethio-AA I, and TD. TD, of course, circulated in both Syria and Egypt at an early date. Since the anaphora in ApTrad Ch. 4 continued to be used in Egypt, though in a modified form, more than in Syria, it is likely that Egypt was the location where the final redaction of ApTrad may have occurred. It is also likely that the text emerged from an Egyptian context because of the way it functioned as "living literature" in the Egyptian tradition and because of close structural parallels to an Egypto-Palestine anaphoral tradition.

268. CA 3, 61, 63, 69, 82, and 86.

269. CA 66–67, in particular 67.

270. Oil of the sick, etc.

Given all the evidence, it seems that the eucharistic practices in ApTrad have the most overlap with the Egyptian tradition. To begin with, it is in Egypt that we see additional materials included in the text and the longest-lasting modifications, like with the rubrics in Chs. 23.4 and 29C.16, as well as additional materials being added, such as from *Didascalia* 12. But the real key indicators are the following:

- With regard to the anaphora (ApTrad Ch. 4)
  - Circulated in Egypt and Syria at an early date
  - Bears a structural resemblance to anaphoral developments shared between Egypt and Palestine in the late third and early fourth century
  - It only really impacted texts within the Egyptian orbit
  - Its unique doxology was preserved in Egyptian-orbit anaphoras and prayers
- Fraction and Communion
  - Developments in ApTrad's fraction rites occurred around the same time as those in Egypt
  - The administration and formulas for the distribution of bread and cup during the initiatory Eucharist in ApTrad Ch. 21.31-32 and 34-36 find near exact parallels in Ethio-MC
- Blessing of foodstuffs in the eucharistic celebration—Egypt
- The prayers in Chs. 5 and 6 appear very similar to Egyptian texts, though Ch. 5 did receive broad adoption as seen in Greek fragments[271]
- Chs. 31–32 appear to have had a long-lasting influence in Egypt, where the offering of the firstfruits continued for a long time
- Milk and honey in the baptismal Eucharist—North Africa, Egypt, Rome

This suggests that Egypt very probably was the place of the final redaction of the eucharistic and meal practices in ApTrad, especially since it was still a living document in the Egyptian milieu.

271. See Table 3 in our Introduction.

# *Chapter 7*

# Treatment of the Sick and Christian Burial

## 1. Treatment of the Sick

There are three central chapters in ApTrad that deal with the care of the sick—Chs. 5, 29B, and 34—as well as Ch. 14, which deals with healers (for more on "healers," see Ch. 3 above), though additional chapters in some way deal with the sick and illness.[1] In fact, as Ric Barrett-Lennard notes, ApTrad is particularly concerned with the sick, illness, and healing, though Barrett-Lennard includes in this category exorcisms, which we will otherwise exclude from consideration here.[2] He identifies three different approaches to the ministry of the sick in the early church: "(1) ministry by the whole community to the sick; (2) ministry by particular individuals with a charism of healing; and (3) ministry to the sick by the leadership of the churches."[3] While the second and third forms of ministry are most clear in ApTrad, the first is also apparent, especially since in Ch. 20 catechumens

1. This includes Ch. 20, which references catechumens visiting the sick during their catechumenate and Ch. 39, which notes that deacons who are ill do not have to come to the daily church gathering.

2. Ric J. S. Barrett-Lennard, *Christian Healing after the New Testament: Some Approaches to Illness in the Second, Third and Fourth Centuries* (Lanham, MD: University Press of America, 1994), Ch. 8.

3. Ric Barrett-Lennard, "The *Canons of Hippolytus* and Christian Concern with Illness, Health, and Healing," *Journal of Early Christian Studies* 13 (2005): 143–44.

are said to visit the sick. The concern for the sick and the ill will, however, become more apparent in ApTrad's derivatives, in particular CH.[4]

The first chapter worth looking at in detail is ApTrad Ch. 5, the prayer for the oil, which would have once been included within the eucharistic liturgy. This prayer is displaced in Ethiopic I as a result of the omission of Ch. 4 and is entirely absent in Arabic I.[5] That this prayer was likely used for healing the sick is clear from the text of the prayer: "As, sanctifying this oil, you give, God, health to those using and receiving [it], whence you have anointed kings, priests, and prophets, so also may it afford strengthening to all tasting [it] and health to all using it."[6] The reference to tasting the oil will be addressed below. In any event, this oil would naturally be used for healing but could have been used for other functions as well. In fact, Stewart argues that originally this prayer could have been for those who were baptized.[7] It seems more likely that this oil was multi-use, being used for treating the sick as well as being used in the rites of initiation. Both Bradshaw and Stewart note that, if this text was for the sick, its inclusion of the phrase "kings, priests, and prophets" would be odd; nevertheless, Bradshaw thinks Stewart's suggestion may better explain the material, while it seems more likely that this oil was multi-use.[8]

There is a good deal of support for the use of this oil in multiple liturgical contexts and rituals. The earliest liturgical witnesses to anointings with oil, particularly the anointing of the sick,[9] are ApTrad, ApCons, the euchologion in the "Barcelona Papyrus," and the sacramentary of Sarapion

4. Barrett-Lennard, "The *Canons of Hippolytus*."

5. Bradshaw, *Apostolic Tradition*, 33–34.

6. Cf. Barrett-Lennard, *Christian Healing*, 240–44. However, *pace* Barrett-Lennard, there is no reason this prayer could not have also been used for the blessing of chrism.

7. Stewart, *On the Apostolic Tradition*, 91–92.

8. Bradshaw, *Apostolic Tradition*, 33. For the treatment by Stewart, see Stewart, *On the Apostolic Tradition*, 91–92.

9. For an overview of the anointing of the sick, see Charles W. Gusmer, *And You Visited Me: Sacramental Ministry to the Sick and the Dying*, Studies in the Reformed Rites of the Catholic Church, vol. 6 (New York: Pueblo, 1984), Ch. 1. For a study that is now somewhat dated, but still quite useful, see Elie Mélia, "The Sacrament of the Anointing of the Sick: Its Historical Development and Current Practice," in *Temple of the Holy Spirit: Sickness and Death of the Christian in the Liturgy; The Twenty-First Liturgical Conference Saint-Serge*, ed. Achille Triacca, trans. Matthew J. O'Connell, Semaine d'études liturgiques (New York: Pueblo, 1983), 127–60. For an overview of the Eastern material, see Stefanos Alexopou

of Thmuis.[10] Distinctions between chrism, in particular, and the oil used in the anointing of the sick are not clear in the early sources. In fact, in the Coptic form of *Didache* 10 there is also a prayer for the anointing of the sick or initiation that was inserted at the end. The oil may have been used in both contexts.[11] Pope Innocent I, for instance, suggests that chrism was the oil used for the anointing of the sick.[12] The prayer for the consecration of chrism in BR-AC and Euch-AC also seems to give this oil a healing function and even suggests that it was used for more than just initiation: "which you have given us for medicine and for other purposes as a desired need."[13] BR-AC also references a post-baptismal anointing "for those who receive the washing and for the sick,"[14] and a parallel practice appears in Euch-AC.[15] Similarly, a connection between chrism (possibly a pre-baptismal chrismation!) and healing appears in the *Passio Sebastiani* 36.[16] Stefan Heid suggests that this anointing may have occurred only for those who were sick.[17] The Barcelona Papyrus also contains a prayer for the exorcism of the individual and for their physical healing, which may

---

and Maxwell E. Johnson, *Introduction to Eastern Christian Liturgies* (Collegeville, MN: Liturgical Press, 2021), Ch. 5.

10. Prebaptismal (Prayer 15); chrism (Prayer 16); oil of the sick (Prayer 5 and 17); see Maxwell Johnson, *The Prayers of Sarapion of Thmuis: A Literary, Liturgical, and Theological Analysis*, Orientalia Christiana Analecta 249 (Rome: Pontifico Istituto Orientale, 1995). See also Barrett-Lennard, *Christian Healing*, 285–303 and 312–16.

11. Kurt Niederwimmer and Harold W. Attridge, *The Didache: A Commentary* (Minneapolis: Fortress Press, 1998), 165–67.

12. See Martin Connell, *Church and Worship in Fifth-Century Rome: The Letter of Innocent 1 to Decentius of Gubbio: Text with Introduction, Translation and Notes*, Joint Liturgical Studies 52 (Cambridge: Grove Books, 2002), 46–47.

13. "Den du uns gegeben hast zur Arznei und zu anderm (Zweck) als erwünschtes Bedürfnis." Alessandro Bausi, "The *Baptismal Ritual* in the Earliest Ethiopic Canonical Liturgical Collection," in *»Neugeboren aus Wasser und Heiligem Geist« Kölner Kolloquium zur Initiatio Christiana*, ed. Heinzgerd Brakmann, Tinatin Chronz, and Claudia Sode (Münster: Aschendorff Verlag, 2020), 79.3-4. Translation ours. For Euch-AC, see Σ53$^{va}$.

14. Bausi, 79.26-27 with a prayer on p. 79.27–81.6.

15. Euch-AC: Σ53$^{vb}$-54$^{ra}$ (H 33.25-34.10; D 94.15-96.7). For more on these prayers, see Ágnes T. Mihálykó, "Healing in Christian Liturgy in Late Antique Egypt: Sources and Perspectives," *Trends in Classics* 13 (2021): 154–94.

16. See *Acta Sanctorum*, January II (Paris: 1863), 635.

17. Stefan Heid, "Die Taufe in Rom nach den frühen römischen Märtyrerlegenden," *Rivista di archeologia cristiana* 89 (2013): 244.

have been associated with the catechumens and, like ApTrad, followed after the anaphora in the papyrus.[18]

In antiquity the use of oil and water in Christian, medicinal, and magical contexts was common,[19] and oil and water were used together in magical healing rituals.[20] Each could be put on the body or ingested. We see the latter in ApTrad Ch. 5, but also in Sarapion Prayers 5 and 6, as well as 17; ApCons 7.29.1-3; and BR-AC (65.22-37).[21] This suggests that references to the tasting of the oil were for healing reasons in these texts. The concern for the sick, as well as the use of oil and water in healing rituals, seems to be particularly strong in Egypt.[22]

The centrality of oil (and water) in healing rituals in antiquity would have also led to a strong connection between the liturgical oils and the oils used in healing centers[23] and collected by pilgrims at shrines.[24] This

18. Reinhold Merkelbach, "V Christlicher Öl-Exorzismus," in *Abrasax: Ausgewählte Papyri Religiösen Und Magischen Inhalts. Band 4: Exorzismen Und Jüdisch/Christlich Beeinflusste Texte*, vol. 17.4, Papyrologica Coloniensia (Opladen: Westdeutcher Verlag, 1996), 64–70; Alistair Stewart, *Two Early Egyptian Liturgical Papyri: The Deir Balyzeh Papyrus and the Barcelona Papyrus with Appendices Containing Comparative Material*, Joint Liturgical Studies 70 (Norwich: Hymns Ancient and Modern, 2010), 27–28; Mihálykó, "Healing in Christian Liturgy," 173–74; Nathan Chase, *The Anaphoral Tradition in the "Barcelona Papyrus,"* Studia Traditionis Theologiae 53 (Turnhout: Brepols, 2023), 69.

19. Béatrice Caseau, "Ordinary Objects in Christian Healing Sanctuaries," in *Objects in Context, Objects in Use: Material Spatiality in Late Antiquity*, ed. Luke Lavan, Ellen Swift, and Toon Putzeys, Late Antique Archaeology 5 (Leiden: Brill, 2007), 625–54; AnneMarie Luijendijk, "'If You Order That I Wash My Feet, Then Bring Me This Ticket': Encountering Saint Colluthus at Antinoë," in *Placing Ancient Texts: The Ritual and Rhetorical Use of Space*, ed. Mika Ahuvia and Alexander Kocar (Tübingen: Mohr Siebeck, 2019), 211–12; Anne Grons, "The Question of the Effectiveness of Coptic Pharmacological Prescriptions," *Trends in Classics* 13 (2021): 122–53; Mihálykó, "Healing in Christian Liturgy"; Korshi Dosoo, "Healing Traditions in Coptic Magical Texts," *Trends in Classics* 13 (2021): 44–94.

20. For how they were used, see Dosoo, "Healing Traditions," 75–78.

21. For more, see Mihálykó, "Healing in Christian Liturgy," 176–79.

22. Barrett-Lennard, "The *Canons of Hippolytus*." For a broader study of early Christian texts, see Barrett-Lennard, *Christian Healing*.

23. See, for example, Caseau, "Ordinary Objects"; Peter Grossmann, "Antinoopolis: The *Area* of St. Colluthos in the North Necropolis," in *Antinoupolis II*, ed. R. Pintaudi (Florence: Firenze University Press, 2014), 241–300.

24. Susan Ashbrook Harvey, *Scenting Salvation: Ancient Christianity and the Olfactory Imagination*, The Transformation of the Classical Heritage 42 (Berkeley: University of California Press, 2006), 228–29; Georgia Frank, "Pilgrimage," in *The Oxford Handbook*

is still carried over in some of the Christian rituals for the sick, which use oil from the lamps in shrines or near altars and icons as the oil used to anoint the sick.[25] At the same time, this would lead to tensions between the use of oil in Christian and magical circles.[26] Likely as a result of these tensions and emerging distinctions, the consecration and distribution of the holy oils, especially chrism, quickly became a key factor in their theology and ecclesiology.[27] The consecration of chrism was already an

---

*of Early Christian Studies*, ed. Susan Ashbrook Harvey and David G. Hunter (Oxford: Oxford University Press, 2008), 833.

25. Mélia, "The Sacrament of the Anointing of the Sick," 129 and 145–46. For more on lamps, see Tomasz Górecki, "Appendix B: Lighting of the Churches' Interior," in *The Alexandrian Church: People and Institutions*, ed. Ewa Wipszycka, The Journal of Juristic Papyrology Supplement 25 (Warsaw: Faculty of Law and Administration of the University of Warsaw, 2015), 343–48; Paul Fouracre, *Eternal Light and Earthly Concerns: Belief and the Shaping of Medieval Society*, Artes Liberales (Manchester: Manchester University Press, 2021), Ch. 1.

26. Dosoo, "Healing Traditions."

27. For an overview, see Nathan Chase, "Oleoculture: The Production, Ritual Use, and Reservation of 'the Fruit of the Olive' in the Early Church," in *On Earth as in Heaven? Liturgy, Materiality, Economics*, ed. Melanie Ross (Collegeville, MN: Liturgical Press, 2025). See the following studies for each liturgical tradition. Byzantine: (a) Constantinople—Miguel Arranz, "La consécration du saint myron," *Orientalia Christiana Periodica* 55 (1989): 317–38; Mark Morozowich, *Holy Thursday in Jerusalem: The Liturgical Celebrations from the Fourth to the Fourteenth Centuries* (Rome: Orientalia Christiana Analecta, forthcoming), Ch. 7. (b) Jerusalem—Morozowich, Ch. 7. Greek Melkite—Alexandra Nikiforova, "The Consecration of Holy Myron in the Near East: A Reconstruction Attempt of the Greek-Melkite Rite (with the Edition of *Sinai Greek NF/E 55+ Fragment E Sine Numero, A.D. 1156*)," *OCP* 85 (2019): 167–216. Coptic Rite—Youhanna Nessim Youssef and Ugo Zanetti, *La Consecration Du Myron Par Gabriel IV, 86e Patriarche d'Alexandrie En 1374 A.D.*, Jerusalemer Theologisches Forum, Bd. 20 (Münster: Aschendorff, 2014); Heinzgerd Brakmann, "ⲃⲁⲡⲧⲓⲥⲙⲁ ⲁⲓⲛⲉⲥⲉⲱⲥ: Ordines und Orationen kirchlicher Eingliederung in Alexandrien und Ägypten," in *»Neugeboren aus Wasser und Heiligem Geist«*, ed. Brakmann, Chronz, and Sode, 85–196. West Syrian—Baby Varghese, *Les onctions baptismales dans la tradition Syrienne*, CSCO 512 (Leuven: Peeters, 1989); Baby Varghese, "Studies in the West Syrian Liturgy of the Consecration of Holy Myron," *The Harp* 6 (1993): 65–80; Baby Varghese, *Baptism and Chrismation in the Syriac Tradition* (Piscataway, NJ: Gorgias Press, 2012); Nikiforova, "Consecration of Holy Myron," 187. Armenian—Tinatin Chronz, Daniel Kölligan, and Heinzgerd Brakmann, "Die Feier der Myronweihe in der armenischen Kirche—mit einer deutschen Übersetzung und liturgiehistorischen Beobachtungen," *Oriens Christianus* 101 (2018): 177–233. Roman—Gerard Austin, *Anointing with the Spirit: The Rite of Confirmation; The Use of Oil and Chrism*

issue with Cyprian, and this continued in later North African sources like the so-called Second Council of Carthage, Canon 3 (c. 390 CE).[28]

Further support for this can be seen in the writings of Shenoute of Atripe, CB, and a pseudo-Athanasian homily (= CC0452) from the seventh or eighth century,[29] as well as the Canons of Clement, which prohibits the use of chrism for medicinal applications (§28).[30] Shenoute, for instance, in a sermon (Acephalous Work A14) derided those who seek the healing waters and oils of magicians over (or in addition to) those of the church:

> In the very moment of suffering, if they fall into poverty or a sickness, or indeed into other temptations, they renounce God and they rush to the feet of enchanters (*refmoute*) and oracles (*ma n-šine)* and do other deceitful deeds, just as I myself saw the head of a snake bound to the hands of certain men, and another with the tooth of a crocodile bound to his arm, another with the claws of a fox bound to his feet—and furthermore, it

(New York: Pueblo, 1985), Ch. 5; Seth Nater Arwo-Doqu, "The *Missa Chrismatis:* A Liturgical Theology" (PhD diss., Washington, DC, The Catholic University of America, 2013). Milanese Rite—Gabriel Ramis Miquel, *Introducción a las liturgias occidentales no romanas*, Bibliotheca ephemerides liturgicae Subsidia 164 (Rome: Ed. Liturgiche, 2013), 96–97. Hispano-Mozarabic—Nathan Chase, "From Arianism to Orthodoxy: The Role of the Rites of Initiation in Uniting the Visigothic Kingdom," *Hispania Sacra* 72:146 (2020): 427–38. There is not a rite for the consecration of chrism in the Hispano-Mozarabic sources; the closest is a blessing for the oil of the sick; see Gabriel Ramis Miquel, *La unción de los enfermos en la liturgia hispánica: estudio teológico litúrgico*, Bibliotheca "Ephemerides liturgicae," "Subsidia" 152 (Rome: CLV edizioni liturgiche, 2009), Ch. 3. The East Syrian uses oil but not myron—George Percy Badger, *The Nestorians and Their Rituals: With a Narration of a Mission to Mesopotamia and Coordistan in 1842–1844*, 2 vols. (London, 1852), II: 195–214 and 407–8; Wilhelm de Vries, *Sakramententheologie bei den Nestorianern*, OCA 125 (Rome: Pontificio Instituto Orientalium Studiorum, 1947), 170–75; Joseph Chalassery, *Holy Spirit and Christian Initiation in the East Syrian Tradition* (Rome: Mar Thoma Yogam, 1995), 93–148; Sebastian Brock, *The Holy Spirit in the Syrian Baptismal Tradition* (Piscataway, NJ: Gorgias Press, 2013), 23–24 and passim.

28. Charles Munier, ed., *Concilia Africae A. 345–A. 525, Corpus Christianorum Series Latina* 149 (Turnhout: Brepols, 1974), 13–14. ET: Charles Joseph Hefele, *A History of the Councils of the Church* (Edinburgh: T&T Clark, 1876), II: 390.

29. Dosoo, "Healing Traditions," 49–56.

30. Wilhelm Riedel, *Die Kirchenrechtsquellen des Patriarchats Alexandrien* (Leipzig: A. Deichert, 1900), 172; Johannes Hofmann, *Unser heiliger Vater Klemens: ein römischer Bischof im Kalender der griechischen Kirche*, Trierer theologische Studien, Bd. 54 (Trier: Paulinus-Verlag, 1992), 36–39.

> was a magistrate (*arkhōn*), who claimed to be wise! For indeed, when I reproached him, saying, "Is it the claws of a fox which will heal (*talkyo*) you?" he said to me, "It was a great monk who gave them to me, saying, 'Bind them to yourself and have relief.'" Listen to these impieties! Fox claws, snake heads, crocodile teeth, and so many other vanities in which men put their faith, saying that they will have relief because of them, while others are led astray by them. And again in this way they anoint (*tōhs*) themselves with oil, or they pour (*pōht*) water on themselves, having received it from enchanters or sorcerers (*refpahre*), together with every other type of deceitful relief. After they have said . . . again, they pour water on themselves, and they anoint themselves with water from the priest of the church, or indeed some monks. [ . . . ] If it is the oracles of demons that are of profit to you, and enchanters and sorcerers and all the other things of this type that do lawless things, indeed, go to their feet so that you will receive a curse on the earth. But if it is the house of God which is of profit to you, the Church, indeed, go there.[31]

Similarly, the pseudo-Athanasian homily mentioned above encourages Christians to go to *martyria* to get oil and water, rather than getting them from magicians.[32] A similar text also appears in CH 21b: "The sick also, it is a healing for them to go to the church to receive the water of prayer and the oil of prayer, unless the sick person is seriously ill and close to death: the clergy shall visit him each day, those who know him."[33] All of this likely also explains some of the references to the blessing of oil and water in early Egyptian liturgical sources like CH, *Sarapion*, BR-AC, and the exorcism of water for any purpose in the Euch-AC (see also Ch. 5 above).[34] The oil and water described in these liturgical sources likely functioned in a similar way and was the Christian corollary to the magical uses for oil and water in the Egyptian tradition.

31. Translation taken from Dosoo, "Healing Traditions," 51–52. For more information, see Stephen Emmel, *Shenoute's Literary Corpus*, 2 vols., Corpus Scriptorum Christianorum Orientalium; Subsidia, vv. 599–600. t. 111–12 (Leuven: Peeters, 2004), II: 692–93.

32. Dosoo, "Healing Traditions," 54.

33. Barrett-Lennard, "The *Canons of Hippolytus*," 154–56.

34. For a summary of the evidence, see Mihálykó, "Healing in Christian Liturgy," 165, 170–71, 173, 176–80, and 187–88. For Euch-AC, see Σ54$^{rb}$ (H 32.3-11; D 90.1-8). See also Barrett-Lennard, "The *Canons of Hippolytus*," 154–56.

While the rituals involving water and oil in churches and *martyria* are not described by Shenoute and the other sources, we can presume they were very similar to the practices surrounding the use of water and oil in pilgrimage shrines and healing centers in this period in Egypt and elsewhere. In Egypt, for example, oil and water were especially important in the St. Colluthos martyrium, as well as the pilgrimage shrines of Menouthis and Abū Mīnā.[35] These material substances were closely associated with healing, and the rituals surrounding water utilized basins for either water storage or ritual washing. Abū Mīnā, for instance, also had extensive bathing complexes, which may have also fulfilled a ritual function.[36] In fact, baths were frequently part of monastic complexes and pilgrimage centers.[37]

Oil and water would even be taken back with pilgrims in ampullae, as is clear from the extant pilgrimage flasks found across the ancient world from different pilgrimage shrines, but particularly those in Egypt and the Holy Land.[38] In fact, the first extant vessels that were definitively used to carry oil in a Christian context were the pilgrims' ampullae used to transport oil collected from the tombs of the martyrs and saints.[39] The largest collection of these ampullae, the "Monza ampullae," were made in the Holy Land from the fifth to seventh centuries and preserved in the

35. Dominic Montserrat, "Pilgrimage to the Shrine of SS Cyrus and John at Menouthis in Late Antiquity," in *Pilgrimage and Holy Space in Late Antique Egypt*, ed. David Frankfurter, Religions in the Graeco-Roman World, v. 134 (Leiden: Brill, 1998), 257–79.

36. Peter Grossmann, "The Pilgrimage Center of Abû Mînâ," in *Pilgrimage and Holy Space in Late Antique Egypt*, ed. David Frankfurter, Religions in the Graeco-Roman World 134 (Leiden: Brill, 1998), 292.

37. See, in particular, the chapters by Pierre-Louis Gatier, Peter Grossmann, and Maria Mossakowska-Gaubert, in Marie-Françoise Boussac, Thibaud Fournet, and Bérangère Redon, eds., *Le bain collectif en Égypte*, Études urbaines 7 (Le Caire [Paris]: Institut français d'archéologie orientale diff. AFPU, 2009).

38. J. Witt, *Werke der Alltagskultur. Teil 1: Menasampullen* (Wiesbaden: Reichert, 2000); M. Gilli, *Le ampolle di San Mena. Religiosità, cultura materiale e sistema produttivo* (Rome: Pontificio Istituto di Archeologia Cristiana, 2002). For more on the use of these flasks, see Harvey, *Scenting Salvation*, 228–29; Frank, "Pilgrimage," 833.

39. For more, see Chase, "Oleoculture." This was often done by pouring oil over the relics. For a possible material witness, see The Metropolitan Museum of Art 49.69.2a, b, https://www.metmuseum.org/art/collection/search/468311. Oil was also taken from the sacred lamps; see Fouracre, *Eternal Light*, Ch. 1.

Monza Cathedral.[40] A good example is the c. 600 CE pilgrim's ampulla in the Cleveland Museum of Art, John L. Severance Fund 1999.46.a (6.3 cm; 4.6; 1.5 cm) (Figure 2).[41] There are also *unguentarium* with episcopal stamps at Saraçhane in Turkey and Marea in Egypt, which are thought to be from pilgrims' ampullae.[42]

Figure 2. A Pilgrim's Ampulla (image courtesy of the Cleveland Museum of Art).

A good example of how water and oil were used in a pilgrimage and healing center can be seen in the cult of St. Colluthos in Antinoopolis, for which we have archaeological and literary evidence. The cult of St. Colluthos gave rise to at least two healing centers in the city: 1) the church

40. André Grabar, *Ampoules de Terre Sainte (Monza, Bobbio)* (Paris: C. Klincksieck, 1958).

41. https://www.clevelandart.org/art/1999.46.a.

42. J. W. Hayes, *Excavations at Saraçhane in Istanbul, 2. The Pottery* (Princeton: Princeton University Press, 1992), 9; Hanna Szymańska and Krzysztof Babraj, "Marea 2007: Eighth Season of Excavations," *Polish Archaeology in the Mediterranean* 19 (2010): 72. For pilgrimage flasks from Abu Menas, see Witt, *Werke der Alltagskultur*; Gilli, *Le ampolle di San Mena*.

complex known as D3, which was constructed in the fifth/sixth century,[43] and 2) the so-called Colluthos martyrium, which dates to the sixth century.[44] The latter is especially noteworthy since it contains a cistern for holy water and there are basins for some sort of washing, likely associated with healing.[45] In fact, the attention to water was common in healing centers,[46] likely stemming from general bathing practice.[47] Literary sources from the St. Colluthos martyrium also indicate that healing washings occurred there. In fact, papyri evidence, mainly oracle tickets, discusses the use of ritual baths, anointing with oil, and the drinking of consecrated water.[48] An oracle ticket from the healing center, for instance, notes this: "+ God of my lord Saint Colluthus, the true physician, if you order that your slave Rufus washes today in the healing bath, bring me the favorable ticket. +"[49]

The water and oil were central to the rites used in these centers, and there was a ritual resonance between these healing uses of water and oil and the rites of Christian initiation. This is not surprising since there is always ritual seepage that occurs between rites within a ritual system.[50] As Kimberly Belcher has pointed out:

43. Peter Grossmann, "New Early Christian Churches at Antinoopolis," in *Copts in the Egyptian Society Before and After the Muslim Conquest: Archaeological, Historical and Applied Studies*, ed. Loaay Mahmoud and Ahmed Mansour (Alexandria: Biblioteca Alexandrina, 2016), 35–36.

44. Grossmann, "Antinoopolis: The *Area* of St. Colluthos"; Aaltje Hidding, *The Era of the Martyrs: Remembering the Great Persecution in Late Antique Egypt*, Millennium-Studien, Band 87 (Berlin: De Gruyter, 2020), Ch. 3.

45. Grossmann, "Antinoopolis: The *Area* of St. Colluthos," 257–59 and 267. A similar phenomenon likely occurred at Menouthis; see Montserrat, "Pilgrimage to the Shrine," 268.

46. Caseau, "Ordinary Objects," esp. 636 and 640; Peter Grossmann, "Churches and Meeting Halls in Necropoleis and Crypts in Intramural Churches," in *Egypt in the First Millennium AD: Perspectives from New Fieldwork*, ed. E. R. O'Connell (Leuven: Peeters, 2014), 93–113, passim.

47. Sadi Maréchal, *Public Baths and Bathing Habits in Late Antiquity: A Study of the Evidence from Italy, North Africa and Palestine A.D. 285–700* (Leiden: Brill, 2020); Sadi Maréchal, "Washing the Body, Cleansing the Soul: Baths and Bathing Habits in a Christianising Society," *Antiquité Tardive* 28 (2020): 167–76.

48. Luijendijk, "If You Order That I Wash My Feet"; Hidding, *The Era of the Martyrs*, 93n376.

49. Luijendijk, "If You Order That I Wash My Feet," 211.

50. For information on ritual systems, see Kimberly Hope Belcher, "Ritual Systems, Ritualized Bodies, and the Laws of Liturgical Development," *Studia Liturgica* 49 (2019): 89–110.

> A ritual system is comprised of rites that are linked by "replicated symbols and gestures that create homologies among different ritual situations." In these cases, "the content or structure of the rites themselves create links that group them into a coherent set." The symbolic links between baptism, monastic profession, dedication of churches, ordination, marriage, viaticum, and funerals (in some cases, sprinkling of water, chrism, or renewal of baptismal promises; in others, new or white garments) create systemic connections between the different rites.[51]

This is the same reason why Shenoute and others were so careful of magicians; it was too familiar to the Christian ritual repertoire. It explains the special initiatory rites for the sick as well as the discussion of catechumens and others bringing oil and water to the church during the forty days (see Ch. 5 above). But it also means that a study of initiation and initiatory spaces within the pilgrimage centers must also be mindful of these other ritual associations.

A number of people are encouraged to visit the sick throughout ApTrad. The first reference to visits to the sick appears in Ch. 20.1, where the catechumens are instructed to visit the sick and widows, as well as to do good works. This instruction makes its way into the corresponding chapters in CH 19b and TD II.6. What the function of the catechumens would have been vis-à-vis the sick is unclear, but what is clear is that they were asked in some way to care for the sick.

The next chapter to discuss who should visit the sick is Ch. 29B (= Ch. 24), which mentions regular visits to the sick by deacons and presbyters. This chapter only appears in Ethiopic I and II, as well as Arabic I, CH 32, and TD II.10-11. Ethiopic I and Arabic I confirm that this passage originally followed Ch. 23.[52] The content of the chapter is a bit odd, especially in its ministerial directives, suggesting some later insertions as Bradshaw notes:

> The function of the deacon as an emergency substitute for the presbyter in this role is somewhat surprising, as the deacon was the normal minister to the sick (see chapter 34). For that reason, it is suggested that certain phrases

51. Belcher, 94.

52. Bradshaw, *Apostolic Tradition*, 85.

> . . . were later insertions made when there was conflict over the relative status of presbyter and deacons in the fourth century (see also chapter 22).[53]

There is also a bit of confusion surrounding the last part of the chapter. Bradshaw notes this, and more or less follows the interpretation of "Reinhard Meßner [who] rendered the latter part of the text as 'let him [the sick person] as often as necessary take from what has been distributed and use it up,' understanding the deacon to have left with the person sufficient consecrated bread to provide for communion over several days."[54] While this seems to be the most logical interpretation of the text, the reference to the "sign" still remains somewhat perplexing.[55] TD II.10 interprets this as baptism, but it could be that this is referring more generally to an anointing. In fact, given the mention of the blessing of oil for the sick in Ch. 5, this signing/sealing in Ch. 29B may be an anointing. It could be that blessed oil for the sick was distributed to the sick, either alongside other foodstuffs and/or the Eucharist, and that a supply of oil was given to the sick person for use over several days as Meßner proposed, but with regard to the Eucharist for communion. As we have seen above, the consuming of oil would be consistent with practices for the sick.

What is clear from the chapter is that presbyters and deacons (if a presbyter is not available) are the ones who normally visit the sick and take food and/or the Eucharist to them. That the presbyter is the normative minister to bring the Eucharist to the sick is clear from Dionysius of Alexandria in the mid-third century.[56] What other ritual(s) may have been done is unclear, though the remaining portion of the chapter concerns gifts given to the widow, sick, those who work for the church, and (presumably) the poor, as indicated in the final part of the chapter. As Bradshaw notes, this section is introduced with a new title in Ethiopic I, and it appears also in CH 32 and TD II.10.[57] What is clear is that those who bring alms need to do so promptly. Failure to do that means that the one bringing the alms should supplement the gift from their own stores.

53. Bradshaw, 85–86. See also Barrett-Lennard, *Christian Healing*, 257–59.

54. Bradshaw, *Apostolic Tradition*, 86; Reinhard Messner, "Die Angebliche *Traditio Apostolica*," *Archiv Für Liturgiewissenschaft* 58–59 (2016): 31n100.

55. *Herm.Com.* 2002, 154–55; Bradshaw, *Apostolic Tradition*, 85.

56. *Herm.Com.* 2002, 155.

57. Bradshaw, *Apostolic Tradition*, 86. See also Stewart, *On the Apostolic Tradition*, 163.

Ch. 34 adds further layers to who is called to minister to the sick.[58] In this chapter, it is clear that while the bishop is ultimately responsible for those who are sick, it is up to the deacons and subdeacons to keep him informed, suggesting that they are the ones making regular visits to the sick. The bishop, however, is also tasked with visiting the sick periodically. The reference to the subdeacon appears to be a development in the text, since the subdeacon is not mentioned in the corresponding parts of CH 24 and TD II.21.[59] In the reception of ApTrad, the bishop takes on a greater role as healer. Barrett-Lennard notes that in CH 24, the corresponding canon to this chapter in ApTrad, "the focus of the ordinance is now on the sick, and particularly the bishop's ministry to the sick," rather than in ApTrad on "the general role of the deacons and subdeacons in waiting on the bishop" with its brief mention of "the particular task of reporting to the bishop the names of any who are ill."[60] Furthermore, throughout the CH the bishop seems to take on the role of a healer, likely pointing to the institutionalization of the charism of healing.[61] CA in canons 14–15 (Arabic) also makes it clear that the bishop was charged with supporting and visiting the poor, orphaned, sick, and widows. In talking about the true bishop, that text states: "Whoso is occupied about the church, the people know that the shadow of his body healeth the sick."[62] The reference to Peter's shadow here from Acts 5:15 also appears in CH 24, again pointing to a greater healing function for the bishop in these texts than in ApTrad.[63] At the same time, especially in Egypt, the support for the sick would also come to include monks and stewards.[64]

58. Barrett-Lennard, *Christian Healing*, 259–60.

59. Bradshaw also sees the mention of the subdeacon as a later development, though his reasons are different; see Bradshaw, *Apostolic Tradition*, 99.

60. Barrett-Lennard, "The *Canons of Hippolytus*," 151.

61. For the bishop as healer in CH, see Barrett-Lennard, "The *Canons of Hippolytus*." On CH and ApCons VIII.16.5, see Barrett-Lennard, *Christian Healing*, 251.

62. Wilhelm Riedel and W. E. Crum, *The Canons of Athanasius of Alexandria: The Arabic and Coptic Versions* (London: Williams and Norgate, 1904), 26.

63. Barrett-Lennard, "The *Canons of Hippolytus*," 152–54.

64. Ewa Wipszycka, "Les confreries dans la vie religieuse de l'Egypte chretienne," in *Proceedings of the Twelfth International Congress of Papyrology*, American Studies in Papyrology 7 (Toronto: A.M. Hakkert, 1970), 513 and 516; Ewa Wipszycka, *The Alexandrian Church: People and Institutions*, The Journal of Juristic Papyrology Supplement 25 (Warsaw: Faculty of Law and Administration of the University of Warsaw, 2015), for

Ch. 14 also describes a class of healers, but there is a clear tension in the text between the healers and the clergy (see Ch. 3 of our commentary).[65] It appears that a transition was underway when ApTrad was written, and the charism of healing was coming to be viewed as a gift of the ordained clergy. As a result, there is a skepticism about healers in the text. Whether this office also included an exorcistic function is also a matter of debate.[66]

## 2. Burial Practices

No funeral or burial practices are explicitly described in ApTrad other than in Ch. 40. This chapter is not concerned about the burial process itself, but about the ability for the Christian poor to have a proper burial and for the proper support of those who dig the graves and take care of the cemeteries. This is all to be supervised by the bishop and a steward who was supported by the bishop. As noted in Ch. 3 of our commentary, this is the only reference to a steward in the text, and as noted in the Introduction to our commentary, this text appears to be a later addition to the original core material of ApTrad.

In terms of the ancient written sources that describe Christian burial and funerary practices,[67] already by the time of Tertullian (third century)

steward, see pp. 111, 114, 199, 256–58, for other support for sick and poor, see Ch. 12. See also Barrett-Lennard, "The *Canons of Hippolytus*," 156–60.

65. Barrett-Lennard, *Christian Healing*, 244–57.

66. Barrett-Lennard, 244–57.

67. For an overview of early Christian funerary practices, as well as their relation to the Greco-Roman practices, see Jon Davies, *Death, Burial, and Rebirth in the Religions of Antiquity* (London: Routledge, 1999), Ch. 13; H. Richard Rutherford and Tony Barr, *The Death of a Christian: The Order of Christian Funerals*, rev. ed. (Collegeville, MN: Liturgical Press, 1991), Ch. 1; Robin Jensen, "Dining with the Dead: From the *Mensa* to the Altar in Christian Late Antiquity," in *Commemorating the Dead: Texts and Artifacts in Context*, ed. Laurie Brink and Deborah Green (New York: Walter de Gruyter, 2008), 107–43; Ann Marie Yasin, "Funerary Monuments and Collective Identity: From Roman Family to Christian Community," *The Art Bulletin* 87 (2005): 433–57; J. Patout Burns and Robin Margaret Jensen, eds., *Christianity in Roman Africa: The Development of Its Practices and Beliefs* (Grand Rapids, MI: William B. Eerdmans, 2014), 126–28, 493–94, 505–8, and 512–13; Eliezer González, *The Fate of the Dead in Early Third Century North African Christianity: The Passion of Perpetua and Felicitas and Tertullian*, Studien Und Texte Zu Antike Und Christentum = Studies and Texts in Antiquity and Christianity 83 (Tübingen: Mohr Siebeck, 2014), Ch. 6; Bradley Daugherty, "The Bishops of North Africa: Rethinking Practice and Belief in Late Antiquity" (Nashville: Vanderbilt University,

there was a distinction between pagan and Christian burial practices, as well as an explicit rejection of the Roman practice of cremation. Cyprian also notes the need for Christians to be buried apart from pagans, and for the church, and the bishop in particular, to supervise the process.[68] Other practices, like burial *ad sanctos* and developments around the cult of the martyrs, also came about in this period. In addition, churches began to appear in Christian cemeteries by the second quarter of the fourth century.[69] At the same time, legislation in the fourth century prohibited burials in intramural churches; however, this did not stop the burial of the dead in some intramural churches in this period.[70]

Exclusively Christian cemeteries are almost unknown in the first to third centuries, though evidence from Egypt, for instance, attests to mixed Christian and non-Christian cemeteries in the third to fourth centuries.[71] Evidence from places like Dakhla in Egypt, for instance, also

---

2015); Sherry Fox and Paraskevi Tritsaroli, "Burial and Human Remains of the Eastern Mediterranean in Early Christian Context," in *The Oxford Handbook of Early Christian Archaeology*, ed. David K. Pettegrew, William R. Caraher, and Thomas W. Davis (New York: Oxford University Press, 2018), 105–26. Two studies, now dated, are still worth consulting; see Bernard Botte, "The Earliest Formulas of Prayer for the Dead," in *Temple of the Holy Spirit*, ed. Triacca, trans. O'Connell, 17–31; Cyrille Vogel, "The Cultic Environment of the Deceased in the Early Christian Period," in *Temple of the Holy Spirit*, ed. Triacca, trans. O'Connell, 259–76. For the Eucharist and *refrigeria* in connection with Christian burial and commemoration, see Jensen, "Dining with the Dead"; Candida Moss, "Christian Funerary Banquets and Martyr Cults," in *The Eucharist, Its Origins and Contexts: Sacred Meal, Communal Meal, Table Fellowship in Late Antiquity, Early Judaism, and Early Christianity*, ed. David Hellholm and Dieter Sänger, vol. 2, Wissenschaftliche Untersuchungen zum Neuen Testament 376 (Tübingen: Mohr Siebeck, 2017), 819–28. For the development of funeral practices in the East, see Alexopoulos and Johnson, *Introduction to Eastern Christian Liturgies*, Ch. 5. See also Andrea Riedl, Elias Haslwanter, and Hans-Jürgen Feulner, eds., *Das Gebet für die Verstorbenen: Zugänge aus Theologie und Praxis* (Münster: Aschendorff Verlag, 2025).

68. The development of Christian burial practices is well documented in North Africa; see Burns and Jensen, *Christianity in Roman Africa*, 118–26, 492–94, 498, 506–8. See also Ch. 11.

69. Grossmann, "Churches and Meeting Halls," 93–95.

70. Peter Grossmann, *Christliche Architektur in Ägypten* (Leiden: Brill, 2002), 128; V. Marinis, "Tombs and Burials in the Monastery Tou Libos in Constantinople," *Dumbarton Oaks Papers* 63 (2009): 150–51; Fox and Tritsaroli, "Burial and Human Remains of the Eastern Mediterranean in Early Christian Context," 108.

71. Ulrich Volp, *Tod und Ritual in den christlichen Gemeinden der Antike* (Leiden: Brill, 2002), 106; Grossmann, "Churches and Meeting Halls," 94. The Dakhla Oasis can serve

reveals some common funerary customs that are not otherwise attested in the written sources.[72] Later liturgical sources like TD II.23[73] and CA 100 (Arabic)[74] further codified Christian burial practices, especially for the poor.[75] However, one of the earliest witnesses to the funeral prayers themselves appears in ApCons.[76] In light of this, this chapter in ApTrad seems to date to a time when there were dedicated Christian cemeteries, or at least areas in the cemeteries dedicated for Christians, but when burial practices had not yet been codified.

Many of the discussions about this chapter have revolved around the mention of "tiles" in the Sahidic and Ethiopic I form of Ch. 40, something that does not appear in Arabic I or II or Ethiopic II versions. Some have argued that the reference to "tiles" points to a Roman context, and not an Egyptian one. Since this was presumably a practice in Rome, some scholars have argued that this may explain the omission of tiles in the

---

as a helpful example. For a summary of the Christian cemeteries discovered in Dakhla to date, see Gillian Bowen, "Christianity in Dakhleh Oasis: An Archaeological Overview," in *The Oasis Papers 9: Proceedings of the Ninth International Dakhleh Oasis Project Conference. Papers Presented in Honour of Anthony J. Mills*, ed. Gillian Bowen and Colin A. Hope (Oxford: Oxford University Press, 2019), 375–77. See also Nicola Aravecchia, *Early Christianity at Amheida (Egypt's Dakhla Oasis): A Fourth-Century Church*, Amheida vii (New York: Institute for the Study of the Ancient World/NYU Press, 2024). For more recent discoveries at El-Bagawwat and in the Fayyum, see respectively F. Dunand, "Changes in Funerary Structures at Kharga from 'Traditional' to 'Christian' Tombs," in *The Oasis Papers 9*, ed. Bowen and Hope, 381–93; K. V. L. Pierce and B. Jensen, eds., *Excavations at the Seila Pyramid and Fag El-Gamous Cemetery* (Leiden: Brepols, 2020).

72. Davies, *Death, Burial, and Rebirth in the Religions of Antiquity*, 199; Gillian Bowen, "Some Observations on Christian Burial Practices at Kellis," in *The Oasis Papers 3. Proceedings of the Third International Conference of the Dakhleh Oasis Project*, ed. Gillian Bowen and Colin A. Hope (Oxford: Oxford University Press, 2003), 169; Bowen, "Christianity in Dakhleh Oasis: An Archaeological Overview," 375.

73. However, this source circulated in Egypt at an early date; see Alessandro Bausi, "Testamentum Domini," in *Encyclopaedia Aethiopica*, ed. Siegbert Uhlig and Alessandro Bausi, vol. 4 (Wiesbaden: Harrassowitz, 2010), 927–28.

74. Riedel and Crum, *The Canons of Athanasius of Alexandria: The Arabic and Coptic Versions*, 65.

75. *Herm.Com.* 2002, 191–93.

76. ApCons 7.30.2; 8.41.1-8; 8.42.1-5. For the English translation, see W. Jardine Grisbrooke, ed., *The Liturgical Portions of the Apostolic Constitutions: A Text for Students*, Alcuin/GROW Liturgical Study 13–14 (Bramcote: Grove Books, 1990), 79–81. See also Vogel, "The Cultic Environment of the Deceased in the Early Christian Period."

Arabic I and II, as well as Ethiopic II versions of ApTrad.[77] However, the use of tiles was common in Egypt as well and can be seen, for instance, in pagan and Christian burials in the third and fourth centuries in cemeteries at Kellis.[78] In any event, this chapter appears to be a later addition to the text, though it does appear in Ethiopic I, and both Ethiopic I and the Sahidic appear to preserve the original text.

While the first half of the chapter clearly denotes the burial process and making burial accessible for the poor, the last part of the chapter is rather intriguing: "And let those who take care of the place and live there be supported by the bishop, *so that it shall not be a burden for those who come*" [emphasis added]. Clearly this is no longer a reference to the burial practice itself but to visitors to the cemeteries. While this chapter is rather light on the specific practices surrounding burial and the commemoration of the deceased, this phrase suggests that here we are dealing with frequent visitors to the cemetery, and so we must look beyond the text to the larger sociocultural context to assess what these Christian visitors may have been doing.

Early Christian funerary practices were rooted in older Greco-Roman observances for the dead, and these Greco-Roman observances may explain why there is a need for a steward to manage the cemeteries for those who come.[79] Greco-Roman funerary practices included ritual meals at the time of burial (*silicernium*), the ninth day after the funeral (*cena novendialis*), as well as on memorials of the anniversary of the death of the deceased (*dies natalis*), and during the festival of the ancestors (*Parentalia*). These meals celebrated at graves or tombs are known generally as *refrigeria*.

These practices were especially influential on Christian funerary meal practices, which are some of the earliest Christian practices witnessed to around Christian burials. Often when these meals were carried over

77. *Herm.Com.* 2002, 191–93.

78. Bowen, "Some Observations on Christian Burial Practices at Kellis."

79. For an overview of Christian funerary practices, and also their relation to the Greco-Roman practices, see Davies, *Death, Burial, and Rebirth in the Religions of Antiquity*, Ch. 13; Jensen, "Dining with the Dead"; Yasin, "Funerary Monuments and Collective Identity: From Roman Family to Christian Community"; Burns and Jensen, *Christianity in Roman Africa*, 126–28, 493–94, 505–8, and 512–13; González, *The Fate of the Dead in Early Third Century North African Christianity*, Ch. 6; Daugherty, "The Bishops of North Africa: Rethinking Practice and Belief in Late Antiquity"; Fox and Tritsaroli, "Burial and Human Remains of the Eastern Mediterranean in Early Christian Context"; Fred Klawiter, *Martyrdom, Sacrificial Libation, and the Eucharist of Ignatius of Antioch* (Lanham, MD: Lexington Books/Fortress Press Academic, 2022).

into Christian practice they became celebrations of the Eucharist. We see this already in the *Didascalia* 26, which calls for the celebration of the Eucharist as part of the funeral liturgy, often at the gravesite:

> But you, in accordance with the Gospel and in accordance with the power of the Holy Spirit, gather in the cemeteries to read the Holy Scriptures and to offer your prayers and your rites to God without observance and offer an acceptable eucharist, the likeness of the royal body of Christ, both in your congregations and in your cemeteries and on the departure of those who sleep.[80]

This would be furthered, in the case of the martyrs, by the construction of shrines and *martyria* over their graves, which are mostly extant from the second quarter of the fourth century.[81] Christians would gather at these shrines for pilgrimages and commemorations, and they would celebrate the Eucharist in them. Moreover, the archaeological evidence supports the continuation of these *refrigeria* beyond the fourth century.[82] In Egypt, for instance, there is ample evidence of *stibadia,* or the semi-circular banquet beds on which these *refrigeria* were celebrated.[83]

It cannot be assumed, however, that these *refrigeria* were the same everywhere, or that they were always eucharistic. As Candida Moss notes:

> Any theory of the relationship between funerary meals held in honor of martyrs and any other form of ancient meal must take into account chronological development, sectarian differences, and geographical variety not

80. Alistair Stewart-Sykes, ed., *The Didascalia Apostolorum: An English Version*, Studia Traditionis Theologiae 1 (Turnhout: Brepols, 2009), 255–56.

81. Grossmann, "Churches and Meeting Halls," 93.

82. Jensen, "Dining with the Dead," 126–28.

83. Semi-circular banquet beds (or *stibadia*) are also attested in late antique funerary contexts, for example, in building 180 (in the past interpreted as a church) at the Christian cemetery of El-Bagawat in Kharga Oasis and in the courtyard of mausoleum 18 (dated to the second half of the fifth century) at the same site; see respectively G. Cipriano, *El-Bagawat: Un cimitero paleocristiano nell'Alto Egitto* (Todi: Tau Editrice, 2008), 74–83 and 68–69, fig. 38 respectively. See also Volp, *Tod und Ritual in den christlichen Gemeinden der Antike*; Karel Innemée, "The Lord's Table, *Refrigerium*, Eucharist, *Agapè*, and Tables for Ritual Meals in al-Bagawat and in Monasteries," in *Christianity and Monasticism in Alexandria and the Egyptian Deserts*, ed. Gawdat Gabrat and Hany N. Takla, Christianity and Monasticism Series (Cairo: American University in Cairo Press, 2020), 281–96.

> only in the practice of Eucharistic meals, but also in the performance of funerary meals in general. The issue is not just one of Christian diversity, but also of Roman diversity of practice.[84]

At the same time, Moss is willing to entertain that frequently these *refrigeria* were "quasi-eucharistic (if not Eucharistic) meals."[85] In those cases, it is likely better to call them non-normative Eucharists.

Nevertheless, the celebration of *refrigeria* by Christians was not without controversy among fourth-century authorities. As Karel Innemée notes: "By the end of the fourth century the celebration of the *dies natalis* . . . of the martyrs could apparently turn into festivities that were considered inappropriate, and as a reaction bishops gradually tried to forbid these or replace them with liturgical celebrations."[86] In other words, in the fourth century there was an attempt to convert these meals—whether they were non-normative Eucharists or more clearly understood as non-eucharistic meals—into normative Eucharists. The same was the case with the funerary meals of ordinary Christians, many of which were non-"normative" Eucharists. But by the fourth century these too were being made normative eucharistic celebrations[87] or *agapes*.[88] It is not exactly clear what visitors were doing in the cemeteries as envisioned by the redactors of ApTrad; however, it seems very likely that the celebration of *refrigeria*, and particularly eucharistic *refrigeria*, would have been one of the practices occurring there.

84. Moss, "Christian Funerary Banquets and Martyr Cults," 822.

85. Moss, 826.

86. Innemée, "The Lord's Table," 285. For more, see Jensen, "Dining with the Dead," 132–43; Alistair C. Stewart, *Breaking Bread: The Emergence of Eucharist and Agape in Early Christian Communities* (Grand Rapids, MI: William B. Eerdmans, 2023), 125–35. See also Arietta Papaconstantinou, *Le culte des saints en Égypte des Byzantins aux Abbassides: L'apport des papyrus et des inscriptions grecs et coptes* (Paris: Éditions CNRS, 2001), 318–22.

87. Stewart, *Breaking Bread*, 135–40 and 143–47. See also Nathan Chase, "Kitchens and Communion: The Eucharist and Communal Meals in the Fourth and Fifth Centuries," forthcoming in *Ex Fonte - Journal of Ecumenical Studies in Liturgy*.

88. Stewart, *Breaking Bread*, 140–41 and 145–47. See also Chase, "Kitchens and Communion."

*Chapter 8*

# Assorted Rituals in the *Apostolic Tradition* and Additional Texts Added into the *Apostolic Tradition* in Ethiopic I

## 1. Introduction

ApTrad has a number of assorted rituals and ritual practices that should also be addressed. This includes the references to fasting practices, the sign of the cross, ritual washings, and other assorted prayers. These will be discussed in this chapter. Ethiopic I also contains a number of texts that are not part of ApTrad in the other versions of the document, but which have been placed within the church order by the redactor of Ethiopic I in such a way that they appear to be part of ApTrad itself.

## 2. Fasting

There are three chapters in ApTrad that deal with fasting: Chs. 23, 33, and 36. In Ch. 23, fasting is viewed as a unique and frequent ministry of the virgins and widows. Bradshaw suggests that their inclusion here might be a later interpolation.[1] While virgins may be a later addition, since "they are

1. Bradshaw, *Apostolic Tradition*, 84.

not otherwise mentioned in [Ethiopic I] except at the end of chapter 18," the reference to widows may indeed be original to the text.[2] The reference to virgins and widows does appear in a fragment of the *Epitome*[3] and CH 32.

Others are also called to fast. The presbyters may fast if they want, and the same is the case with the laity. Ethiopic II specifically mentions deacons as well. The exclusion from this discussion on fasting of deacons—except in Ethiopic II—and other ministers is interesting, and it may indicate that deacons and the other offices in ApTrad were considered part of the laity. The fasting practice of the bishop is unique. The bishop can only fast when everyone fasts presumably because the bishop needs to make the eucharistic offering for those who want it and to participate in other communal meals (see also Ch. 6 above).[4] Stewart actually sees this chapter as thoroughly anti-Montanist, since the Montanists legislated fasts and here the fasts are determined by the individual.[5] Similarly, *Herm.Com.* 2002 observes that "the absence of any explicit reference to specific, regular fast days observed by all may perhaps be a sign of the antiquity of this passage, or at least its origin in a Christian community that did not follow what was becoming the mainstream custom."[6] This seems also to be confirmed by the fact that not all of the ministries listed throughout ApTrad are included here. This is either the result of a lack of consistency in the redaction of ApTrad, which is common for the document, or a sign of the antiquity of this chapter.

Later sources in Egypt, for instance, will provide more details about fasting. CA 31 (Arabic) and 49 (Arabic and Coptic) refer to fast days on Wednesday and Friday, and CA 57 (Arabic and Coptic) gives directions for priests, readers, and the laity during Pascha. This appears to be more developed than the fasting practices outlined in ApTrad, but not as developed as the fasting practices prescribed in SD II.9-14 and 17 and V.1.[7] Further directives on fasting are found in the additional texts added to the document in Ethiopic I and II (see below).

2. Bradshaw, *Apostolic Tradition*, 84.

3. Franz Xaver Funk, *Didascalia et Constitutiones Apostolorum*, 2 vols. (Turin: Bottega d'Erasmo, 1979), II:112. See also our Introduction.

4. Bradshaw, 84.

5. Stewart, *On the Apostolic Tradition*, 161–62.

6. *Herm.Com.* 2002, 140.

7. H. Hyvernat, "Le Syntagma Doctrinae," in *Studia Patristica: Études d'ancienne Littérature Chrétienne*, ed. Pierre Batiffol (Paris: Leroux, 1890), 123 and 125.

Ch. 33 deals with the fast before Easter. The sick and pregnant are exempt from the fast, except for the Sabbath. They are only to eat bread and water (and salt in Sahidic and CH 22). The mention of salt provides an interesting connection to Philo's description of the community at Therapeutae (*De vita contemplativa* 66–81).[8] This chapter also discusses what should happen to those who miss the fast, in particular sailors and travelers. They are to observe the fast after the fifty days of Easter. Ethiopic I and Arabic I support the authenticity of the phrase "for it is not a Pascha that we observe," thus setting up a distinction between Jews who miss the Passover and Christians who miss Easter.[9] The reference to Pentecost, as Bradshaw notes, points to a third-century context.[10] At the same time, it must be noted that with regard to the Paschal fast, no reference is made either to baptismal preparation or to the rite of baptism itself, thus underscoring that there is no connection between Easter and baptism in ApTrad.

Ch. 36 gives information on fasting practices before receiving the Eucharist. While Bradshaw notes that this likely originally referred to the reception of communion at home during the week,[11] presumably this same stipulation would have applied whenever someone received communion (see Ch. 6 above for more). Regardless, it points to a need to abstain from eating food before receiving the Eucharist. The last part of the chapter attests to the apotropaic quality of the Eucharist, something that appears at an early date, as can be seen in the writings of Ignatius of Antioch: "the medicine of immortality, the antidote preventing death" (*Ephesians* 20.2).[12]

## 3. Sign of the Cross

There are two chapters that discuss the sign of the cross directly, Chs. 38B and 42; however, there is a brief mention in Ch. 41.14 as well. Ch. 38B is very similar to Ch. 42, and so one of these is a duplication of the other. The former is known as the short ending and the latter as the long ending.

8. Philo of Alexandria, *The Contemplative Life*, Loeb Classical Library, vol. 363 (Boston: Harvard University Press, 1991), 153–67.

9. *Herm.Com.* 2002, 174–75.

10. Bradshaw, *Apostolic Tradition*, 98.

11. Bradshaw, 100.

12. Bradshaw, 101.

There has been some discussion about which chapter, 38B or 42, is the earlier one.[13] Ch. 38B only appears in the Latin. The chapter deals not only with the sign of the cross as in Ch. 42 but also contains additional material taken from Ch. 43. As a result, the consensus has been that the Latin version with the short ending is likely the result of an attempt "to conflate a longer and a shorter version of the Church order."[14] Ethiopic I and Arabic I only contain the longer ending of the document, which at first provides further support to this consensus.[15] The material in Ch. 38B and Chs. 42 and 43, however, are largely the same, except for a key difference below, making determining the original form of the text more difficult. The reference to "striking" in Ch. 38B.2 and "spitting" in Ch. 42.2 has caused some confusion. Bradshaw argues that Ethiopic I confirms the theory "offered by Dix and Hanssens . . . that there had been confusion in the original between the Greek for 'striking,' *tuptontos*, and 'spitting,' *ptuontos*."[16] This appears to also be affirmed by Arabic I.

In both chapters, the sign of the cross is to be made on the forehead and is a shield-like protection against the devil, i.e., apotropaic in nature. It appears that it is the inner Spirit in the person given through baptism that allows this to be an effective defense against the devil. This is then seen as analogous to the smearing of the blood on the doorposts of the Israelites. This analogy is quite old and is also found in Origen.[17]

There is one other brief mention of the sign of the cross in Ch. 41.14 during the discussion of daily prayer: "Through consignation with moist breath and catching your spittle in your hand, your body is sanctified down to your feet. For when it is offered with a believing heart, just as from the font, the gift of the Spirit and the sprinkling of washing sanctifies him who believes." Ethiopic I and Arabic I are close to the Sahidic here. This sign of the cross also uses the breath of the mouth and protects your whole body through the gift of the Holy Spirit which lives in the faithful by virtue of their baptism.[18] This closely mirrors what can be seen in Ch. 38B in the Latin and the corresponding text in Ch. 42.2 in Ethiopic I

13. *Herm.Com.* 2002, 218.

14. *Herm.Com.* 2002, 187.

15. Bradshaw, *Apostolic Tradition*, 103 and 114–16.

16. Bradshaw, 115. For more, see also Stewart, *On the Apostolic Tradition*, 196 and 211.

17. *Herm.Com.* 2002, 220.

18. *Herm.Com.* 2002, 204–5 and 211–12. See also the commentary in Stewart, *On the Apostolic Tradition*, 204 and 207–8.

and Arabic I. The other versions of Ch. 42.2 make this a reference to the "likeness of the Word." Interestingly, however, in Ch. 41.14 spittle is seen as assisting in this process, whereas in Chs. 38B.2 and 42.2 it is not.[19] This passage has a clear similar to material found in Origen, but more particularly Tertullian.[20]

## 4. Ritual Washings

Ritual baths for purification appear already in pagan and Jewish sources,[21] but they also appear quite early in Christian sources. A ritual washing can be seen in two places in ApTrad. The first is in ApTrad Ch. 20.5, which talks about the preparation of the catechumens for baptism: "And let those who are appointed for baptism be taught to wash and make themselves free, and wash themselves on the fifth day of the week." The Sahidic and Ethiopic II forms of this passage in ApTrad imply that there is something exorcistic about this ritual;[22] however, this is not the case in CH 19b or in Ethiopic I and Arabic I,[23] which might imply a ritual washing for purity in the later Egyptian tradition. CH 19b, for instance, has "Those who are to be baptized are to bathe in water on the fifth day of the week and eat."

The second place a ritual washing occurs is in ApTrad Ch. 41.1 and 11-14:

> [41.1] And every faithful man and woman, when they arise early from sleeping, before they touch any work, let them wash their hands and pray to God, and in this way let them proceed to their work.
> [41.11-14] And rising about midnight, wash your hands with water and pray. And if your wife is also present, pray both together; but if she is not yet a believer, withdrawing into another room, pray and return again to your bed. And do not be lazy about praying. He who is bound in marriage

19. *Herm.Com.* 2002, 211.

20. *Herm.Com.* 2002, 211.

21. Everett Ferguson, *Baptism in the Early Church: History, Theology, and Liturgy in the First Five Centuries* (Grand Rapids, MI: Eerdmans, 2009), Chs. 2 and 4.

22. *Herm.Com.* 2002, 104 and 108.

23. Alessandro Bausi, "La 'nuova' versione ethiopica della *Traditio apostolica*: Edizione e traduzione preliminare," in *Christianity in Egypt: Literary Production and Intellectual Trends*, ed. Paola Buzi and Alberto Camplani (Rome: Institutum Patristicum Augustinianum, 2011), 41/43.

> is not defiled. For those who have washed do not have necessity to wash again, because they are clean. Through consignation and moist breath and catching your spittle in your hand, your body is sanctified down to your feet. For when it is offered with a believing heart, just as from the font, the gift of the Spirit and the sprinkling of washing sanctifies him who believes.

This is reproduced in CH 25b and 27:

> [25b] Each person in the order of Christians is to pray when he rises from sleep in the morning—they are to wash their hands when they wish to pray, before doing anything.
> [27] The Christian is to wash his hands each time he prays. He who is bound by marriage is also to pray, even if he rises from beside his wife, because marriage is not impure and there is no need of a bath after second birth, except for the washing of the hands only, because the Holy Spirit marks the body of the believer and purifies him completely.[24]

Commenting on the corresponding passage in ApTrad, *Herm.Com.* 2002 notes that both Tertullian and Clement of Alexandria were critical of a ritual washing of the hands and distinguished it from Jewish practices of ritual purity.[25] But there also appears to be a practice among some Christians of not only washing their hands as an act of ritual purity but also of taking a full bath. In fact, this is also attested in the Pseudo-Clementine literature and among the Ebionites and within Jewish Christianity.[26] Additionally, this is implied by the way that ApTrad and CH critique those who give too high a status to a ritual bath, paralleling it to baptism.

Evidence for this ritual purity bath may also be contained in CH 38, which describes the need for a water bath before the celebration of the Easter Vigil:

> As for the night of the resurrection of our Lord, one is to take great care that absolutely no one sleeps until morning. They are to wash their bod-

24. Nathan Chase and Maxwell Johnson, *The Origins of the Canons of Hippolytus* (Collegeville, MN: Liturgical Press Academic, 2024).

25. *Herm.Com.* 2002, 210–12; Bradshaw, *Apostolic Tradition*, 107. See also Stewart, *On the Apostolic Tradition*, 204–5 and 207–8.

26. Alistair Stewart, *The Canons of Hippolytus: An English Version, with Introduction and Annotation and an Accompanying Arabic Text* (Macquarie Centre: SCD Press, 2021), 149n169; Ferguson, *Baptism*, 248–51.

> ies with water before celebrating the Pascha, and all the people should be illuminated, because at this hour the Savior made all creation free and subdued heaven and earth and all that is in them, because he rose from the dead, ascended into heaven, and is seated at the right hand of God. He will come in the glory of his Father and of his angels, and he will reward each according to his deeds, those who have done good [with the] resurrection of life, and those who have done evil [with the] resurrection of condemnation, as it is written.[27]

This canon is one of the expansions made by CH to ApTrad and points to a local liturgical practice. Bradshaw asks: "Was this simply because they had presumably also abstained from the bath during the pre-paschal week of fasting (see canon 22), or did it have some ritual significance?"[28] In fact, CA 31 notes a fasting from bathing during Lent.[29]

It is worth considering where these washings, especially those that imply a full bath, may have taken place. In her work on baptismal fonts in North African pilgrimage centers, in particular Bir Ftouha, Jensen has pushed back on the idea that baptism in pilgrimage shrines would have been a common occurrence, especially as adult baptism gave way to infant baptism.[30] She notes also that for adults, traveling to be baptized was mortally risky. As a result, Jensen

> is tempted to propose other uses for Bir Ftouha's monumental baptistery and font—perhaps the reception of a special blessing, the collecting of holy water, or even participating in a ritual of purification or baptismal renewal sought by penitents. Pilgrimage to a martyr's shrine was a common undertaking of penitents and their reconciliation might have included some sense of reaffirming the baptismal promises.[31]

27. Chase and Johnson, *The Origins of the Canons of Hippolytus*, p. 103.

28. Bradshaw, 35.

29. Wilhelm Riedel and W. E. Crum, *The Canons of Athanasius of Alexandria: The Arabic and Coptic Versions* (London: Williams and Norgate, 1904), 31.

30. Robin Jensen, "Baptismal Practices in North African Martyrs' Shrines," in *Ablution, Initiation, and Baptism in Early Judaism, Graeco-Roman Religion, and Early Christianity*, ed. David Hellholm et al. (Berlin: Walter de Gruyter, 2011), 1673–95; Robin Jensen, "When Is a Baptistery Not a Baptistery?," in *Explorations in Christian Initiation from the East*, ed. Stefanos Alexopoulos, Nathan Chase, and Anna Petrin (Washington, DC: The Catholic University of America Press, forthcoming). See also *Baptisteries of the Early Christian World*, ed. Robin Jensen, Nathan Dennis, and Nathan Chase (Turnhout: Brill, forthcoming), Cat. #VIII.11.

31. Jensen, "Baptismal Practices," 1681.

She argues that these may have been a type of ablution pool, a form of *baptism ad sanctos*.[32] Extending this, Jensen has more recently suggested:

> It seems reasonable to suppose that petitioners would come to such shrines hoping for reconciliatory healing as much as physical cures. If this was the case, would some kind of water ritual be a symbolic cleansing act, perhaps as a kind of reminder of baptism that was thought to be central to the reconciliation of repentant sinners in the same way that the minister's imposition of hands on the baptizand is repeated in the gesture of offering absolution and restoration of divine indwelling?[33]

Jensen points to the use of footwashing and other ablution rituals as a way of washing away sins, perhaps indicating that these "fonts" were used for rituals other than baptism. Similarly, Gabriel Radle, for instance, has argued for the use of these basins for charitable baths of the diakonia,[34] which was part of the larger connection between baths and churches in antiquity.[35] This may even be supported by the presence of some heated fonts in this period.[36] It is also not inconceivable that these bore some resemblance to the basins at the entrance to some churches for the washing of the hands, face, and feet.[37]

It is clear from the Egyptian evidence, for instance, that washings, including footwashings, occurred in these centers.[38] Abū Mīnā, for instance,

32. Jensen, 1692–93.

33. Jensen, "When Is a Baptistery."

34. Gabriel Radle, "Liturgy and Charitable Ministration in Late Antiquity: Diakonia Prayers in the Earliest Euchologion Manuscripts," *Ex Fonte - Journal of Ecumenical Studies in Liturgy* 2 (2023): 259–96, esp. 277 and 280–88.

35. Dallas DeForest, "Baths, Christianity, and Bathing Culture in Late Antiquity," in *The Oxford Handbook of Early Christian Archaeology*, ed. David K. Pettegrew, William R. Caraher, and Thomas W. Davis (New York: Oxford University Press, 2019), 189–206.

36. See, for example, Abū Mīnā Western House Chapel Phase 2—Font 2 (Cat. #X.1.5P2, sixth century) and Kellia, (QIsa 366)—Basilica (Cat. #X.1.20) in *Baptisteries of the Early Christian World*, ed. Robin Jensen, Nathan Dennis, and Nathan Chase (Brill, forthcoming). Heated fonts appear throughout the ancient Christian world; see ibid.

37. Annewies van den Hoek and John J. Herrmann, *Pottery, Pavements, and Paradise: Iconographic and Textual Studies on Late Antiquity*, Supplements to Vigiliae Christianae, vol. 122 (Leiden: Brill, 2013), Ch. 1, esp. 9–17, 18, 22–27, and 43–63.

38. AnneMarie Luijendijk, "'If You Order That I Wash My Feet, Then Bring Me This Ticket': Encountering Saint Colluthus at Antinoë," in *Placing Ancient Texts: The Ritual and Rhetorical Use of Space*, ed. Mika Ahuvia and Alexander Kocar (Tübingen: Mohr Siebeck, 2019), 205 and 211–14. Footwashing of guests at monasteries is also a well-known practice;

also had extensive bathing complexes, which may have also fulfilled a ritual function.[39] In fact, baths were frequently part of monastic complexes and pilgrimage centers.[40] It is very possible that Jensen is right and that these "fonts" were used for multiple purposes. While in bigger shrines, monasteries, and other places it may have been possible to have dedicated spaces for baptism and other rituals, like healing rites—there were separate bathing facilities at Abū Mīnā, for instance[41]—in smaller or less prominent places this may not have been possible or even desired. It is also very possible that many of the baptismal fonts in these spaces, but also in regular churches, were re-used outside of the baptismal season for ritual washings associated with ritual purity.[42]

## 5. Additional Texts in Ethiopic I

In Ethiopic I, there are some additional materials included between Ch. 43.3 in ApTrad and before Ch. 43.4.[43] Ch. 43.4 states that: "If there is therefore anything we have overlooked, our brethren, let the Lord reveal it to those to whom it suits, while he governs the holy church in a quiet

---

see Peter Grossmann, "Badeeinrichtungen in ägyptischen frühchristlichen Klöstern," in *Le bain collectif en Égypte*, ed. Marie-Françoise Boussac, Thibaud Fournet, and Bérangère Redon, Études urbaines 7 (Le Caire [Paris]: Institut français d'archéologie orientale diff. AFPU, 2009), 287–95; Maria Mossakowska-Gaubert, "Les bains et les moines: Le rôle hygiénique, thérapeutique et symbolique de la toilette corporelle dans la vie des moines égyptiens durant les premiers siècles du mouvement monastique," in *Le bain collectif en Égypte*, ed. Boussac, Fournet, and Redon, 297–303. See also in the Egyptian context the c. fourth-century *Syntagma Doctrinae* §II.21; see Hyvernat, "Le Syntagma Doctrinae," 124.

39. Peter Grossmann, "The Pilgrimage Center of Abû Mînâ," in *Pilgrimage and Holy Space in Late Antique Egypt*, ed. David Frankfurter, Religions in the Graeco-Roman World 134 (Leiden: Brill, 1998), 292.

40. See, in particular, the chapters by Pierre-Louis Gatier, Peter Grossmann, and Maria Mossakowska-Gaubert in Boussac, Fournet, and Redon, eds., *Le bain collectif en Égypte*.

41. See n. 36.

42. Nathan Chase, "Breaking Down the 'Golden Age' of Initiation: Baptism in Monasteries, Pilgrimage Centers, and Cemeteries in the Nile Valley," in *Proceedings from the Liturgies of the Church of Alexandria: From Late Antique Origins to the Medieval Heritage* (Washington, DC: The Catholic University of America Press, forthcoming).

43. See our introduction, as well as Alessandro Bausi, "The >so-called *Traditio apostolica*<: Preliminary observations on the new Ethiopic evidence," in *Volksglaube im antiken Christentum*, ed. Theofried Baumeister and Andreas Merkt (Darmstadt: WBG, Wissenschaftliche Buchgesellschaft, 2009), 297.

harbor" (Ethiopic I). This closing statement makes the additional material added into Ethiopic I appear to be part of ApTrad, despite not being found in the other versions of the text. Horner's edition of Ethiopic II does duplicate Ch. 43.4 after this material in the collection, despite also having Ch. 43.4 in its traditional location after Ch. 43.3 (see Table 3 in our Introduction). As a result, it is really only Ethiopic I that has tried to extend the ending of ApTrad to include this material.

The first text added into Ethiopic I is the so-called *Decree of the Apostles*, which is against idols and idolatry. It is taken from Acts 15:20 and John 19:36 and has been the source of much debate among biblical scholars.[44] In Ethiopic I it is titled "Concerning Idols," and in this way appears to be part of the text of ApTrad, though it was not. In many ways, this text is an extension of material contained in Ch. 16 (see Ch. 5 of our commentary). Its inclusion here must be because of its interest in the Egyptian and/or Ethiopic churches, since it is contained only in these versions.

Following this is a composite text taken from *Didache* 11.3-5, 7-12; 12.1-5; 13.1, 3-7; 8.1-2. This material is given a quasi-title of "Concerning the apostles and prophets, according to the rule of the gospel let them do so." This material concerns the reception of prophets, what is a true prophet, the reception of newcomers and travelers, giving of the firstfruits to the prophets or the poor, fasting on Wednesdays and Fridays, and praying the Lord's Prayer. The material on the prophets in many ways mirrors the caution in Ch. 14 against blindly trusting healers. The material on fasting provides more concrete directives on fasting than what is seen in the other treatments of fasting in ApTrad (see above). This material mirrors what is seen in CA 31, though it is also not as developed as what is seen in SD II.9-14 and 17 and V.1.

The final additional text comes from the *Didascalia* 12 and is a discussion on how the worship space should be organized. In many ways, this parallels what is seen in ApTrad Ch. 18, but here we have more specificity (see also Ch. 6 of our commentary). It addresses not only the seating of men and women, but also the sick, the youth, presbyters, deacons, bishops, and others. Undoubtedly this was included in order to provide further guidance on the organization of the worship space.

44. For the reception of Acts 15 in the early church, see Marcel Simon, "The Apostolic Decree and Its Setting in the Ancient Church," *Bulletin of the John Rylands Library* 52 (1970): 437–60.

# *Chapter 9*

# Conclusion

In this commentary, we have approached the study of ApTrad in light of two undertreated witnesses—Ethiopic I and Arabic I—and to study the church order along thematic lines, rather than chapter by chapter. This, we believe, allows for a better sense of the interests and concerns of those who shaped the text and the liturgical reforms, practices, and standards they were setting. It remains to be seen whether this document represented the liturgical practices of any particular community. We will try to assess that throughout this conclusion, after first articulating some general insights that this study has uncovered.

A close look at the various witnesses to ApTrad, including its derivatives, reveals that ApTrad was a much more fluid tradition than has traditionally been realized. We see differences in the various versions of ApTrad and also in its derivatives. These differences are not always attributable to local variation (like with CH and TD, or even the Ethiopic witnesses). Thus, we are not looking at a single Greek exemplar, but possibly several Greek versions that attest to signs of development of this church order. We are looking particularly for a Greek version that influenced CH, and one that was closer to (though not exactly like) what we see in the Latin version and Ethiopic I. In light of this, further work needs to be done on Arabic I, which provides yet another unique witness to this church order. Such work is luckily already underway by Martin Lüstraeten and will likely lead to new understandings of ApTrad and its development beyond the preliminary remarks on the text made here.

What is also clear is that ApTrad, as is common of the church orders, is a type of "living literature," the result of layers of development across a long textual tradition. In the case of ApTrad, that development appears to span several centuries and possibly several geographical locations. *Herm. Com.* 2002 concluded that ApTrad was compiled with contents ranging across different times and places, a process with which we tend to agree here. At the same time, if its contents come from different places, its final redaction can be pinpointed with more specificity. That is, although the materials that were drawn together to form the document likely came from different places, those materials were brought together very intentionally within a particular context and continued to be shaped in that context. There are no indications, for instance, that ApTrad was passed around and accumulated different layers of materials from local church contexts. Rather, the documents and their derivatives give the appearance of having been engaged continually on a local level. In this way, it again represents a form of "living literature," here not understood as a piece of masking tape that picks up liturgical practices from everywhere it circulated, but rather a document that evolved within the ever-changing context in which it was initially composed.

In this way, Alistair Stewart's work on ApTrad provides a helpful critique to *Herm.Com.* 2002.[1] The document does appear to have been compiled and redacted in a single location even if the core parts of the document may have originally come from different ecclesial contexts. The issue with Stewart's work, as we see it, is that he does not allow a significant enough length of time for the development of the text. He proposes several redactions all within the space of the third century and within a Roman context. The issue with this approach is that it is clear that the redactions made to ApTrad must have spanned at least the third and fourth centuries, likely taking up between a century to a century and a half of changes, and as our commentary has consistently shown, these could not have occurred in a Roman context. In fact, even Stewart argues that the Hippolytean school in which ApTrad was supposedly redacted was of Asiatic origin. In any event, the layers of temporal development in the text would have required more time than Stewart proposes and would necessarily have continued into the fourth century. Our summaries

1. Stewart, *On the Apostolic Tradition*.

for each of thematic sections in the document will make this clear. These indicate that (1) the time of the text's redaction was quite long, (2) it was a multi-stage process, and (3) it more likely occurred in the East than the West. But before turning to those summaries, it is worth looking first at the general development of the text.

## 1. General Development of ApTrad

It should be noted that generally speaking we can see that the document began from a core set of material that was gradually expanded, something more or less affirmed by all who study the document. As noted in our Introduction, *Herm.Com.* 2002 posits that the document consisted of three core sections, likely three sources of original material, that were combined together:[2]

- Directives about appointment to ministry:
  - 2.1-4; 7.1; 8.1; 9.1-2(?); 10.1-3; 11; 12*; 13; 14
- Directives about the initiation of new converts:
  - 15; 16; 17; 18; 19; 20; 21.1-5, 12-18, 20, 25-26
- Directives about community meals and prayer:
  - 23*; 24 (=29B); 25 (=29C*); 26(?); 27; 28.4-6; 29A; 30A; 31; 32; 33; 35

The rest of the material found in ApTrad represents expansions[3] or additions[4] to this earlier core. The chapters above with an asterisk (*) may not, however, have been part of the original source material used to initially compile ApTrad.

The expansion and additions made to these core materials were not, as this commentary has shown, made all at once, but occurred gradually over time. In the case of the directives about appointment to ministry, for instance, we see the gradual development of the offices of bishop, presbyter, and deacon. In the first layer of development, we see only

2. *Herm.Com.* 2002, 14–15.

3. 2.5; 7.2-5; 8.2-12; 9.2-5; 10.4-5; 21.6-11, 19, 21-24, 27-40; 28.1-3.

4. 1; 3; 4; 5; 6; 22; 29D; 30B; 34; 36; 37; 38A; 38B; 39; 40; 41; 42; 43.

rubrics for the development of these offices. Then at some point, and this had to be first, a prayer for the ordination of a bishop (ApTrad Ch. 3) and possibly the deacon (ApTrad Ch. 8.10-12) was added to the text, with the prayer of the presbyter being the same as that of the bishop. In a subsequent layer of development, the prayer for the presbyter was added (ApTrad Ch. 7.2-5). But these prayers also show layers of development, which may or may not have been contemporaneous with their introduction into the text. This also does not begin to address the edits made to the rubrics, which may or may not have been contemporaneous with the addition of the prayers or their reformulation. All of this would have taken more time than what is accounted for by Stewart, at least, from $^{R}$El to $^{R}$CN (both operating according to Stewart in the first half of the third century),[5] and certainly continued into the fourth century. These changes are, however, likely indicative of changes being made to the document within the same local context.

Compounding these complications is the fact that some derivatives of ApTrad, like CH, appear to preserve intermediate stages in the development of these layers. To borrow one example, again from the ordination rites, CH (along with Arabic I!) seems to preserve an older form of rubrical instructions for the ordination of a bishop in ApTrad Ch. 2 than in the received text of ApTrad as given in all the other versions of the text.[6] This makes a broad circulation of the document and its accumulation of material (*pace Herm.Com.* 2002) less likely, but also undercuts the short temporal development of the document as posited by Stewart. Additionally, given that CH is placed around 336–340 CE (mid-fourth century at the very latest),[7] this makes Stewart's early dating to the first half of the third century also highly unlikely. Furthermore, it suggests that

5. It is actually an even narrower period. $^{R}$El is often attributed to a figure writing around the time of "pope" Callistus I (r. c. 218 to 222/223 CE); see Alistair Stewart-Sykes, "The Integrity of the Hippolytean Ordination Rites," *Augustinianum* 39 (1999): 104–5. $^{R}$CN is attributed to a figure writing around the time of "pope" Pontianus (c. 230–235 CE); see Stewart, *On the Apostolic Tradition*, 61. Stewart does allow for a second-century set of material known as "P" that was edited first by $^{R}$El; see Stewart, 23 and 60–62. But the redactional layers are extremely short, at most (and this is a conservative number) 25 years, and all, again, within the first half of the third century.

6. See Ch. 3.

7. Nathan P. Chase and Maxwell E. Johnson, *The Origins of the Canons of Hippolytus* (Collegeville, MN: Liturgical Press Academic, 2024).

a look at the location of the derivatives of ApTrad, in particular CH, is more important to questions about ApTrad's own provenance than they at first appear due to their "derivative" status. If the CH was redacted in Egypt, as we have recently argued,[8] and if that text at times preserves an intermediate layer of development in ApTrad, then this likely points to an Egyptian context for the location of ApTrad's redaction.

In fact, there are multiple instances in which CH appears to be derived from an intermediate version of ApTrad. As has been noted already, the relationship between ApTrad and CH has long been explored, most recently by Stewart[9] and by us.[10] What is clear is that CH is one of the earliest derivatives of ApTrad. At the same time CH appears to know of an earlier form of ApTrad, preserving that form's reading in places:

- CH, along with TD and Ethiopic I, attests to transitional forms in the development of ApTrad that indicate that at least in some cases CH preserves an earlier form of ApTrad than some witnesses to ApTrad
- CH 2, along with Arabic I, seems to preserve an older form of rubrical instructions for the ordination of a bishop in ApTrad Ch. 2
- CH 4 also preserves the older rubric for the ordination of a presbyter in ApTrad Ch. 7.1
- The absence of the ordination prayer for a presbyter from ApTrad Ch. 7.2-5 in CH 2 points to the antiquity of CH
- CH 8, supported by Arabic I, may attest to an early form of ApTrad Ch. 14
- One of the manuscripts of CH 19c may indicate that the original form of CH and ApTrad's initiatory rites did not include a second postbaptismal anointing
- CH 30-31 attests to ApTrad Ch. 22 alongside Ethiopic I and II, as well as TD II.10, indicating that this chapter was in some cases original to ApTrad

8. Chase and Johnson.

9. Alistair Stewart, *The Canons of Hippolytus: An English Version, with Introduction and Annotation and an Accompanying Arabic Text* (Macquarie Centre: SCD Press, 2021).

10. Chase and Johnson, *The Origins of the Canons of Hippolytus.*

- In the corresponding sections within CH (5, 20, 30, and 32-33) describing the communal meals in ApTrad Chs. 26, 27, and 29C, it is clear that CH preserves their original eucharistic connotations more than the received texts of ApTrad
- CH 3c preserves the earlier practice of blessing all the firstfruits after the eucharistic prayer
- CH 5, 30, and 32 confirms that ApTrad Ch. 29B (= Ch. 24) was originally part of ApTrad
- CH 5 and 24, alongside TD II.21, appears to know an older form of ApTrad Ch. 34 which lacks a reference to the subdeacon

Since CH has firmly been placed in Egypt,[11] its use of an early form of ApTrad points to the early circulation of ApTrad in Egypt, and may even suggest that CH was a localized attempt at providing a final redaction to that early circulating form of ApTrad.

But it is not just ApTrad's derivatives that attest to layers of development. So, too, do the various linguistic witnesses. As noted in Ch. 2, ApTrad has two different endings, a short (Ch. 38B) and a long (Chs. 42 and 43) ending. This has led *Herm.Com.* 2002 (and for the most part also Stewart) to argue that Chs. 39–41 are a later addition to the text, with Chs. 39 and 40 expanding Ch. 35.[12] In explaining this development they suggest the presence of some intermediate stages in the development of ApTrad:

> All these variants can best be explained by the hypothesis of a gradual expansion of the material, with at least four stages: (1) a shorter version lacking chaps. 39–41 altogether; (2) an intermediate version, in which chap. 34 was replaced by an earlier form of what are now chaps. 39 and 40 (which are an adaptation of chap. 34), and chap. 35 was replaced by an earlier form that became the expanded chap. 41—the order apparently known to the compilers of the *Canons of Hippolytus* and of the *Testamentum Domini*; (3) a composite version, in which chaps. 34 and 35 were retained and chaps. 39–41 were instead inserted into the shorter version just before the conclusion (chaps. 42–43), thus creating the form underlying the oriental-language texts; and (4) the longer version, represented

11. Chase and Johnson.
12. *Herm.Com.* 2002, 16 and 188.

> by the Latin alone, in which the final portion of the composite version (chap. 39 to the end) was appended to the conclusion of the shorter version, resulting in a duplication of chaps. 42 and 43.[13]

As argued above in Ch. 2, Ethiopic I, CH, and TD seem to be witnesses to a number of intermediate forms in what the *Herm.Com.* 2002 describes as stages 2 and 3. Thus, there was likely not a single composite version of the text, but rather a mixture of several transitional forms, which is in keeping with Messer's caution against attempting to create a single archetype of the document.[14] Nevertheless, one of these transitional versions appears to have been known to the redactor of the Latin version, which seems to have taken a short version of the text and combined it with one of the longer composite versions to form the Latin text. That transitional version cannot be the same as Ethiopic I because of disparities between the texts. For the same reason, it also cannot be the transitional version known to CH and TD. This would, in fact, suggest another transitional version. The production of these intermediate forms must have taken some time and precludes a quick development, especially in the third century, as implied by Stewart.

Now what makes this especially interesting for questions of ApTrad's provenance is that Ethiopic I and CH, and perhaps even TD—the provenance of which is very much open to interpretation—all clearly emerged within the Egyptian orbit. Ethiopic I appears to be a product of Alexandria, while CH appears to be the result of the localization of ApTrad to another Egyptian context.[15] TD's provenance is unclear, but it may have emerged in a Palestinian context,[16] which is well known to have borne a number of similarities to Egyptian liturgical practices and development alongside them into the fourth century.[17] In any event, TD is also

13. *Herm.Com.* 2002, 16, see also pp. 178, 187, 188–89, 202, 218, and 221.

14. Reinhard Messner, "Die Angebliche *Traditio Apostolica*," *Archiv Für Liturgiewissenschaft* 58–59 (2016): 26.

15. Chase and Johnson, *The Origins of the Canons of Hippolytus*.

16. See our Introduction.

17. Geoffrey Cuming, "The Shape of the Anaphora," *Studia Patristica* 20 (1989): 333–45. Cuming expands on the relationship between MARK and JAS in "The Anaphora of St. Mark: A Study in Development," *Le Muséon* 95 (1982): 115–29. Bryan Spinks, "The Jerusalem Liturgy of the Catecheses Mystagogicae: Syrian or Egyptian?" *Studia Patristica* 18 (1989): 391–95; Juliette Day, *The Baptismal Liturgy of Jerusalem: Fourth- and Fifth-Century*

known to have circulated in Egypt at an early date, placing this witness not far from the Egyptian orbit as well. This leaves all of the intermediate witnesses to ApTrad within an Egyptian orbit, and because of this, it strongly suggests that Egypt was the place where, at the very least, the final redaction of ApTrad was made. In other words, ApTrad was still "living" within the Egyptian milieu. Otherwise, why would so many Egyptian-orbit languages and texts preserve intermediate forms of ApTrad?

Finally, we must account for the circulation of ApTrad beyond Egypt, particularly in the Latin version of the text and in ApCons. This is not actually that difficult to explain. As with all of the church orders, their geographical spread moved beyond their initial location of redaction. What at first glance appears more difficult to explain is why the Latin version contains all of the prayers for bishop, presbyter, deacon, and the anaphora, and why ApCons also clearly was influenced by the prayers for the bishop, presbyter, and the anaphora (but not the prayer for the deacon), while not all the other versions contain these prayers. This would seem to point to ApTrad's final redaction outside of Egypt. However, there is one Egyptian-orbit text that contains all of these prayers and that is Ethiopic II. This text indicates that all of these prayers were known together as part of ApTrad within the Egyptian orbit. Moreover, Arabic I has the incipit for all of these prayers except the anaphora. But the anaphora is known to have circulated in the Egyptian orbit at a very early date since it was known to Ethiopic I, though not included in the text of ApTrad. Instead, it was

---

*Evidence from Palestine, Syria and Egypt* (Burlington, VT: Ashgate, 2007); John Paul Abdelsayed, "Liturgical Exodus in Reverse: A Reevaluation of the Egyptian Elements in the Jerusalem Liturgy," in *Issues in Eucharistic Praying in East and West*, ed. Maxwell Johnson (Collegeville, MN: Liturgical Press, 2010), 139–60; Maxwell Johnson, "The Origins of the Anaphoral Sanctus and Epiclesis Revisited: The Contribution of Gabriele Winkler and Its Implications," in *Crossroad of Cultures: Studies in Liturgy and Patristics in Honor of Gabriele Winkler*, ed. Hans-Jürgen Feulner, Elena Velkovska, and Robert Taft, Orientalia Christiana Analecta 260 (Rome: Pontificio Istituto Orientale, 2000), 405–42; Anna Adams Petrin, "The Egyptian Connection: Egyptian Elements in the Liturgy of Jerusalem" (PhD diss., Notre Dame, University of Notre Dame, 2018), esp. Ch. 4; Nathan Chase, "From *Logos* to Spirit Revisited: The Development of the Epiclesis in Syria and Egypt," *Ecclesia Orans* 39 (2022): 29–64; Nathan Chase, *The Anaphoral Tradition in the "Barcelona Papyrus,"* Studia Traditionis Theologiae 53 (Turnhout: Brepols, 2023); Nathan Chase, "The Anaphoras of the Barcelona Papyrus, St. Mark, and St. James: An Anaphoral Hydra?" in *Symposium on the Liturgy of Saint James, Regensburg, Germany, June 2022*, forthcoming.

conflated with MARK to form Ethio-AA I and placed after ApTrad in Euch-AC. In light of the complicated reception of these prayers, it is worth summarizing which versions are missing which prayers:

- Prayer for the ordination of a bishop (Ch. 3): missing in Sahidic, Arabic II
- Prayer for the ordination of a presbyter (Ch. 7.2-5): missing in Sahidic, Arabic II, Ethiopic I, as well as CH
- Prayer for the ordination of a deacon (Ch. 8.9-12): missing in Sahidic, Arabic II, Ethiopic I, as well as CH
- Anaphora (Ch. 4): missing in Sahidic, Arabic I and II, and Ethiopic I (though it clearly was known to Ethiopic I since it was used to form Ethio-AA I), as well as CH 3b.

What is clear is that the Latin and Ethiopic II represent the most developed form of ApTrad, though Ethiopic II lacks the double ending. It is also clear that the absence of many of these prayers from the Egyptian-orbit language witnesses is the result of their intentional omission, like the absence of the anaphora. The Sahidic and Arabic II also appear to have universally excised the prayers, but these prayers were known to their redactors. In some cases, like the absence of the prayer for the ordination of a presbyter in Ethiopic I and CH 4, this was likely the result of these being witnesses to a true intermediate stage of development in ApTrad. Again, it is only within the Egyptian-orbit witnesses that we see intermediate versions, with the Latin and whatever version influenced ApCons representing well-developed forms of ApTrad.

## 2. Summaries of the Development of Each Part of ApTrad

Having looked at the general development of ApTrad, it is worth now turning to the various liturgical sections treated by the document. Each of these provides further insights into the development of the text that can help answer questions about its dating and provenance.

### *2.1. Ordination and Ministries (Ch. 3)*

- The material on ordination and ministry is clearly the product of several layers of development.

- The possible dating and provenance of the offices and ministries in ApTrad is difficult to establish, but the final redaction of the ministerial sections of the text seems to suggest a late third- or early fourth-century context.
- The instructions in the text have their roots in an earlier period in which a more federated style of ecclesial leadership predominated.
- While the original core of the episcopal, presbyteral, and diaconal prayers may date to before the third century or earlier, the final redactions of these prayer also seem to belong to the early fourth century.
- There are still tensions in the text between the three foundational orders of ministry—bishop, presbyters, and deacons—as well as other ministries, particularly the confessors, healers, and teachers.
- As far as provenance is concerned, there is nothing that is particularly unique to any region. Nevertheless, we can say a few things about provenance:
    - A school context—either in Rome or Alexandria—is hard to sustain.
    - There is nothing that supports a Roman, or even Western, provenance for the text.
    - There are a few indications that point away from a North African context.
    - There are a number of parallels here to an Egyptian context; however, there are also challenges to an Egyptian provenance. Overall, however, the evidence points to an Egyptian provenance.
- Given all this, it seems that the text was frozen in the early fourth century and Egypt remains the most likely location for its final redaction.

### *2.2. Daily Horarium (Ch. 4)*

- The daily horarium in ApTrad is clearly the product of several layers of development.
- The following is the shape of daily prayer in ApTrad according to its final redaction:
    - Prayer at rising/cockcrow

  - A communal catechesis and prayer, or a private reading of "holy books"
  - [Possibly a morning reception of the Eucharist, perhaps in conjunction with prayer at the third hour]
  - Prayer at the third hour
  - Prayer at the sixth hour
  - Prayer at the ninth hour
  - [A weekly(?) Eucharist/Evening Prayer]
  - Prayer before bed
  - Prayer in the middle of the night

- What we see in ApTrad is a slightly later development from that seen in Egyptian sources (like Origen and Clement), as well as North African sources (like Tertullian and Cyprian).

- In ApTrad we see the merging one tradition of prayer at morning, noon, evening, and midnight, and another of prayer at the third, sixth, and ninth hours, as well as midnight.

- ApTrad's horarium is addressed primarily towards the laity within an ecclesiastical setting.

- The morning instructional prayer found in ApTrad may represent a movement towards the common synaxes in the morning and evening in what are later termed the cathedral and monastic forms before these traditions diverged. If so, ApTrad represent a time when only morning prayer was a communal prayer.

- North Africa could be the source of ApTrad's horarium, or perhaps the location of one of the traditions that forms the basis for ApTrad's conflated horarium. But there are also strong indications that ApTrad is Egyptian, at least in its current formulation.

- It appears that in ApTrad's horarium we see a form of daily prayer contemporaneous with, or slightly after, Tertullian, Cyprian, Origen, and Clement. If after, it likely represents in its current form an Egyptian tradition before or around the same time as Pachomius.

## *2.3. Initiation (Ch. 5)*

- As with all other sections of ApTrad, the materials on Christian initiation also display various layers or strata of development, at the very least an earlier level with no explicit reference to the identity of ministers, followed next by rites pertaining to the bishop, and last by those rites pertaining to presbyters and deacons.

- Explicit parallels to the catechumenate and those prohibited from baptism are in Tertullian, but also in both *Didache* and Origen of Alexandria.

- Reference to daily exorcism appears to be a fourth-century innovation and is not documented before the *Catechesis* ascribed to Cyril of Jerusalem.

- References to a three-year catechumenate in all versions of ApTrad or to forty days in CH, the earliest derived document from ApTrad, all seem to point to an Egyptian context before fourth-century developments in the catechumenate.

- Elements belonging to an earlier core appear to include a rather general description of baptism in Ch. 20 with a more detailed rite associated with the ministries of bishops, presbyters, and deacons beginning anew in Ch. 21.

- The interrogatory form of baptism appears to have been widespread in early Christian Egypt and there is no reason to doubt that the core of ApTrad here comes from Egypt, which has been expanded with further creedal development.

- The postbaptismal rites of ApTrad, in light of later Egyptian developments, including CH, Sarapion, BR, Euch-AC, CB, Arb-TD.B, and even the current CR, probably had a postbaptismal anointing and handlaying prayer, the pneumatic content of which was expanded from an earlier epiclesis for grace to a full-fledged epiclesis for the Holy Spirit.

- If provenance cannot be demonstrated for the rites of Christian initiation alone, there is no question but that prior to the influence of this document in the West, after the fifth century at the earliest, its influence is Eastern, especially Egyptian, and, hence, Egypt again emerges as the likely place for its final redaction.

### *2.4. Eucharist and Meal Practices (Ch. 6)*

- It is clear that the discussion of meal and eucharistic practices in ApTrad is the result of several layers of development from different times and possibly different places.
- All of the eucharistic and meal practices described in ApTrad have their origins in a variety of older Greco-Roman meal practices, like *symposia*, *collegia*, the morning *salutationes*, and *refrigeria*.
- The final redaction of ApTrad's sections on the Eucharist and meal practices dates to the mid-fourth century.
- Five different ritual practices can be seen in these sections:
  1. The Eucharist proper (Chs. 4; 21.25-29 and 31-37; 22; 33; 36-38A);
  2. The blessing of foodstuffs in conjunction with the Eucharist (Chs. 5; 6; and 21.27-29);
  3. The blessing of firstfruits (Chs. 31-32);
  4. Rules surrounding communal meals (Chs. 23–32),
  5. in particular the communal meal in the evening (Ch. 29C).
- The discussion of the Eucharist proper points to several layers of development.
  - Concerning the anaphora in ApTrad Ch. 4:
    - It is possible that the core of the anaphora dates to the second or third centuries.
    - There are several early fourth-century developments in the prayer, mainly the addition of the institution narrative, a pneumatological epiclesis, and some creedal language.
  - Concerning communion:
    - Within Chs. 21.25-29 and 31–37 there is some development in the administration of the cup. This appears to be the result of third- to fourth-century developments in the understanding and theology of the Eucharist, which has led to changes in how the bread and cups are administered.

    - Other later additions include the ministerial directions in Chs. 21.25-29 and 31-37, and for a similar reason most of Ch. 22.
    - Chs. 36–38A may preserve remnants of older traditions, but they have also been developed in the fourth century as a result of changes in eucharistic theology.
    - Changes in patronage practices and the desire to see the bishop as the central patron of the Christian community may have also motivated the explicit references to the role of the bishop in the distribution of the Eucharist and other foods in ApTrad.
  - Concerning the gifts:
    - In the final form of ApTrad there is a clear separation of the blessing of fruits from the blessing of foodstuffs, which likely represents a later development, perhaps of the late third or early fourth century.
    - At an earlier point, these were likely all blessed together in the context of the eucharistic liturgy just as the foodstuffs in ApTrad Chs. 5–6 are described.
    - Moreover, these likely were also all vestiges of an even earlier practice of celebrating the Eucharist as a meal. This practice ceased in most places at the end of the third century, but in others into the fourth century.
- The rules surrounding communal meals:
  - In the earliest period, there was no separation between the communal meals and the eucharistic celebrations.
  - The rules surrounding communal meals are clearly fourth-century developments but are likely vestiges of earlier second- or third-century rules surrounding a eucharistic meal. They have been reformulated as general meal rules as a result of the shift from a eucharistic meal to a token distribution of bread and wine.
- Concerning the provenance of these sections in ApTrad:
  - There is nothing unique enough in the sections on the meal practices to indicate where these may have come from.
  - The anaphora in ApTrad Ch. 4:
    - The anaphora circulated in Egypt and Syria at an early date, but its influence was mostly confined to Egypt.

        - It shares a number of developments with Egyptian and Palestinian texts of the late third and early fourth century.
        - Its unique doxology was preserved in Egyptian-orbit anaphoras.
        - The early core of the prayer in ApTrad Ch. 4 is even more difficult, if not impossible, to place. There is nothing in the core of the prayer that points to any particular region.
    - The prayers in Chs. 5 and 6 appear very similar to Egyptian texts, though Ch. 5 did receive broad adoption as seen in Greek fragments.
    - The administration and formulas for the distribution of bread and cup during the initiatory Eucharist in ApTrad Ch. 21.31-32 and 34-36 find near exact parallels in Ethio-MC.
    - The section on the blessing of foodstuffs, however, points to an Egyptian context. The Egyptian tradition maintained a strong connection between the blessing of foodstuffs apart from oil—which continued to be blessed close to the Eucharist in most places[18]—and the Eucharist into the fourth century. Chs. 31–32 appear to have had a long-lasting influence in Egypt, where the offering of the firstfruits continued for a long time.
    - The practice of giving milk and honey with the baptismal Eucharist occurs in a few specific locations, namely North Africa, Egypt, and Rome.
- Given all the evidence, Egypt is very probably the place of the final redaction of the eucharistic and meal practices in ApTrad.

### *2.5. Treatment of the Sick and Christian Burial (Ch. 7)*

- Treatment of the sick:
    - References to the care of the sick occur throughout ApTrad, but are usually not clearly defined.
    - The oil prayers in Ch. 5 may have been used for the care of the sick.
    - Oil and water often were multi-use in Christian, other religious, and secular contexts—in Christian ritual (for the sick and in initiation) as well as in medicinal and magical contexts.
    - ApTrad also prescribes meals and visits to the sick.

18. Oil of the sick, etc.

  - Those charged with caring for the sick include catechumens, subdeacons, deacons, presbyters, and bishops.
  - A class of healers is also described in ApTrad, though these appear to have been diminishing in importance by the time of ApTrad's final redaction.
  - Nothing points to a particular location or date for these materials, though there are Egyptian parallels.

- Christian burial:
  - There is no reference to the actual practice of burial in ApTrad.
  - It is clear from ApTrad that Christians had some sort of specialized tomb, or burial care, that was taken care of by the church.
  - It is also clear that visitors would go to the tomb, likely to celebrate *refrigeria*.
  - Again, nothing points to a particular location or date, and theories that the reference to tiles can only refer to a Roman context are not true.

### *2.6. Assorted Rituals in ApTrad and Additional Texts in Ethiopic I (Ch. 8)*

- Fasting:
  - ApTrad takes up a few instances of fasting:
    - General fasting
    - A fast before Easter
    - Fasting before the Eucharist
  - With the exception of Ethiopic I, these fasts are not well defined. Ethiopic I adds additional material on fasting specific to the Egyptian context.
  - There is nothing that points to a particular time or place, except in Ethiopic I which has parallels to the Egyptian context.

- Sign of the cross:
  - There is nothing that points to a particular time or place for this material on the sign of the cross with the exception that there are

some parallels to Tertullian and Origen in the discussion of the use of spittle with the sign of the cross.

- Ritual washings:
    - ApTrad discusses three different instances of ritual washings:
        - By the catechumens before baptism
        - When rising from sleeping at night and in the morning
        - For everyone before the Easter Vigil
    - Here again there is nothing that points to a particular time or place from which these materials emerged.

## 3. Summary

What we see then is that while ApTrad is a somewhat unruly church order with a complicated textual history, the editors of the document were likely trying to compose something that mirrored in some way the lived realities of the community using this church order. At the same time, elements of ApTrad likely remain fictitious or aspirational. The development of ApTrad clearly shows layering in the text, layers that must have developed throughout the third and fourth centuries, since portions of the text may go back as far as the second century. The most likely place for the compilation and redaction of the text is Egypt, from which we see a number of intermediate versions (e.g., Ethiopic I, Arabic I) and derivatives (e.g., CH) that were also from the intermediate stage. It is from Egypt that this church order would spread to the West and other parts of the East. Originally called, after its discovery in the nineteenth century, "The Egyptian Church Order," we would like to suggest here that such an appellation may well have been accurate.